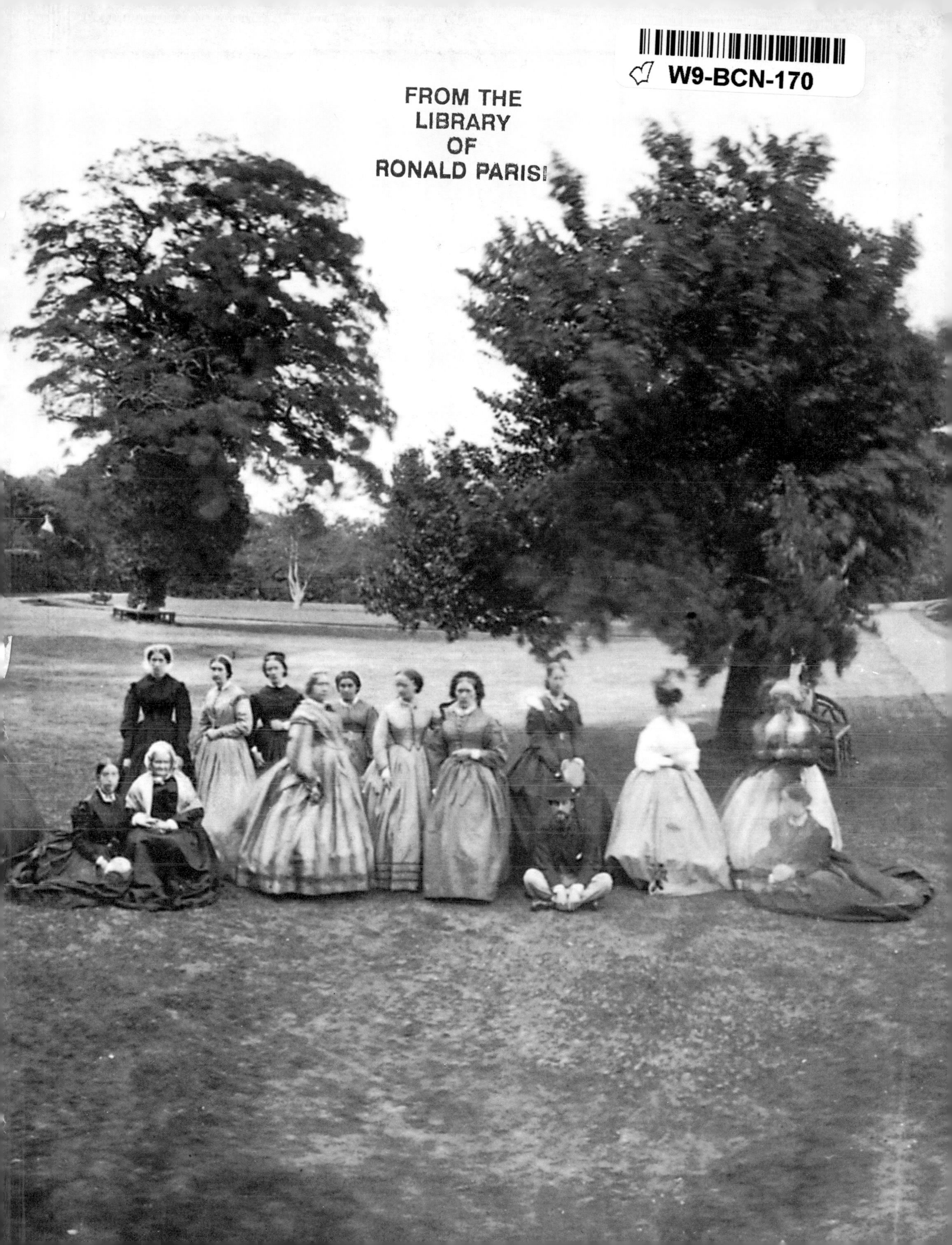

TO JOHN HARRIS

Best of Country House Companions

A COUNTRY HOUSE
COMPANION

MARK GIROUARD

YALE UNIVERSITY PRESS

NEW HAVEN and LONDON

Published in Great Britain 1987 by Century Hutchinson
Publishing Group Ltd.
Published in the United States 1987 by Yale University Press.

Printed in Great Britain.

Library of Congress cataloging card number: 87–50445
International standard book number: 0–300–04083–0

10   9   8   7   6   5   4   3   2   1

Contents

INTRODUCTION

Anthologies are designed to instruct and to entertain, and tend to lean one way rather than the other. Mine is angled firmly in the direction of entertainment, although I hope that those who are entertained may pick up a little instruction by the way. I have tried to put it together like a menu, or series of menus, contrasting period with period and attitude with attitude, breaking up the main course with appetizers, and setting one savour against another.

In general, my aim has been to take the reader into country houses as an invisible tourist, and allow him or her to see them through the eyes of the people who lived in or visited them, to look over their shoulders as they write, to peer through windows into rooms as they were furnished many hundred years ago, to attend parties, watch dramas unfold, look down dinner tables, or overhear the gossip and grumbles in the servants' hall.

Our knowledge of English country houses, and of the life lived in them, derives from a mass of different sources, apart from the first and basic one, the evidence of the fabric and contents of the houses themselves. But these only tell a limited story, unless other sources are used to illuminate them. Bills, letters, account books, diaries, household regulations, inventories, newspaper reports, descriptions of country houses and poems about them, all add piece by piece and little by little to our knowledge of the way houses were built and why they were built, of the people who lived in them and how they lived in them.

Added to these is the visual evidence of plans, architects' drawings, old photographs, and paintings and drawings of all kinds, from views and conversation pieces commissioned from professional artists to sketches made by children or amateurs. Much of this evidence can still be found in the country houses themselves, hanging on their walls, pasted in their visitors' books and photo-graph albums, or preserved in their muniment rooms. Much has found its way into public collections. Much has been published, but often in obscure or inaccessible publications. Much still remains unpublished or in manuscript.

I have collected what I find entertaining, unusual or instructive from all kinds of different places, and grouped them together under twelve heads, to give the anthology a little shape. In general, each section is arranged chronologically, but I have not hesitated to go out of the general chronological sequence when I want to illustrate different reactions to one house over the centuries. I have tried to avoid quotations and illustrations which featured in my *Life in the English Country House*. Sometimes, however, I have included a full, or fuller version, of passages which were quoted there only in part. A few of the entries seemed to need elucidation, which I have added either before the entries themselves, or in the introductions to each section. The index at the end gives the location of houses referred to, when this is not given in the text, and an appendix gives the source for each entry in detail. Spelling has been modernized throughout.

The thousands of pieces of evidence out of which an overall picture of the country house can be constructed are like the bits and pieces in a kaleidoscope. Shake them up and a new pattern emerges. Although the patterns may be quite different from one another in the impression they give even of the same house, they are not necessarily misleading or untrue.

One shake of the kaleidoscope, and country houses seem like visions in a dream: visions bathed in sunlight, melting in the mist, or gleaming under the moon. The architecture is frozen, the trees cast long shadows, the houses hover at the end of golden glades, the fruit hangs heavy and abundant in the orchards, the flowers along the garden walks rise in spires drenched and gleaming with dew. This dream-like quality has been felt and described by some of the authors in this anthology – by Marvell in the garden at Appleton House, for instance, by William Howett in the still forecourt of Wootton Lodge, by Henry James looking out from the window at Wroxton Abbey and seeing 'the great soft billows of the lawn melt away into the park'.

Another shake, and another pattern emerges; a pattern of happi-ness, a memory or picture of country houses as places where life is good. It infuses Ben Jonson's poem on Penshurst, with a strength that must reflect a personal reaction by the poet, and not just a desire to please a powerful patron. It is present in Katherine Mansfield's description of Garsington, of 'long conversations between people wandering up and down in the moonlight'. Perhaps it tends to come more often in the form of far-off memories tinged by nostalgia, but none the less vivid, like Constance Sitwell's memory of driving back from Edwardian cricket parties and of the brakes packed with tired boys and girls singing as the horses trotted through the twilit Norfolk lanes. Those who have lived in country houses will have similar memories; certainly I have them myself.

Another twist, and one is looking at a way of life infinitely remote, at customs and ceremonies which seem as unlike our own experi-

(left) *View from the south portico at Stowe House, Buckinghamshire* (detail). Jacques Rigaud, c.1734.

ences as the tribal rituals in the South Sea islands. Elizabethan servants smother the food, dishes, napkins and tablecloths of their employers with ceremonial kisses; Jacobean ladies pelt each other with eggshells filled with rosewater; in the eighteenth century the Duke of Chandos sits on a marble water-closet beneath a gilded ceiling; in the nineteenth century the Duchess of Rutland's steward, riding a black horse hung with black, carries his dead mistress's coronet on a scarlet cushion; Edwardian footmen soap their hair, and then powder it with powder puffs.

Yet another twist and another change. Everything comes alive. The houses are filled with real people, often far from nice, who behave exactly like ourselves, or like people we know. House guests are bored, and bitchy about their host and hostess. Young Elizabethan bloods in Yorkshire behave just as badly as young bloods at a hunt ball today. That tough old matriarch, Bess of Hardwick, sits in her bedroom surrounded by as much clutter as a retired governess who has taken all her bits and pieces with her into a bedsitting room in North London; and, just like a retired governess eking out her gas fire, she has screens and hangings everywhere, in an endeavour to keep out the unbearable cold of Hardwick in the winter. A hundred years later Lady Gardiner complains that her stepdaughter stays out dancing all night, that her boyfriend is a bad lot, and, worst of all, that she brings his laundry back to be washed by Lady Gardiner's servants.

It is all true. Country houses and country-house life evoke a nostalgia and romanticism today – understandably so, perhaps, but to an extent of which it is easy for anyone who studies country houses to have a surfeit. For although, in some moods and under some circumstances, they are magical places, country-house life was far from pure gold all the way through.

There is a mythology of the English country house which runs something as follows. The English upper-classes, unlike their continental counterparts, have always been firmly rooted in their estates. They know the land, and enjoy its ways and its sports. They look after their tenantry and their servants, and have an easy and natural relationship with working-class people. At the same time they have a sense of duty, which leads them to devote much of their lives to public service, with no thought of personal gain. Their lives are a happy mean between country sports and pastimes, public service, and the cultivation of the mind. Their houses are filled with beautiful pictures and fine furniture. Their libraries are well stocked with books bound in vellum or tooled leather; temples and classical monuments dot their parks. They share their life with their friends, in a free hospitality which results in one of the most enviable ways of life ever devised.

Such a picture corresponds with an ideal, and the elements out of which it is made can be matched through the centuries in individual country houses or the lives of individual owners. But anyone who has studied country houses will know how often the picture is a different one. There were, and are, many dull or ugly country houses. The ideal of the great landowner who serves the public for nothing out of a sense of duty is a nineteenth-century one; most

earlier country-house owners took anything they could get out of the
public purse. The servants and dependants of country-house owners
have a way, when one can find their own comments, of turning out
much less appreciative and admiring of their employers than their
employers might like to think; and much of the prosperity and
beauty of country houses in the eighteenth and nineteenth centuries
rested on the basis of massive enclosures of agricultural land, which
reduced many agricultural workers to a life of misery and near
starvation.

Henry James's dry remark on finding the 'happy occupants' of
Wroxton Abbey away from home – 'Happy occupants, in England,
are almost always absent' – has a strong basis of truth in it. Through
the centuries country-house owners with the means to do so have
readily left their country houses, often for years at a time. They have
gone off to live in Bath or Brighton, or to travel and live on the
continent, or sail round the world; they have spent most of the year
in London, filling their houses there with fine pictures and contents
which have often ended up, in this century, in the country houses.
Some have gone away because careers in politics, government or the
armed forces took them away, others simply because they were
bored, and had the means to leave.

They were also, very often, boring. They had enough money to
do nothing, and many of them did nothing. Doing nothing is not a
recipe which produces interesting people. Staying in country houses
could be a highly enjoyable or even idyllic experience, but it could
also be, as numerous letters or descriptions testify, a dull or
disillusioning one. Accounts of this nature feature prominently in
this anthology, perhaps because accounts which have a touch of acid
in them are more entertaining to read. They should not always be
taken too seriously, however. Guests who have been invited to stay

9

A teaparty at Elveden Hall, Suffolk, c.1910.

with very rich or powerful people have a habit of communicating their good fortune to friends who have not been invited, but at the same time keeping their end up by not being too impressed. Raymond Asquith's comment from Chatsworth is a perfect example of this genre: 'There is only *one* bathroom in the house, which is kept for the King'.

What all this amounts to is that country-house life is and has been full of variety. It is the variety which makes it interesting. There is variety as between individual country houses and variety as between country houses of different periods: a gradual change between ideals of state and formality, which came to their peak in the seventeenth century, and ideals of informality and ease, which gradually replaced them in the course of the eighteenth and nineteenth centuries. There is the variety of different reactions, conditioned by period or background, which make the same houses fill some visitors with enthusiasm and others with indignation or disdain.

This anthology aims to give a sample of this variety. It is an invitation to enter the houses, and savour their life. Sit at the kitchen table at Knole along with Diggory Dyer, Marfidy Snipt and John Morockoe the Blackamoor. Enjoy a lively weekend with Evelyn Waugh and the Sitwells at Renishaw, where 'the household was very full of plots'. Meet the Miss Philippses at Picton Castle, 'all honest good kind of girls in their way', and Philip Morrell at Garsington 'with a glassy geniality gleaming in his eyes'. Read Elizabeth George's account of Queen Victoria at Stowe, and wonder whether, under the veil of euphemism, she is really saying that the Queen was provided with a gold chamber pot.

It is a mixed story, full of odd bits and pieces. Some are entertaining, some regrettable, some sad, some silly; but much of the story deserves the description applied to Queen Elizabeth's entertainment at Elvetham in 1591: 'The melody was sweet and the show stately'.

Blickling Hall, Norfolk, as depicted on a jug of *c.*1800.

(right) *Wisbech Castle, Cambridge* (detail). Unidentified artist, *c.*1658.

1
Arrivals
&
Impressions

*L*arge numbers of people have always been coming and going at country houses, at every kind of level. They can be heirs coming to claim their inheritance, brides coming to be married, servants coming to work, guests coming to stay or to be entertained, tenants coming to pay their rent, tradesmen coming to deliver goods or do a job, or just curious people, coming to have a look. Until lodge gates, parks and drives appeared in the eighteenth century anyone could get close to country houses, however grand, and any well-spoken person could probably get past the porter at the entrance, and have a look inside. In the eighteenth century the concept of privacy began to develop, but the same period saw the beginning of organized country-house visiting, complete with tickets, tours and guides, at a considerable number of the larger or more famous houses.

Many of these visitors left a record of their reactions or their impressions. Some produced long poems of praise or celebration, usually to please the owners; these were an especial feature of the seventeenth and early eighteenth centuries. Many wrote up the houses for publication, or committed full descriptions to their diaries or letters. Others made casual comments that can be just as revealing. Descriptions and memories can be soaked with nostalgia, or steeped in acid. Not surprisingly, the same house can provoke widely different reactions, depending on the nature of the visitor or the period of the visit.

Country and country-house pursuits on a painted screen of c. 1720.

(right) Porter's Lodge, Longford Castle, Wiltshire, engraved after Robert Thacker, c. 1860.

Janua Longo Vadensis Icon; quæ Atriensi, ascribitur.
The Porters Lodg att Longford.

R. Thacker delin. &c. I. Collins fecit

ARRIVALS

LORD BURGHLEY VISITS HOLDENBY

BUT approaching to the house, being led by a large, long, straight fair way, I found a great magnificence in the front or front pieces of the house, and so every part answerable to other, to allure liking. I found no one thing of greater grace than your stately ascent from your hall to your great chamber; and your chamber answerable with largeness and lightsomeness, that truly a Momus could find no fault. I visited all your rooms, high and low, and only the contentation of mine eyes made me forget the infirmity of my legs.

LORD BURGHLEY TO SIR CHRISTOPHER HATTON, 1579

13

DEFOE COMES TO CHATS-WORTH AS A TRAVELLER

NOTHING can be more surprising of its Kind, than for a Stranger coming from the North, . . . and wandering or labouring to pass this difficult Desert Country, and feeling no End of it, and almost discouraged and beaten out with the Fatigue of it, (just such was our Case) on a sudden the Guide brings him to this Precipice, where he looks down from a frightful height, and a comfortless, barren, and, as he thought, endless Moor, into the most delightful Valley, with the most pleasant Garden, and most beautiful Palace in the World.

DANIEL DEFOE, *Tour through Great Britain* (1727)

I left London by the Comet Coach for Chesterfield; and arrived at Chatsworth at half-past four o'clock in the morning of the ninth of May, 1826. As no person was to be seen at that early hour, I got over the green-house gate by the old covered way, explored the pleasure grounds and looked round the outside of the house. I then went down to the kitchen gardens, scaled the outside wall and saw the whole of the place, set the men to work there at six o'clock; then returned to Chatsworth and got Thomas Weldon to play me the water works and afterwards went to breakfast with poor dear Mrs Gregory and her niece, the latter fell in love with me and I with her, and thus completed my first morning's work, at Chatsworth before nine o'clock.

Handbook to Chatsworth and Hardwick (1845)

Belton House, Lincolnshire (detail). Unidentified artist, c. 1720.

HERE I arrived, and found the lodge; a fine old Elizabethan house, situated in as solemnly striking a solitude as one can well conceive. It stood up aloft, on a natural terrace overlooking a deep winding glen, and surrounded by sloping uplands, deep masses of wood, and the green heights of Weaver, in a situation of solitary beauty which extremely delighted me. Not a person was visible throughout the profoundly silent scene, scarcely a house was within view. I ascended to the front of the lodge, and stood in admiration of its aspect. Its tall square bulk of dark grey stone, with its turreted front, full of large square mullioned windows; its paved court, and ample flight of steps ascending to its porched door; its old garden, with terraces and pleached hedges on the south slope below it, and deep again below that, dark ponds visible amongst the wild growth of trees. The house stood, without a smoke, without a sign of life, or movement about it, in the broad sunshine of noon. I advanced and rung the bell in the porch, but no one answered it. It was, for all the world, like a hall of old romance laid under an enchanted spell. I rung again, but all was silent. I descended the flight of steps, and paced the grey pavement of the court, and was about to withdraw, when an old woman opened a casement in the storey and said, in a slow dreamy voice, 'I am coming down.'

WILLIAM HOWETT, *Visits to Remarkable Places* (1840)

15

Looking across the lake to Wilton House, Wiltshire. Detail from the painting by Richard Wilson, c. 1758.

A

NEW

DUKE

OF

PORTLAND

COMES

TO

WELBECK

ABBEY

1879

WE travelled in a saloon carriage, arriving at Worksop on a dark, windy winter evening. Outside the station there was a little crowd of people waiting to see the young Duke arrive. Their white faces and dark clothes caught the light of the dim oil lamps as they pressed round the door of the old-fashioned carriage, while my little brother Charlie was lifted carefully into a second carriage. Then a long dreary drive to Welbeck, till at last we arrived before the house. The road in front was a grass-grown morass covered with builders' rubbish, and to allow the carriage to reach the front door they had had to put down temporary planks. The hall inside was without a floor and here also planks had been laid to allow us to enter.

Why the house had been allowed to get into this state I do not know, unless it was that the old Duke was so absorbed with his vast work of digging out and building underground rooms and tunnels that he was oblivious of everything else. He pursued this hobby at the cost of every human feeling, and without any idea of beauty, a lonely, self-isolated man. It was always thought that his love of tunnels was due to a dislike of being seen. Even round the garden of Harcourt House, where he lived in London, he erected high frosted-glass screens, so that he could not be overlooked; and when he travelled he never left his own carriage, but had it placed on a railway truck at the end of the train, keeping the green silk blinds closely drawn.

Naturally rumours spread that he was a leper or suffered from some other terrible disease, but I have talked to his old servants and they tell me that he had a delicate and lovely skin, and was an extremely handsome man, tall and thin, with a proud, aristocratic air. My mother had a bust of him made from a cast after his death, and from this he certainly appears to have been a remarkably handsome man, of a thin, clear-cut type, not very unlike the Duke of Wellington, but with a harder and more selfish face.

We were met at the front door by some of the heads of departments – McCallum, the Steward, a tall Scotsman; Tinker, the Clerk of Works, and others – and shown up to the few rooms that were fit to live in. The late Duke had only inhabited four or five rooms opening into each other in the West Wing of the house. Here he lived, slept and ate; indeed, it was said that he began his nights in one room, and if unable to sleep had a bath and went into another, keeping up fires in each room. To these rooms, which were scantily and almost poorly furnished, the little family party, all dressed in black, was solemnly ushered up, and my brother Charlie was put to bed.

Next day began the journey of discovery of the house. The suite of rooms that we were living in had double sets of brass letter-boxes in the doors: one to push the letters in, and the other to push the letters out. Two of these rooms were quite charming: a large west room and a little room known as the north closet adjoining, which had

been used by the second Duchess of Portland (Matthew Prior's noble, lovely little Peggy) who brought Welbeck into the family, and was a great collector of antiques and a highly cultivated woman. It was here that she and Mrs. Delany sat, embroidered and talked. I remember the smell of these rooms now.

All the rest of the rooms in the house were absolutely bare and empty, except that almost every room had a water-closet in the corner, with water laid on and in good working order, but not enclosed or sheltered in any way. All the rooms were painted pink, and the large drawing-rooms decorated with gold; but no furniture or pictures were to be seen. At last, in a large hall, decorated rather

View from under the North Portico, Stowe House, Buckinghamshire. J.C. Nattes, 1805.

beautifully in the manner of Strawberry Hill, was found a vast gathering of cabinets all more or less in a state of disrepair.

Then on by an underground passage and up through a trap-door into the building that had originally been the Duke of Newcastle's riding school and had been lined by the late Duke with mirrors and crystal chandeliers hanging from every point of the raftered roof, which was painted to represent the bright rosy hues of sunset; but the sudden mood of gaiety that had made him decorate it as a ballroom must have soon faded, leaving the mock sunset to shine on a lonely figure reflected a hundred times in the mirrors. For stacked here were all the pictures belonging to the house – pictures that had come down from generation to generation, but taken out of their frames and set up two or three deep against gaunt 'wooden horses'. The frames were afterwards found hidden away in a storehouse.

In a similar building opposite this, which had been the stables of the Duke of Newcastle's famous horses, was the kitchen where the late Duke's perpetual chicken had been kept roasting on a spit, one chicken following another so that whenever he should call for it one should be ready roasted and fit for eating. From this kitchen the food was lowered by a lift into a heated truck that ran on rails pushed by a man through a long underground passage to the house – a method of transit which I believe still continues. Another passage branching off from this one took us to three underground rooms, all very large, and one that seemed quite immense. These also were painted pink with parquet floors; heated by hot air, and lit from the top by mushroom lights level with the ground, vast empty rooms, built down instead of up, and except for the top lighting you would not have been aware that they were under the level of the ground. Along the side of them was a glass corridor intended for statues, but with no statues.

Then back we came to the house through more underground passages. Starting from these passages was the walking tunnel, about a mile long and wide enough for two or three people to walk abreast, that led from the house to the stables and gardens; and a little way off and parallel to it was another rather rougher one for the use of the gardeners and workmen; for the Duke did not wish to meet anyone walking in the same tunnel as himself. Then there was the great driving tunnel, more than a mile long, which was the only direct road to Worksop. It had been dug out under the old drive and was wide enough for two carriages to pass each other. In the daytime it was lit from the top by small mushroom windows which threw a ghostly light upon it, except where it dipped down under the lake, and there it was lit by jets of gas, as the whole tunnel was at night.

The collection of buildings, hunting stables, riding school, coach-houses, dairy, laundry and offices with a number of cottages and a covered tan gallop, about a quarter of a mile long, made a small town in themselves. They were all built in the same grey stone in dull heavy architecture, and stood without trees or flowers – flowers indeed were banished from the place – expressing only grandeur and pomp. The riding school was said to be the largest in the world. The vegetable gardens were on an equally huge scale – a series of square gardens, each surrounded by high walls, and of an average size of about eight acres.

The poor deluded owner seemed to assert his power and pride in making all the buildings as large and lonely as possible, banishing grace and beauty and human love and companionship, and leaving his fellow-beings in order to hide in tunnels. He even cut down every tree within a considerable distance of the house.

He was kind to the hundreds of labourers who came from all the villages around to take part in these vast excavations, providing them with donkeys to carry them to and from their work, and with large silk umbrellas to shelter them from the rain.

LADY OTTOLINE MORRELL

AN

ODD

VISIT

TO

HAM

1944

I walked down the long drive to Ham House. The grounds are indescribably overgrown and unkempt. I passed long ranges of semi-derelict greenhouses. The garden is pitted with bomb craters around the house, from which a few windows have been blown out and the busts from the niches torn away. I walked round the house, which appeared thoroughly deserted, searching for an entrance. The garden and front doors looked as though they had not been used for decades. So I returned to the back door and pulled a bell. Several seconds later a feeble rusty tinkling echoed from distant subterranean regions. While waiting I recalled the grand ball given for Nefertiti Bethell which I attended in this house some ten years or more ago. The door was roughly jerked open, the bottom grating against the stone floor. The noise was accompanied by heavy breathing from within. An elderly man of sixty stood before me. He had red hair and a red face, carrot and port wine. He wore a tail coat and a starched shirt front which had come adrift from the waistcoat. 'The old alcoholic family butler,' I said to myself. He was not affable at first. Without asking my name, or business, he said, 'Follow me.' Slowly he led me down a dark passage. His legs must be webbed for he moved in painful jerks. At last he stopped outside a door, and knocked nervously. An ancient voice cried, 'Come in!' The seedy butler then said to me, 'Daddy is expecting you,' and left me. I realized that he was the bachelor son of Sir Lyonel Tollemache, aged eighty-nine. As I entered the ancient voice said, 'You can leave us alone, boy!' For a moment I did not understand that Sir Lyonel was addressing his already departed son.

Sir Lyonel was sitting in an upright chair. He was dressed, unlike his son, immaculately in a grey suit, beautifully pressed, and wore a stock tie with large pearl pin. I think he had spats over black polished shoes. A very decorative figure, and very courteous. He asked me several questions about the National Trust's scheme for preserving country houses, adding that he had not made up his mind what he ought to do. After several minutes, he rang the bell and handed me over to the son who answered it.

The son showed me hurriedly, I mean as hurriedly as he could walk, round the house, which is melancholy in the extreme.

JAMES LEES-MILNE, *Ancestral Voices*

IMPRESSIONS

Newburgh Priory, North Yorkshire. Unidentified artist, c. 1695.

THOU art not, Penshurst, built to envious show,
Of touch, or marble; nor canst boast a row
Of polish'd pillars, or a roof of gold:
Thou hast no lantern, whereof tales are told;
Or stair, or courts; but stand'st an ancient pile,
And these grudg'd at, art reverenc'd the while.
Thou joy'st in better marks, of soil, of air,
Of wood, of water: therein thou art fair.
Thou hast thy walks for health, as well as sport:
Thy Mount, to which the Dryads do resort,
Where Pan, and Bacchus their high feasts have made,
Beneath the broad beech, and the chest-nut shade;
That taller tree, which of a nut was set,
At his great birth, where all the Muses met.
There, in the writhed bark, are cut the names
Of many a Sylvan, taken with his flames.
And thence, the ruddy Satyrs oft provoke
The lighter Fauns, to reach thy Ladies oak.
Thy copse, too, nam'd of Gamage, thou hast there,
That never failes to serve thee season'd deer,
When thou would'st feast, or exercise thy friends.
The lower land, that to the river bends,
Thy sheep, thy bullocks, kine, and calves do feed:
The middle grounds thy mares, and horses breed.
Each bank doth yield thee coneyes; and the tops
Fertile of wood, Ashore, and Sydney's copse,
To crown thy open table, doth provide
The purpled pheasant, with the speckled side:
The painted partridge lies in every field,
And, for thy mess, is willing to be kill'd.
And if the high swollen Medway fail thy dish,
Thou hast thy ponds, that pay thee tribute fish,
Fat, aged carps, that run into thy net.
And pikes, now weary their own kind to eat,
As loth, the second draught, or cast to stay,
Officiously, at first, themselves betray.
Bright eels, that emulate them, and leap on land,
Before the fisher, or into his hand.
Then hath thy orchard fruit, thy garden flowers,
Fresh as the air, and new as are the hours.
The early cherry, with the later plum,
Fig, grape, and quince, each in his time doth come:
The blushing apricot, and woolly peach
Hang on thy walls, that every child may reach.
And though thy walls be of the country stone,
They're rear'd with no man's ruin, no man's groan,
There's none, that dwell about them, wish them down;
But all come in, the farmer, and the clown:
And no one empty-handed, to salute
Thy lord, and lady, though they have no suit.
Some bring a capon, some a rural cake,

Some nuts, some apples; some that think they make
The better cheeses, bring them; or else send
By their ripe daughters, whom they would commend
This way to husbands; and whose baskets bear
An emblem of themselves, in plum, or pear.
But what can this (more than expresse their love)
Add to thy free provisions, far above
The need of such? whose liberal board doth flow,
With all, that hospitality doth know!
Where comes no guest, but is allow'd to eat,
Without his fear, and of the lord's own meat:
Where the same beer, and bread, and self-same wine,
That is his Lordship's, shall be also mine.
And I not fain to sit (as some, this day,
At great men's tables) and yet dine away.
Here no man tells my cups: nor, standing by,
A waiter, doth my gluttony envy:
But gives me what I call, and lets me eat,
He knows, below, he shall find plenty of meat,
Thy tables hoard not up for the next day,
Nor, when I take my lodging, need I pray
For fire, or lights, or livery: all is there;
As if thou, then, wert mine, or I reign'd here:
There's nothing I can wish, for which I stay.
That found King James, when hunting late, this way,
With his brave son, the Prince, they saw thy fires
Shine bright on every hearth as the desires
Of thy Penates had been set on flame,
To entertain them; or the country came,
With all their zeal, to warm their welcome here.
What (gear, I will not say, but) sudden cheer
Did'st thou, then, make them! and what praise was heap'd
On thy good lady, then! who, therein, reap'd
The just reward of her high housewifery;
To have her linen, plate, and all things nigh,
When she was far: and not a room, but dressed
As if it had expected such a guest!
These, Penshurst, are thy praise, and yet not all.
Thy lady's noble, fruitful, chaste withal.
His children thy great lord may call his own:
A fortune, in this age, but rarely known.
They are, and have been taught religion: Thence
Their gentler spirits have suck'd innocence.
Each morn, and even, they are taught to pray,
With the whole household, and may, every day,
Read, in their virtuous parent's noble parts,
The mysteries of manners, armies, and arts.
Now, Penshurst, they that will proportion thee
With other edifices, when they see
Those proud, ambitious heaps, and nothing else,
May say, their lords have built, but thy lord dwells.

BEN JONSON, *To Penshurst*

REACTIONS TO HARDWICK 1610–1953

HIGHER yet in the very East frontier of this county, upon a rough and a craggy soil standeth Hardwick, which gave name to a family which possessed the same: out of which descended Lady Elizabeth Countess of Shrewsbury, who began to build there two goodly houses joining in a manner one to the other, which by reason of their lofty situation show themselves a far off to be seen, and yield a very goodly prospect.

WILLIAM CAMDEN, *Britannia, translated Holland* (1610)

Never was I less charmed in my life. The house is not Gothic, but of that betweenity, that intervened when Gothic declined and Palladian was creeping in – rather, this is totally naked of either ... The gallery is sixty yards long, covered with bad tapestry and wretched pictures.

HORACE WALPOLE, 1760

Some of the Apartments are large, but ill fitted up, & the general Disposition of the Rooms is awkward ... I took notice of a good deal of old Stucco in the State Room representing Hastings, & the figures coloured, but it is very ugly.

PHILIP YORKE, LORD HARDWICKE, 1763

Like a great old castle of romance ... Such lofty magnificence! And built with stone, upon a hill! One of the proudest piles I ever beheld.

JOHN BYNG, LORD TORRINGTON, 1789

... at about 10 we set off [from Chatsworth] for Hardwick Hall ... arrived at about 1, and went over the house which is very curious and old but yet so *liveable* that it looks as if it was not so old as it is.

Extract from Princess Victoria's Journal, Monday, 22 October, 1832

We went to Hardwick – a vilely ugly house but full of good needlework.

EVELYN WAUGH, *Diary*, 1930

We turn round and there Hardwick stands before us at another angle, and we see the lead statues and yew alleys of its haunted garden. To what can we compare it? To Chambord, but only for its fantastic roof, where the ladies sat to watch François Premier hunting in the forest. Not for its interior beauties, for it has none, except the twisting stairway. Yet Chambord is the most beautiful of the French châteaux. The only great house of the Renaissance to which Hardwick could be compared is Caprarola; but its faded frescoes of the Farnese family are as nothing to this hunting frieze; the moss-grown giants, the tritons and Atlantes, are not more magical than the needlework, more romantic than the hand of Mary Stuart; even the faun caryatids, mysteriously smiling, under the full baskets of ripe figs and grapes upon their heads, some of them whispering to their neighbour statue, are not more beautiful than Summer resting on the corn stooks, to watch the golden harvest. From Caprarola you can see Soracte and the Volscian mountains. The dome of St. Peter's floats in the distance over Rome. But we would sooner the view of the collieries outside the park. What wonders we have come from! All hidden, all enclosed behind the leaded windows, under the towers of Hardwick, looking out for all weathers on the stag-antlered trees.

SACHEVERELL SITWELL, *British Architects and Craftsmen* (1945)

It is of a consistency and hardness which must have suited the old woman entirely. And as the house stands on the flattened top of the hill, there is nothing of surrounding nature either that could compete with its uncompromising unnatural, graceless, and indomitable self-assertiveness. It is an admirable piece of design and architectural expression: no fussing, no fumbling, nor indeed any flights of fancy.

NIKOLAUS PEVSNER, *The Buildings of England* (1953)

Elizabeth, Countess of Shrewsbury ('Bess of Hardwick'). Detail from the portrait at Hardwick.

SEE, sir, here's the grand approach,
This way is for his Grace's coach;
There lies the bridge, and here's the clock,
Observe the lion and the cock,
The spacious court, the colonnade,
And mark how wide the hall is made!
The chimneys are so well design'd,
They never smoke in any wind.
This gallery's contriv'd for walking,
The windows to retire and talk in;
The council chamber for debate,
And all the rest are rooms of state.
Thanks, sir, cried I, 'tis very fine,
But where d'ye sleep, or where d'ye dine?
I find by all you have been telling
That 'tis a house, but not a dwelling.

ALEXANDER POPE (attributed), *Upon the Duke of Marlborough's House at Woodstock*

NOBODY had told me that I should at one view see a palace, a town, a fortified city, temples on high places, woods worthy of being each a metropolis of the Druids, the noblest lawn in the world fenced by half the horizon, and a mausoleum that would tempt one to be buried alive; in short I have seen gigantic places before but never a sublime one.

HORACE WALPOLE TO GEORGE SELWYN, AUGUST 12, 1772

...BUT PRINCE PÜCKLER-MUSKAU IS LESS IMPRESSED 1827
On my journey I visited Castle Howard, the seat of Lord Carlisle. It is one of the English 'show places', but does not please me in the least. It was built by Vanbrugh, an architect of the time of Louis the Fourteenth, who built Blenheim in the same bad French taste. That, however, imposes by its mass, but Castle Howard neither imposes nor

(right) Badminton House, Gloucestershire. Detail from the painting by Antonio Canaletto, 1748.

pleases. The whole park, too, has something to the last degree melancholy, stiff, and desolate. On a hill is a large temple, the burial-place of the family. The coffins are placed around in cells, most of which are still empty; so that the whole looks like a bee-hive, only indeed more silent and tranquil.

The park, planted in large stiff masses, is remarkably rich in arch-ways: I passed through about seven before I reached the house. Over a muddy pond, not far from the Castle, is a stone bridge of five or six arches, and over this bridge – no passage. It is only an 'object'; and that it may answer this description thoroughly, there is not a tree or a bush near it or before it. It seems that the whole grounds are just as they were laid out a hundred and twenty years ago. Obelisks and pyramids are as thick as hops, and every view ends with one, as a staring termination. One pyramid is, however, of use, for it is an inn.

PÜCKLER-MUSKAU, *Tour* (1830)

LOWTHER! in thy majestic Pile are seen
Cathedral pomp and grace, in apt accord
With the baronial castle's sterner mien;
Union significant of God adored,
And charters won and guarded by the sword
Of ancient honour; whence that goodly state
Of polity which wise men venerate,
And will maintain, if God his help afford.
Hourly the democratic torrent swells;
For airy promises and hopes suborned
The strength of backward-looking thoughts is
   scorned.
Fall if ye must, ye Towers and Pinnacles,
With what ye symbolise; authentic Story
Will say, Ye disappeared with England's Glory!

     WILLIAM WORDSWORTH, *Itinerary Poems* (1833)

THE house itself somehow seemed full of significance, tinged with melancholy, and steeped in romance; the owls always hooted there in the evenings, there were always white tobacco-plants planted under the windows. It was a very big house, grey, and spreading itself about, with a gallery stretching from one end of it to the other – a place of ample fire-places and log fires, comfort and warmth, the browns and reds of leather chairs, and dark pictures in gilt frames, with a piano at one end and untidy pile of music on the ottoman beside it. The stables were full of horses, the kennels full of greyhounds; from the windows one used to watch a party going off cubbing or hunting, and the dog-boys leading a string of greyhounds across the rather bare and ragged park. Hunting, the famous partridge-shooting, and cricket marked the seasons very distinctly.

CONSTANCE SITWELL, *Bright Morning*

HENRY

JAMES

ON

WROXTON

ABBEY

1905

AND what shall I say of the colour of Wroxton Abbey, which we visited last in order and which in the thickening twilight, as we approached its great ivy-muffled face, laid on the mind the burden of its felicity? Wroxton Abbey, as it stands, is a house of about the same period as Compton Wynyates – the latter years, I suppose, of the sixteenth century. But it is quite another affair. The place is inhabited, 'kept up', full of the most interesting and most splendid detail. Its happy occupants, however, were fortunately not in the act of staying there (happy occupants, in England, are almost always absent), and the house was exhibited with a civility worthy of its merit. Everything that in the material line can render life noble and charming has been gathered into it with a profusion which makes the whole place a monument to past opportunity. As I wandered from one rich room to another and looked at these things, that intimate appeal to the romantic sense which I just mentioned was mercilessly emphasised. But who can tell the story of the romantic sense when that adventurer really rises to the occasion – takes its ease in an old English country-house while the twilight darkens the corners of expressive rooms and the victim of the scene, pausing at the window, turns his glance from the observing portrait of a handsome ancestral face and sees the great soft billows of the lawn melt away into the park?

HENRY JAMES, *English Hours*

LOOKING

BACK

1942

THOSE serene country houses of pre-war years! Looking back at them, they seem to swim in a haze of sunshine and ease, their parks with the light striking across the slopes of open grass as one drove up to the door in the evenings; trout streams, and king-cups, and shallow fords with the cows standing knee-deep in the water; someone fishing in the distance, the sinking sun flushing trees and sward with rich gold green; gardens and familiar gardeners who looked just the same year after year; ancient mulberry trees with their branches propped up from below; bee-hives in a row in the orchard; the mossy broken-down seats in shrubberies. How much indeed of the summer holidays passed going into the garden, pinching and eating fruit; the plums and greengages were visited every day, and the ground in front of them became worn into a path; the leisurely, laughing tennis; the slippery polished staircases and halls, which smelt of bees-wax and azaleas; the big tables with hats and sticks and hunting crops and fishing-rods laid on them and, when one looked out of the window after coming up to bed, there was a twilight lawn and the incense of the evening came up, breathed from garden and grass-land and streams far and near.

CONSTANCE SITWELL, *Bright Morning*

THE DUCHESS OF DEVONSHIRE ON CHATSWORTH 1984

THE charm, attraction, character, call it what you will, of the house is that it has grown over the years in a haphazard sort of way. Nothing fits exactly, none of the rooms except the Chapel is a set-piece, like those in many houses which were built and furnished by one man in the fashion of one time. It is a conglomeration of styles and periods, of furniture and decoration. You find a hideous thing next to a beautiful thing, and since taste is intensely personal you would probably disagree with me as to which is which. It is a decorator's nightmare, unless that decorator has exceptionally catholic taste. There is no theme, no connecting style. Each room is a jumble of old and new, English and foreign, thrown together by generations of acquisitive inhabitants and standing up to change by the variety of its proportions and the strength of its cheerful atmosphere.

Likewise the outside. There is something surprising to see wherever you look; nothing can be taken for granted. Some of the house is like a mongrel dog, bits too long and bits too short, a beautiful head with an out of scale tail, and in the garden there are buildings and ornaments of so many dates and tastes you begin to wonder who was in charge here and when.

DEBORAH, DUCHESS OF DEVONSHIRE, *The House*

28

(right) The Harden family at Brathay Hall, Westmorland. John Harden, 1810.

2
The
Family

Mr and Mrs Tasburgh, of Burghwallis Hall in Yorkshire, lived seven years in the same house without meeting or speaking to each other. The only contact between them was when Mr Tasburgh was walking on the lawn outside the house; his wife would lean out of her bedroom window to spit on him. She had been an heiress, and they were at odds about her property.

Owning land dominated the lives of country-house families. It made them the feudal, or semi-feudal, overlords of hundreds or even thousands of people. Land was the basis of their power and wealth, a frequent reason for their marriages, a source of feuds between families and within families. Buying and selling land, improving it, planting it, farming it or hunting over it, occupied much of their time.

But their wealth and their position as a ruling class constantly pulled them away from their land – to attend court, or parliament, or the London season, to fill government offices, to travel, or just to have a good time. All kinds of options were open to them, and all kinds of different families resulted. There were hunting and shooting families, political families, intellectual families, domestic families and dissipated families. There were families who never went to London, families who seldom left it, and families who vanished for years to Europe. There were wives who went one way, and husbands another. In most counties there were one or two notably 'clever' families, such as the Trevelyans in Northumberland, who were looked at a little askance by their sporting neighbours. All kinds met constantly together, in country or London society, knew each other, criticized each other, and gossiped about each other.

In the background lurked an ideal of perfect balance between town and country, sport and culture, responsibility and fun. A few families or individuals came close to reaching it. Lord Egremont was one, except perhaps for his string of illegitimate children – owner of Petworth, paternal landlord of many thousand acres, patron of Turner and other artists, tireless sportsman, genial host, individual to the point of eccentricity. But eccentricity has always been tolerated in country houses, and the space, time, money and deference built into their way of life has even encouraged it. If the fifth Duke of Portland chose to go underground like a millionaire mole, no-one was going to stop him.

Elizabeth Spencer was a great heiress, the daughter of an extremely rich London merchant, and was in a strong bargaining position.

ELIZABETH SPENCER MAKES THINGS CLEAR TO HER FIANCÉ LORD COMPTON 1594

MY sweet life, Now I have declared to you my mind for the settling of your estate, I suppose that it were best for me to bethink and consider within myself what allowance were meetest for me ... I pray and beseech you to grant to me, your most kind and loving wife, the sum of £2600. quarterly to be paid. Also I would, besides that allowance, have £600. quarterly to be paid, for the performance of charitable works; and those things I would not, neither will be accountable for. Also, I will have three horses for my own saddle, that none shall dare to lend or borrow: none lend but I, none borrow but you.

Also, I would have two gentlewomen, lest one should be sick, or have some other let. Also, believe it, it is an undecent thing for a gentlewoman to stand mumping alone, when God hath blessed their lord and lady with a great estate. Also, when I ride a hunting, or a hawking, or travel from one house to another, I will have them attending; so, for either of those said women, I must and will have for either of them a horse. Also, I will have six or eight gentlemen; and I will have my two coaches, one lined with velvet to myself, with four very fair horses; and a coach for my women, lined with cloth and laced with gold, or otherwise with scarlet and laced with silver, with four good horses.

Also, I will have two coachmen; one for my own coach, the other for my women. Also, at any time when I travel, I will be allowed not only caroches and spare horses, for me and my women, and I will have such carriages as be fitting for all, orderly, not pestering my things with my women's, nor theirs with either chambermaids, nor theirs with washmaids. Also, for laundresses, when I travel, I will have them sent away before with the carriages, to see all safe. And the chambermaids I will have go before, that the chamber may be ready, sweet and clean. Also, that it is undecent for me to crowd up myself with my gentleman-usher in my coach, I will have him to have a convenient horse to attend me, either in city or country. And I must have two footmen. And my desire is, that you defray all the charges for me. And for myself besides my yearly allowance, I would have twenty gowns of apparel; six of them excellent good ones, eight of them for the country, and six other of them very excellent good ones. Also, I would have to put in my purse £2000 and £200, and so, you to pay my debts. Also I would have £6000 to buy me jewels; and £4000 to buy me a pearl chain.

Now, seeing I have been, and am so reasonable unto you, I pray you do find my children apparel, and their schooling, and all my servants, men and women, their wages. Also, I will have all my

(left) Sir Thomas Cave of Stanford Hall, Leicestershire, and family, c. 1770. Silhouette by Toroend.
Elizabeth Vernon, Countess of Southampton. Unidentified artist, c. 1600.

'Fledges' are probably pillows or quilts filled with feathers or down. 'Darnix' is a fabric originally made in Tournai, probably of wool and linen. 'Fustian' is a cloth or cloth blanket with a linen warp and cotton weft.

BESS
OF
HARDWICK'S
BEDROOM
1601

IN my Lady's Bed Chamber: two pieces of tapestry hangings with people and forest work fifteen feet and a half deep, a bedstead, the posts being covered with scarlet laid on with silver lace, bed head, tester and single valance of scarlet, the valance embroidered with gold studs and tassels, striped down and laid about with gold and silver lace and with gold fringe about, three Curtains of scarlet striped down with silver lace and with silver and red silk buttons and loops, five Curtains of purple baize, a mattress, a featherbed, a bolster, a pillow, two little pillows, two quilts whereof one linen, the other candlewick, three pairs of fustians, Six spanish blankets, eight fledges about the bed, two Curtains of red Cloth for the windows, three Coverlets to hang before a window, a Coverlet to hang before a door, a Counterpoint of tapestry before another door, a cupboard inlaid and Carved, a little folding table, a turkey Carpet to it, a chair of russet satin striped with silver and with silver and russet silk fringe, two foot-stools of wood, two foot Carpets of turkey work, a covering for the russet satin Chair of scarlet embroidered with flowers of petit point, a stool and a footstool of scarlet suitable to the same, a high joined stool, two other Joined stools, an inlaid stool.

A long cushion of cloth of gold on both sides, a long cushion of needlework of Crewel with pansies and lined with green says, a little needlework cushion with my Lady's Arms in it lined with red velvet, my Lady's books viz: Calvin upon Job, covered with russet velvet, the resolution, Solomon's proverbs, a book of meditations, two other books covered with black velvet, a looking glass, an hour glass, two brushes, a pair of pulleys lined with black taffeta, a great Iron Chest painted, three great trunks, two little trunks, three Desks covered with leather whereof one a great one, a little desk to write on gilded, a little Coffer gilt, a little Coffer covered with leather, a little Coffer covered in black velvet, three flat Coffers covered

houses furnished, and my lodging chambers to be suited with all such furniture as is fit; as beds, stools, chairs, suitable cushions, carpets, silver warming-pans, cupboards of plate, fair hangings, and such like. So for my drawing-chamber in all houses, I will have them delicately furnished, both with hangings, couch, canopy, glass, carpet, chairs, cushions, and all things thereunto belonging. Also, my desire is, that you would pay your debts, build up Ashby house and purchase lands, and lend no money, as you love God, to my lord chamberlain, who would have all, perhaps your life from you . . .

So, now that I have declared to you what I would have, and what it is that I would not have, I pray you, when you be an earl, to allow me £2000 more than I now desire, and double attendance.

HARLEIAN MSS.

Perseverance, attendant to Penelope. Detail from the 'Heroines and Virtues' embroideries at Hardwick Hall.

Col. Pl. I (top) Barbara, Lady Sidney, with six children. Marcus Gheeraerts the Younger, 1596.
Col. Pl. II Lord and Lady Beauchamp and family in the staircase hall at Madresfield Court, Worcestershire. W.B. Ranken, 1924.

with leather, a box painted and gilded with my Lord's and my Lady's Arms on it, a Yellow Cotton to cover it, an other box covered with green velvet, two trussing Coffers bound with Iron, five wood boxes, a wicker screen, a pair of Copper Andirons, a pair of Iron Andirons, a fire shovel, a pair of tongs, a pair of bellows, My Lady Arbell's bedstead, a Canopy of darnix blue and white with gilt knobs and blue and white fringe, a Cloth of Checker work of Crewel about the bed, a mattress, a feather bed, a bolster, a quilt, four spanish blankets, a pair of fustians. In a pallet there: a mattress, a featherbed, two bolsters, two blankets, a Coverlet, wainscot under the windows.

HARDWICK INVENTORY

Lady Gardiner describes the behaviour of her stepdaughter Ursula Stewkeley at Preshaw, Hampshire.

TROUBLE

WITH

THE

YOUNGER

GENERATION

1674

I wish he [her husband] had stayed at home, but your sex will follow their inclinations which is not for women's convenience. I should be more contented if his daughter Ursula were not here, who after 8 month's pleasure came home unsatisfied, declaring Preshaw was never so irksome to her, and now hath been at all the Salisbury races, dancing like wild with Mr Clark whom Jack can give you a character of, and came home of a Saturday night just before our Winton [Winchester] races, at near 12 o'clock when my family was abed, with Mr Charles Turner (a man I know not, Judge Turner's son, who was tried for his life last November for killing a man, one of the number that styles themselves Tyburn Club), and Mr Clark's brother, who sat up 2 nights till near 3 o'clock, and said she had never been in bed since she went away till 4 in the morning, and danced some nights till 7 in the morning. Then she borrowed a coach and went to our races, and would have got dancers if she could, then brought home this crew with her again, and sat up the same time. All this has sufficiently vexed me.

Her father was 6 days of this time from home, and she lay out 3 nights of it, and Friday she was brought home and brought with her Mr Turner's linen to be mended and washed here and sent after him to London, where he went on Saturday, to see how his brother Mun is come of his trial for killing a man just before the last circuit. And since these were gone, I reflecting on these actions, and she declaring she could not be pleased on the 24, and taking it ill I denied in my husband's absence to have 7 ranting fellows come to Preshaw to bring music, was very angry and had ordered where they should all lie, she designed me to lie with Peg G., and I scaring her and contradicting her, we had a great quarrel.

LADY GARDINER TO HER BROTHER, SIR RALPH VERNEY, 4 MAY, 1674

Col. Pl. III (top left) The Sneyd family dancing in the hall at Keele Hall, Staffordshire, 1882.
Col. Pl. IV (left) Sir Rowland and Lady Winn in the library at Nostell Priory, Yorkshire. Unidentified artist, c.1767.
(above) Sir John Trevelyan of Wallington Hall, Northumberland, and his family. Arthur Devis, c. 1770.

A

DUKE

AND

DUCHESS

AT

HOME:

THE

BEAUFORTS

AT

BADMINTON

1680

AS for the duke and duchess, and their friends, there was no time of the day without diversion. Breakfast in her gallery that opened into the gardens; then, perhaps, a deer was to be killed, or the gardens, and parks, with the several sort of deer, to be visited; and if it required mounting, horses of the duke were brought for all the company. And so, in the afternoon, when the ladies were disposed to air, and the gentlemen with them, coaches and six came to hold them all. At half an hour after eleven the bell rang to prayers, so at six in the evening; and, through a gallery, the best company went into an aisle in the church (so near was it), and the duke could see if all the family were there. The ordinary pastime of the ladies was in a gallery on the other side, where she had divers gentlewomen commonly at work upon embroidery and fringe-making; for all the beds of state were made and finished in the house.

ROGER NORTH. *Lives of the Norths*

AN iron stove w. furniture, 1 Moon Lanthorne, 1 steel crossbow, a iron chest, 1 old squab and cushion, 1 table, 3 cane chairs, 1 old green cushion, 1 pair of old window curtains and rod, 10 pairs of leather bags, 5 dozen money bags, 1 portmanteau, a male pillion, 3 trooping saddles & bridles, housing & holsters, 3 pad saddles, 1 snaffle bridle, 1 fine saddle with red embroidered furniture, & the furniture of a saddle of blue with gold embroidery, 2 tin money shovels and a chain to measure land, 2 swords, 1 sumpter saddle, 1 bridle and 2 hampers.

INVENTORY OF LANGLEYS, ESSEX

(right) Catherine Allan at Brathay Hall. John Harden, 1805

AN

EVENING

WITH

SIR

JOHN

PHILIPPS

AND

HIS

FAMILY

AT

PICTON

CASTLE

PEMBROKESHIRE

1754

THE cloth was just gone, and the clock had struck ten
When Moll, who hates idleness, took up a pen;
No aid she implored, no muse she'd invoke,
For she never attempted to write save in joke.
The subject she chose was her friends round the fire,
For her genius, alas! would never reach higher.
The party consisted of no more than five,
And a list'ner would scarcely have thought them alive,
Such undisturbed silence there reigned, so profound,
That no mortal creature could hear the least sound.
The Knight, as superior, first appears on the stage,
He was carefully turning o'er many a page
While sleep did her Ladyship kindly engage.
The next were her daughters, nor handsome nor gay,
But all honest good kind of girls in their way.
I have only a right to precedence by birth,
I'm honest and free, and love innocent mirth,
And freely submit to my sisters in worth,
Miss Betty all meekness and mildness, and merit,
Miss Kitty, though good, has a little more spirit.
So much for their characters; now I'm to say
How they were employed; not in romping and play,
But instead of all that, and flirting and stuff,
Miss Betty was dextrously making a ruff.
And instead of crying eagerly, who'd cut old shuffle,
Miss Kitty was busily altering a ruffle.
While silently thus our time steals away
We're envied by none, and despised by the gay.
But my comfort is this, we *may* make good wives,
For men say that flirts are the plague of their lives.
Now Sir John shuts his book, and my Lady's awake,
The chambermaid's called for the candles to take.
My pen I must quit, to wish you good night,
May I give you more pleasure the next time I write.

From a Poem by Molly Philipps

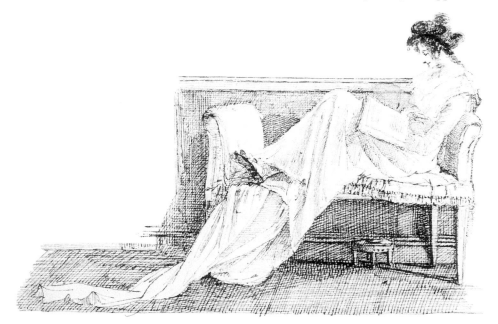

A girl tries on her mother's garland. Watercolour by one of the Drummond children, of Denham, Buckinghamshire, c. 1830.

... **A**ND this day we have been all sitting together in the drawing room going on with our various little employments – Mrs Sneyd by turns making net for one of the Miss Leicester's and a pantin [puppet] for one of the Leicester children – Emma rummaging in a box for new ribbons from Lichfield to find what will suit half a dozen nets – all the ribbons so pretty that they make ones eyes water – Fanny in the library by her recluse philosophical self for some time – Then joining the vulgar herd in the drawing room – Honora on Fanny's appearance quitting her drawing table where she was copying Mr. J. Sneyd's Captain Moneygawl and joining Fanny on the sofa and reading out of one book (and that book too small for any one person) Ariosto, translating it much to their mutual satisfaction both saying the lines at a time and hoping 'Aunt Sneyd and Maria we don't disturb you' ...

Enter Mr Sneyd, to whom as if he was just landed from Naples both the Italian scholars ran with their book and 'Oh uncle! Oh Mr. Sneyd! You'll explain this' ...

Luncheon – damson pie – pork pie – mutton steaks – hot mashed potatoes – puffs – unnoticed – brawn untouched – cold roast beef on sideboard – seen to late! Observation by Mrs Sneyd – Not well bred ever you know to put the gravy on the meat when you serve anybody – No because you should leave the person at liberty to eat it or not as they please.

MARIA EDGEWORTH

SUCH is Lord Egremont. Literally like the sun. The very flies at Petworth seem to know there is room for their existence, that the windows are theirs. Dogs, horses, cows, deer and pigs, peasantry and servants, guests and family, children and parents, all share alike his bounty and opulence and luxuries. At breakfast, after the guests have all breakfasted, in walks Lord Egremont; first comes a grandchild, whom he sends away happy. Outside the window moan a dozen black spaniels, who are let in, and to them he distributes cakes and comfits, giving all equal shares. After chatting with one guest, and proposing some scheme of pleasure to others, his leather gaiters are buttoned on, and away he walks, leaving everybody to take care of themselves, with all that opulence and generosity can place at their disposal entirely within their reach. At dinner he meets everybody, and then are recounted the feats of the day. All principal dishes he helps, never minding the trouble of carving; he eats heartily and helps liberally. There is plenty, but not absurd profusion; good wines, but not extravagant waste. Everything solid, liberal, rich and English. At seventy-four he still shoots daily, comes home wet through, and is as active and looks as well as many men of fifty.

BENJAMIN ROBERT HAYDEN, *Journals*

TWO GENERATIONS AT WALLINGTON 1862

*S*EPT. 24. – Sir Walter is a strange-looking being, with long hair and moustache, and an odd careless dress. He also has the reputation of being a miser. He is a great teetotaller, and inveighs everywhere against wine and beer: I trembled as I ran the gauntlet of public opinion yesterday in accepting a glass of sherry. Lady Trevelyan is a great artist. She is a pleasant, bright little woman, with sparkling black eyes, who paints beautifully, is intimately acquainted with all the principal artists, imports baskets from Madeira and lace from Honiton, and sells them in Northumberland, and always sits upon the rug by preference.

Blind man's buff. Water-colour by one of the Drummon children, c. 1830.

Sept. 26. – Such a curious place this is! and such curious people! I get on better with them now, and even Sir Walter is gruffly kind and grumpily amiable. As to information, he is a perfect mine, and he knows every book and ballad that ever was written, every story of local interest that ever was told, and every flower and fossil that ever was found – besides the great-grandfathers and great-grandmothers of everybody dead or alive. His conversation is so curious that I follow him about everywhere, and take notes under his nose, which he does not seem to mind in the least, but only says something more quaint and astonishing the next minute. Lady Trevelyan is equally unusual. She is abrupt to a degree, and contradicts everything. Her little black eyes twinkling with mirth all day long, though she says she is ill and has 'the most extraordinary *feels*;' she is 'sure no one ever had such extraordinary feels as she has.' She never appears to attend to her house a bit, which is like a great desert with one or two little oases in it, where by good management you may possibly make yourself comfortable. She paints foxgloves in fresco and makes little sketches à la Ruskin in the tiniest of books.

AUGUSTUS HARE, *The Story of my Life*

.... AND 1940

Lady Trevelyan speaks succinctly, carefully and measuredly, using the north country clipped 'a', and is distinctly 'clever'. Gertrude Bell was her sister. Lady T. is handsome in a 'no nonsense about appearances' manner, and looks as though she may have been the first woman chairman of the L.C.C. I don't know if she ever was this. She is authoritarian, slightly deaf, and wears pince-nez. The two daughters are abrupt and rather terrifying. Mrs. Dower paints water-colours, competently. After dinner I am worn out, and long for bed. But no. We have general knowledge questions. Lady T. puts the questions one after the other with lightning rapidity. I am amazed and impressed by her mental agility, and indeed by that of the daughters, who with pursed lips shoot forth unhesitating answers like a spray of machine-gun bullets. All most alarming to a tired stranger. At the end of the 'game', for that is what they call this preparatory school examination, they allot marks. Every single member of the family get 100 out of 100. The son-in-law gets 80, Matheson (who is also a clever man) gets 30. I get 0.

JAMES LEES-MILNE, *Ancestral Voices*

Playing billiards in the long gallery, Capesthorne, Cheshire. James Johnson, c. 1840 (detail).
(right) A corner of the library at Wootton Hall, Staffordshire. Detail from an anonymous water-colour, c. 1850.

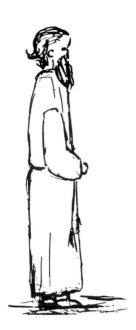

THEN every evening we used to go up to bed at 10, when we reached the landing Granny used to sit down on a chair, and we all stood round and gossiped, perhaps for ten minutes or a quarter of an hour, quite a large party of us, then we all used to go away into our rooms, my Mother used to go away into her room, Pris into hers, Granny into hers, Aunt Emily into hers, Sally into hers and me into mine, and when we were all undressed and in our neat dressing gowns we used again to go and see one another once or twice before we got into bed. Even Uncle Charles used to come and see us, in his dressing-gown, looking more like a man in Noah's Ark than anything else I have ever seen. I have drawn a picture of him, and Father used to come and see us too but he didn't look so much like a man in Noah's Ark because he hasn't got a long beard like Uncle Charles.

ELLEN BUXTON, *Diary*

SIR

ROUNDELL

PALMER

MOVES

INTO

HIS

NEW

HOUSE

AT prayers where we mustered now a large party before kneeling down R. made one of his nice addresses to the whole household, explaining how he came to be in possession by God's blessing on his labour, that we were to remember that we were the first to come and live here, that we must not only try to be a help to our poor neighbours, but examples too and that as there would be always plenty *in* the house he wished never to see or hear of any one of his servants being seen or heard of at a public house – he did it kindly but very firmly.

DIARY OF LADY PALMER, BLACKMOOR HOUSE, HAMPSHIRE, 19 OCTOBER, 1866

AS she grew older her clothes became most remarkable. Some neighbours, calling on her at Deene, found her dressed in Lord Cardigan's red military riding trousers and cuirass with a leopard skin thrown over her shoulders. Her visitors looked rather surprised at this get up, and were still more astonished when she told them it was her bicycling costume! Sometimes she would come down attired as a Spanish dancer, with a coloured skirt covered with lace and a mantilla and high comb, when she would dance the cachoncha, playing the castanets with great skill and verve. Another evening she would flit round the great hall dressed like the Grey Nun who was supposed to haunt the place, when it behoved her guests to show alarm by hiding under the tables and chairs. In every-day life she wore a wig composed of golden curls with a scarlet geranium fixed behind her ear. Many years after she had given up riding she would drive to the Meet in her brougham dressed for hunting in a smart habit and high hat. Stepping lightly out of her carriage she would survey the scene, and then remark to anyone near her that her stupid groom had taken her horse to the wrong Meet. For several years before her death she kept her coffin in the inner hall and would order her butler, Knighton, to lift her into it so that she might be certain that it was comfortable.

LADY AUGUSTA FANE, *Chit-Chat*

(left) Uncle Charles Buxton in his dressing gown, and the Buxton children reciting verses to Papa. Drawings by Ellen Buxton, 1864 and 1865.
(above) The Duchess of Marlborough in her boudoir at Blenheim. George Scharf, 1864.

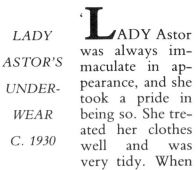

'LADY Astor was always immaculate in appearance, and she took a pride in being so. She treated her clothes well and was very tidy. When she changed she hung her discarded clothes on a hanger, put her hat on the hat stand and trees in her shoes. She was particularly fastidious about her underwear. It was kept in sets in silk pouches which I had to make and decorate in his lordship's racing colours, blue and pink. Every evening I would leave one pouch on her stool and she would fold her underwear into it and tie the ribbon, and so it would be sent to be laundered ... Her ladyship's underwear was hand made in France, at some school for crippled girls, from a silk and wool mixture for winter, with knickers fitting above the knee, and of triple ninon for the summer, beautifully appliquéd and sewn.

R. HARRISON *Rose: My Life In Service*

The 3rd Lord Leconfield in the garden at Petworth, c. 1950.
(right) the 9th Duke of Devonshire and seventeen grandchildren at Chatsworth, Christmas, 1931.

STATELY and strange it stood, the Nabob's house,
Indian without and coolest Greek within,
Looking from Gloucestershire to Oxfordshire;
And, by supremest landscape-gardener's art,
The lake below the eastward slope of grass
Was made to seem a mighty river-reach
Curving along to Chipping Norton's hills.
   Crackle of gravel! in the entrance-hall
Boot-jacks and mattocks, hunting mackintosh,
And whips and sticks and barometric clock
Were Colonel Dugdale's; but a sheaf of bast
And gardening-basket told us of his wife.
'Camilla Russell – Bridget King-Tenison –
And Major Attlee – Patsy Rivington –
Shall we go in? I think it's rather late.'
   Dear Mrs Dugdale, mother of us all,
In trailing and Edwardian-looking dress,
A Sargent portrait in your elegance,
Sweet confidante in every tale of woe!
She and her son and we were on the Left,
But Colonel Dugdale was Conservative.
From one end of the butler-tended board
The Colonel's eyes looked out towards the hills,
While at the other end our hostess heard
Political and undergraduate chat.
'Oh, Ethel,' loudly Colonel Dugdale's voice
Boomed sudden down the table, 'that manure –
I've had it shifted to the strawberry-beds.'
'Yes, Arthur . . . Major Attlee, as you said,
Seventeen million of the poor Chinese
Eat less than half a calory a week?'
       How proud beneath the swelling dome
           I sang Lord Ullin's daughter
           At Mrs Dugdale's grand At Home
               To Lady Horsbrugh-Porter
So Sezincote became a second home.

The love between those seeming opposites,
Colonel and Mrs Dugdale, warmed their guests.
The paddock where the Colonel's favourite mare,
His tried companion of the '14 war,
Grazed in retirement – what is in it now?
New owners wander to the Temple Pool
Where Mrs Dugdale snipped exotic shrubs
With secateurs as on and on I talked.
The onion dome which listened all the time
To water filling after-tennis baths,
To water splashing over limestone rock
Under the primulas and thin bamboo,
The cottages and lanes and woods and paths
Are all so full of voices from the past
I do not dare return.

JOHN BETJEMAN, *Summoned by Bells*

Mrs Ronald Greville on the verandah at Polesden Lacey,
Surrey, c. 1940.
(right) Arthur Williams-Wynn learning to ride a bicycle when
staying at Milton House, Northamptonshire, c. 1890.

3
Guests

*H*aving people to stay is made easy when there is abundance of space and servants. Since both were to be found in country houses, guests have featured prominently in country-house life from the Middle Ages onwards. To begin with, when roads were almost non-existent, distances great, and horse or foot the only means of transport, anyone who came to a house on business or for a meal almost automatically stayed the night. This was less the case as transport improved, but on the other hand improved transport made it easier to bring invited guests across long distances for short periods. The coming of the railways marked the great breakthrough. As a result it was in nineteenth-century country-houses that the house-party entered on its apogee, especially in the form of the 'Saturday to Monday' (the expression 'weekend' was considered vulgar in Victorian and Edwardian days).

At country stations all over the British Isles trains disgorged crowds of ladies and gentlemen from first class compartments, valets and lady's maids from third class compartments, leather trunks and (in the days of the late Victorian bicycling craze) bicycles from the luggage van. All were conveyed in fleets of carriages (for the gentry) and 'brakes' (for the servants) to neighbouring country houses to spend two or three days, or sometimes two or three weeks together. House parties were not necessarily held just for pleasure. They could be a way of pushing social or political ambitions, or putting one's daughters in company with eligible young men. Their make-up was as carefully worked out as the make-up of a dinner-party, and the names of the guests were listed in the social columns of the London newspapers. To have thirty or forty house guests was nothing out of the ordinary in a big country house.

Much of our knowledge of country houses comes from the letters or diaries written by guests. To have the freedom of a big house set in several square miles of woods and parkland, to share it with congenial company, to hunt, shoot, fish, gossip, argue, sightsee, flirt or play games together, could add up to one of the pleasantest ways of passing time ever devised. But the ideal was not always attained; some house parties were more an affair of rich people eating too much and being bored together in the rain. Some guests were uninvited or unwillingly invited; some were more censorious or difficult than others.

THEN it must be seen if strangers shall be brought to chamber, and that the chamber be cleanly apparelled and dressed according to the time of year, as in winter time fire, in summer time the bed covered with pillows and head-sheets in case that they will rest. And after this done, they must have cheer of novelties in the chamber, as junket, cherries, pippins and such novelties as the time of year requireth; or else green ginger comfits, with such things as winter requireth; and sweet wines, as hippocras, tyre, muscadell, bastard, vernage, of the best that may be had, to the honour and laud of the principal of the house.

'FOR TO SERVE A LORD', FROM A MANUSCRIPT OF
C. 1450–1500.

ON Tuesday the 26th Aug. Sir Thomas Hoby was standing in his hall at Hackness, when there came in Sir W. Eure's footboy and said that his master and sundry other gentlemen would come that night. Sir Thomas answered that he was sorry, his wife was ill and he not so well provided for them as he wished, and desiring the footboy to tell his master as much, he answered that his master was hunting in the forest of Pickering Lyth, so as he knew not where to find him.

About two hours after, the above-named, Mr. Dawnay excepted, came to Hackness with sundry other servants and boys, and Sir Thomas hearing they were come into his dining-room went to them and told them they were welcome. Presently after this Sir William Eure's footboy took forth cards and laid them on the table, wherewith some of the gentlemen were exercised until supper. In the beginning of supper, Mr. Eure pretending he had come to hunt, Sir Thomas sent for his servant that had charge of his deer, who dwelt three miles from him, to come the next morning, and so continued with them all the time at supper, which was spent by the gentlemen partly in discoursing of horses and dogs, sports whereunto Sir Thomas never applied himself, partly with lascivious talk where every sentence was begun or ended with a

(left) A frisky horse: an incident when staying with Mr and Mrs Snow, Langton Lodge, Dorset. Diana Sperling, 1823.

great oath, and partly in inordinate drinking unto healths, abuses never practised by Sir Thomas.

In supper time came in a footboy whom they had sent for Mr. Dawnay, and brought word he would come in the morning. After supper Sir Thomas willed to have their chambers made ready, and came himself to bring them to their lodgings, but they being at dice told him they would play awhile, so he did leave them and went down and set his household to prayers as they were accustomed. When Sir Thomas and his family had begun to sing a psalm, the company above made an extraordinary noise with their feet, and some of them stood upon the stairs at a window opening into the hall, and laughed all the time to prayers.

The next morning they went to breakfast in the dining-room, and Sir Thomas hearing them call for more wine, sent for the key of the cellar and told them . they should come by no more wine from him. Presently Sir Thomas sent to Mr. Eure to know how he would bestow that day, and told him if he would leave disquieting him with carding, dicing and excessive drinking, and fall to other sports, they should be very welcome. After this message Mr. Eure sent to Sir Thomas's wife that he would see her and begone, whereunto she answered she was in bed and when she was ready she would send him word.

At his coming she prayed him to depart the house in quietness, and going to the rest of the company, he called a servant of Sir Thomas, and said 'Tell thy master he hath sent me scurvy messages, and the next time I meet him I will tell him so, if he be upon the bench, and will pull him by the beard.' Coming to the uttermost court, Mr Eure said he would go to the top of the hill and fling down mill-stones ... at the same time throwing stones at the windows and breaking four quarrels of glass.

Hatfield MSS

VISITING

IN

CORNWALL

1602

ALL Cornish gentlemen are cousins ... They converse familiarly together, and often visit one another. A gentleman and his wife will ride to make merry with his next neighbour, and after a day or twain those two couples go to a third, in which progress they increase like snowballs, till through their burdensome weight they break again.

RICHARD CAREW, *The Survey of Cornwall*

LORD

GUILDFORD'S

BROTHER

MEETS

THE

ALDERMEN

AT

WROXTON

ABBEY

1684

BUT after dinner in came my old acquaintance the mayor and aldermen, with the council of the neighbour corporation of Banbury. And my brother came out to them and received their compliment, and having answered and drank to them retired to his better company, and left them to me in charge to make welcome. I thought that sack was the business and drunkenness the end, and the sooner over the better; so I ordered two servants to attend us with salvers, glasses and bottles, and not to leave us wherever we went. Then I plied them sitting, standing, walking in all places with the creatures (for I walked them all over the house to shew the rooms and buildings, and sometimes we sat and sometimes stood) until I had finished the work, took leave and dismissed them to their lodgings in ditches homeward bound. But having had a load at dinner, which made me so valiant in this attack, and such a surcharge after, it proved not only a crapula but a surfeit. And I made my way like a wounded deer to a shady moist place, and laid me down all on fire as I thought myself upon the ground; and there evaporated for four or five hours, and then rose very sick, and scarce recovered in some days.

ROGER NORTH, *Lives of the Norths*

IT is the place that of all others I fancy . . . I write an hour or two every morning, then ride out a hunting upon the Downs, eat heartily, talk tender sentiments with Lord Bathurst, or draw plans for houses and gardens, open avenues, cut glades, plant firs, contrive water-works, all very fine and beautiful in our own imagination. At night we play at commerce and play pretty high: I do more, I bet too; for I am really rich, and must throw away my money if no deserving friend will use it. I like this course of life so well that I am resolved to stay here till I hear of somebody's being in town that is worth coming after.

ALEXANDER POPE TO THE MISSES BLOUNT, CIRENCESTER PARK, GLOUCESTERSHIRE, 8 OCTOBER, 1718

...AND OF STOWE 1739

This garden is beyond all description in the new part of it. I am every hour in it, but dinner and night, and every hour envying myself the delight of it.... Every one takes a different way, and wanders about till we meet at noon. All the mornings we breakfast and dispute; after dinner, and at night, music and harmony; in the garden, fishing; no politics and no cards, nor much reading. This agrees exactly with me; for the want of cards sends us early to bed. I have no complaints, but that I wish for you and cannot have you.

ALEXANDER POPE TO THE MISSES BLOUNT, STOWE,
BUCKINGHAMSHIRE, 4 JULY, 1739.

Henry Fox and his friends, perhaps in the garden at Water Eaton House, Oxfordshire. William Hogarth, c. 1738.

POPE

CONDOLES

WITH

TERESA

BLOUNT

ON

A

COUNTRY

VISIT

1714

SHE went to plain work, and to purling brooks,
Old fashion'd halls, dull aunts, and croaking rooks:
She went from opera, park, assembly, play,
To morning walks, and prayers three hours a day;
To part her time 'twixt reading and bohea,
To muse, and spill her solitary tea,
Or o'er cold coffee trifle with the spoon,
Count the slow clock, and dine exact at noon;
Divert her eyes with pictures in the fire,
Hum half a tune, tell stories to the squire;
Up to her godly garret after seven,
There starve and pray, for that's the way to heaven.
  Some squire, perhaps, you take delight to rack,
Whose game is whisk, whose treat a toast in sack;
Who visits with a gun, presents you birds,
Then gives a smacking buss, and cries – no words;
Or with his hounds comes hallooing from the stable,
Makes love with nods, and knees beneath a table;
Whose laughs are hearty, though his jests are coarse,
And loves you best of all things – but his horse.

From ALEXANDER POPE, TO A YOUNG LADY, ON HER LEAVING
THE TOWN AFTER THE CORONATION, 1714

SIR

ROBERT

WALPOLE

ENTERTAINS

FRIENDS

AND

NEIGHBOURS

AT

HIS

BIANNUAL

'CONGRESS'

AT

HOUGHTON

1731

THE base, or rustic story, is what is chiefly inhabited at the Congress. There is a room for breakfast, another for supper, another for dinner, another for afternooning, and the great arcade with four chimneys for walking and quid-nuncing. The rest of this floor is merely for use, by which your Royal Highness must perceive that the whole is dedicated to fox-hunters, hospitality, noise, dirt and business ... We have a whole house full of people, but every body does so much what he pleases, that one's next room neighbour is no more trouble to one here than one's next door neighbour in London ...

Our company swelled at last into so numerous a body that we used to sit down to dinner a little snug party of about thirty odd, up to the chin in beef, venison, geese, turkeys, etc.; and generally over the chin in claret, strong beer and punch. We had Lords spiritual and temporal, besides commoners, parsons and freeholders innumerable. In public we drank loyal healths, talked of the times, and cultivated popularity; in private we drew plans and cultivated the country.

LORD HERVEY TO FREDERICK, PRINCE OF WALES, HOUGHTON HALL, NORFOLK, 14, 16, AND 21 JULY, 1731

LORD

BYRON'S

HOUSE-

PARTY

AT

NEWSTEAD

ABBEY

1809

OUR party consisted of Lord Byron and four others, and was, now and then, increased by the presence of a neighbouring parson. As for our way of living, the order of the day was generally this:- for breakfast we had no set hour, but each suited his own convenience, – every thing remaining on the table till the whole party had done; though had one wished to breakfast at the early hour of ten, we would have been rather lucky to find any of the servants up. Our average hour of rising

was one. I, who generally got up between eleven and twelve, was always, – even when an invalid, – the first of the party, and was esteemed a prodigy of early rising. It was frequently past two before the breakfast party broke up. Then, for the amusements of the morning, there was reading, fencing, single-stick, or shuttlecock, in the great room; practising with pistols in the hall; walking – riding – cricket – sailing on the lake, playing with the bear, or teasing the wolf. Between seven and eight we dined; and our evening lasted from that time till one, two, or three in the morning. The evening diversions may be easily conceived.

I must not omit the custom of handing round, after dinner, on the removal of the cloth, a human skull filled with burgundy. After revelling on choice viands, and the finest wines of France, we adjourned to tea, where we amused ourselves with reading, or improving conversation, – each, according to his fancy, – and, after sandwiches, etc., retired to rest. A set of monkish dresses, which had been provided, with all the proper apparatus of crosses, beads, tonsures, etc., often gave a variety of our appearance, and to our pursuits.

C.S. MATTHEWS TO HIS SISTER, 22 MAY, 1809

An artist painting at Petworth, c. 1828, sketched by J.M.W. Turner when a fellow guest.

TODAY, for instance, I observed the company was distributed in the following manner. Our suffering host lay on the sofa, dozing a little; five ladies and gentlemen were very attentively reading in various sorts of books (of this number I was one, having some views of parks before me); another had been playing for a quarter of an hour with a long-suffering dog; two old Members of Parliament were disputing vehemently about the 'Corn Bill'; and the rest of the company were in a dimly-lighted room adjoining, where a pretty girl was playing on the piano-forte, and another with a most perforating voice, singing ballads.

. . . A light supper of cold meats and fruits is brought, at which everyone helps himself, and shortly after midnight all retire. A number of small candlesticks stand ready on a side-table; every man takes his own, and lights himself up to bed; for the greater part of the servants, who have to rise early, are, as is fair and reasonable, gone to bed.

PRINCE PÜCKLER-MUSKAU, *Tour*

AS far as tobacco is concerned it is said that the Duke of Wellington would only allow smoking in his house after the ladies had retired to bed. He would then inform the gentlemen that those who wished to indulge in the objectionable pastime could do so in the Servant's Hall.

JOHN JAMES, *Memoirs of a House Steward*

Edward Lear's impression of himself sketching at Nuneham Park, Oxfordshire, c. 1860.

SWINBURNE

READS

HIS

POEMS

AT

FRYSTON

1863

IN April of that year Lady Ritchie recalls for me that the Houghtons stimulated the curiosity of their guests by describing the young poet who was to arrive later. She was in the garden on the afternoon of his arrival, and she saw him advance up the sloping lawn swinging his hat in his hand, and letting the sunshine flood the bush of his red-gold hair. He looked like Apollo or a fairy prince . . . On Sunday evening after dinner he was asked to read some of his poems. His choice was injudicious; he is believed to have recited *The Leper*; it is certain that he read *Les Noyades*! At this the Archbishop of York made so shocked a face that Thackeray smiled and whispered to Lord Houghton, while the two young ladies, who had never heard such sentiments expressed before, giggled aloud. Their laughter offended the poet, who, however, was soothed by Lady Houghton . . . *Les Noyades* was then proceeding on its amazing course, and the Archbishop was looking more and more horrified when suddenly the butler – 'like an avenging angel', as Lady Ritchie says – threw open the door and announced 'Prayers, my Lord!'

EDMUND GOSSE, *Swinburne*

HENRY

JAMES

STAYS

WITH

THE

PORTS-

MOUTHS

1878

I am paying a short visit at what I suppose is called here a 'great house', viz. at Lord Portsmouth's. Lady P., whom I met last summer at Wenlock Abbey, & who is an extremely nice woman, asked me a great while since to come here at this point, for a week. I accepted for three days, two of which have happily expired – for when the moment came I was very indisposed to leave London. That is the worst of invitations given you so long in advance, when the time comes you are apt to be not at all in the same humour as when they were accepted. . . .

The place and country are of course very beautiful & Lady P. 'most kind'; but though there are several people in the house (local gentlefolk, of no distinctive qualities) the whole thing is dull. This is a large family, chiefly of infantine sons and daughters (there are 12!) who live in some mysterious part of the house & are never seen. The one chiefly about is young Lord Lymington, the eldest son, an aimiable youth of 21, attended by a pleasant young Oxford man, with whom he is 'reading'. Lord P. is simply a great hunting and racing magnate, who keeps the hounds in this part of the country, and is absent all day with them. There is nothing in the house but pictures of horses – and awfully bad ones at that.

The life is very simple and tranquil. Yesterday, before lunch, I walked in the garden with Lady Rosamund, who is not 'out' & doesn't dine at table, though she is a very pretty little pink and white creature of 17; & in the p.m. Lady P. showed me her boudoir which she is 'doing up', with old china &c.; & then took me to drive in her phaeton, through some lovely Devonshire lanes. In the evening we had a 'ballet'; i.e. the little girls, out of the schoolroom, came down into the gallery, with their governess, & danced cachuckas, minuets, &c. with the utmost docility & modesty, while we sat about & applauded.

To-day is bad weather, & I am sitting alone in a big cold library, of totally unread books, waiting for Lord Portsmouth, who has offered to take me out & show me his stables & kennels (famous oncs), to turn up. I shall try & get away tomorrow, which is a Saturday; as I don't think I could stick out a Sunday here . . . It may interest you [to] know, as a piece of local color that, though there are six or seven resident flunkeys here, I have been trying in vain, for the last half hour, to get the expiring fire refreshed. Two or three of them have been in to look at it – but it appears to be no-one's business to bring in coals . . .

I have come to my room to dress for dinner, in obedience to the bell, which is just being tolled. A footman in blue & silver has just come in to 'put out' my things – he almost poured out the quantum of water I am to wash by. The visit to the stables was deferred till after lunch, when I went the rounds with Lord P. and a couple of men who were staying here – 40 horses, mostly hunters, & a wonderful pack of foxhounds – lodged like superior mechanics!

HENRY JAMES TO HIS FATHER, EGGESFORD HOUSE, NORTH DEVON, OCTOBER 18, 1878

MR

COBDEN-

SANDERSON

LEAVES

NAWORTH

CASTLE

1892

A row blew up between my mother and Cobden-Sanderson, which (as I learnt long after) arose from a stormy argument on whether or not the middle class were 'all snobs' and aristocrats 'unsurpassingly charming'. Both were furious, both were insulting. She 'turned him out of the house', he 'would not stay under her roof another hour'. Not even in a time of desperate anxiety [his children had bad influenza] would either of these fiery fighters make allowance for each other's hot temper. Cobden-Sanderson took himself off to an

Detail from a photograph of a shooting party at Blenheim, 1896. The Prince and Princess of Wales seated, A.J. Balfour 3rd from the left in the back row.

inn in the little town of Brampton, leaving his boy and girl to be looked after in the harassed castle. Every morning he got a Brampton fly to drive him over to Naworth. He stood for some twenty minutes in the courtyard signalling and gesticulating to the window where his children were ill. He was a tiny little man, dressed in a pinkish Norfolk jacket and knickerbockers, with thin little legs in black stockings, and a deer-stalker cap. It was a fascinating sight – and when by child-magic we knew the show was ready, we watched it from a window. That was the last of the Cobden-Sandersons; but his version of the story is too good to leave out. My mother, he said, having ordered him out of the house on the spot, and the children being too ill to move, my mother refused to feed them. So every day a basket was lowered to the courtyard from their high-up bedroom window, and he put food that he had brought from Brampton into it for them.

DOROTHY HENLEY, *Rosalind Howard Countess of Carlisle*

MR BALFOUR IS BLASÉ AT BLENHEIM 1896

THERE is here a big party in a big house at a big park beside a big lake. To begin with . . . 'the Prince of Wales and the rest of the Royal family –' or if not that, at least a quorum, namely himself, his wife, 2 daughters and a son-in-law. There are two sets of George Curzons, the London-derrys, Grenfells, Gosfords, H. Chaplin, etc. etc. We came down by special train – rather cross most of us – were received with illuminations, guards of honour, cheering and other follies, went through agonies about our luggage, but finally settled down placidly enough.

Today the men shot and the women dawdled. As I detest both occupations equally, I stayed in my room till one o'clock and then went exploring on my bike, joining everybody at luncheon. Then again after the inevitable photograph, I again betook myself to my faithful machine and here I am writing to you. So far you perceive the duties of society are weighing lightly upon me.

LETTER FROM A. J. BALFOUR TO LADY ELCHO, 1896

A ROUGH AWAKENING AT CHATSWORTH C. 1900

THE Ante-Room. This was the telephone room when the only telephone was in a sort of shrine. In spite of the size of the house it was not unknown to lodge a male guest here when there was a big party. In the Eighth Duke's time a friend of the Duke of Portland's slept here on a camp bed and was much amused when early in the morning the letter bags were thrown on top of him and the postman shouted, 'Get up you lazy devil, you've overslept again!'

DEBORAH, DUCHESS OF DEVONSHIRE, *The House*

RAYMOND ASQUITH TAKES AGAINST CHATSWORTH 1906

HOW you would loathe this place! It crushes one by its size and is full of smart shrivelled up people. Lady Helen Vincent is the only beauty here and Lady Theo Acheson the only girl – quite nice but not very interesting. I have been a long walk with her in the snow this afternoon – sometimes up to our waists: but I never found it necessary to lift her out of a drift. There is some very mild tobogganing and a good deal of bridge, but shooting and skating are prevented by the snow, and there is only *one* bathroom in the house, which is kept for the King.

RAYMOND ASQUITH TO KATHERINE HORNER, CHATSWORTH, 29 DECEMBER, 1906

. . . . AND ENJOYS (ON THE WHOLE) CLOVELLY, 1901
I am so sorry when I think of you at Brighton and myself here that I cannot help writing to you, though in a few hours from now – damnably few – I shall be lifting my aching bones from a couch which has hardly had time to take the impress of my body and preparing for the great adventure of the day. For it is the custom of the house to plunge *en échelon* into the Atlantic Ocean as near the centre of it as may be at precisely 5 minutes before 8 every morning. We are rowed out in purple bathing dresses by bronzed descendants of Armada heroes

until there is no land in sight but the Island of Lundy and then at a given signal we leap into the blue and bottomless swell and are borne hither and thither like helpless jelly fish in the racing tide.

Having sustained ourselves in the waves so long as our strength holds out we crawl again into the boats and are ferried back to a great lugger anchored off the harbour mouth where we find our clothes elegantly disposed by careful valets; we cover our bodies; light cigarettes and are taken back to land where we find a herd of black thoroughbred Dartmoor ponies; each man and woman selects a mount and we clamber up a sheer precipice where the occasional ash give a perilous foothold and so over a rolling park back to the house where we are welcomed by a smoking mass of lobsters and great dishes of honey and Devonshire cream.

It is a curious life, and being a poor swimmer I find it a little tiring – But the place is so beautiful as to repay any fatigues imposed on one by a barbarous tradition. It really is so marvellously beautiful that description is impotent. If you can imagine the softer glories of an Italian lake crowned by a clean Greek sky and the strong northern air which has fed our Drakes and Hawkins', our Jervises, Collingwoods and Rodneys for countless generations – crimson cliffs thickly mantled with oaks and rhododendrons sliding into a cerulean sea – you have some faint idea of the place. Add to this a square white house standing 400 feet above the sea in a park dappled with fallow-deer, surrounded by smooth lawns and dewy terraces glistening with sun-dials of Parian marble, great trees and luscious shrubs and red garden walls glowing with peaches and nectarines, and shade so cunningly arranged that you can be cool at mid-day and hot in the setting sun and you will admit that Brighton cannot equal it.

The cook is good, the wines are good, the servants are good; at ¼ past 7 every morning a handsome rascal in red plush breeches lays by one's bedside a plate of raspberries and a glass of milk with 6 drops of brandy in it to fortify one for the sea, and large flagons of icy cup are alluringly disposed throughout the day in the mossy shadows of ancient beeches. In the morning one reads at length on cushions in the bright air and in the afternoon we shoot deer and rabbits in the bracken or pull in mackerel from the decks of red sailed boats . . .

RAYMOND ASQUITH TO H.T. BAKER, CLOVELLY COURT, DEVON, 1 AUGUST, 1901

House-party on ice at Eastwell Park, Kent, c. 1860

GARSINGTON:

DAVID

GARNETT

REMEMBERS

1955

GARSINGTON was on the slope of a hill. The approach was down a lane with farm buildings on the right hand side, screening it, so that the lovely dignified front of the Tudor Manor House came as a surprise. It was noble, even grand, yet it was the very reverse of ostentatious.

Inside there were several large panelled rooms, which had, I surmise, been a mixture of genuine seventeenth-century and Victorian baronial styles before Ottoline [Morrell] descended upon them. She had transformed them, stamping her personality ruthlessly everywhere. The oak panelling had been painted a dark peacock blue-green; the bare and sombre dignity of Elizabethan wood and stone had been overwhelmed with an almost oriental magnificence: the luxuries of silk curtains and Persian carpets, cushions and pouffes. Ottoline's pack of pug dogs trotted everywhere and added to the Beardsley quality, which was one half of her natural taste. The characteristic of every house in which Ottoline lived was its smell and the smell of Garsington was stronger than that of Bedford Square. It reeked of the bowls of pot-pourri and orris-root which stood on every mantelpiece, side table and windowsill and of the desiccated oranges, studded with cloves, which Ottoline loved making. The walls were covered with a variety of pictures. Italian pictures and bric-à-brac, drawings by John, water-colours for fans by Conder, who was rumoured to have been one of Ottoline's first conquests, paintings by Duncan and Gertler and a dozen other of the younger artists.

Greeting us was Philip Morrell in riding breeches and rat-catcher coat with a glassy geniality gleaming in his eyes and his head thrown so far back that the high bridge of his nose was level with his forehead. And the pugs barked their welcome.

DAVID GARNETT *The Flowers of the Forest*

GUESTS REACT, 1916–19.

I came here with the notion of working. Mon Dieu! There are now no intervals between the weekends – the flux and reflux is endless – and I sit quivering among a surging mess of pugs, peacocks, pianolas, and humans – if humans they can be called – the inhabitants of this Circe's cave. I am now faced not only with Carrington and Brett

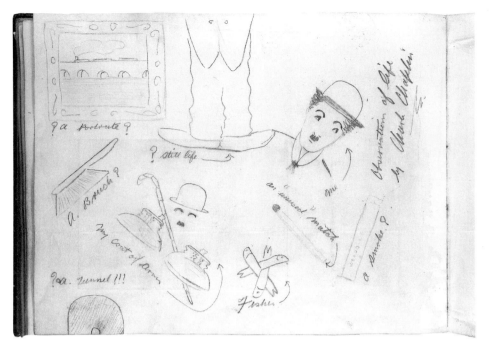

(more or less permanencies now) but Gertler, who
. . . is at the present moment carolling a rag-time in
union with her Ladyship. I feel like an open boat in
a choppy sea – but thank goodness the harbour is
in sight.

LYTTON STRACHEY TO BARBARA HILES, 17 JULY, 1916

KATHERINE MANSFIELD WRITES A THANK-YOU NOTE

My memory of the days we had spent together
was as perfect as ever – as bright as untroubled. I
still saw the blue spears of lavender – the trays of
fading scented leaves, you in your room, and your
bed with the big white pillow – and you coming
down in the garden swinging the gay lantern.

KATHERINE MANSFIELD TO OTTOLINE MORRELL,
11 AUGUST 1917

VIRGINIA WOOLF WRITES TO OTTOLINE

Katherine Mansfield describes your garden, the
rose leaves drying in the sun, the pool, and long
conversations between people wandering up and
down in the moonlight.

VIRGINIA WOOLF TO OTTOLINE MORRELL, 15 AUGUST, 1917

VIRGINIA WRITES TO HER SISTER

The worst of a weekend on that scale is that one
gets rather stupefied before it is over. I had a
private talk with Ott: and on the whole I think that
she has been slightly maligned. At least she was
more vivacious and malicious and less vapourish
than I expected . . . There were endless young men
from Oxford, and Brett and Lytton and Aldous
Huxley who talks too much about his prose
romances for my taste, and falls into deep gloom
when, according to Ott: he is thinking of Maria.

VIRGINIA WOOLF TO VANESSA BELL, 27 NOVEMBER, 1917

VIRGINIA WRITES TO JANET CARE

. . . after two days of it, the discomfort is con-
siderably worse than mere boredom. There are, of
course, visits by night to ones bedroom; and then
if one can't come up to the scratch the poor old
creature gets more and more harassed and desperate; her paint runs too, and her powder blows
off . . .

VIRGINIA WOOLF TO JANET CARE, JULY 23, 1919

ONE

DUCHESS

TEASES

ANOTHER

C. 1920

THE winter shooting parties
and Christmas were the busiest
time at Chatsworth. Every
November the Duke and
Duchess of Portland came over
from Welbeck for four or five
days' pheasant shooting. Although the two duchesses were
friends there was some rivalry
between them over their houses and the things in
them. For these parties a great display of gold and

60

Charlie Chaplin's signature in Sir Philip Sassoon's visitors' book, Port Lympne, Kent.

silver was put on in the dining room. Winnie Portland, well aware that every piece was out on show, used to tease Evie Devonshire by waiting for a pause in the conversation and saying, 'Evie, will you take us down to the strongroom after dinner and show us the plate?'

DEBORAH, DUCHESS OF DEVONSHIRE *The House*

A HOUSE-PARTY AT RENISHAW 1930

WENT to Renishaw. Travelled down with Robert [Byron] who made me go third class. He says he only travels first class abroad because he thinks it is expected of Englishmen. We arrived at Chesterfield Station and found Sachie and Georgia [Sitwell] there to meet us. Also Willie Walton, Harold Monro, a young man, very mad and conceited, called Gaspard Ponsonby (son of Fritz). At Renishaw we found Francis Birrell, Arthur Waley, a nasty man called Roderick and the entire family.

Renishaw very large and rather forbidding. Arterial main roads, coal mines, squalid industrial village, then a park, partly laid out as a golf course, and the house; north front, discoloured Derbyshire stone, castellated. Very dark hall. Many other rooms of great beauty, fine tapestry and Italian furniture. Ginger [Sir George Sitwell] in white tie and tail coat very gentle. Ginger and Lady Ida never allowed to appear together at meals. The house extremely noisy owing to shunting all round it. The lake black with coal dust. A finely laid out terrace garden with a prospect of undulating hills, water and the pit-heads, slag heaps and factory chimneys.

Georgia exquisitely dressed among all these shabby men. G.P. in love with her. She got very much stouter during the ten days I was there chiefly because of bathing and the very good food (chef from Ritz) about which all the family complained. Most of the party left after the weekend. Robert shut himself in his bedroom most of the day. Later Ankaret and William Jackson arrived. I summoned Alastair who had returned to England. The household was very full of plots. Almost everything was a secret and most of the conversations deliberately engineered in prosecution of some private joke. Ginger, for instance, was told

that Ankaret's two subjects were Arctic exploration and ecclesiastical instruments; also that Alastair played the violin. Sachie liked talking about sex. Osbert very shy. Edith wholly ignorant. We talked of slums. She said the poor streets of Scarborough are terrible but that she did not think that the fishermen took drugs very much. She also said that port was made with methylated spirit; she knew this for a fact because her charwoman told her.

The servants very curious. They live on terms of feudal familiarity. E.g., a message brought by footman to assembled family that her ladyship wanted to see Miss Edith upstairs. 'I can't go. I've been with her all day. Osbert, you go.' 'Sachie, you go.' 'Georgia, you go', etc. Footman: 'Well, come on. One of you's got to go.' Osbert's breakfast was large slices of pineapple and melon. No one else was allowed these. Osbert kept cigars and smoked them secretly. I brought my own. The recreations of the household were bathing, visiting houses, and Osbert's Walk. We went to Hardwick – a vilely ugly house but full of good needlework. Osbert's Walk consisted of driving in the car a quarter of a mile to Eckington Woods, walking through them, about half an hour (with bracken), the car meeting him on the other side

and taking him home. He did this every day. There was a golf club where we had morning drinks. This too was a secret. Georgia is the centre of all the plots.

EVELYN WAUGH, Diaries 1930

A HOUSE-PARTY AT CLIVEDEN 1930

DOWN to Cliveden. A dark autumnal day. Thirty-two people in the house. Cold and draughty. Great sofas in vast cathedrals: little groups of people wishing they were alone: a lack of organisation and occupation: a desultory drivel. The party is in itself good enough. Duff and Diana [Cooper], Tom Mosley and Cimmie. Oliver Stanley and Lady Maureen, Harold Macmillan and Lady Dorothy, Bracken, Garvin, Bob Boothby, Malcolm Bullock. But it does not hang together. After dinner, in order to enliven the party, Lady Astor dons a Victorian hat and a pair of false teeth. It does not enliven the party.

Diary of Harold Nicolson, 29 November, 1930

Family and guests at Madresfield Court, Worcestershire, in the 1920s. (Left to right) Evelyn Waugh, Hamish Erskine, Dorothy Lygon, Hubert Duggan.
(right) Menu card, Wilden House, 17 January, 1879.

WILDEN
JANUARY 15 1879

Mock Turtle Soup.
Turbot with Lobster Sauce.
Oyster Patés.
Stewed Kidneys.
Boiled Turkey – Tongue with
Oyster Sauce.
Roast Haunch of Mutton.
Pheasants à la Gitana.
Roast Hare.
Plum Pudding.
Mince Pies.
Jellies &c.   Cheesecakes &c.

4
Eating
&
Drinking

Food and drink had a symbolic role in country houses. To consume it, or cause others to consume it, in enormous quantities suggested power, wealth and hospitality at one go. From the Middle Ages onwards the hecatombs that vanished down the throats of guests at feasts and funerals were carefully recorded.

It was a sign of status for an individual to be served more food than he or she could conceivably eat. In the Middle Ages food came up in what were called 'messes'; each mess contained the same amount of food, but could be served to one great man or six or more lesser persons. The former ate what he felt like; what was left over was passed down the hierarchy until the final remnants reached the beggars at the gate. Consuelo, Duchess of Marlborough, records how this medieval procedure was still lingering on at Blenheim in the 1890s. The vast spreads at country-house breakfasts, as described by Harold Nicolson, were an example of conspicuous waste adapted for Edwardian life.

The route taken by food was part of the symbolism. Serving up a meal became a ritual. The distance between kitchen to dining room was often vast, through deliberate choice rather than bad planning: it allowed for a grand procession, and reduced smells and danger of fire. To want the food to be hot seems to have been a nineteenth-century refinement. Appearance was perhaps more important than taste; certainly, care was lavished on the visual conceits which diversified great feasts, and were the predecessors of the fancy wedding cakes of today.

It can be a relief to move from the orgies being prepared in the kitchen to the refinements of the still room. The stills known as alembics were the equivalent of microwave cookers in the late sixteenth and early seventeenth centuries: new toys with which the mistress of the house personally distilled cordials, medicines and toilet waters. Other forms of medicine were also prepared in the still room, along with dessert delicacies which were the ancestors of the cakes, preserves and biscuits which furnished Edwardian tea-tables.

By then, however, the still room had long since been taken over by the housekeeper. In the late eighteenth and nineteenth centuries the dairy was the place where the mistress of the house amused herself. It was on show to guests who would never have thought of penetrating to the kitchen. Dairy maids could go far. Lady Fetherstonhaugh, the owner of the great house of Uppark in Sussex in the late nineteenth century, had started life as one, her buxom arms busy at the churn catching the fancy of her baronet employer.

Medieval cooks, from the *Luttrell Psalter*.

Col. Pl. V William Brooke, 10th Lord Cobham and his family. Unidentified artist, 1567.

Col. Pl. VI (following page top) The Sperling family at dinner at Dynes Hall, Essex. Diana Sperling, c.1812–13.

Col. Pl. VII (following page bottom) A tea-party at St Fagan's. Detail from the painting of Lord and Lady Windsor and family by Sir John Lavery, 1905.

WEDDING FOOD IN THE FIFTEENTH CENTURY

FOR TO MAKE A FEAST FOR A BRIDE

The first course
Brawn with the boar's head, lying in a field, edged about with
a scripture saying in this wise:
>Welcome you brethren goodly in this hall
>Joy be unto you all
>That on this day it is now fall.
>That worthy lord that lay in an ox stall
>Maintain your husband and you, with your guests all.

Frumenty with venison, swan, pig, pheasant, with a great custard,
with a subtilty: a lamb standing in scripture, saying in this wise:
>I meekly unto you, sovereign, am sent
>To dwell with you and ever be present.

The second course
Venison in broth, viand Ryalle, venison roasted, crane, cony,
a baked meat, leche damask, with a subtilty: an antelope sitting
on a selc that sayeth with scripture:
>Be-eth all glad and merry that sitteth at this mess,
>And prayeth for the king and all his.

The third course
Cream of almonds, losynge in syrup, bittern, partridge, plover,
snipe, powder veal, leche veal, whelks in subtilty, roches in subtilty,
place in subtilty: a baked meat with a subtilty: an angel with a
scripture:
>Thank all, God, of this feast.

The fourth course
Payne puff, cheese freynes, bread hot, with a cake, and a wife lying
in child-bed, with a scripture saying in this wise:
>I am coming toward your bride
>If ye durst once look to me ward
>I ween you needs must.

Another course or service
Brawn with mustard, umblys of a deer or of a sheep; swan, capon,
lamb.

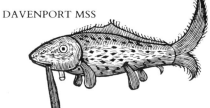

DAVENPORT MSS

HINTS

FROM

THE

COUNTESS

OF

KENT

1653

AGAINST melancholy. Take one spoonful of gilliflowers, the weight of seven barley corns of Bezer-stone, bruise it as fine as flour, and so put it into two spoonfuls of syrup of gilliflowers, and take it four hours after dinner, this will cheer the heart.

To take away a hoarseness. Take a turnip, cut a hole in the top of it, and fill it up with brown sugar-candy, and so roast it in the embers, and eat it with butter.

To take away the head-ache. Take the best salad oil, and the glass half full with the tops of poppy flowers which groweth in the corn, set this in the sun a fortnight, and so keep it all the year, and anoint the temples of your head with it.

For a cough. Take salad oil, *Aqua vitae*, and sack, of each in equal quantity, heat them altogether, and before the fire rub the soles of your feet with it.

THE COUNTESS OF KENT'S *Choice Manual*

THE

COUNTESS

OF

DORSET'S

RECIPE

FOR

WHITE

METHEGLIN

1668

TAKE Rosemary, Thyme, Sweet-bryar, Penny-royal, Bays, Water-cresses, Agrimony, Marshmallow leaves, Liver-wort, Maiden-hair, Betony, Eyebright, Scabious, the bark of the Ash-tree, Eringoroots, Green-wild-Angelica, Ribwort, Sanicle, Roman-worm-wood, Tamarisk, Mother-thyme, Sassafras, Philipendula, of each of these herbs a like proportion; or of as many of them as you please to put in. But you must put in all but four handfuls of herbs, which you must steep one night, and one day, in a little bowl of water, being close covered; the next day take another quantity of fresh water, and boil the same herbs in it, till the colour be very high; then take another quantity of water, and boil the same herbs in it, until they look green; and so let it boil three or four times in several waters, as long as the Liquor looketh any thing green.

Then let it stand with these herbs in it a day and night. Remember the last water you boil it in to the proportion of herbs, must be twelve gallons of water, and when it hath stood a day and a night, with these herbs in it, after the last boiling, then strain the Liquor from the herbs, and put as much of the finest and best honey into the Liquor, as will make it bear an Egg. You must work and labour the honey and liquor together one whole day, until the honey be consumed.

Then let it stand a whole night, and then let it be well laboured again, and let it stand again a clearing, and so boil it again a quarter of an hour, with the whites of six New-laid-eggs with the shells, the yolks being taken out; so scum it very clean, and let it stand a day a cooling. Then put it into a barrel, and take Cloves, Mace, Cinnamon, and Nutmegs, as much as will please your taste, and beat them altogether; put them into a linen bag, and hang it with a thread in the barrel. Take heed you put not too much spice in; a little will serve. Take the whites of two or three New-laid-eggs, a spoonful of balm, and a spoonful of Wheat-flower, and beat them altogether, and put it into your Liquor into the barrel, and let it work, before you stop it.

Then afterwards stop it well, and close it well with clay and Salt tempered together, and let it be set in a close place; and when it hath been settled some six weeks, draw it into bottles, and stop it very close, and drink it not a month after: but it will keep well half a year, and more.

The Closet of Sir Kenelm Digby

FANCY

COOKING

FOR

CHRISTMAS

AND

FEASTS

1660

MAKE the likeness of a Ship in Paste-board, with Flags and Streamers, the Guns belonging to it of Kickses [kickshaws], bind them about with pack-thread, and cover them with close paste proportionable to the fashion of a Cannon with Carriages, lay them in places convenient as you see them in Ships of war, with such holes and trains of powder that they may all take fire; Place your Ship firm in the great Charger; then make a salt round about it, and stick therein eggshells full of sweet water, you may by a great Pin take all the meat out of the egg by blowing, and then fill it up with the rose-water, then in another Charger have the proportion of a Stag made of coarse paste, with a broad Arrow in

To make a Pheasant *of a* Rabbit, *truſs'd in ſuch a manner, that it will appear like a* Pheasant, *and eat like one, with its Sauce.* This is called, by the topping Poulterers, *a* Poland-Chicken, *or a* Portugal-Chicken. But it is moſt like a Pheasant, *if it is larded. From Mrs.* Johnſon, *at the famous Eating-Houſe in* Devereux-Court *near the* Temple.

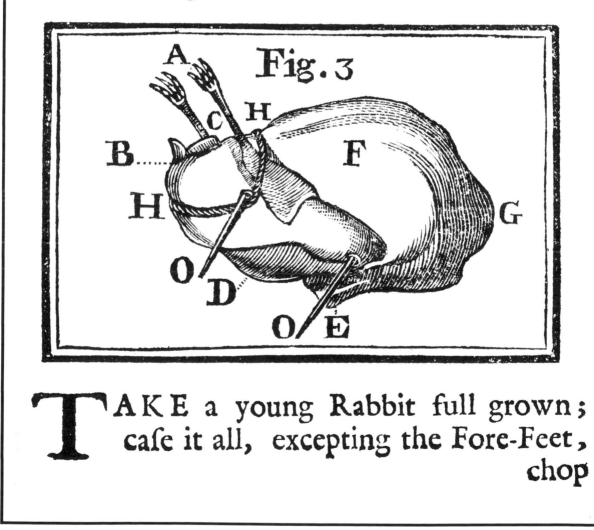

TAKE a young Rabbit full grown; caſe it all, excepting the Fore-Feet, chop

'To make a pheasant.' From R.S.B. Bradley *The Country Lady's Directory*, 1727.

the side of him, and his body filled up with claret-wine; in another Charger at the end have the proportion of a Castle with Battlements, Portcullises, Gates and Draw-Bridges made of Paste-board, the Guns and Kickses, and covered with coarse paste as the former; place it at a distance from the ship to fire at each other. The Stag being placed betwixt them with egg shells full of sweet water placed in salt.

At each side of the Charger wherein is the Stag, place a Pie made of coarse paste filled with bran, and yellowed over with saffron or the yolks of eggs, gild them over in spots, as also the Stag, the Ship, and Castle; bake them, and place them with gilt bay-leaves on turrets and tunnels of the Castle and Pies; being baked, make a hole in the bottom of your pies, take out the bran, put in your Frogs, and Birds, and close up the holes with the same coarse paste, then cut the Lids neatly up; To be taken off the Tunnels; being all placed in order upon the Table, before you fire the trains of powder, order it so that some of the Ladies may be persuaded to pluck the Arrow out of the Stag, then will the Claret-wine follow, as blood that runneth out of a wound.

This being done with admiration to the beholders, after some short pause, fire the train of the Castle, that the pieces all of one side may go off, then fire the Trains of one side of the Ship as in a battle; next turn the chargers; and by degrees fire the trains of each side as before. This done, to sweeten the stink of powder, let the Ladies take the egg shells full of sweet-waters and throw them at each other. All dangers being seemingly over, by this time you may suppose they will desire to see what is in the pies; where lifting first the lid off one pie, out skip some Frogs; which make the Ladies to skip and shriek; next after the other pie, whence come out the birds, who by a natural instinct flying in the light, will put out the Candles, so that what with the flying Birds and skipping Frogs; the one above, the other beneath, will cause much delight and pleasure to the whole company: at length the Candles are lighted, and a banquet brought in, the Music sounds, and every one with much delight and content rehearses their actions in the former passages. These were formerly the delights of the Nobility, before good Housekeeping had left *England*, and the Sword really acted that which was only counterfeited in such honest and laudable exercises as these.

ROBERT MAY, *The Accomplisht Cook*

A WEDDING MENU, 1683

A Bisque of Pigeons
A Sirloin of Beef Royal with Fillets Larded
A Pastry of Venison in Blood
Carps Curbouisson
Pigs darling with Olives of Veal larded
Hams and Tongues. Chi'nered Cold
Crayfish Pottage
Geese Roasted
A Patty Royal
A Haunch of Venison roasted, marinated
with a neck of Veal

A fresh Salmon Colvert with marinated
Fish
A Bisquet of Veal ragou'd
A Joale of Sturgeon marinated with other
Fish
A Patty of Lumber with Trouts about it
Pickled Pullets in Jelly
6 legs of Lamb a la Daube
6 Lambs heads Larded and broiled
Potage de Sante

For ye Middle of ye Table

A square dish of sweet meats
2 dishes of China oranges with each 100

2 pyramids of Fruits
2 pryramids of Sweet meats

To Remove etc. 3 Pottage

1 chine of mutton and veal with Cutlets
a pike Roasted with other Fish about it
A Westphalia Ham with pullets roasted
A chine of Beef upon ye side Table
4 dishes of Hot fowle
2 of Pulpitoons
1 Calves head hashed with Livers Larded
A dish of Boiled Salads
A dish of Marrow puddings
A patty of Eels
A Dish of Blanched beans and Bacon Fried
2 Fricasses of Chickens
A Tart de Moij

A dish of veal with sweet bread, roasted
and Larded with a Ragout
Pigeons du Poviage
Mackerels Broiled
Whitings buttered with eggs
A Tongue and udder roasted
A Dish of Scotch Collops
A Capon in ye Bladder boiled
A dish of Chardons
Chickens foried
Ducklings foried at la Daube
Eggs in Gravy
Pullets hashed

The Cold Messes

6 Comperts from ye Confectioners
6 of Creames
2 of Pistachios ⎫
2 of Chocolate ⎬ Creames
2 of Ice creame
Potts of Lampries
Collered Eel
Crayfish
Collered Pigg
2 Dishes of Jellyes

2 of Blanc-mange
2 Cold Pigeon Pies
2 of Tarts
2 of Morcills and Truffles
2 of Artichokes
2 of Peas
2 of Champinions
19 Dishes of Porcelain with Small meats
    interspersed

The Whole 180 dishes of meat all upon ye Table at one time
The Table 5 yards long and 3 yards broade

BILL OF FARE AT WEDDING OF MRS LEVESON'S DAUGHTER TO MR WYNDHAM

A TABLE OF FOWL

Moſt Proper and in Seaſon for the Four Quarters of the Year.

March, April, May.	June, July, Auguſt.	Sept.br, Octo.br, Novem.br	Decem.br, January, Feb.ry
Turkeys with Eggs	Ruffs Reeves Godwits	Wild Ducks	Chickens
Pheasants with Eggs	Knotts Quails Rayls	Teals	Woodcocks
Partridges n.th green Corn	Pewets Dottrells	Wild Geese	Snipes
Pullets with Eggs	Pheasant Polts	Barganders	Larks
Green Geese	Young Partridges	Brandgeese	Plovers
Young Ducklins	Heath Polts, Black or	Widgeons	Curlews
Tame Pidgeons	Red Game	Shrilldraks	Redshanks
Squab Pidgeons	Turkey Caponetts	Cackle Ducks	Sea Pheasants
Young Rabbets	Flacking Ducks	Cygnets	Sea Parrots
Young Leverets	Wheat Ears	Pheasants	Shuflers
Caponetts	Virgin Pullets	Partridges	Divers
Chicken Peepers	Young Herons	Gronse	Ox Eyes
Young Turkeys	Young Bitterns	Hares	Pea Cocks & Hens
Tame Ducks	Young Bustards	Rabbets	Bustards
Young Rooks	Pea Polts	Ortelans	Turkeys
Young Sparrows	Wild Pidgeons	Wild Pidgeons	Geese
	Young Coots	Capons	Blackbirds
		Pullets	Feldefares, Shrushes.

USED

MEATS:

THE

PORTER

AT

ASHRIDGE

1652

HE is also to attend diligently at private suppers to receive the meat at the yeomans usher's hands that comes from my table; and place it orderly upon the parlour table for the gentlewomen, that what comes from my table they may make their suppers with.

ASHRIDGE HOUSEHOLD REGULATIONS

... AND THE USHER OF THE HALL AT CANNONS, 1721
That he likewise takes care all the meat that remains not fit for any other use be laid up to be delivered to the poor upon the day or days of the week mentioned in the Instructions.

INSTRUCTIONS TO SERVANTS, CANNONS

... AND AN AMERICAN DUCHESS AT BLENHEIM, 1896
It was the custom at Blenheim to place a basket of tins on the side table in the dining room and here the butler left the remains of our luncheon. It was my duty to cram this food into the tins, which we then carried down to the poorest in the various villages where Marlborough owned property. With a complete lack of fastidiousness it had been the habit to mix meat and vegetables and sweets in a terrible jumble in the same tin. In spite of being considered impertinent for not conforming to precedent, I sorted the various viands into different tins, to the surprise and delight of the recipients.

MEMOIRS OF CONSUELO VANDERBILT

GARLIC, ALLIUM; ... 'tho both by Spaniards and Italians, and the more southern people, familiarly eaten with almost everything ... we absolutely forbid its entrance into our salleting, by reason of its intolerable rankness, and which made it so detested of old that the eating of it was (as we read) part of the punishment for such as had committed the horrid'st crimes. To be sure, 'tis not fit for ladies' palates, nor those who court them, farther than to permit a light touch on the dish with a clove thereof.

Lettuce, LACTUCA SATINA ... ever was, and still continues the principal foundation of the universal tribe of sallets [salads] ... it allays heat, bridles choler, extinguishes thirst, excites appetite, kindly nourishes; and, above all, represses vapours, conciliates sleep, mitigates pain; besides the effect it has on the morals, temperance, and chastity.

Thistle, CARDUUS MARIAE; our Lady's milky or dappled thistle, disarmed of its prickles, and boiled, is worth esteem, and thought to be great breeders of milk, and proper diet for women who are nurses. The young stalk, about May, being peeled and soaked in water, to extract the bitterness, boiled or raw, is a very wholesome sallet, eaten with oil, salt and pepper: some eat them sodden in proper broth or baked in pies, like the artichoke; but the tender stalk boiled or fried, some prefer; both nourishing and restorative.

JOHN EVELYN, *Acetaria: a discourse of sallets* (1699)

(top left) Table of Fowl, from Charles Carter *Complete Cook*, 1730.
(left) Silhouette of an unidentified family at table, c. 1760.

ADDISON

IS

INSPIRED

1720

ADDISON, according to the tradition of Holland House, used, when composing, to walk up and down the long gallery there, with a bottle of wine at each end of it, which he finished during the operation.

THOMAS MOORE, *Diary*

THE

FUNCTIONS

OF

A

DINING-

ROOM

1778

THEIR [the French] eating rooms seldom or never constitute a piece in their great apartments, but lie out of the suite, and in fitting them up, little attention is paid to beauty of decoration. The reason of this is obvious; the French meet there only at meals, when they trust to the display of the table for show and magnificence, not to the decoration of the apartment; and as soon as the entertainment is over, they immediately retire to the rooms of the company. It is not so with us. Accustomed by habit, or induced by the nature of our climate, we indulge more largely in the enjoyment of the bottle. Every person of rank here is either a member of the legislation, or entitled by his condition to take part in the political arrangements of his country, and to enter with ardour into those discussions to which they give rise; these circumstances lead men to live more with one another, and more detached from the society of the ladies. The eating rooms are considered as the apartments of conversation, in which we are to pass a great part of our time. This renders it desirable to have them fitted up with elegance and splendour, but in a style different from that of other apartments. Instead of being hung with damask, tapestry, they are always finished with stucco, and ordained with statues and paintings, that they may not retain the smell of the victuals.

ROBERT AND JAMES ADAM, *Works*

CON-

SPICUOUS

CONSUMP-

TION

AT

BELVOIR

CASTLE

1839

CONSUMPTION of Wine and Ale, Waxlights, &c. from December, 1839, to April, 1840, or about eighteen weeks: Wine, 200 dozen; Ale, 70 Hogsheads; Waxlights, 2330; Sperm-oil, 630 gallons.

Dined at his Grace's table, 1997 persons; in the steward's room, 2421; in the servant's hall, nursery, and kitchen departments, including comers and goers, 11,312 persons.

Of loaves of bread there were consumed 3333; of meat, 22,963 lbs., exclusive of game. The quantity of game killed by his Grace and friends, and consumed at Belvoir Castle alone, was 2589 head.

REV. IRVIN ELLER, *History of Belvoir Castle*

Refreshments in the garden of an unidentified house. Detail from the water-colour by Thomas Robbins, c. 1750.

AFTER-NOON TEA 1849

THERE was no gathering for five o'clock afternoon tea in those days, but most ladies took an hour's rest in their rooms before the six or seven o'clock dinner, retiring thither with their books. Later, young ladies persuaded their maids to bring them surreptitious cups of tea from the housekeeper's room, a practice to which they dared not confess for fear of being well scolded by their elders. Married ladies did not conceal the luxurious habit, as many indulgences were allowed to them which would have been thought highly unnecessary for younger people. It was not till about 1849 or 1850, when I was about twenty-six or twenty-seven that five o'clock tea in the drawing-room was made an institution, and then only in a few fashionable houses where the dinner hour was as late as half-past seven or eight o'clock.

MEMORIES OF GEORGIANA CAROLINE SITWELL

HIGH LIVING BELOW STAIRS C. 1880

IT was a great treat for us children to be allowed to have tea in the housekeeper's room; where all the choicest cakes, hot toasted buns and every variety of jam were to be found in far greater profusion than in the drawing-room or school-room. There is a story about the great Lord Derby (15th Earl) who complained to his butler about the badness of dinner, and said gravely: 'I do not expect to have as good food as you have in the housekeeper's room, but I must insist on its being the same as in the servant's hall.'

LADY AUGUSTA FANE, *Chit Chat*

EDWARDIANS AT BREAKFAST C. 1910

ONLY the really improper Edwardians had breakfast in their rooms. The others met, on that Sunday morning, in the dining-room. The smell of last night's port had given place to the smell of this morning's spirits of wine. Rows of little spirit lamps warmed rows of large silver dishes. On a table to the right between the windows were

(right) Breakfast in the Carved Room, Petworth House, Sussex. Detail from the water-colour by Mrs Percy Wyndham, c. 1865.

Tea on the terrace before an unidentified country house, c. 1900.

grouped Hams, Tongues, Galantines, Cold Grouse, ditto Pheasant, ditto Partridge, ditto Ptarmigan. No Edwardian meal was complete without Ptarmigan. Hot or Cold. Just Ptarmigan. There would also be a little delicate rectangle of pressed beef from the shop of M. Benoist. On a further table, to the left between the doors, stood fruits of different calibre, and jugs of cold water, and jugs of lemonade. A fourth table contained porridge utensils. A fifth coffee, and pots of Indian and China tea. The latter were differentiated from each other by little ribbons of yellow (indicating China) and of red (indicating, without *arrière pensée*, our Indian Empire). The centre table, which was prepared for twenty-three people, would be bright with Malmaisons and toast-racks. No newspapers were, at that stage, allowed.

The atmosphere of the Edwardian dining-room at nine-thirty was essentially daring. A pleasant sense of confederacy and sin hung above the smell of the spirit-lamps. For had they not all been brought up to attend family prayers? And had they not all eluded that obligation? It was true, of course, that the host and hostess, with their niece, had at nine proceeded to the family chapel and heard the butler reading a collect for the day. But the guests had for their part evaded these Victorian obligations. This corporate evasion gave to the proceedings an atmosphere of dash. There was no insincerity in the bright gaiety with which they greeted each other, with which they discussed how he or she had slept. 'A little kedjiree, Lady Maude?' 'Oh, thank you, Mr Stapleton.' Evidently it was all going very well.

Edwardian breakfasts were in no sense a hurried proceeding. The porridge was disposed of negligently, people walking about and watching the rain descend upon the Italian garden. Then would come whiting and omelette and devilled kidneys and little fishy messes in shells. And then tongue and ham and a slice of Ptarmigan. And then scones and honey and marmalade. And then a little melon, and a nectarine or two, and just one or two of those delicious raspberries. The men at that stage would drift (I employ the accepted term) to the smoking-room. The women would idle in the saloon watching the rain descend upon the Italian garden. It was then 10.30.

HAROLD NICOLSON, *Small Talk*

BOWOOD
PICNICS
IN
THE
1920s

ONE custom particularly delighted us at Bowood. It was a sort of survival of the former *fêtes champêtres*. Lady Lansdowne ('Granny Maud', as she was called by her grandchildren) would ask the guests after breakfast whether they would like a picnic lunch as a change if 'Daddy Clan' (Lord Lansdowne) thought it would be fine enough. On his approval being given, the arrangements were made. On the first occasion I assumed that this would entail a walk or drive, by car or carriage, and perhaps an uncomfortable but agreeable lunch in a wood or on the side of a hill. As the hours . . . passed I began to wonder what was going to happen. At one o'clock we were ready to start, and the little company walked about two or three hundred yards from the house to the lake. At the lakeside was a boat-house, and a kind of chalet or summer-house . . . The luncheon had been carried down; the tables were arranged in the same silver and glass and napery as would have been used in the house. The butler and one or two footmen were there to serve. In fact the picnic was no different from an ordinary lunch, except that we ventured a few hundred yards from the mansion, and sat above the boat house. After luncheon and all the suitable wines had been served and coffee drunk, we processed back to the house. The great expedition had taken place.

HAROLD MACMILLAN, *Winds of Change*

Breakfast at Sunningdale Park, Berkshire, photographed by Alexandra, Princess of Wales, c. 1889.
(right) The Duke of Clarence and Princess Mary of Teck, photographed in the conservatory of Luton Hoo, Bedfordshire, after their engagement in December 1891.

5
Love,
Lust
&
Marriage

Up till the eighteenth century almost all country-house marriages were arranged. From then on, if not arranged they were at least engineered. Daughters were introduced to the right young men, and vice versa. Lady Stanley of Alderley could afford to write indulgently about her daughter's courtship in the 1860s. It was an earl who was courting her.

Many arranged marriages turned out happily. Conscientious parents would not push their children into marrying someone with whom they were obviously imcompatible. However, country-house life allowed couples who had merged on the basis of property and good connections, rather than love or even respect, to go their own way after marriage – within reason. They could move into different parts of the same house, or into different houses. Husbands could keep mistresses, as long as they were not kept in the same house as their wives. It was acceptable, and even usual, for a mistress to be of a lower social class, but unacceptable, in this case, for her lover to marry her. Lady Harington's isolation was largely due to the fact that she had been both an actress and her husband's mistress before marriage. County society would never have visited her at Elvaston Castle, had it been invited.

Upper-class wives could take lovers, as long as they were reasonably discreet about it – and had produced a *bona-fide* heir first. Wilfred Scawen Blunt was keeping the conventions by creeping secretly across the moonlit hall at Parham – but breaking them because he was heading for a newly-married wife. Lady Caroline Lamb broke all the conventions because she made her feelings about Byron public – even doing such silly things as slashing her wrists in front of him at a London ball. She was frozen out of London as a result.

There were plenty of exceptions to the general pattern. There were love-matches and elopements, from the earliest years. There were couples who stayed devoted to each other all their lives. And there were county girls who went completely to the bad, like Bess Broughton, who ran off from a Herefordshire manor house in the seventeenth century, and became one of the most notorious of London prostitutes.

OLAVE SHARINGTON WINS A HUSBAND AT LACOCK ABBEY

DAME Olave, a daughter and co-heir of Sir Henry Sharington, of Lacock, being in love with John Talbot, a younger brother of the Earl of Shrewsbury, and her father not consenting that she should marry him; discoursing with him one night from the battlements, said she, I will leap down to you. Her sweetheart replied, he would catch her then; but he did not believe she would have done it. She leapt down, and the wind, which was then high, came under her coats and did something break the fall. Mr Talbot caught her in his arms, but she struck him dead: she cried out for help, and he was with great difficulty brought to life again. Her father told her that since she had made such a leap she should e'en marry him. She was my honoured friend Col. Sharington Talbot's grandmother, and died at her house at Lacock about 1651, being about an hundred years old.

JOHN AUBREY, *Brief Lives*

THE COUNTESS OF PEMBROKE AT WILTON C. 1580

SHE was a beautiful lady and had an excellent wit, and had the best breeding that that age could afford. She had a pretty sharp-oval face. Her hair was of reddish yellow.

She was very salacious, and she had a contrivance that in the spring of the year when the stallions were to leap the mares they were to be brought before such a part of the house, where she had a *vidette* to look on them and please herself with their sport; and then she would act the like sport herself with *her* stallions. One of her great gallants was crookback't Cecil, earl of Salisbury.

JOHN AUBREY, *Brief Lives*

(left) Madame Baccelli, mistress of the 3rd Duke of Dorset, being painted by Gainsborough in the ballroom at Knole. From a drawing of c. 1782, possibly by Ozias Humphrey.

A young man serenading a lady before Aylesford Friary, Kent. Detail from a painting of c.1650 by an unidentified artist.

MISTRESS Elizabeth Broughton was daughter of Broughton in Herefordshire, an ancient family. Her father lived at the manor-house at Canon-Peon. Whether she was born there or no, I know not: but there she lost her maiden-head to a poor young fellow, then I believe handsome, but, in 1660, a pitiful poor old weaver, clerk of the parish. He had fine curled hair, but grey. Her father at length discovered her inclinations and locked her up in the turret of the house, but she gets down by a rope; and away she got to London, and did set-up for her self.

She was a most exquisite beauty, as finely shaped as nature could frame; and had a delicate wit. She was soon taken notice of at London, and her price was very dear.

JOHN AUBREY, *Brief Lives*

A match had been arranged between Philip Carteret and Lady Jemima Montagu, daughter of Pepys's patron and former employer, the Earl of Sandwich. In July 1665 Pepys took the young man to meet his future wife at Dagnans, in Essex.

JULY 15, 1665 . . . but Lord, what silly discourse we had by the way as to matter of love-making, he being the most awkward man ever I met withal in my life as to that business. Thither we came by time it begin to be dark, and were kindly received by my Lady Wright and my Lord Crew; and to discourse they went, my Lord discoursing with him, asking him questions of travel, which he answered well enough in a few words. But nothing to the lady from him at all. To supper, and after supper to talk again, he yet taking no notice of the lady. My Lord would have had me have consented to leaving the young people together tonight to begin their amours, his staying being but to be little. But I advised against it, lest the lady might be too much surprised. So they led him up to his chamber, where I stayed a little to know how he liked the lady; which he told me he did mightily, but Lord, in the dullest insipid manner

that ever lover did. So I bid him good-night, and down to prayers with my Lord Crew's family . . .

July 16. LORD'S DAY . . . Having trimmed myself, down to Mr Carteret; and he being ready, we down and walked in the gallery an hour to two . . . Here I taught him what to do; to take the lady always by the hand to lead her; and telling him that I would find opportunity to leave them two together, he should make these and these compliments, and also take time to do the like to my Lord Crew and Lady Wright. After I had instructed him, which he thanked me for, owning that he needed my teaching him, my Lord Crew came down and family, the young lady among the rest; and so by coaches to church . . .

Thence back again by coach – Mr Carteret having not had the confidence to take this lady once by the hand, coming or going; which I told him of when we came home, and he will hereafter do it. So to dinner . . . Then to walk in the gallery and to sit down. By and by my Lady Wright and I go out (and then my Lord Crew, he not by design); and lastly my Lady Crew came out and

left the young people together. And a little pretty daughter of my Lady Wright's most innocently came out afterward, and shut the door to, as if she had done it, poor child, by inspiration – which made me without have good sport to laugh at.

They together an hour; and by and by church time, whither he led her into the coach . . . So home again and to walk in the gardens, where we left the young couple a second time . . .

July 17. Up, all of us, and to billiards . . . By and by the young couple left together. Anon to dinner . . . Before we went, I took my Lady Jem apart and would know how she liked this gentleman and whether she was under any difficulty concerning him. She blushed and hid her face awhile, but at last I forced her to tell me; she answered that she could readily obey what her father and mother had done – which was all she could say or I expect . . .

July 24 . . . I find Mr Carteret yet as backward almost in his caresses as he was the first day.

The wedding took place on July 31. Pepys set out for it 'being in my new coloured-silk suit and coat, trimmed with gold buttons and gold broad lace

A bedroom in the Nostell Priory doll's house, c. 1740.

round my hands, very rich and fine.' *Owing to a muddle over the coach, he missed the service. However:-* ... so to dinner, and very merry we were ... At night to supper, and so to talk and, which methought was the most extraordinary thing, all of us to prayers as usual, and the young bride and bridegroom too. And so after prayers, soberly to bed; only, I got into the bridegroom's chamber while he undressed himself, and there was very merry – till he was called to the bride's chamber and into bed they went. I kissed the bride in bed, and so the curtains drawn with the greatest gravity that could be, and so goodnight.

SAMUEL PEPYS, *Diary*

A young girl dreams of balls and Byron at her dressing table. From the drawing by Olivia de Ros, c. 1820.

LADY CAROLINE LAMB HOLDS AN AUTO-DA-FÉ AT BROCKET HALL 1812

BYRON at last was sick of her. When their intimacy was at an end, and while she was living in the country, she burned, very solemnly, on a sort of funeral pile, *transcripts* of all the letters which she had received from Byron, and a *copy* of a miniature (his portrait) which he had presented to her; several girls from the neighbourhood, whom she had dressed in white garments, dancing round the pile, and singing a song which she had written for the occasion.

SAMUEL ROGERS, *Table Talk*

Lady Caroline recited the following verses by the bonfire, dressed in her favourite costume as a page.

> See here are locks and braids of coloured hair
> Worn oft by me, to make the people stare;
> Rouge, feathers, flowers, and all those tawdry things,
> Besides those Pictures, letters, chains, and rings –
> All made to lure the mind and please the eye,
> And fill the heart with pride and vanity –
> Burn, fire, burn; these glittering toys destroy.
> While thus we hail the blaze with throats of joy.
> Burn, fire, burn, while wondering Boys exclaim,
> And gold and trinkets glitter in the flame.
> Ah! look not thus on me, so grave, so sad;
> Shake not your heads, nor say the Lady's mad.
> Judge not of others, for there is but one
> To whom the heart and feelings can be known.
> Upon my youthful faults few censures cast.
> Look to the future – and forgive the past.
> London, farewell; vain world, vain life, adieu!
> Take the last tears I e'er shall shed for you.
> Young tho' I seem, I leave the world for ever,
> Never to enter it again – no, never – never!

LORD

AND

LADY

HARRING-

TON

AT

HOME

1835

ANOTHER castle with which I was very familiar was Elvaston, near Derby, where year after year I stayed with the late Lord and Lady Harrington. Originally a red-brick manor house, it was castellated in the days of Wyatt; and though architects of today would smile at its artificial Gothic, it may now for this very reason be regarded as an historical monument. It is a monument of tastes and sentiments which have long since passed away. It represents not only a vanished taste in architecture, but sentiments also which are now even more remote. The Earl of Harrington, under whom the Gothic transfiguration was accomplished, seems to have regarded himself as a species of knight-errant. Round the fluted pillars by which the roof of the hall is supported – a hall which he christened 'the hall of the fair star' – were strapped imitation lances, and the windows were darkened by scrolls which all bore the same motto, 'Loyal to Honour and to Beauty'. This Lord Harrington had married a very beautiful wife, for whose pleasure he surrounded the house with a labyrinth of clipped yew hedges, the trees having been brought full grown from every part of England. Animated by a romantic jealousy, he never permitted this lady to stray beyond the park gates, and a little pavilion at the end of a yew avenue contains, or contained till lately, a curious something which is a vivid revelation of his mind. It consists of an image in plaster-of-Paris of his lady-love, together with one of himself kneeling at her feet and gazing at her, his hands being about to commit his adoration to the strings of a guitar.

W. H. MALLOCK, *Memoirs of Life and Literature*

Love on a bicycle. Detail of a frieze at Paddockhurst House, Sussex, designed by Walter Crane, *c.*1897.

BARBARA
TASBURGH
ELOPES
FROM
BURGH-
WALLIS
HALL
1839

I was greatly grieved to leave my poor, long-suffering mother, who had been so unvariedly kind to me. I hardly know how I kept from breaking down. She always went to bed early, and after kissing her as usual on parting for the night I retired to my own room, locked myself in, and changed my light-coloured summer frock for one of a dark *cachemire*.

As for the watch-dog that was kennelled under my bedroom window to keep guard over my slumbers, the good Mrs Firth gave it some harmless drug which removed the danger from that direction. At half-past eleven I lit up my room, opened wide the window, and sat down to wait. At a quarter to midnight, on Wednesday the 19th June, William was under my window, having posted from Doncaster and left the chaise at the end of the lane so that the noise of wheels should not disturb the house. I threw my soft bundle of belongings out of the window, and then by means of torn-up sheets fastened to a heavy, old-fashioned sofa, I swung out and, wonderful to say, got down without a scratch. We ran for our lives to where the chaise was standing, the object of getting posters from Doncaster instead of from Robin Hood's Well (only a mile from Burgh-wallis) being to leave no clue behind for pursuit in the morning.

We posted through the night,

and all next day, until we reached the Blacksmith's house at Gretna Green at 6 p.m. on the evening of June 20th, when we became man and wife.

L.E.O. CHARLTON, *Recollections of a Northumbrian Lady*

(left) The Marquess and Marchioness of Lansdowne at a window of Bowood House, Wiltshire, in 1870, shortly after their marriage.
(above) A young man plays his flute for the ladies at Dynes Hall. Diana Sperling, *c.*1815–20.

THE

EARL

OF

AIRLIE

PROPOSES

AT

ALDERLEY

HALL

1851

AUGUST 3.

He never leaves her side for a moment, & she seems very well pleased, & they are now, between 12 & 1, sitting on the lawn with a book each, but I can see by the reflection in the window that he is not reading. I do not know why he does not settle it, Blanche says she gives him every opportunity, but her manner is rather brusque and perhaps he is a little afraid, & she every now & then says very odd things. But all is in a right train & I hardly think she would make such a slave of him if she did not mean to reward him.

August 4.

It is all settled, & I do hope it will be for our darling's happiness – I never saw more deep feeling than on his part, & tho' Blanche is very nervous yet she is glad it is settled. During their ride he asked her if she would care for a dog, if he gave her one, & when she came home she went upstairs to rest. I saw at dinner he was very nervous & that he was most anxious to speak. I had given her a red carnation (like those I used to give you) to give him, at first she said she would not, but she came down with the heath in her hair he had got for her & waited on the stair case to give him the flower – he never spoke but looked very pale. After dinner he rushed after her, & she went with him to sit on two chairs under the brown beech, & then we all walked out, they turned up the Fernhill & we walked all about the boy's walk. When we came home I saw him alone & he came & took my arm & walked me away in the dark, & he could not speak so I was obliged to begin, & then he told me he had spoken to her & that 'she had no great objection', that he loved her very much – had done so for two years – that he had been very unhappy the last week because he thought she never would like him. I said then why *would* you go to Goodwood – he said he was obliged to do so. After some talk I left him to go to Blanche, & found her on her knees in her room, very nervous, but much happier, & then she told me how it all happened, that they went off walking & he never spoke all the time till she grew so faint & cold she said she must sit down. He then said he hoped she would not be

angry but he must speak – she covered her face with her hands & he went on & said he was neither as good nor as clever as she was, but that he loved her very much, & she never answering till she says he took her hand & spoke in such agony & told her she frightened him, & then she answered that she would try to make him happy, but she said her voice sounded cold & different to his. She then asked him if he cld. give up the thing he liked best for her, meaning racing, & he said he would, & she asked him if he had ever loved Lady Rachel at which he laughed & said never. She also asked him if he had ever liked anyone & he said he had been in love with Martia Fox, & she was kind enough to say that she did not mind that as she was dead, & was very good – & after such talk she went upstairs.

LADY STANLEY OF ALDERLEY TO LORD STANLEY

'Doll' is Lady Zouche, recently and unhappily married. She ran off from her husband shortly after this incident – but not with Blunt. His account is a mixture of reminiscence, and diary entries made at the time.

A

SUSSEX

AFFAIR:

WILFRED

SCAWEN

BLUNT

FALLS

FOR

HIS

HOSTESS

AT

PARHAM

1875

THE week that followed

was a week of extravagant amusement, one of sublime unreason in an Earthly Paradise, for Parham is in all Sussex, and therefore in all England, the perfectest and best, the most ideal framework of romance. Its old park and its ancient trees, its oaks and thorns and knee deep fern, set at the foot of the downs, from which ten minutes takes a rider to the top where he will meet the breezes from the sea, the wide heaths stretching northwards, the great fir wood where the herons breed, and the Tudor glories of the house, all these beautiful and noble things were then combined, to make a play ground for us during just that week, a week of riotous profanity which grieves my conscience yet, and was then to be shut up for us and lost for ever . . . I was ensorcelled with Doll's gipsy face, with her sudden love for me and the romance of

Gentlemen of the Bootle-Wilbraham family paying homage before Lathom House, Lancashire, 1904.

the situation. To have foregone playing the leading part in such a drama when thus thrust upon me was an impossibility of what was in my nature. During that enchanted week I saw her as the sleeping beauty to be called to life by her prince of fairyland and I resolved it should be my hand to wake her. If it was not mine it would be another's, this was clear. Robin had lost all control over the situation; he seemed already to have abdicated his marital right, and she was too pretty to be long without a lover . . .

The week went by in imitation of the wild life we were supposed to be about to lead in Abyssinia. The weather was perfect for the purpose and we were to live as far as possible out of doors. Doll was in her nature a gipsy and this was entirely to her mind.

September 13 . . . Suddenly it was resolved we should sleep tonight in the North Park Woods and we fixed on the heronry as our place of encampment. Beds were robbed of their blankets, the kitchen of its cooking pots, a cart was ordered to the door and loaded with the spoils . . . We made our fire under the giant fir trees, ranging our sleeping places round it, while Pompey roasted partridges upon a wooden spit. One huge bed was spread for all the party which we called the 'Bed of Ware', and we sat talking far into the night. Doll in her ulster coat a true gipsy, had hung a piece of looking glass near her on a tree and was tired now after her long day of violent life, and sad and tender. She sat watching me with great black eyes in the firelight . . . At last we lay down, our pillows almost touching and our faces. It was long before we slept. The fire burned at first too brightly and the moon was nearly at its full. After the rest were silent we two were still awake and always when I looked at her her eyes were wide and fixed on mine. There were rooks above us which fidgeted overhead, and once a heron coming back to roost settled a moment, then with a ghostly croak seeing there were strangers there flapped hurriedly away . . . At last the fire burned down and the moon set . . . That was our marriage night . . .

The days and nights that followed were hardly less an enchantment. Parham was a ghostly house in which to wander by moonlight and every night I passed from the East Wing where my room was placed to hers in the West Wing, descending a stair and then ascending, and passing between the two stairs through the uncurtained hall watched by the moon and by the effigies in armour. In this lay the romance close bound up with the risk, the dangers of discovery. She, reckless child, feared nothing. All she asked was to be free of the last tie that bound her to her legal lord. He had been useless to her as a husband, and she held him cheap. When at our last night's end Sept. 19, it was time for us to go home, Doll tearful at parting made me take with me her wedding ring. I am to give her another in its place. We are to love each other for ten years, since it is best to fix a limit to all human happiness, and we are to meet again in London on Tuesday, and on the 30th for another week at Crabbet.

BLUNT MSS, FITZWILLIAM MUSEUM

AN UNFORTU-NATE MISTAKE C. 1880

EVEN the craftiest did not always succeed in his stratagems. Lord Charles Beresford told my grandfather that on one occasion he tiptoed into a dark room and jumped into the vast bed shouting 'Cock-a-doodle-doo', to find himself, when trembling hands had lit a paraffin lamp, between the Bishop of Chester and his wife. The situation seemed very difficult to explain and he left the house before breakfast next morning.

ANITA LESLIE, *Edwardians in Love*

(right) Lord Nelson and Emma Hamilton entering the grounds of Fonthill Abbey, Wiltshire, 1801.

6
Parties

*P*arties in country houses originated to celebrate particular events: feasts, especially
Christmas and the New Year; births, marriages,
and funerals; and the paying of rent by tenants.
They invariably involved eating and drinking, and
were sometimes followed by dancing. A party was
no good unless it involved gorging and getting
drunk.

Over the centuries the range and types of parties were extended. House-warming parties, servants' balls and coming-of-age parties all appeared in the eighteenth century, and perhaps a little before. Garden parties were a nineteenth-century development. They were a response to increasing numbers of middle-class families living in country neighbourhoods, who were too grand to be invited to tenant's balls and not grand enough to be asked to dinner. Hence the abbreviation GPO, for 'Garden Party Only' which Mrs Sothill in Evelyn Waugh's *Put Out More Flags* affixed to certain names in her address book.

In earlier days there was a distinction between parties in country houses, which were attended by all classes, and parties in London, which were aimed at the fashionable. Funerals took place in the country, christening and parties to launch daughters were more often held in London. The right kinds of godparents and young men could more easily be gathered together there.

As transport improved, and the lesser gentry learned social graces in provincial assembly rooms, London-type parties began to be introduced to the country. The eighteenth-century type of ball was a London invention: the emphasis was on dancing rather than eating or drinking, and only upper-class guests were invited. Towards the end of the century, balls began to be given in country houses; but the reaction of guests to the ball at Fawley Court, in 1777, is still 'Sure, we are in London'.

The belief that landowners had a duty to entertain their tenantry, especially at Christmas, dates back to the Middle Ages. In the early seventeenth century James I attacked country-house owners for getting too fond of London life. He issued a series of edicts, ordering them to return to their houses for Christmas, and entertain their tenantry in the traditional manner. There is, in fact, a long history behind the parties for tenants or the village described with such different inflections by Dorothy Henley and Cecil Beaton.

The Hellfire-Club fancy-dress party at West Wycombe Park, Buckinghamshire, June, 1953. Sir John and Lady Dashwood with the Marchioness of Dufferin and Ava, Roy and Billa Harrod and other friends.

The setting is probably Apthorpe, in Northamptonshire

HARVEST-HOME AT THE EARL OF WESTMORLAND'S

COME, Sons of Summer, by whose toil,
We are the Lords of Wine and Oil:
By whose tough labours, and rough hands,
We rip up first, then reap our lands.
Crown'd with the ears of corn, now come,
And, to the Pipe, sing Harvest home.
Come forth, my Lord, and see the Cart
Dressed up with all the Country Art.
See, here a *Maukin*, there a sheet,
As spotless pure, as it is sweet:
The Horses, Mares, and frisking Fillies,
(Clad, all, in Linen, white as Lilies.)
The Harvest Swains, and Wenches bound
For joy, to see the *Hock-cart* crown'd.
About the Cart, hear, how the Rout
Of Rural Younglings raise the shout;
Pressing before, some coming after,
Those with a shout, and these with laughter.
Some bless the Cart; some kiss the sheaves;
Some prank them up with Oaken leaves:
Some cross the Fill-horse: some with great
Devotion, stroke the home-borne wheat:
While other Rusticks, less attent
To Prayers, than to Merryment,
Run after with their breeches rent.
Well, on, brave boys, to your Lord's Hearth,
Glitt'ring with fire; where, for your mirth,
Ye shall see first the large and chief
Foundation of your Feast, Fat Beef:
With Upper Stories, Mutton, Veal
And Bacon, (which makes full the meal)
With sev'rall dishes standing by,
As here a Custard, there a Pie,
And here all-tempting Frumentie.
And for to make the merry cheer,
If smirking Wine be wanting here,
There's that, which drowns all care, stout Beer:
Which freely drink to your Lords health,
Then to the Plough, (the Common-wealth)
Next to your Flails, your Fanes, your Fats;
Then to the Maids with Wheaten-Hats:
To the rough Sickle, and crook Scythe,
Drink, frolic, boys, till all be blyth.

From ROBERT HERRICK, *The Hock-cart or Harvest Home*

I dined at Stowe yesterday, Nelly Denton and Jock Stewkeley went with me. We met Sir Harry Andrews, & his lady and daughter, his only child there, as also cousin Risley & his lady & Jack Doddington, & 3 sisters of Lady Temple, & Mr Stanion, husband to one of them, & Ned Andrews and Groves his father-in-law, & Thomas Temple & another old Temple with 3 or 4 very drunken parsons, which made up our company. Lady Baltinglass was invited & promised to be there but failed. We saw Sir Richard and his fine lady wedded, & flung the stocking, & then left them to themselves, & so in this manner was ended the celebration of his Marriage à la mode. After that we had Music, Feasting, Drinking, Revelling, Dancing & Kissing: it was two of the clock this morning before we got home.

EDMUND VERNEY TO SIR ROBERT VERNEY, 26 AUGUST, 1675

On Thursday last Jacob Houblon, of Hallingbury in Essex, Esq., member of Parliament for Colchester, baptized his new born son with the greatest magnificence imaginable. Most of the gentlemen within 15 or 20 miles of Mr Houblon's seat in Essex were present, and most of the common people within 4 or 5 miles were made so welcome that they lay in heaps round his house dead drunk. There were three courses of upwards of 200 dishes each, and two tables, at which were 400 persons serv'd all at once, with all sorts of rarities and sweetmeats. Sir John Hynd Cotton and Sir Robert Abdy, Barts, were godfathers, the latter being proxy for Dr Houblon, and the child was nam'd Jacob. There was a grand concert of music at dinner, and a noble ball at night, from which the company did not break up till the next morning. There were 20 Knights and Baronets, and 150 gentlemen, and about as many ladies.

Daily Gazetteer, 14 SEPTEMBER, 1736

Col. Pl. VIII (right) Preparations for a tenant's dinner in the Great Hall, Cotehele, Cornwall. Lithograph after Nicholas Condy, c.1840.

SIR

WATKIN

WILLIAMS

WYNN

COMES

OF

AGE

AT

WYNNSTAY

1770

At noon, not less than twenty thousand visitants were assembled ... among the hecatombs sacrified to his friends, an enormous ox was roasted whole, which being placed upon a kind of triumphant car, ornamented with garlands and streamers, was drawn, by six little mountaineers, to the amphitheatre in the midst of which was erected a Bacchanalian altar, crowned with a cask, the size of which presented a suitable emblem of that unbounded hospitality so long renowned at Wynnstay ... When Sir Watkin, from an eminence, gave his guests a general salute in a bumper, their repeated acclamations, mixed with the thunder of cannon, might fairly be said to make the adjacent Welsh mountains tremble. While the populace here regaled, the numerous visitants of superior rank were summoned, by sound of trumpet, to dinner ...

DIARY OF ELIZABETH, DUCHESS OF NORTHUMBERLAND

Sir Watkin Williams Wynn's private theatre at Wynnstay, Denbighshire, from an engraved ticket of 1782.
Col. Pl. IX (left) An assembly at Wanstead House, Essex, 1729. Detail from the painting by William Hogarth.

MRS

PHILIP

LYBBE

POWYS

GOES

TO

SUPPER

AT

FAWLEY

PARK

1777

ON the Wednesday, Mr. and Miss Pratt, my brother, and ourselves got to Freemans' a little after eight. So great a crowd, or so fine a house to dispose them in, you don't often see in the country . . . Their usual eating-room not being large enough, the supper was in the hall, so that we did not come in thro' that, but a window was taken out of the library, and a temporary flight of steps made into that, from which we passed into the green breakfast-room (that night the tea-room), thro' the pink paper billiard-room, along the saloon, into the red damask drawing-room. Though none sat down, this room was soon so crowded as to make us return to the saloon. This likewise very soon fill'd, and as the tea was carrying round, one heard from every one, 'Fine assembly,' 'Magnificent house,' 'Sure we are in London.'

They danc'd in the saloon. No minuets that night; would have been difficult without a master of the ceremonies among so many people of rank. Two card-rooms, the drawing-room and eating-room. The latter looked so elegant lighted up; two tables at loo, one quinze, one vingt-une, many whist. At one of the former large sums pass'd and repass'd. I saw one lady of quality borrow ten pieces of Tessier within half-an-hour after she set down to vingt-une, and a countess at loo who ow'd to every soul round the table before half the night was over. They wanted Powys and I to play at 'low loo,' as they term'd it, but we rather chose to keep our features less agitated than those we saw around us, for I always observe even those who have it to lose have no less a tinge of the rouge in their countenances when fortune does not smile. Oh! what a disfiguring thing is gaming, particularly to the ladies.

The orgeat, lemonade, capillaire, and red and white negus, with cakes, were carried round the whole evening. At half an hour after twelve the supper was announced, and the hall doors thrown open, on entering which nothing could be more striking, as you know 'tis so fine a one, and was then illuminated by three hundred colour'd lamps round the six doors, over the chimney, and over the statue at the other end. The tables were a long one down the room, terminated by a crescent at each end, and a crescent table against the two doors in the middle; the windows were sideboards. The tables had a most pleasing effect, ornamented with everything in the confectionery way, and festoons and wreaths of artificial flowers prettily disposed; all fruits of the season, as grapes, pines, &c.; fine wines (Freeman is always famous for); everything conducted with great ease – no bustle. Their servants are particularly clever on these occasions, indeed are annually used to it, and none of those of the company admitted, which generally creates confusion.

Ninety-two sat down to supper. Everybody seem'd surpris'd at entering the hall. The house had before been amazingly admir'd, but now there was one general exclamation of wonder. This, you may be certain, pleas'd the owners, particularly as many of the nobility there now never saw it before. The once so beautiful Lady Almeria, I think, is vastly altered. She and Lady Harriot Herbert had the new trimmings, very like bell-ropes with their tassels, and seemingly very inconvenient in dancing. Lady Villiers had a very pretty ornament on, which was the girdle 'Lady Townly' wore, fasten'd round the robing of her gown, and hung down as a tippet. After supper they return'd to dancing, chiefly then cotillons, till near six.

CAROLINE POWYS *Letters,* 13 JANUARY, 1777

Mr Richard Edgcumbe entertaining his guests before the Garden House at Mount Edgcumbe, Cornwall. Thomas Badeslade, 1735.

MAGIC

AT

STOWE:

PRINCESS

AMELIA

ENTERTAINED

1764

ALL day a number of people were preparing the grotto and garden for Her Highness and company to sup there . . . At ten the gardens were illuminated with above a thousand lights, and the water before the grotto was covered with floating lights. At the farther end of the canal on the ship, which was curiously figured with lights, was a place for the music, which performed all supper-time . . . Her Highness walked down to the grotto at half-past ten, and was pleased and delighted with the grand prospect which was presented to her view; nothing was seen but lights and people, nothing was heard but music and fireworks, and nothing was felt but joy and happiness.

GRENVILLE PAPERS

100

Peasants dancing under the portico of Stowe House, Buckinghamshire, at the coming–of–age of Earl Temple, February, 1818.

On Wednesday a small Vauxhall was acted for us at the grotto in the Elysian fields, which was illuminated with lamps as were the thicket and two little barks on the lake. The evening was more than cool, and the destined spot anything but dry. There were not half lamps enough, and no music but an ancient militia man who played cruelly on the squeaking tabor and pipe. As our procession descended the vast flight of steps into the garden, in which was assembled a crowd of people from Buckingham and the neighbouring villages, I could not help laughing as I surveyed our troop, which, instead of tripping lightly to such an Arcadian entertainment were hobbling down by the balustrades, wrapped in cloaks and great coats, for fear of catching cold ... We were none of us young enough for a pastoral.

HORACE WALPOLE TO GEORGE MONTAGU, 7 JULY, 1770

LORD NELSON AND EMMA VISIT FONTHILL ABBEY 1801

THEY all proceeded slowly and in order, as the dark of the evening was growing into darkness. In about three quarters of an hour, soon after having entered the great wall which includes the abbey-woods, the procession passed a noble Gothic arch ... and hence, upon a road winding through the woods of pine and fir, brightly illuminated by innumerable lamps hung in the trees, and by flambeaux moving with the carriages, they proceeded betwixt two divisions of the Fonthill volunteers, accompanied by their band playing solemn marches, the effect of which was much heightened by the continued roll of drums placed at different distances on the hills ...

The company on their arrival at the Abbey could not fail to be struck with the increasing splendour of lights and their effects, contrasted with the deep shades which fell on the walls, battlements, and turrets, of the different groups of the edifice. Some parts of the light struck on the walls and arches of

the great tower, till it vanished by degrees into an awful gloom at its summit . . .

The parties, alighting in orderly succession from their carriages, entered a groined Gothic hall through a double line of soldiers. From thence they were received into the great saloon, called the Cardinal's parlour, furnished with rich tapestries, long curtains of purple damask before the arched windows, ebony tables and chairs studded with ivory, of various but antique fashion; the whole room in the noblest style of monastic ornament, and illuminated by lights on silver sconces. At the moment of entrance they sat down at a long table, occupying nearly the whole length of the room (53 feet), to a superb dinner, served in one long line of enormous silver dishes, in the substantial *costume* of the ancient abbeys, unmixed with the refinements of modern cookery. The table and side-boards glittering with piles of plate and a profusion of candle-lights, not to mention a blazing Christmas fire of cedar and the cones of pine, united to increase the splendour and to improve the *coup'-d'oeil* of the room . . .

Dinner being ended, the company removed up stairs to the other finished apartments of the abbey. The staircase was lighted by certain mysterious living figures at different intervals, dressed in hooded gowns, and standing with large wax-torches in their hands. A magnificent room hung with yellow damask, and decorated with cabinets of the most precious japan, received the assembly. It was impossible not to be struck, among other objects, with its credences, (or antique buffets) exhibiting much treasure of wrought plate, cups, vases, and ewers of solid gold. It was from this room they passed into the Library, fitted up with the same appropriate taste. The Library opens by a large Gothic screen into the gallery . . . This room, which when finished will be more than 270 feet long, is to half that length completely fitted up, and furnished in the most impressively monastic style. A superb shrine, with a beautiful statue of St. Anthony in marble and alabaster, the work of Rossi, placed upon it, with reliquaries studded with brilliants of immense value, the whole illuminated by a grand display of wax-lights on candlesticks and candelabras of massive silver gilt, exhibited a scene at once strikingly splendid and awfully magnificent . . .

As the company entered the gallery a solemn music struck the ear from some invisible quarter, as if from behind the screen of scarlet curtains which backed the shrine, or from its canopy above, and suggested ideas of a religious service; ... After the scenic representation a collation was presented in the library, consisting of various sorts of confectionery served in gold baskets, with spiced wines, &c. whilst rows of chairs were placed in the great room beyond, which had first received the company above stairs. A large vacant space was left in the front of the seats. The assembly no sooner occupied them than Lady Hamilton appeared in the character of Agrippina, bearing the ashes of Germanicus in a golden urn, and as presenting herself before the Roman people with the design of exciting them to revenge the death of her husband ... Lady Hamilton displayed, with truth and energy, every gesture, attitude, and expression of countenance, which could be conceived as Agrippina herself, best calculated to have moved the passions of the Romans in behalf of their favourite general. The action of her head, of her hands and arms in the various positions of it, in her manner of presenting before the Romans, or of holding it up to the gods in the act of supplication was most classically graceful ... The company delighted and charmed broke up, and departed at 11 o'clock ... On leaving this strange nocturnal scene of vast buildings and extensive forest, now rendered dimly and partially visible by the declining light of lamps and torches, and the twinkling of a few scattered stars in a clouded sky, the company seemed, as soon as they had passed the sacred boundary of the great wall, as if waking from a dream, or just freed from the influence of some magic spell ...

Gentleman's Magazine, APRIL, 1801

Tenants and labourers being feasted in front of Stowe, February 1818.

THE cricket matches were the highlights of the summer holidays, one eleven staying in the house, and a neighbouring house bringing over the other ... The first steps of making friends with strangers took longer than nowadays; we did not plunge into Christian names and familiarity all at once, by any means, and dinner on the first night when the cricket eleven had collected was often stiff and rather painful; everybody sat looking straight in front of them, or at their plates, while laborious conversation was conscientiously made. On the first evening no one was ever found who could sing, or play, or do any tricks, but all this ice melted after one day's cricket, and by the second evening all kinds of latent powers were discovered in the guests, prodigies who could bend backwards, or could pick up an orange with their teeth from the floor, or play entrancingly on their combs. All through the day in the sun, or, worse, in a chill wind, we sat riveted by the game, going through agonies of despair and sympathy with the unsuccessful players. In the evening plates of redcurrants and sugar were brought out – the grooms and boot-boys came to watch at the end of the day's work, and photographs were taken of the eleven as they came in after an innings. How important it all seemed, and the photographs looked at now, faded and discoloured, show round-faced and simple boys, who seemed to us then such mysterious and exciting beings.

Or, if ours was the visiting team, there was the drive back in the brake with its pair of horses after the match was over; two boys would sit on a box beside the coachman, and, sitting packed on the seats which faced each other, the rest of us crowded in – muslin dresses and white flannels – the boys wearing grey felt hats and the girls hats of straw with flowers. Trotting along the country roads, through the summer evenings, we broke into song to pass the time if the drive was long, and especially if our side had won. 'Shine, shine, moon, while I dance with Dinah dear', or 'Lousiana Lou', – 'dream, dream, dream of me, and I'll dream of you' we sang, and the villagers stopped to look at the turn-out rattling along and smile at its singing load.

CONSTANCE SITWELL *Bright Morning*

TENANTS'

BALLS

AND

CHRISTMAS

TREE

PARTIES

AT

NAWORTH

CASTLE

C. 1890–1900

THE balls were held in the great hall, with its stone floor overlaid by a temporary wooden one ... The band of twelve sat on the big oak table opposite the fireplace. The Hall was lit by huge chandeliers hanging from the roof trusses, each carrying forty-two candles, and round each corbel was a half chandelier with twenty-one ... They were all thickly festooned with chains of evergreens. So was the dais South wall, and some other parts. Gardeners and woodmen were at work for days on this lovely job.

All the food was cooked in the house. Refreshments, i.e. tea, coffee, lemonade, orangeade, stone ginger beer, cakes, biscuits, bunlets, and quarter oranges to suck, were served all night through in the Glen room. The magnificent cold suppers in regular 'sittings' were eaten in the billiard room – hams, turkeys, geese, beef, mutton, jellies, puddings, pastries, macedoine-of-fruit (not 'fruit salad' in those aristocratic days). Do children of all generations put away two, if not three suppers? We might sup, dance, doze on an empty sofa, at will. We danced a lot, with whoever would dance with us, and we were there to the finish. My mother never danced in my time, though she said she had loved it. My father danced the night through ... In my day the balls began at 8 or 8.30, and went on till 4.30 or 5. My mother said they used to go on longer – but I don't know how the candles could have lasted much more than ten hours. She said they had once gone on till 7. In later years I have been to two other families' 'Tenants' and 'Servants' balls. In both cases the Family left at midnight, 'when,' they said, 'the real ball begins.' I am dead certain that if our family, Parents and Young, had left at midnight, the 'real ball' would have ended. It was the kind of family and the kind of guests that made our presence essential to gaiety and good company ... The balls ended with 'Auld Lang Syne' sung in a huge running circle by everyone.

There were the exciting great Christmas Tree parties. The highest tree recorded was under the Dome at Castle Howard, 24 feet high ... My most constant memory is of the Naworth trees, twenty

(right) Lord Tredegar and parrot at a garden party at Tredegar Park, Monmouthshire, in the 1930s.

to twenty-three feet high. My mother was the moving spirit in all this. She bought vast quantities of toys for every boy and girl in every school on the estate and in Brampton. It was not 'one toy per child' but lashings over, to give a reasonable choice. They ranged from good concertinas to mouth organs; books to tin soldiers; paints, painting books, stories, tea-sets, tops, whips, hoops, skipping-ropes, dolls, dolls' beds made by 'Hop o' my Thumb' (John Hope, beloved joiner). My mother was in the midst of it all – hanging coloured glass balls of all shapes and sizes, and threading heavy red apples and oranges to weigh down the spruce branches. Our six boys, and the Bulkeley five (of Lanercost vicarage) took their share in creating the trees. Threaders hung apples and balls on rods. Hangers placed them on the tree. Artistic helpers made things: gold paper ships and stars. Needlewomen dressed dolls and upholstered cradles. We were an army of family, maids, governesses, vicar's wife, coachman's wife – anyone who liked a party came to sew, to gum gold and silver paper into massive chains, to decorate, and to place the scores of candles on the tree. From early days I claimed it as my privilege to dress the Fairy for the tree top.

DOROTHY HENLEY, *Rosalind Howard: Countess of Carlisle*

THE DUCHESS OF HAMILTON ENTERTAINS AT FERNE HOUSE 1931

AT last we found ourselve marshalled into the drawing room, where a spindly Christmas tree stood decorated with tinsel toys and illuminated by coloured balls. Soon the village children from Berwick St John trooped in by invitation – fifty or sixty of them standing like a military unit. They had large heads, pale, weedy complexions, and goggle eyes. An overfat schoolmaster, crimson in the face, conducted a hymn while his minions sang with only a remote interest in the proceedings. The Duchess stood to attention surrounded by many ugly, grey-haired women, including a few deaf mutes. The village children, puny and unattractive, made a startling contrast to the healthy ducal offspring.

Her Grace then spoke a few words, welcoming the local children and giving them a dissertation on the advantages of country over city. Each leaf, she explained, was different in the country. There were many things to watch; they must appreciate and preserve its rustic joys.

One boy was asked the main difference between town and country and ruggedly replied, 'Oi think the moine difference is that in the cities there is so much dust and doirt and muck. In the country, the air is different and there are flewers.'

'Quite right, that is excellent.' The Duchess seemed a stalking crane in her off-white flannel skirt, socks and gym shoes. Finally she excoriated those who are cruel to the animals. 'Above all you must be kind to birds.'

The children were then encouraged to give bird calls for Father Christmas. They moved joylessly into the pitchpine panelled hall and intoned at the top of their melancholy screechy voices. After delays, and hitches and whispered commands from the family, and repeated shouts in unison from the children, Father Christmas materialised in the form of the Duke who was wheeled on to the scene by Geordie, his stalwart son. The Duke was dressed in red flannel with hood and a wig of white cotton wool. The children were told to line up in order of their ages. Those who were twelve years old must head the proccssion and be given a present.

A few mumbled words, then the village children were given orders to troop as a platoon into the frigid drawing-room. Each child took an orange and an apple from fruit-filled Tate sugar boxes placed near the door.

Everyone waited: grey-haired women, deaf mutes, refugee cats and dogs, and children of all ages. Then the lights went out; a few of the smaller village children began to whimper. The ducal grandchildren crawled in and out of the legs, human and animal, while outside the French windows their handsome parents could be seen for a flash or two, as they ran in the stormy darkness with matches and beacons. Suddenly a Catherine wheel hissed; then in the rain appeared a shower of 'golden rain'; squibs popped; jumping crackers exploded on the wet ground; chinesc crackers went off in a series of half-hearted reports.

The whimpering village children now burst into screams of alarm. Terrificd of the darkness and the noise, they howled, bellowed, shrieked with each new explosion. Babies cried, dogs barked, oranges and apples rolled on the floor. From exploding rockets blinding flashes revealed a maggot-crawling mass of panicking children and dogs. The hysteria reached a terrifying crescendo when a spurting, spluttering 'sparkler' came flying indoors.

CECIL BEATON, *The Wandering Years*

(right) The Princesses Louisa, Victoria and Maud on a visit to Sir William and Lady Armstrong at Cragside, 1884. From the water-colour by H. H. Emmison.

7
Royal
Visits

A royal visit has been the dream and night-mare of country-house owners from the Middle Ages up till the present day. What was the protocol? How could one avoid making some appalling bloomer? Where was the line between providing too much and too little? The stakes were especially high in the centuries before constitutional monarchy, when the king or queen was the fount of jobs, honours and perquisites, and could make or mar the fortunes of a family.

In the sixteenth century Sir Nicholas Bacon ran up a new wing at his house at Gorhambury, in preparation for a visit by Queen Elizabeth; in the nineteenth century the de Murrieta family more than doubled the size of Wadhurst Park in Sussex, in order to entertain the Prince of Wales. In both

cases the visits took place. The unfortunate Sir Christopher Hatton turned Holdenby in Northamptonshire into a house the size of Chatsworth, in anticipation of putting up Queen Elizabeth. He ruined his estate, and she never came.

Others did not go so far, but most sizeable country houses had a suite of state rooms, one of the main functions of which was to provide for possible royal visits. The culminating feature of all such suites was a state bed, the more magnificent the better. In grand houses, even if the rest of the suite was sometimes used on other occasions, the bed was reserved for royalty. In some cases this meant that it was never slept in at all.

Then, at Wilton in 1779, the absurd situation arises of a state-bed being borrowed for a visit by George III and Queen Charlotte, who arrive with their own much more modest one. It is just about then, in fact, that one begins to notice a lack of fit between what hosts provide and royal guests desire. The latter are beginning to want to be treated more like ordinary mortals. The change becomes especially obvious in the account of Queen Victoria's visit to Stowe in 1845, as related by Elizabeth George, the daughter of a tenant farmer, who picked up the gossip from the Stowe servants.

Of course, there has always been a difference between a king or queen just looking in, as it were, for a hour or two, and coming for a night or a week, with an entourage, perhaps, of several hundred people. And visits from a Prince or Princess of Wales have tended to be more relaxed affairs; monarchy in embryo is less constricting than monarchy in fact.

Painting of Thomas Williams 'A Plasant Fool That Died In The Year 1687.' He was servant to Lord Coningsby, Hampton Court, Herefordshire.

EDWARD

III

FALLS

FOR

THE

COUNTESS

OF

SALISBURY

AT

WARK

CASTLE

1341

AS soon as the lady knew of the king's coming, she set open the gates and came out so richly bedizened that every man marvelled of her beauty, and could not cease to regard her nobleness, with her great beauty and the gracious words and countenance that she made. When she came to the king she knelt down to the earth, thanking him of his succour and so led him into the castle to make him cheer and honour as she that could right well do it. Every man regarded her marvellously; the king himself could not withold his regarding of her, for he thought that he never saw before so noble nor so fair a lady; he was stricken therewith to the heart with a sparkle of fine love that endured long after; he thought no lady in the world so worthy to be beloved as she.

Thus they entered into the castle hand in hand; the lady led him first into the hall, and after into the chamber nobly apparelled. The king regarded so the lady that she was abashed; at last he went to a window to rest him, and so fell into a great study. The lady went about to make cheer to the lords and knights that were there, and commanded to dress the hall for dinner. When she had all devised and commanded them she came to the king with a merry cheer, (who was in a great study) and she said Dear Sir, why do you study so. . . . Then the king said, Dear lady, know for truth that since I entered into the castle there is a study come to my mind so that I can not choose but to muse, nor I can not tell what shall fall thereof; put it out of my heart I cannot . . . surely your sweet behaving, the perfect wisdom, the good grace, nobleness and excellent beauty that I see in you, hath so sore surprised my heart that I cannot but love you, and without your love I am but dead. Then the lady said, Right noble prince for God's sake mock nor tempt me not; I can not believe that it is true that you say, nor that so noble a prince as you be would think to dishonour me and my lord my husband, who is so valiant a knight.

. . . Therewith the lady departed from the king and went into the hall to have dinner; then she

Queen Elizabeth out hunting. Engraving from *The Book of Faulconrie* by George Turbeville (1575).

returned again to the king and brought some of his knights with her, and said, Sir, if it please you to come into the hall, your knights abideth for you to wash; you have been too long fasting. Then the king went into the hall and washed and sat down among his lords and the lady also. The king ate but little, he sat still musing, and as he did so he cast his eye upon the lady . . . All that day the king tarried there and wyst not what to do. In the morning he arose and took leave of the lady saying, My dear lady to God I commend you till I return again, requiring you to advise you otherwise than you have said to me. Noble prince, quoth the lady, God the father glorious be your conduct, and put you out of all villain thoughts. Sir I am and ever shall be ready to do your grace service to your honour and to mine. Therewith the king departed all abashed.

FROISSART *Chronicles*

QUEEN

ELIZABETH

VISITS

LORD

HERTFORD

AT

ELVETHAM

1591

... **H**IS honor with all expedition set artificers a work, to the number of three hundred, many days before her Majesty's arrival, to enlarge his house with new rooms and offices ...

First there was made a room of estate for the Nobles, and at the end thereof a withdrawing place for her Majesty. The outsides of the walls were all covered with boughs, and clusters of ripe hazel nuts, the insides with arras, the roof of the place with works of ivy leaves, the floor with sweet herbs and green rushes.

Near adjoining unto this, were many offices new builded, as namely, Spicery, Lardery, Chandlery, Winecellar, Ewery, and Pantry: all which were tiled.

Not far off was erected a large hall, for the entertainment of Knights, Ladies and Gentlemen of chief account.

There was also a several place for her Majesty's footmen, and their friends.

Then there was a long bower for her Majesty's guard. Another for other servants of her Majesty's house. Another for my Lord's Steward, to keep his table in. Another for his Gentlemen that waited.

Most of these foresaid rooms were furnished with tables, and the tables carried twenty-three yards in length.

Moreover on the same hill there was raised a great common buttery. A Pitcher-house. A large Pastry, with five ovens new built, some of them fourteen feet deep. A great Kitchen, with four ranges, and a boiling place for small boiled meats. Another Kitchen, with a very long range, for the waste, to serve all comers. A Boiling-house, for the great boiler. A room for the Scullery. Another room for the Cook's lodgings. Some of these were covered with canvas, and other some with boards.

Between the Earl's house and the foresaid hill, where these rooms were raised, there had been made in the bottom, by handy labour, a goodly Pond, cut to the perfect figure of a half moon. In this Pond were three notable grounds, where hence to present her Majesty with sports and pastimes. The first was a *Ship Isle*, of a hundred foot in length, and four-score foot broad, bearing

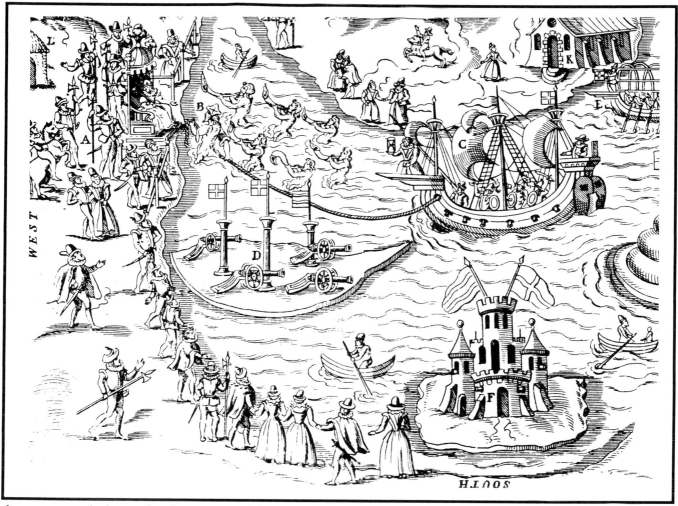

three trees orderly set for three masts. The second was a *Fort* twenty foot square every way, and overgrown with willows. The third and last was a *Snail Mount*, rising to four circles of green privy hedges, the whole in height twenty foot, and forty foot broad at the bottom. These three places were equally distant from the sides of the pond, and every one, by a just measured proportion, distant from the other. In the said water were divers boats prepared for music: but especially there was a pinnace, full furnished with masts, yards, sails, anchors, cables, and all other ordinary tackling, and with iron pieces; and lastly with flags, streamers, and pendants, to the number of twelve, all painted with divers colours and sundry devices.

Part of the Second Day's Entertainment
Presently after dinner, the Earl of Hertford caused a large canopy of estate to be set at the pond's head, for her Majesty to sit under, and to view some sports prepared in the water. The canopy was of green satin, lined with green taffeta sarcenet; every seam covered with a broad silver lace; valanced about, and fringed with green silk and silver, more than a hand-breadth in depth; supported by four silver pillars movable; and decked above head with four white plumes, spangled with silver. This canopy being upheld by four worthy knights (Sir Henry Grey, Sir Walter Hungerford, Sir James Marvin and Lord George Carew), and tapestry spread all about the pond's head, her Majesty, about four of the clock, came and sat under it, to expect the issue of some device, being advertised that there was some such thing towards.

At the further end of the pond, there was a bower, close built to the brink thereof; out of which there went a pompous array of sea persons, which waded breast-high or swam till they approached near the seat of her Majesty. Nereus, the Prophet of the Sea, attired in red silk, and having a cornered-cap on his curled head, did swim before the rest, as their pastor and guide. After him came

111

Queen Elizabeth's entertainment at Elvetham. Detail from an engraving of 1591.

the pond, all along the middle of the current, the Tritons sounded one half of the way; and then they ceasing, the cornets played their Scottish jigs. The melody was sweet, and the show stately.

JOHN NICHOLS, *Progresses of Queen Elizabeth*

ON Monday, [Aug 17, 1591] at eight of the clock in the morning, her Highness took horse, with all her train, and rode into the park: where was a delicate bower prepared, under the which her Highness's musicians played, and a crossbow by a Nymph, with a sweet song, delivered to her hands, to shoot at the deer, about some thirty in number, put into a paddock, of which number she killed three or four, and the Countess of Kildare one.

JOHN NICHOLS, *Progresses of Queen Elizabeth*

YESTERDAY the Queen and all the Royal Family dined at Claremont & I dined with the Duke and Sir Robert, &c. His Royal Highness came to us as soon as his and our dinner was over & drank a bumper of rack punch to the Queen's health which ye may be sure I devotedly pledged, & he was going on with another but Her Majesty sent in word that she was a going to walk in the garden, so that broke up the company. We walked till candle-light, being entertained with very fine french horns, then returned into his Great Hall, and everybody agreed that never was any thing finer lit. Her Majesty and Princess Charlotte, Lady Charlotte Roucy, Mr Shutz played there at quadrille, in the next room the Prince had the fiddlers and danced, and did me the honour to ask me if I could dance country dances, & told him yes, & if there had been a partner for me, I should have made one in that glorious company . . .

The Queen came from her cards to see that sight . . . there stood at the farther end of that room a table with bottles of wine for the dancers to drink.

PETER WENTWORTH TO LORD STRAFFORD, 21 AUGUST, 1729

five Tritons breast-high in the water, all with grisly heads, and beards of divers colours and fashions, and all five cheerfully sounding their trumpets. After them went two other Gods of the sea, Neptune and Oceanus, Phoreus and Glaucus, leading between them that pinnace whereof I spoke in the beginning of this treatise.

In the pinnace were three Virgins, which, with their cornets, played Scottish jigs, made three parts in one. There was also in the said pinnace another Nymph of the Sea, named Nedera, the old supposed love of Sylvanus, a God of the Woods. Near to her were placed three excellent voices, to sing to one lute, and in two other boats hard by, other lutes and voices, to answer by manner of echo. After the pinnace, and two other boats which were drawn after it by other sea-gods, the rest of the train followed breast-high in the water, all attired in scaly marine suits, and every one armed with a huge wooden squirt in his hand; to what end it shall appear hereafter. In their marching towards

112

Charles II being presented with a pineapple at an unidentified country house, c. 1675.

THE PRINCE OF WALES VISITS HARDWICK, 1619

The visit took place on August 9. The total cost was £91.13.2 (several thousand pounds in modern currency), mainly made up of presents to the royal entourage and to the servants of neighbours who sent gifts of food.

My Lord Darcy's man bringing a peacock	2s 0d
Sir William Kniveton's man bringing a fat cow	10s 0d
Mr Lee's man bringing fish and fowl	5s 0d
My Lady Stanhope's man bringing cheeses	2s 0d
Mr Bagshawe's man bringing powts	2s 0d
Sir Francis Wortley's man bring 2 rois	5s 0d
Mr Hunloke's bringing a calf	2s 0d
To Sir Thomas Momson's man bringing apples, apricocks, &c.	5s 0d
To the guard 6 pieces [a piece = £1.3s.6d], to the footmen 2 pieces, to the waggoner a piece, to the yeoman of the cellar a piece, [yeoman of the] pantry a piece, [yeoman of the] ewery a piece, Butler a peice, master cook 4 pieces, yeoman cook a piece, yeoman of the pastry a piece, yeoman of the robes a piece, the saddler & helper a piece, Sir Francis Fullerton's man (cook) 11s 0d, to the waiter of the back stairs 11s 0d	£26.19.0d
To my Lady to play with the Prince at cards	£5.10.0
To John Bartram the London cook for himself, his workmen and a boy	£12.0.0
Given by my Lady to Mr Cave	£1.2.0
To the musicians that came from court	£2.4.0
More given to them playing at my Lady's chamber window	5s 0d
Mr Wright's man of Foston bringing a pannet of fish and fowl	5s 0d
To Mr Markham's man of Ollerton bringing half a stag	10s 0d
To my Lady which his honour gave away to the Prince's servants	£24.4.0
Wages paid to 15 several cooks employed at Hardwick at the Prince's coming	£13.5.8
Scullery labourers, turnspits, &c.	£3.15.6

ACCOUNT BOOK, 1ST EARL OF DEVONSHIRE

THE King dined in the new Dining Room, the Queen in the Cube Room; the Aide de Camp in the Breakfast Corner Room below stairs; Miss Herbert at which were Mrs Hegerdorn, the Queen's old Nurse, I believe, alias Mistress of the Robes, Her Majesty's Secretary and Comptroller Mr Harris, Ld Pembroke's Chaplain Dr & Mrs Eyre, in Lord Pembroke's old long dressing room over the Steward's Room; the Pages in the Coffee Room below Stairs; the Highlife below Stairs Gentry in the Stewards Room; the King's Footmen, Coachmen etc. in the Room over the Manège; & the rest of the Party-coloured Race in the Servants Hall, which will, I believe, give a good account of the eight Tables mentioned in the Papers sent to you by Lord Pembroke.

To accommodate their Majesties with a good Bed, I made interest with Mr Hill, Mr Beckford's Steward, to lend us his superb State Bed, which we brought to Wilton, slung on the Carriage of a Waggon, without the least damage, at no small expense, but what signifies money, when we were to entertain the Princes of the Land. I wish you had the list this Business cost, and His Majesty no worse, God Bless him, and I think you would not be very sorry. But it was necessary to get things decent and in order, and when we had bustled our hearts out for a week before the time, lo, and behold! when they arrived, they brought a snug double Tent Bed, had it put up in the Colonade Room, where the State Bed was already placed, in a crack, and slept, for any thing I know to the contrary, extremely quiet and well, directly under Ld & Lady Pembroke's & yr honour's Picture by Sir Joshua Reynolds.

The King dressed in the Hunting Room, where there was a fireplace made for the occasion, & now continues, and the Queen had the Corner Room for her Dressing Room, ornamented in the Toilette way, with Gold Candlesticks, & the Devil knows what which I cannot describe to you. The Blue Closet within was for her Majesty's private purposes, where there was a red new velvet Close Stool, and a very handsome China Jordan, which I had the honour to produce from an old collection, & you may be sure, I am as proud as Punch, that her Majesty condescended to piss in it.

DR EYRE TO LORD HERBERT, 1 JANUARY, 1779

PERHAPS you may have seen in the newspapers that our Fawley environs was then honour'd by the royal visitors. The servants at Fawley Court heard of them about two miles off; of course thought they were coming there, as they often did in his uncle's time, but to the no small disappointment of the nephew, as well as the domestics, they pass'd by, and went up to the Dowager Mrs Freeman's at Henley Park, not so noble a house, but all elegance, and one of the most beautiful situations imaginable. She most unluckily had been some time confined to her house with a violent cold; and the butler came running up to her dressing-room, saying, 'The King and Queen, M'am.' 'Don't alarm me, William' (you know her delicate manner); 'they are not coming here, but to Fawley Court, no doubt.' However, another footman followed immediately, saying the carriages were just driving up, and he had got a good fire in the drawing-room. She had only time to say, 'A smart breakfast, William,' and to throw on a huge cloak, and was down just as the King, Queen, two Princesses, Lady Louisa Clayton, and two gentlemen entered. They stayed two hours and a half, talked incessantly, seemed vastly pleased, and knew every family and their concerns in this neighbourhood, Mrs Freeman said, better than she did herself! The worst of these great visitors are that no servants must appear, and you are obliged to wait on them yourself; this, ill as she then felt, was very fatiguing; besides, not knowing the art, one must do it awkwardly. Mrs Freeman, after standing up in the corner to make the tea in the same spot, she handed a dish to her Majesty, and was carrying one to the Princess Royal, who laughingly said, 'I believe you forgot the King.' Mrs Freeman, in some agitation, was ready to laugh too, as she says she had at the moment completely forgotton that kings were to be served before ladies; but immediately rectified her mistake, and it was received in perfect good-humour; but what next vexed her sadly was that she had no opportunity of giving the least refreshment to Lady Louisa, and the two gentlemen, who stood behind all the time, and were out so early in the morning, and to be at home so late, but she knew in the same room with their Majesties it was not to be attempted; therefore if you know of it, another breakfast is prepared in another room in case opportunity offers to let their attendants partake of it.

CAROLINE POWYS, *Letters*, 30 DECEMBER, 1785

THE

PRINCE

OF

WALES

IS

JOVIAL

AT

HINCHING-

BROKE

1789

AT Christmas, 1789, His Royal Highness visited that bon vivant, the Earl of Sandwich, satirized by Churchill under the name of Jemmy Twitcher, at his seat at Hinchingbroke, where a numerous party annually assembled during the holidays. The mornings were devoted to concerts, at which his Royal Highness performed on the violincello; Madame Mara, then at the zenith of her ability, came from Burleigh with the Earl of Exeter to join the party; an excellent band, led by Ashley, was engaged, and his lordship assisted as usual on the kettledrums ... An elegant theatre was fitted up for the evening amusements, when *Love-à-la-Mode, the Mock Doctor, Virgin Unmasked, High Life below Stairs*, &c. were performed by amateurs; and an occasional prologue, written by his lordship in honour of his Royal Highness' visit, was spoken by L. Brown, Esq., M.P. for Huntingdonshire. After supper the evening concluded with catches and glees. His Royal Highness remained with the Earl one week, and on departing said, he had often heard of his lordship's hospitality, but could not have expected to have experienced so much gratification and pleasure in such a very numerous and diversified assemblage.

ROBERT HUISH, *Memoirs of George IV*

(below) Queen Victoria arriving at the railway station for a visit to Castle Howard, 1850.

(top right) The Prince of Wales at a shooting party at Elveden Hall, Suffolk, 1876.

(right) The Prince of Wales (second from left) at a meet before Easton Neston, Northamptonshire, October 1887.

unbounded trouble to receive her Majesty with the greatest magnificence. Every part of his noble and vast mansion had been, in part, newly furnish'd and decorated, even articles that are generally made of cheap materials, and for the commonest every day wear – were of gold or silver if intended for the Queen's use.

Perhaps the Duke thought to surprise and gratify her Majesty by such delicate flattery, if so, he could hardly have been pleased when she said 'I am sure *I* have no such splendid apartments in either of my palaces' – considering who was the Speaker such an observation must be regarded as a very equivocal compliment.

The expensive and elaborate preparations were so evident that the very idea of having caused so serious an outlay must have been oppressive and unpleasant to her Majesty.

We were told that the Queen would have been far better pleased had her bedroom and dressing room been more simply furnished.

The head housemaid conducted the Royal pair to the apartments especially set apart for their private use, and she reported that the moment the Queen enter'd the bedroom she turn'd to the Prince and said 'O Albert, I know this carpet I have seen it before – it was offered to me, but I did not like to spend so much money on one carpet.' Then she told Mrs. Bennett to bring a drugget and lay over the carpet before she came to bed – adding 'I shall feel quite uncomfortable if it is not cover'd.'

DIARY OF ELIZABETH GEORGE

QUEEN VICTORIA IS SOUR AT STOWE 1845

AFTER hearing many details of the Royal visit, I cannot help thinking it was not quite satisfactory either to the Duke or his Guest. The Duke had been at great expense and had given himself

The Duchess of Teck descends the stairs of Trafford Park, near Manchester, with Sir Humphrey de Trafford, 1897. Behind her is her daughter Princess May, the future Queen Mary.
(top right) Prince Henry of Prussia shooting duck at Lyme Park, Cheshire, 1910.
(right) The Duke of York (later George V) out shooting at Elveden Hall, Suffolk, c. 1900.

AN

EMBARRASS-

ING

DOG

AT

HALTON

I was at Mr Alfred's first house-party when he opened Halton. The Prince of Wales was there, and Mr Alfred exhibited a number of small Japanese dogs, which had been taught to perform. Great confusion was aroused by the fact that, although the chief little dog performed, it was not according to the programme.

HALTON REMINISCENCES, 1880

THE

PRINCESS

OF

WALES

IS

STARTLED

WHEN the Princess of Wales, afterwards Queen Alexandra, visited Newstead, as the guest of the Duke and Duchess of St Albans at Bestwood, she was shown the haunted room, in which there was a cupboard let into the wall, with its door slightly ajar. Being always full of fun, H.R.H. said, 'I think the ghost must be in here,' and opened the cupboard door. Noticing a long curtain inside, she poked it with her parasol – and then drew back with a very startled '*Oh!*' For a faint scream came from behind the curtain and out rushed two housemaids, who had evidently hidden there to obtain a good view of the Royal visitor.

DUKE OF PORTLAND, *Men Women and Things*

The house is not identified; the dancer sounds like Margot Tennant, the future wife of H. H. Asquith.

THE Prince had a very keen sense of humour [but] he hated any of his friends made fun of; and, for example, was extremely displeased with a well-known peeress's sister because, when after some of her fantastic dancing, she playfully knelt before him and he smilingly said: 'Thank you, Lady Salome. Have you come to claim half of my Kingdom?' she replied – 'No, King Herod, but do give me Sir Ernest Cassel's head on a charger.'

JULIAN OSGOOD FIELD *Uncensored Recollections*

Queen Mary with Lord and Lady Lansdowne at Bowood House, Wiltshire, in 1922. (right) William Beckford's dwarf in front of Fonthill Abbey, Wiltshire.

8
Servants

*F*or at least five centuries complaining about their servants was one of the favourite pastimes of the English upper classes. The complaints have varied over the years. In the early centuries it was the treachery or disloyalty of upper servants that was the commonest theme. In those days upper servants were gentlemen or ladies by birth, often distantly related to the great people who employed them; they presided over lower echelons of yeomen or grooms, and acted as companions, agents, or business assistants to their employers, as well as playing cards or backgammon with them in the Great Chamber, or waiting on them at table. The opportunities for betraying vital secrets, setting husbands against wives or pushing their own interests were very great. In later centuries the status and social rank of upper servants changed, and the complaints changed too, to grumbles about drunkenness, slothfulness, unreliability or petty dishonesty, of the kind so brilliantly put across by Jonathan Swift, in his satirical *Directions to Servants*.

Such complaints went on into this century. But increasingly one gets the other side of the picture. Servants' own letters or memoirs begin to surface, and include their views of the gentry, not always complimentary ones. But of course there were endless variations in these teeming and highly stratified communities: there were loyal and loved servants, as well as dishonest or incompetent ones, kind and considerate employers, as well as cruel or aloof ones.

On the average, both size and ceremony decreased over the centuries. In late medieval and Tudor households, the ceremony involved in serving up meals is almost unbelievable. Even the minor business of supplying an earl with a bedside snack for the night involved ten servants in a ritual of bowing, kissing and processing all over the house. By the eighteenth century ritual had largely disappeared; but vestiges survived into Edwardian days, as in the dinner procession of upper servants from servants' hall to housekeeper's room. In general, the self-importance of upper servants derived from the fact that their predecessors had once been gentry.

At the Earl of Dorset's great house at Knole, 111 servants regularly sat down to dinner in the early seventeenth century. This was nothing out of the ordinary at the time, but by Edwardian days numbers even in the grandest houses seldom exceeded thirty or forty. The 1939–45 war was generally supposed to have dealt a death-blow to large staffs. But when the Earl of Derby's footman went berserk with a machine gun in 1952, one of the aspects of the drama which fascinated the public was that he drew coveys of servants out of the corridors and backstairs of Knowsley, on a scale which was thought to have gone for ever. As Winston Churchill is said to have remarked, 'It's nice to hear of a house where you can still get a left and right at a butler.'

(right) Musicians depicted in the frieze of the Great Chamber, Gilling Castle, North Yorkshire, c. 1585.

HOW

TO

GIVE

YOUR

MASTER

A

BATH

C. 1460

IF your sovereign will to the bath, his body to wash clean,
Hang sheets round about the roof. This is how I mean,
Every sheet full of flowers and herbs sweet and green,
And look you have sponges five or six, thereon to sit or lean.
Look there be a great sponge, thereon your sovereign to sit,
And on it a sheet, so he may bathe him there a fit,
Under his feet also a sponge, if there be any to put,
And always be sure of the door, and see that it is shut.
Take a basin in your hand full of hot herbs and fresh
And with a soft sponge in hand [start] his body to wash.
Rinse him with rose water warm and fair upon his flesh
Then let him go to bed, but see that it's sweet and nesh [soft]
But first set on his socks, his slippers on his feet,
That he may go fair to the fire, there to take his foot sheet,
Then with a clean cloth to wipe away all wet.
Then bring him to his bed, his troubles there to beat.

JOHN RUSSELL, *The Boke of Nurture*

*The following ceremony involved four household depart-
ments, each of which had a yeoman in charge of it: the
ewery, where linen, napkins, and basins and ewers for
washing were kept; and the pantry, buttery, and cellar,
which were responsible for bread, beer and wine respect-
ively. The procession was marshalled by the usher of the
chamber, assisted by attendant grooms. The earl is
referred to as 'the Estate'. To 'give saye' means to give
something to someone for trying out or tasting; it was a
test of quality and precaution against poison.*

BRINGING

UP

AN

EARL'S

'ALL-NIGHT'

C. 1500

THEN one of the grooms goeth into the ewery and calleth for all-night. The yeoman of the ewery giving him a towel, kisseth it and layeth it upon the groom's left shoulder, and after the basin and ewer with water (the groom giving him saye) then delivereth him a torch of wax lighted, if it be winter, and if it be not, unlighted. And so cometh he [the groom] to the pantry bar, where the yeoman usher with divers yeomen of the chamber do give attendance.

The bar put to, the usher calleth for all-night. The yeoman of the pantry bareheaded bringeth, in a napkin, one manchet and one cheate loaf, folded as one would wind it at the head and foot, laying the napkin plain over the one side. The usher giving him saye, and the said panter kissing the napkin and bread, the usher delivereth it to one of the yeomen and so goeth to the buttery bar, calling in like manner for all-night.

The yeoman of the buttery coming bareheaded bringeth the Estate's drinking cup covered, and a cup of saye, and a drinking cup for the Lady in like manner, and a great jug of silver covered all filled with beer. The usher, giving him saye of them all, after delivereth the said cups and jug to two other yeomen. Then he calleth for a cup of beer and so drinketh and giveth to all the servants in like manner. Then goeth he forth to the cellar (if the torch be lighted the groom [going] foremost with the torch and basin and ewer), so coming to the cellar bar in like manner calleth for all-night.

The yeoman of the cellar bringeth a cupboard cloth and a cup of state covered, and a cup of saye, and two great pots of wine, the usher giving him saye. If the torch be lighted the usher causeth the yeoman to kiss the cupboard cloth, and giveth it to the groom, laying it on his left shoulder, and giveth the two pots to one other yeoman, and taketh in his own hand the cup of state with the cup of saye: the torchlight foremost, the usher next, the bread next to him, the beer cup for the Estate next him, the cup of beer next and last the wine pots.

In this manner they go to the bedchamber. If the torch be not lighted then he with the torch and basin goeth behind last, and the usher foremost with the cupboard cloth on his right shoulder. Coming to the cupboard, the usher making curtsey, the torch standing at the nether end of the cupboard, and the chamberer being ready taketh the light off the cupboard and standing at the upper and holdeth the same in her hand. The usher, setting down the cup of state upon the cupboard [and] kissing the cupboard cloth, spreadeth it abroad upon the cupboard. If the groom has the cupboard cloth then he kisseth it. Then he [the usher] taketh the bread of the yeoman, he kissing it. So unfolding the napkin, foldeth it plain, setting the bread in it, and giveth saye thereof to the yeoman. Then he covereth the bread with the one end of the napkin, so setteth it at the upper end of the cupboard.

Then, taking the Estate's drinking cups, giving the yeoman sayes, he setteth them next the bread; then the jug of beer, setting it next the cups; then the pots of wine, giving sayes, setteth them next the jugs; and then he taketh the towel from the shoulder of the groom, kissing it, and raiseth it upon his own left shoulder, and giveth saye to the groom of the water. Then setteth last the basin and ewer down, and kissing the towel layeth it upon the ewer.

Then he uncovereth the Estate's cup, setting it and the cup of saye covered in the middle of the cupboard, most to the over end. Then taketh the wax light from the chamberer and setteth it upon the cupboard. And so all with curtsies depart and avoid the chamber. Then the usher of the chamber giveth charge of the cupboard to one of the gentlewomen of presence, if the Lady lieth with the Estate, or else one of the grooms hath the charge.

HARLEIAN MSS, ORDERS OF SERVICE BELONGING TO THE
DEGREE OF AN EARL

(left) Bradford table cloth, early seventeenth century, from Weston Park.

TABLE SEATING
The Household Of The Earl Of Dorset At Knole, In Kent, 1613–24

At My Lord's Table

My Lord

My Lady

My Lady Margaret

My Lady Isabella

Mr. Sackville

Mr. Frost

John Musgrave

Thomas Garret

At The Parlour Table

Mrs. Field

Mr. Wooldridge

Mrs. Grimsditch

Mr. Cheyney

Mrs. Fletcher

Mr. Duck, Page

Mrs. Willoughby

Mr. Josiah Cooper, a

Mrs. Stewkly

Frenchman, Page

Mrs. Wood

Mr. John Belgrave, Page

Mr. Dupper, Chaplain

Mr. Billingsley

Mr. Matthew Caldicott, my
  Lord's favourite

Mr. Graverner, Gentleman
Usher

Mr. Edward Legge, Steward

Mr. Marshall, Auditor

Mr. Peter Basket, Gentleman of
  the Horse

Mr. Edwards, Secretary

Mr. Drake, Attendant

Mr. Marsh, Attendant on my
  Lady

At The Clerks' Table In The Hall

Edward Fulks and John
  Edwards, Clerks of the
Kitchen

Benjamin Staples, Groom of the
  Great Chamber

Thomas Petley, Brewer

Edward Care, Master Cook

William Turner, Baker

William Smith, Yeoman of the
  Buttery

Francis Steeling, Gardener

Richard Wicking, Gardener

Henry Keble, Yeoman of the
  Pantry

Thomas Clements, Under
  Brewer

John Mitchell, Pastryman

Samuel Vans, Caterer

Thomas Vinson, Cook

Edward Small, Groom of the
  Wardrobe

John Elnor, Cook

Ralph Hussie, Cook

Samuel Southern, Under Baker

John Avery, Usher of the Hall

Lowry, a French boy

Robert Elnor, Slaughterman

The Nursery

Nurse Carpenter

Widow Ben

Jane Sisley

Dorothy Pickenden

At The Long Table In The Hall

Robert Care, Attendant on my Lord
Mr. Gray, Attendant likewise
Mr. Rogert Cook, Attendant on my Lady Margaret
Mr. Adam Bradford, Barber
Mr. John Guy, Groom of my Lord's Bedchamber
Walter Comestone, Attendant on my Lady
Edward Lane, Scrivener
Mr. Thomas Poor, Yeoman of the Wardrobe
Mr. Thomas Leonard, Master Huntsman
Mr. Woodgate, Yeoman of the Great Chamber
John Hall, Falconer
James Flennel, Yeoman of the Granary
Rawlinson, Armourer
Moses Shonk, Coachman
Anthony Ashly, Groom of the Great Horse
Griffin Edwards, Groom of my Lady's Horse
Francis Turner, Groom of the Great Horse
William Grynes,　　"　　"
Acton Curvett, Chief Footman
The Armourer's Man
Ralph Wise, his Servant
John Swift, the Porter's Man

James Loveall, Footman
Sampson Ashley,　　"
William Petley,　　"
Nicholas James,　　"
Paschal Beard,　　"
Elias Thomas,　　"
Henry Spencer, Farrier
Edward Goodsall
John Sant, the Steward's Man
Ralph Wise, Groom of the Stables
Thomas Petley, Under Farrier
John Stephens, The Chaplain's Man
John Haite, Groom for the Stranger's Horse
Thomas Giles, Groom of the Stables
Richard Thomas, Groom of the Hall
Christopher Wood, Groom of the Pantry
George Owen, Huntsman
George Vigeon,　　"
Thomas Grittan, Groom of the Buttery
Solomon, the Bird-Catcher
Richard Thornton, the Coachman's Man
Richard Pickenden, Postillion
William Roberts, Groom
John Atkins　⎰ Men to
Clement Doory ⎱ carry wood

The Laundry-Maids' Table

Mrs. Judith Simpton
Mrs. Grace Simpton
Penelope Tutty, the Lady Margaret's Maid
Anne Mills, Dairy-Maid
Prudence Butcher
Anne Howse

Faith Husband
Elinor Thompson
Goodwife Burton
Grace Robinson, a Blackamoor
Goodwife Small
William Lewis, Porter

The Kitchen And Scullery

Diggory Dyer
Marfidy Snipt
John Watson

Thomas Harman
Thomas Johnson
John Morockoe, a Blackamoor

LADY

WILLOUGHBY

SPEAKS

HER

MIND

TO

A

SERVANT

1594

THOU hast used thy pleasure in bad speeches of the Countess of Shrewsbury, and Mr Thomas Spencer's wife, and others. Thou hast practised dissensions betwixt my husband and me from the beginning. Thou hast set my father and him at jars, because thou mightest the better fish and enrich thyself, as thou hast done, with their spoils. Thou wouldst (being in thy house) have married me to thy cousin Cludd, a poor cozening knave of my father's, that came lousy to him, and theretofore in thy heart couldst never since abide me, tho' hitherto I have concealed it.

I was once before for thy pleasure and persuasions little better than hurled out of this house [Midleton Hall, Warwickshire], being great bellied, when thou didst hope both by that means might have perished.

... And notwithstanding all this and much worse than this, thy ordinary protestation is by the faith of an honest man. Malicious knave thou art that canst not spare poor gentlewomen and infants with thy tongue and practices; gentleman thou know'st thyself to be none, and tho' at this instant I have no better means of revenge than a little ink and paper, let thy soul and carcass be assured to bear and taste of these injuries in other sort and terms than from and by the hands of a woman.

BRIDGET, LADY WILLOUGHBY, TO CLEMENT FISHER, 1594

TIPS

ABOUT

SERVANTS

FROM

SIR

WILLIAM

WENTWORTH

1604

FOR servants be very careful to keep only those that be born of good and honest friends and be well willing, humble, diligent and honest. Take heed what you speak before them, if you be wise, especially touching any great person ... Yet in any case trust them not more than you needs must in matters that may greatly concern your danger. For almost all treacheries have been wrought by servants and the final end of their service is gain and advancement,

Col. Pl. X (right) Servants at Tichborne House, Hampshire. Detail from the painting of the distribution of the Tichborne Dole. Gillis van Tilborch, 1670.

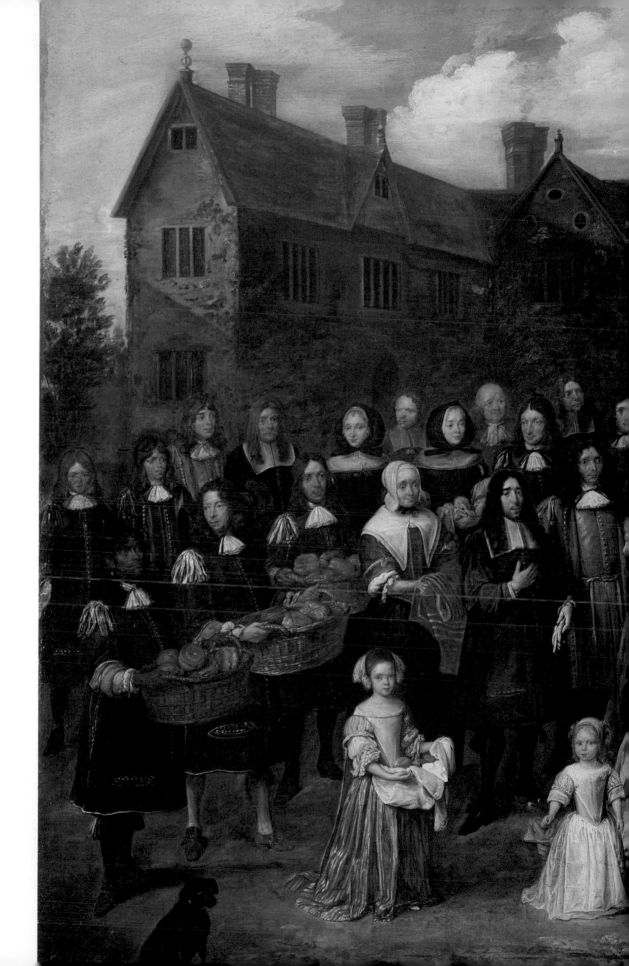

Col. Pl. XI–XIV Gardeners at Hartwell House, Buckinghamshire. Details from the paintings by Balthasar Nebot, 1738.

Col. Pl. XV Killing flies at Dynes Hall, Essex. Diana Sperling, c. 1815–20.

which, offered by any to them that wants it and longs for it, brings a dangerous temptation. Only some ancient honest servants of your father's whose wealth and credit depend most upon your house and are seated on your ground are like to be fast and true to you than other hirelings &c. Yet build no judgement upon things they speak, though they be honest; for ordinarily such men do mistake and misreport matters for want of learning and sounder judgment, though they be honest and mean truth.

SIR WILLIAM WENTWORTH OF WENTWORTH WOODHOUSE

DUTIES

OF

A

TRUMPETER

1610

WHEN the Earl is to ride a journey, he is early every morning to sound, to give warning, that the officers may have time to make all things ready for breakfast and the grooms of the stable to dress and meat the horses. When it is breakfast time, he is to make his second sounding: breakfast ended, and things in a readiness, he is to sound the third time, to call to horse. He is to ride foremost, both out and into any town, sounding his trumpet. Upon the way he may sound for pleasure. But if he see the day so spent that they are like to bring late to their lodging, he is to sound the tantara, to move them to hasten their pace . . . He and the Drummer are to go often into the stable, to acquaint the horses with the sound of the trumpet, and the noise of the drum.

ROBERT BAINBRIDGE, *Some Rules and Orders for the Government of the House of an Earle*

Serving an al fresco meal to Queen Elizabeth, from an engraving of *c.*1570 from *The Book of Faulconrie* by George Turbeville (1575).

MY COOK TO WRITE READ AND MAKE BREAD 1653

PERHAPS my cook comes down tomorrow. Show him what brass baking pans there are in my house and also latten pans for puddings or tarts. If there is not wooden dishes to make white bread, buy a dozen, he will show you the size. Buy a bushel of white wheat for bread and crust. If you find not good, it may be had about Wendover. Persuade my cook to write and read to keep him from worse employment, tell him I bid you pay for his learning and agree what he shall give.

Let him try 2 or three times to make French bread and after the first or second time send me a loaf of each sort to judge of. I have bid him make me 2 or 3 hare pies but he must not kill them this month and I tell him I will have none killed till I come, but for those pies he is wild to get a gun, but I will not have my game destroyed . . . I shall suffer no man that's either debauched or unruly in my house, nor do I hire any servant that takes tobacco, for it not only stinks up my house, but is an ill example to the rest of my family.

SIR RALPH VERNEY TO WILLIAM ROADES, SUMMER 1653

Schedule For The Housekeeper And Others At Bank Hall, 1677

Mondays – look out the foul cloths and call the maids and sit or stay by them till they be all mended.

Tuesdays – clean the rooms, and chairs from the great room to the nursery and the beds on the top and bottom; and dust the feathers.

Wednesdays – clean all the rooms, chairs and beds under and top with the feathers, from the nursery to the Eagle Chamber.

Thursdays – clean the hall and parlours, windows, tables, chairs and pictures below stairs.

Fridays – scour all the grates tongs and hand-irons.

Saturdays – clean the store house shelves and dressers.

Every day – once for one hour in the forenoon go through all the rooms and see it doth not rain into them and dust them all down; and sweep them.

Dairy maid – wash your dairy every day; and for your milk and butter do as you will be directed; Churn – Tuesdays and Fridays. Serve the swine and poultry night and morning; and for the hogsmeat any of the servant men shall carry them out for you. Observe well the time for setting out all sorts of your poultry, once every week make the house bread; and same shall help you to knead. To help them wash when washing day comes; Milk your cows in good time.

Cook maid – wash your kitchen every night, and the Larders every other day, shelfs and dressers and scour the pewter we use every Friday night, and all the rest of the pewter once every month. Keep your Kitchen extraordinary clean. To help upon washing days the rest of the maids to wash. And make all the maids bring down their candle-sticks first thing in a morning to be made clean.

REGULATION FOR THE HOUSEHOLD OF THE MOORE FAMILY, BANK HALL, NEAR LIVERPOOL

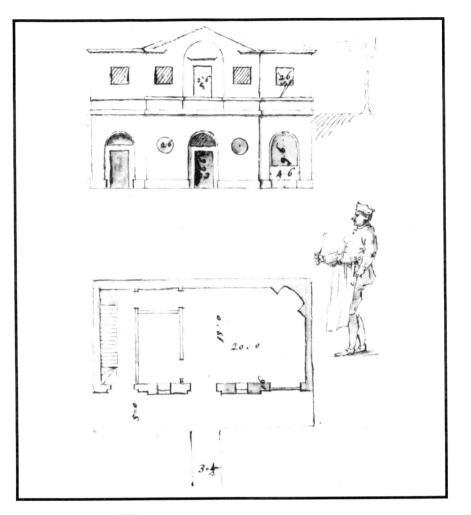

LADY

JUDITH

LOOKS

FOR

A

CHAMBER

MAID

C. 1704

PRAY inquire for a Chamber Maid for us, & that you may fully acquaint her with our business I have sent you an account of what it is that we expect from her. First, she must work plain work very well, Sr. Ab: wears very fine linen & she must make & mend for him & me & for my son & sister, she must wash & smooth all the fine linens & muslins & dress our heads, & keep our chambers neat & clean, & do all that belongs to the Chamber maid's place. The Dairy maid, when her cows are milked, the poultry & swine fed & done the business that belongs to her Dairy, shall help her wash, & likewise to help her to wash that part of the house that is not in constant use; but our Lodging Chambers that we lie in every night, she must do them by herself. We would not have a young raw finical Lass, for then she will mind nothing so much as the dressing up of herself, but a plain discreet staid servant, one that has been used to such business & is able to perform it. If you can hear of such an one for us, that will undertake to do this,

Design for an unidentified country-house kitchen, by William Kent, c. 1730.

we shall think our selves much oblig'd to you for your endeavours herein.

vants being allowed to go into the cellar with them but the under butler only.

DUCAL

WELCOME

AT

CANNONS

1721

. . .

SEPTEMBER 11, 1721. For the future all Gentlemen's Livery Servants that come to the house be taken into the cellar by the Under Butler and have there one horn of strong beer or ale given to each of them and if their masters dine here that this be done after dinner, none of his Grace's ser-

. . . and lack of it at Welbeck, c.1769
We Your Grace's servants whose names are here enclosed beg leave to petition for ale; not for ourselves particular, but for the servants of Your Grace's friends, which we have been frequently refused by Mr Martin, Your Grace's butler, without giving any reason for the same, but in saying I am Master and you shall have none.

The kitchen in the Nostell Priory doll's house, c. 1740.

then take care to fill them up again with clean water, that you may not lessen your master's liquor.

That the salt may lie smooth in the salt-cellar, press it down with your moist palm.

When a gentleman is going away after dining with your master, be sure to stand full in his view, and follow him to the door, and as you have opportunity look full in his face, perhaps it may bring you a shilling; but if the gentleman has lain there a night, get the cook, the housemaid, the stable-men, the scullion, and the gardener, to accompany you, and to stand in his way to the hall in a line on each side him: If the gentleman performs handsomely, it will do him honour, and cost your master nothing.

You need not wipe your knife to cut bread from the table, because, in cutting a slice or two it will wipe itself.

JONATHAN SWIFT, *Directions to Servants*

'Lucy' had retired to Warwickshire because Byron had made her pregnant. The gap after 'the Girls on the Manor' is due to an excision made by Thomas Moore, Byron's editor; the original letter does not survive.

DEAN SWIFT ON A BUTLER'S DUTIES 1745

IF an humble companion, a chaplain, a tutor, or a dependent cousin happen to be at table, whom you find to be little regarded by the master, and the company, which no body is readier to discover and observe than we servants, it must be the business of you and the footman, to follow the example of your betters, by treating him many degrees worse than any of the rest; and you cannot please your master better, or at least your lady.

If any one calls for small-beer towards the end of dinner, do not give yourself the pains of going down to the cellar, but gather the droppings and leavings out of the several cups, and glasses, and salvers onto one; but turn your back to the company, for fear of being observed.

When you clean your plate, leave the whiting plainly to be seen in all the chinks, for fear your lady should believe you have not cleaned it.

If you are curious to taste some of your master's choice bottles, empty as many of them just below the neck as will make the quantity you want; but

LORD BYRON IMPROVES HIS FEMALE STAFF 1811

I am plucking up my spirits, and have begun to gather my little sensual comforts together. Lucy is extracted from Warwickshire; some very bad faces have been warned off the premises, and more promising substituted in their stead; the partridges are plentiful, hares fairish, pheasants not quite so good, and the Girls on the Manor ...... Just as I had formed a tolerable establishment my travels commenced, and on my return I found all to do over again; my former flock were all scattered; some married, not before it was needful. As I am a great disciplinarian, I have just issued an edict for the abolition of caps; no hair to be cut on any pretext; stays permitted, but not too low before; full uniform always in the evening; Lucinda to be commander – *vice* the present, about to be wedded (*mem*, she is 35 with a flat face and a squeaking voice), of all the makers and unmakers of beds in the household.

BYRON TO FRANCES HODGSON, 25 SEPTEMBER, 1811

Servants of the Drummond family, at Denham, Buckinghamshire, as drawn by one of the Drummond children, c. 1830.

ADVICE

TO

A

FOOTMAN

1825

WHILE waiting at dinner, never be picking your nose, or scratching your head, or any other part of your body; neither blow your nose in the room; if you have a cold, and cannot help doing it, do it on the outside of the door; but do not sound your nose like a trumpet, that all the house may hear when you blow it; still it is better to blow your nose when it requires, than to be picking it and snuffing up the *mucus*, which is a filthy trick. Do not yawn or gape, or even sneeze, if you can avoid it; and as to hawking and spitting, the name of such a thing is enough to forbid it, without a command. When you are standing behind a person, to be ready to change the plates, &c., do not put your hands on the back of the chair, as it is very improper; though I have seen some not only do so, but even beat a kind of tune upon it with their fingers. Instead of this, stand upright with your hands hanging down or before you, but not folded. Let your demeanour be such as becomes the situation which you are in. Be well dressed, and have light shoes that make no noise, your face and hands well washed, your finger-nails cut short and kept quite clean underneath; have a nail-brush for that purpose, as it is a disgusting thing to see black dirt under the nails. Let the lapels of your coat be buttoned, as they will only be flying in your way.

T. COSNETT, *Footman's Directory*

GOINGS-

ON

AT

HESLEYSIDE

1840s

NO wine was ever served at dinner, though this did not touch me, as at that time I drank nothing. Water, drunk out of black glass, was the family beverage. Nevertheless, the butler and his pantry cronies appeared to indulge freely in wine! In that way it was hardly possible to find a more drunken establishment; Hesleyside was simply a house of public refreshment for the neighbourhood and, I am sorry to say, remained so when William and I later had it to ourselves. Mauxwell, the butler, a sober enough man himself, gave drink out, he said, for the honour of the family! And my poor husband, who laboured latterly for the effervescent popularity of the lower orders, well knew that drink was a high road to their hearts. How mercilessly was his mistaken generosity taken advantage of! Most certainly Hesleyside in those days was a rum and disorderly establishment.

There was a still in the garden-shed for the distillation of mint, as was the custom in old-fashioned gardens, and which, as far as we knew, was used for no other purpose. But in Hodgson's time as gardener this was not the case. It was in the days of home-brewing, and the brewing refuse was always thrown to the pigs. Hodgson, however, begged it from his unsuspecting master for the raising of carrots, which did not thrive in the Hesleyside garden soil, and had to be bought. Some fine carrots were duly produced as evidence of what a manufactured soil could do, although in reality they had been introduced from outside. For Hodgson was using the refuse for the distillation of something a good deal more potent than peppermint, and the inmates of the saddle-room were in the secret with him.

L.E.O. CHARLTON, *Memoirs of a Northumbrian Lady*

PROTOCOL

AMONG

UPPER

SERVANTS

AT

HENHAM

HALL

SUFFOLK

C. 1870

ANOTHER of our amusements was to hide and watch the upper servants march from the servant's hall to 'The Room' [the housekeeper's room]; this was a serious ceremony: the butler and housekeeper and lady's maid had their meat course in 'the hall', the butler carving whilst the hall-boy waited. When the sweets were handed, the upper servants rose from the table each carrying a plate of pudding in one hand and a glass of beer in the other, and walked majestically out of the room in single file, according to the rank of their master or mistress.

The ladies' maids and valets were always addressed amongst themselves by the name of their employers. A friend of mine arrived late at a country house and as he was hurriedly changing into his evening clothes he heard a valet call to the lady's maid in the next room: 'Hurry up, Ripon, you'll be late for supper, both the Abercorns are down.'

LADY AUGUSTA FANE, *Chit-Chat*

POWDERING

NO

FUN

C. 1890

POWDER money used to be allowed in some houses, while in others the powder itself was provided and was always of the best. Footmen of the younger generation should be thankful that this daily powdering of the hair has gone out of fashion, for it was indeed a very unpleasant business. After the hair had been moistened, soap was put on and rubbed into a stiff lather, and the combing was done so that the teeth marks would show evenly all over. Powder was then applied with a puff and the wet mass allowed to dry on the head until it became quite firm. In the evening the hair was always to be washed and oiled to prevent its becoming almost fox colour, and I remember I was hardly ever free from colds in houses where this hair-powdering was the regulation.

JOHN JAMES, *Memories of a House Steward*

ORDER

OF

LIVERIES

1900

LIVERIES are given 1st April and 1st October of each year. Evening Liveries every Twelve Months. Tweed Jackets every Twelve Months (except the Hall Porter and Steward's Room Boy, they have a Tweed Suit). Hats, Gloves, and Stockings every Six Months, except on special occasions, such as Drawing Rooms, Weddings, etc. Orders for Gloves and Stockings for them will be issued from time to time as required. Macintoshes are given according to wear.

When Evening Liveries have been worn Six Months from date of entry into service, the wearer is entitled to a New Suit on the 1st of April prox. If within Six Months the wearer is not entitled to a New Suit until the following April. When Morning Liveries have been worn Three Months from date of entry, the wearer is entitled to a New Suit either in April or October, according to date of entry, but if not worn Three Months the wearer is not entitled to a Suit until the next term, or issue of Liveries.

Overcoats have to be worn Twelve Months before the wearer is entitled to another on the aforesaid date, 1st of April.

The same rule applies to giving up Liveries on leaving service. Within the above periods they are

Maid in the basement corridor at Stowe House, Buckinghamshire. By J.C. Nattes, 1807.

Lord Salisbury's property, over those periods they are the wearer's property.

Stable Liveries are given and retained on the same system.

HOUSEHOLD REGULATIONS FOR HATFIELD HOUSE, 1900

MEMORIES

OF

BELVOIR

CASTLE

1905

THE gong man was an old retainer, one of those numberless ranks of domestic servants which have completely disappeared and today seem fabulous. He was admittedly very old. He wore a white beard to his waist. Three times a day he rang the gong – for luncheon, for dressing-time, for dinner. He would walk down the interminable passages, his livery hanging a little loosely on his bent old bones, clutching his gong with one hand and with the other feebly brandishing the padded-knobbed stick with which he struck it. Every corridor had to be warned and the towers too, so I suppose he banged on and off for ten minutes, thrice daily.

Then there were the lamp-and-candle men, at least three of them, for there was no other form of lighting. Gas was despised, I forget why – vulgar, I think. They polished and scraped the wax off the candelabra, cut wicks, poured paraffin oil, and unblackened glass chimneys all day long. After dark they were busy turning wicks up or down, snuffing candles, and dewaxing extinguishers. It was not a department we liked much to visit. It smelt disgusting and the lampmen were too busy. But the upholsterer's room was a great treat. He was exactly like a Hans Andersen tailor. Cross-legged he sat in a tremendous confusion of curtains and covers, fringes, buttons, rags and carpets, bolsters, scraps (that could be begged off him), huge curved needles like scimitars, bodkins, hunks of beeswax to strengthen thread, and hundreds of flags. The flags on the towertop, I suppose, got punished by the winds and were constantly in need of repair. I never saw him actually at work on anything else. There were slim flags for wind, little ones for rain, huge ones for sunshine, hunting flags, and many others.

The water-men are difficult to believe in today. They seemed to me to belong to another clay.

Servants at Erddig Hall, Denbighshire, in the late nineteenth century: William Hughes, woodman, William Gittus, foreman carpenter, Jane Brown, housekeeper, and an unidentified gamekeeper, with his son.

They were the biggest people I had ever seen, much bigger than any of the men of the family, who were remarkable for their height. They had stubbly beards and a general Bill Sikes appearance. They wore brown clothes, no collars, and thick green baize aprons from chin to knee. On their shoulders they carried a wooden yoke from which hung two gigantic cans of water. They moved on a perpetual round. Above the ground floor there was not a drop of hot water and not one bath, so their job was to keep all jugs, cans, and kettles full in the bedrooms, and morning or evening to bring the hot water for the hip-baths. We were always a little frightened of the water-men. They seemed of another element and never spoke but one word, 'Water-man', to account for themselves.

LADY DIANA COOPER, *The Rainbow comes and goes*

TROUBLES

OF

A

FOOTMAN

1910

NOW it was while I was at this place in Devon that I met the girl who was to become my wife. She was then head kitchen-maid and in her pale blue uniform she looked so lovely that I fell in love with her. This was all right, but courting while in service was then strictly forbidden. We hadn't to be seen talking, so we used to leave notes under the lamp room mat; or we'd get up at four in the morning and slip out for a walk in the woods. I saved up for a ring (and on £26 a year that took some doing), though I knew very well that Nellie must never be seen wearing it. I think it mostly got worn in those days between four and nine in the morning. It was sometimes possible for us to meet secretly outside for a few minutes in the evening and neither of us will ever forget the time when Nellie, having as usual nipped out of the larder window, went to cross a five-foot plank which the builders had left to cover a trench. It had been a very wet day and what wasn't water in that trench was wet clay and sloshy mud. Nellie (in pale blue) slipped in and I'd a devil of a tug o' war with the mud before it would let her go. Of course this spoilt our little evening's courtship.

MEMORIES OF GERALD HORNE

LAMENT

OF

A

LAUNDRY-

MAID

1911

THERE are 22 servants in the house, of course that does not include those who come into work every day. There is a man in the kitchen who works all the meat (the butcher he is called). He prepares all the meat. Then there is a man in the scullery, also a woman kept for washing up, and two stillroom maids, and a woman comes every day to bake the bread. So there are five in the kitchen and two regularly in the scullery. I am afraid Miss Brown that sounds very much like a fairy tale, but when I tell you there are fourteen cold meats sent up every day for my Lord's luncheon including four or five hot dishes, you will understand there is some work to be done in the kitchen alone! Then my Lord has a clean table cloth for every meal. Is it not ridiculous? Sometimes when he is alone we have twenty three table clothes in the wash in a week and when he has a lot of company we have anywhere from thirty six to forty. His sister is Lady Hereford of Ludlow, and when she and her daughters come here there is plenty of work for everyone. The sideboard cloths are changed three or four times a week and my Lord has a clean cloth, on every tray

taken up to him. I often say if cleanliness would keep any one alive, then Viscount Tredegar would never die.

LETTER TO A FRIEND FROM A LAUNDRY-MAID AT TREDEGAR HOUSE, MONMOUTHSHIRE, 1911

LORD

ASTOR'S

BUTLER

C. 1930

Y ET Mr Lee could be unexpectedly kind. At a dinner there was once nearly a disaster which could have turned into a social scandal. A public figure of some standing was talking to Lady Astor as a footman was serving him. 'I need a skivvy for my kitchen, can any of your servants recommend one, do you think?'

Give her ladyship her due, she tried to temper his speech. 'What kind of servant do you want?'

'Oh, any little slut will do.' The footman stepped back and went white as a sheet. 'I had some sort of sixth sense that things weren't what they should be with him,' Mr Lee told me. 'I moved over as quickly as I could and caught him just as he was about to pour the hot sauce over the guest's head. There was no doubt about it, he told me that was what he was going to do when I got him outside.'

Mr Lee didn't so much as reprimand him when he'd heard his story. He didn't say a word; he went to his sideboard, poured a glass of port, handed it to the footman, patted him on the back and said, 'Come back in when you feel you can.' Mr Lee saw Lady Astor the following day and complained of her guest's conversation. 'He had no right to

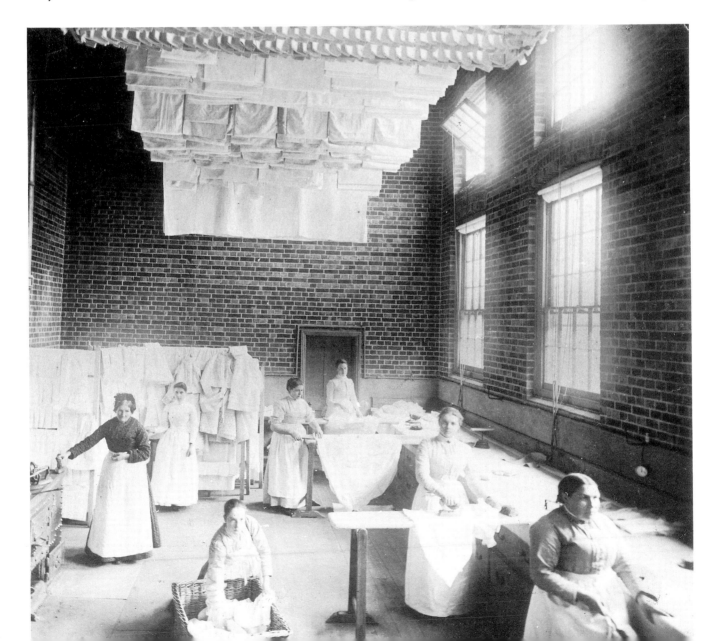

speak like that about servants, even behind their backs, my lady, and in our hearing, it's unforgivable.' He didn't mention the footman's reaction to what had been said.

'You're quite right, Lee, and that man will never visit us again.' She asked for the footman to be sent to see her, and she apologized to him.

ROSINA HARRISON, *Rose: my life in service*

Henry Moate, butler to Sir George Sitwell at Renishaw Hall, Derbyshire. C.R.W. Nevinson, 1918, detail.

(left) The laundry at Petworth House, Sussex, c. 1890.

REDUCTION

OF

STAFF

AT

KNOWSLEY

1952

ON October 7, when at Hoylake, Winstanley [Harold Winstanley, footman to the Earl of Derby at Knowsley, in Lancashire] bought a Schmeisser gun and some hundreds of rounds of ammunition from a friend for a pair of trousers and £3. On November 5, about 8.15 a.m., Lady Derby was sitting in the smoking-room having dinner. Behind her was a door to the second library. About 8.15 the door from the first library opened and there stood Winstanley. The first thing that Lady Derby noticed was that he was smoking a cigarette. She rose from her chair and faced him, and then saw that he was holding a gun which was pointed directly at her. He told her to turn round and she did so and immediately the gun fired. Lady Derby felt a blow on her neck. She fell forward with the force of it.

Lady Derby could hear Winstanley moving about behind her. She kept still, and that may have saved her life. A few moments or a few minutes later she heard Stallard, the butler, say: 'Harold.' Immediately there was a burst of fire and she felt a thud as he fell.

The suspense went on and she could hear Winstanley moving about the room. She heard someone say: 'No,' and that was followed by two bursts of fire and then all was quiet. That no doubt was Stuart, the under-butler. The next thing Lady Derby knew was that she was being attended to by her maid . . .

Having finished in the smoke-room and library, Winstanley walked out into the inner hall, and he there saw Sullivan, Lord Derby's valet, halfway down the stairs from the floor above. Sullivan had heard the first firing from the room immediately below where he was working. Realizing that something was wrong, he ran downstairs and

Winstanley went after him. As Sullivan ran along a corridor downstairs a burst of firing followed him, and he was hit in the hand. He collapsed into an opening at the bottom of the lift. It was there in that opening that the rest of the staff collected. When Winstanley came along the corridor he stood over Sullivan and pointed the gun at him.

Mrs Turley, the housekeeper, and Miss Campbell, the assistant housekeeper, ran along the passage from their room, and housemaids from upstairs came down in the lift. During the confusion Mrs Turley tried to pacify Winstanley, and Sullivan managed to get away and ran into the kitchen corridor. Winstanley said to the people standing there – all of them women: 'Don't be frightened, I wouldn't hurt any of you girls. The three of them are in there dead, Douglas, Mr Stallard, and her Ladyship.' Miss Doxford, Lady Derby's maid, and the housemaids made their way upstairs to the smoke room . . .

Another person attracted to the scene was M. Dupuis, the chef. He tried to reason with Winstanley, and then saw Winstanley go to his room and come out wearing his mackintosh. He walked with Winstanley down one corridor into another, at the end of which was a door leading out into the grounds. In that passage M. Dupuis tried to snatch the gun from Winstanley, but received a blow on the head with the butt of it. When that blow was struck the gun went off, spraying the wall with bullets.

When the police arrived they went to the smoke-room and found Lady Derby. She had been shot and Winstanley could well be forgiven for thinking her dead. A bullet had entered the back of her neck, but had come out just below the left ear. Stallard was dead. He had five bullet wounds, two of which would certainly have killed him. Stuart also had been hit by five bullets, four of which would have killed him, in the head, chest, and abdomen .... Thirty-seven shots were fired in the house that night.

The Times, 6 NOVEMBER, 1952

Luggage van with chauffeur at Polesden Lacey, Surrey, c. 1914.
(right) 'Cabbage Castle', the castellated house designed for his guinea-pigs by Charles Lamb at Beauport House, Sussex, c. 1830.

Cabbage Castle.
The ancient residence of the Counts of
Valerian Cabbage — built by the
Emperor Ermineus I. year 10 - 11 -
In the year 18. having become ruinous
it was taken down & a very splendid
edifice erected on the same site by
Enceladus 4th Count of the house of
Waloi -

9
Animals

Medieval castles and country houses made much use of animals. Dogs for hunting and guarding proliferated, as did hawks for hunting or horses for war, sport and transport. The animal population of a medieval complex may have exceeded its human one, even excluding the deer in the deer park or the sheep and cattle who sheltered in the outbuildings or grazed in the adjacent fields.

But they were anonymous animals, and left little permanent mark. No distinctive stable buildings survive from the period. With the exception of cats for scavenging and dogs to turn kitchen spits, they were forbidden the main house. The image of dogs rootling for bones on the rush-strewn floors of medieval halls is a fantasy invented by Walter Scott and his generation. In any well-conducted medieval or sixteenth-century hall, dogs were not allowed in.

Domestic pets may have arrived in the fifteenth century, or even earlier, but it is not until the late sixteenth and early seventeenth centuries that they begin to feature in English portraits. Their presence was dramatically illustrated at the execution of Mary, Queen of Scots, when her little dog fled for security beneath the dress of his decapitated mistress. Pets begin to appear in literature at about the same time – Lady Harington's dog, for instance. The first impressive English stables were built in the early seventeenth century. At much the same time William Cavendish, later Duke of Newcastle, was perhaps the first English landowner to make a cult of horses – to write about them and commission portraits of them, as well as building lavish stables and riding schools for them.

Even so, at Woburn in the seventeenth century, for instance, dogs are still featuring in letters and account books in a purely functional capacity. It was probably not until the eighteenth century that sporting, as opposed to lap, dogs began to be allowed into the house. Monuments to dogs and horses appeared at about the same time. Occasional menageries added an exotic note. Animal portraits abounded. Animals were becoming the companions, rather than servants, of the upper classes.

The 2nd Lord Rothschild and his team of zebras at Tring Park, Hertfordshire, c. 1900.

SIR

GERVASE

AND

THE

BEAR

1601

Sir Gervase Clifton being at a bear baiting in Nottinghamshire: when the bear broke loose and followed his son up a stairs towards a gallery where himself was, he opposed himself with his rapier against the fury of the beast, to save his son.

JOHN CHAMBERLAIN, *Letters*

DOGS

TO

BE

KEPT

OUT

OF

THE

HOUSE

1605

He [the usher of the hall] is to see that no dogs be suffered to tarry in the hall, for they will be robbers of the alms tubs. The groom [of the hall] is to have a whip with a bell, to fear them away withall; for dogs of all kinds must be kept in their kennels and out places fit for them.

RULES FOR THE HOUSE OF AN EARL, 1605

THE

DUKE

OF

NEWCASTLE

AND

HIS

HORSES

1667

So great a love hath my Lord for good horses! And certainly I have observed, and do verily believe, that some of them had also a particular love to my Lord; for they seemed to rejoice whensoever he came into the stables, by their trampling action, and the noise they made; nay, they would go much better in the Mannage, when my Lord was by, than when he was absent; and when he rode them himself, they seemed to take much pleasure and pride in it. But of all sorts of horses, my Lord loved Spanish horses and barbes best, saying, That Spanish horses were like princes, and barbes like gentlemen, in their kind.

DUCHESS OF NEWCASTLE, *Life of William Cavendish, Duke, Marquess and Earl of Newcastle*

Francis Russell, 4th Earl of Bedford, with his hawk and dogs. Detail from a picture attributed to Robert Peake, c. 1600.

145

Sir John Harrington lived at Kelston Hall in Somerset, and this episode probably took place there.

LADY

HARINGTON'S

DOG

YOUR little dog, that barked as I came by,
I strake by hap so hard I made him cry;
And straight you put your finger in your eye,
And louring sat. I asked the reason why.
'Love me, and love my dog,' thou didst reply.
'Love as both should be loved.' – 'I will,' said I,
And sealed it with a kiss. Then by and by,
Cleared were the clouds of thy fair frowning sky.
Thus small events, great masteries may try.
For I, by this, do at their meaning guess,
That beat a whelp afore a lioness.

SIR JOHN HARINGTON, *To his wife, for striking her dog,*
Epigrams, 1618

TO the Memory
of
SIGNOR FIDO
an *Italian* of good Extraction;
who came into *England*,
not to bite us, like most of his Countrymen,
but to gain an honest livelihood.
He hunted not after Fame,
yet acquired it;
regardless of the Praise of his Friends,
but most sensible of their Love.
Tho' he lived amongst the Great,
he neither learned nor flattered any Vice.
He was no Bigot,
Though he doubted of none of the 39 Articles.
And, if to follow Nature,
and to respect the Laws of Society,
be Philosophy,
he was a perfect Philosopher;
a faithful Friend,
an agreeable companion
a loving Husband,
distinguished by a numerous Offspring,
all which he lived to see take good Courses.
In his old Age he retired
to the house of a Clergyman in the Country,
where he finished his earthly Race,
And died an Honour and an Example to the whole Species.
Reader,
This Stone is guiltless of Flattery
for he to whom it is inscribed
was not a Man
but a
GREYHOUND.

INSCRIPTION ON THE SHEPHERD'S COVE, STOWE.

(far left) A hound in front of Hutton Bonville Hall, Yorkshire. Unidentified artist, c. 1725.
(top) Lord Southampton's cat. Detail from the portrait of Henry Wriothesley, 3rd Earl of Southampton, attributed to John de Critz, 1603.
(left) 'Lord Foppington', William Beckford's dog at Fonthill Abbey, Wiltshire.

148

(top) Deer in front of Averham Park, Nottinghamshire. Detail from a picture by an unidentified artist, c. 1719.
The hunting lodge in the park of Ledston Hall, Yorkshire, with attendant cows. John Settringham, 1728.

DOGS AT CANNONS 1731

ORDERED: that all dogs whatever about the house be sent away except his Grace's be allowed to come into the parlours, and the setting dog, the mastiff bitch & kitchen garden bitch & Lord Carnarvon's little liver-coloured bitch.

HOUSEHOLD ORDERS, DUKE OF CHANDOS, 20 APRIL, 1731

MR PUREFOY'S DOGS AT SHALSTONE

1744   Dec. 30   This afternoon about 2 a clock died my pretty little bitch Chloe.

1750   May 14   Gave our Thos. Clarke for burying Killbuck, 0.0.6d.

1755   Oct. 30   To the lanes by Rawlins's house (where we lost Jewel)

Purefoy Papers

A MENAGERIE AT HORTON 1763

IN the garden or park, is a good artificial river, in which is a sloop and 2 or 3 boats; there are 2 temples, one with a portico, the other round, a triumphal arch, a Gothic bridge and a menagerie at a good distance, in which are kept a variety of wild beasts and birds: a young tiger not bigger than a cat, a bear, one monstrous large eagle, and an eagle with a white head.

REV. WILLIAM COLE, *Account of Tour with Horace Walpole*

Horses in an unidentified country-house stable, c. 1740.

A MENAGERIE AT HARDWICK C. 1800

THE late Duke used to dine here, as he supp'd at Brooks's, with his hat on, which his friends gave as the reason for his being so fond of Hardwick. His son turned the recess where the billiard table now stands into a kind of menagerie: a fishing net nailed up under the curtain confined the rabbits, hedgehogs, squirrels, guinea pigs, and white mice, that were the joy of his life from 8 to 12 years old, the smell caused by these quadrupeds was overpowering . . . but he would have been very much surprised had any objection been made to their residence here. A tree stood in the middle for the unhappy birds – caught by John Hall the gamekeeper – to perch on, and an owl made its melancholy hooting in one of the corners.

6TH DUKE OF DEVONSHIRE, *Handbook*

FAITHFUL DOGS AT FONTHILL 1812

THE poor animals Caroline and Spotty, recognising the carriage from a distance, shot towards me like arrows and, jumping on my lap, showed their genuine delight by innumerable barks and licks. They're lovelier and more attractive than ever, and I adore them – a hundred times more than the other limited, chilly, touchy members of my family. Goodbye, goodbye, I'm going out for a walk with them . . .

WILLIAM BECKFORD

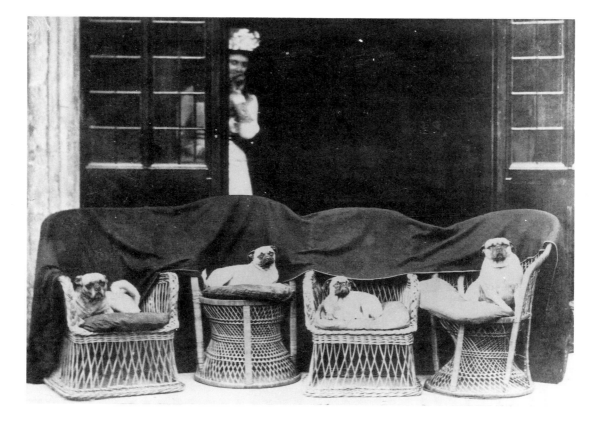

150

Pugs at Wilton House, Wiltshire, in the 1860s. Gladys Herbert in the background.
(right) A formal garden, engraved on the frontispiece of *Catalogus Plantarum . . .*, published by the Society of Gardeners, 1730.

10
Parks
&
Gardens

*T*he image of abundance is one of the most powerful of those connected with country houses: abundance flowing into the houses, for the benefit of the families who lived in them and their guests, and out of them to the families living on their estates; abundance derived from woods, fields, lakes, and rivers; and above all abundance of flowers, fruits and vegetables in and from country-house orchards and gardens.

Ben Jonson celebrated the abundance of fruit at Penshurst; and the letters of Lady de l'Isle, mistress of Penshurst in Jonson's time, are full of references to fruit being sent up from its orchards to her husband in London or at court. A sense of abundance impregnates descriptions of sixteenth- and seventeenth-century gardens, and the numerous bird's-eye views of country houses which were painted in the first half of the eighteenth century.

This abundance seemed like a recreation of Paradise to contemporaries. But it existed in a framework of formal paths, clipped trees, statues and artificial grottoes. In the course of the eighteenth century another image of Paradise, equally powerful in its own way, largely replaced the old one. This was a paradise of Arcadian seclusion, of what appeared to be untouched nature, of magical demesnes hidden from the outside world by walls or encircling belts of trees and enclosing great Palladian mansions at their heart. Within the walls was open grassland dotted with clumps of noble trees, sweeping lakes reflecting the sky, or tree-lined glades in which herds of deer freely roamed and grazed in the shadow of classical temples. The image was a seductive one, but it did not seduce everyone. There were those, like the painter Constable, who distrusted it because its effect was to cut houses off from the real country and the real world.

Flower gardens came back into favour in the nineteenth century. A new phenomenon appeared; the owner-gardeners, emerging with baskets and secateurs to weed, cut and plant in the gardens themselves. This was the world of Gertrude Jekyll. She designed for many country houses, although she did not own one herself. I cannot resist quoting her remarks about the comments of visitors to gardens; they will strike a sympathetic chord in many country-house gardeners of today.

View from the north partico at Stowe House, Buckinghamshire (detail). Engraved after Jacques Rigaud, 1739.

PARADISE

AT

KENILWORTH

1575

A garden then so appointed, as wherein aloft upon sweet shadowed walk of trees, in heat of Summer, to feel the pleasant whisking wind above, or delectable coolness of the fountain spring beneath: to taste of delicious strawberries, cherries, and other fruits, even from their stalks: to smell such fragrancy of sweet odours, breathing from the plants, herbs, and flowers: to hear such natural melodious music and tunes of birds: to have in eye, for mirth, sometimes these under-springing streams; then, the woods, the waters (for both pool and chase were hard at hand in sight), the deer, the people (that out of the East arbour in the base court also at hand in view), the fruit trees, the plants, the herbs, the flowers, the change in colours, the birds fluttering, the fountain streaming, the fish swimming, all in such delectable variety, order, dignity; whereby, at one moment, in one place, at hand, without travel, to have so full fruition of so many God's blessings, by entire delight unto all senses (if all can take) at once: for etymon of the word worthy to be called Paradise.

JOHN LANEHAM, *The Queen at Killingworth Castle*

Killingworth is the old name for Kenilworth, Warwickshire

RICHARD

CAREW

CELEBRATES

HIS

FISH

POND

AT

ANTONY

AND

HIS

PLANS

FOR

IT

1610

I wait not at the lawyer's gates,
Nor shoulder climbers down the stairs;
I vaunt not manhood by debates,
I envy not the miser's fears;
 But mean in state, and calm in sprite,
 My fishful pond is my delight.
There sucking mullet, swallowing bass,
Side-walking crab, wry-mouthed fluke,
And slip-fist eel, as evenings pass,
For safe bait at due place do look,
 Bold to approach, quick to espy,
 Greedy to catch, ready to fly.

I carried once a purpose to build a little wooden banqueting house on the island in my pond, which because some other may (perhaps) elsewhere put in execution, it will not do much amiss to deliver you the plot as the same was devised for me by that perfectly accomplished gentleman, the late Sir Arthur Champernowne.

 The island is square, with four rounds at the corners, like Mount Edgecumbe. This should first have been planched over, and railed about with balusters. In the midst there should have risen a boarded room of the like fashion but lesser proportion, so to leave sufficient space between that and the rails for a walk round about. This square room should withinside have been ceiled roundwise, and in three of the places where the round joined with the square, as many windows should have been set; the fourth should have served for a door. Of the four turrets shut out by this round, one should have made a kitchen, the second a storehouse to keep the fishing implements, the third a buttery, and the fourth a stair for ascending to the next loft; which next loft should have risen on the flat roof of the lower, in a round form, but of a lesser size again, so to leave a second terrace like the other. And as the square room below was ceiled round, so should this upper round room be ceiled square, to the end that where the side walls and ceiling joined, three windows and a door might likewise find their places. The void spaces between the round and square he would have turned to cupboards and boxes, for keeping other necessary utensils towards these fishing feasts.

RICHARD CAREW, *The Survey of Cornwall*

(Left, and elsewhere at borders). John Evelyn's garden tools, from his unfinished and unpublished *Elysium Britannicum*.

William Lawson may have served as gardener to Sir Henry Bellasis, of Newburgh Priory, Yorkshire, to whom his book is dedicated.

THE

DELIGHTS

OF

AN

ORCHARD

1618

WHAT can your eye desire to see, your ears to hear, your mouth to take, or your nose to smell, that is not to be had in an Orchard, with abundance of variety? What more delightsome than an infinite variety of sweet smelling flowers decking with sundry colours, the green mantle of the earth, the universal mother of us all, so by them despotted, so dyed, that all the World cannot sample them, and wherein it is more fit to admire the Dyer, than imitate his Workmanship, colouring not only the earth, but decking the air, and sweetening every breath and spirit.

The Rose red, Damask, Velvet, and double double Province-Rose, the sweet Musk-Rose double and single, the double and single white-Rose: The fair and sweet-scenting Woodbine, double and single, and double double. Purple Cowslips, and double Cowslips, and double double Cowslips, Primrose double and single. The Violet nothing behind the best, for smelling sweetly. A thousand more will provoke your content.

And all these by the skill of your Gardener, so comelily and orderly placed in your borders and squares, and so intermingled, that one looking thereon, cannot but wonder to see, what Nature, corrected by Art, can do.

When you behold in divers corners of your Orchard *Mounts* of stone or wood, curiously wrought within and without, or of earth covered with Fruit-trees, Kentish Cherries, Damsons, Plums, &c. with stairs of precious workmanship; and in some corner (or more) a true Dial or Clock, and some Antick works; and especially silver-sounding Music, mixed Instruments, and Voices, gracing all the rest: How will you be rapt with Delight?

Large Walks, broad and long, close and open, like the *Tempegroves* in *Thessaly*, raised with gravel and sand, having seats and banks of Camomile; all this delights the mind, and brings health to the body.

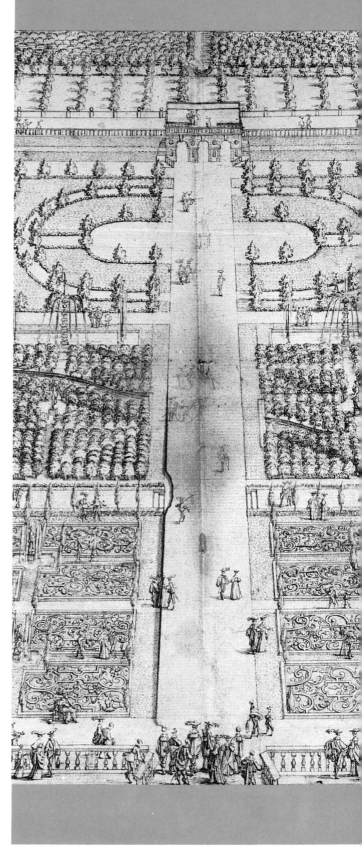

155

Design for the garden at Wilton House, Wiltshire, by Isaac de Caus, late 1630s (detail).

View now with delight the works of your own hands, your Fruit-trees of all sorts, loaden with sweet blossoms, and fruit of all tastes, operations, and colours: your trees standing in comely order, which way soever you look.

Your border on every side hanging and dropping with Feberries, Raspberries, Barberries, Currants, and the Roots of your trees powdered with Strawberries, Red, White, and Green, what a pleasure is this! Your Gardener can frame your lesser wood to the shape of men armed in the field, ready to give battle; of swift-running Greyhounds, or of well-scented and true-running Hounds to chase the Deer, or hunt the Hare. This kind of hunting shall not waste your Corn, nor much your Coin.

Mazes well framed a man's height, may perhaps make your friend wander in gathering of Berries till he cannot recover himself without your help.

To have occasion to exercise within your Orchard, it shall be a pleasure to have a bowling-Alley, or rather (which is more manly, and more healthful) a pair of Butts, to stretch your Arms.

Rosemary and sweet Eglantine are seemly Ornaments about a Door or Window, and so is Woodbine . . .

And in mine own opinion, I could highly commend your Orchard, if either through it, or hard by it, there should run a pleasant River with silver streams, you might sit in your Mount, and angle a peckled Trout, sleighty Eel, or some other dainty Fish. Or Moats, whereon you may row with a Boat, and fish with Nets.

Stores of Bees in a warm and dry Bee-house, comely made of Firboards, to sing, and sit, and feed upon your flowers and sprouts, make a pleasant noise and sight. For cleanly and innocent Bees, of all other things, love, and become, and thrive in an Orchard . . .

WILLIAM LAWSON, *A New Orchard and Garden*

156

(right) The garden at Denham Place, Buckinghamshire. Detail from a painting of c. 1705 by an unidentified artist.

LORD

AND

LADY

FAIRFAX

TAKE

A

MORNING

WALK

WITH

THEIR

DAUGHTER

1651

WHEN in the east the morning ray
Hangs out the colours of the day
The bee through these known alleys hums,
Beating the dian with its drums.
Then flowers their drowsy eyelids raise,
Their silken ensigns each displays,
And dries its pan yet dank with dew,
And fills its flask with odours new.

These, as their governor goes by,
In fragrants volleys they let fly;
And to salute their governess
Again as great a charge they press:
None for the virgin nymph; for she
Seems with the flowers a flower to be.
And think so still! though not compare
With breath so sweet, or cheek so fair.

Well shot ye firemen! Oh how sweet
And round your equal fires do meet;
Whose shrill report no ear can tell,
But echoes to the eye and smell.
See how the flowers, as at parade,
Under their colours stand displayed:
Each regiment in order grows,
That of the tulip, pink and rose.
But when the vigilant patrol
Of stars walk round about the pole,
Their leaves, that to the stalks are curled,
Seem to their staves the ensigns furled.
Then in some flower's beloved hut
Each bee as sentinel is shut;
And sleeps so too: but if once stirred
She runs you through, nor asks the word.
FROM ANDREW MARVELL, *Upon Appleton House*

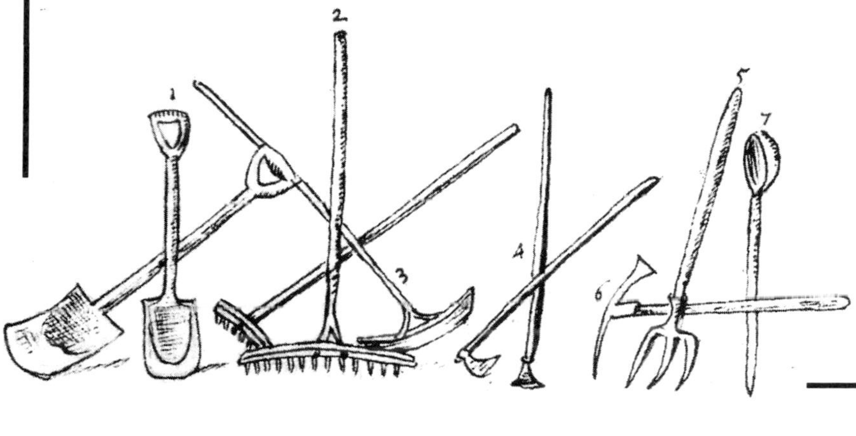

THOMAS

BUSHELL'S

GROTTO

AT

ENSTONE

1667

AFTER his master the lord chancellor died, he married and lived at Enston, Oxon; where having some land lying on the hanging of a hill facing the south, at the foot whereof runs a fine clear stream which petrifies, and where is a pleasant solitude, he spoke to his servant Jack Sydenham to get a labourer to clear some boscage which grew on the side of the hill, and also to dig a cavity in the hill to sit, and read or contemplate . . . The workman had not worked an hour before he discovers not only a rock, but a rock of an unusual figure with pendants like icicles as at Wookey Hole, which was the occasion of making that delicate grotto and those fine walks.

Here in fine weather he would walk all night. Jack Sydenham sang rarely: so did his other servant, Mr Batty. They went very gent. in clothes, and he loved them as his children.

In the time of the civil wars his hermitage over the rocks at Enston were hung with black-bayes; . . . When the queen-mother came to Oxon to the king, she either brought (as I think) or somebody gave her an entire mummy from Egypt, a great rarity, which her majesty gave to Mr Bushell, but I believe long before this time the dampness of the place has spoiled it with mouldiness. The grotto below looks just south; so that when it artificially

Fountain in a Formal Garden, from Stephen Switzer *An Introduction to Hydrostaticks and Hydraulics*, 1729.

rains, upon the turning of a cock, you are entertained with a rainbow. In a very little pond (no bigger than a basin) opposite to the rock, and hard by, stood a Neptune, neatly cut in wood, holding his trident in his hand, and aiming with it at a duck which perpetually turned round with him, and a spaniel swimming after her.

JOHN AUBREY, *Brief Lives*

The grotto at Enstone, from Plot's *Natural History of Oxfordshire*, 1677.

Col. Pl. XVI A Gothick
Pavilion at Painswick
House, Gloucestershire.
Thomas Robbins,
c.1760.

THEREFORE either in the side of some decline of a Hill, or under some Mount or Terrace artificially raised, may you make a place of repose, cool and fresh in the greatest heats. It may be arched over with stone or brick and you may give it what light or entrance you please. You may make secret rooms and passages within it, and in the outer room may you have all those before-mentioned water-works, for your own or your friends' divertisements. It is a place capable of giving you so much pleasure and delight, that you may bestow not undeserved'ly what cost you please on it, by paving it with marble or immuring it with stone or rock-work, either natural or artificially resembling the excellencies of nature.

JOHN WOOLRIDGE, *Systema Horticultura*

MARCH. Now you may set your oranges, lemons, myrtles, oleanders, *lentisci*, dates, aloes, amomums, and like tender trees and plants on the portico, or with the windows and doors of the greenhouses and conservatories open, for eight or ten days before April, or earlier, if the season invite (that is, if the sharp winds be past) to acquaint them gradually with the air; I say gradually and carefully; for this change is the most critical of the whole year; trust not therefore the nights too confidently, unless the weather be thoroughly settled.

JOHN EVELYN, *Kalendarium Hortense*

EVERY fortnight look on Saturday to your seed and root boxes, to air & preserve them from mouldiness & vermin. Look every month (the last day of it) & see in what state the Bee-hives are: and every day, about noon if the weather be warm, and the Bees hang out for swarms; having your hives prepared & ready dressed.

The Tools are to be carried into the Toolhouse, and all other instruments set in their places, every night when you leave work: & in wet weather you are to cleanse, sharpen, & repair them.

The heaps of Dung, & Magazines of Mould &c: are to be stirred once every quarter, the first week.

In April, Mid-August, clip Cypress, Box, & generally most evergreen hedges: & closes, as quick-sets.

Prune standard-fruit & Mural Trees the later end of July, & beginning of August for the second spring: Vines in January & exuberant branches that hinder the fruit ripening in June.

The Gardener is every night to ask what Roots, salading, garnishing, &c will be used the next day, which he is accordingly to bring to the Cook in the morning; and therefore from time to time inform her what garden provision & fruit is ripe and in season to be spent.

He is also to Gather, & bring in to the House-Keeper all such Fruit of Apples, pears, quinces, Cherries, Grapes, peaches, Apricots, Mulberries, strawberry, Raspberries, Corinths, Cornelians, Nuts, Plums, & generally all sort of Fruit, as the season ripens them, gathering all the windfalls by themselves: That they may be immediately spent, or reserved in the Fruit & store-house.

He may not dispose of any the above said Fruit nor sell any Artichoke, Cabbages, Asparagus, Melons, strawberries, Raspberries, Wall, or standard & dwarf fruit, Roses, Violets, Cloves, or any Greens, or other flowers or plants, without first asking, and having leave of his Master or Mistress; nor till there be sufficient of all garden furniture for the Grounds stock and families use.

JOHN EVELYN, *Directions for the Gardiner at Sayes Court*

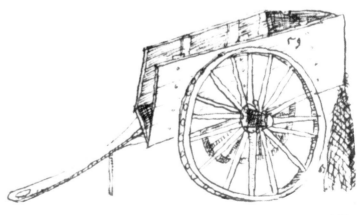

Col. Pl. XVII (left) Garden bridge at Chiswick House, Middlesex. Detail from the picture by P. A. Rysbrack, c.1729–30.

GARDEN GEAR AT HOLKHAM, 1761

In the Pleasure Grounds and Orangery

20	Barrow Chairs	20	Small Winsor Chairs
3	Double Seated Chairs	6	Compass Back Chairs

Plants and Trees in Tubs and Pots

250	Pines in Pots [pineapples]	25	Double and Single Leafed
4	Citrons in Tubs		Myrtles in Pots
46	Orange Trees in Tubs	70	Seedling Oranges in Pots
9	Lemon Trees in Pots	13	Aloes in Pots
3	Broad Leafed Myrtles in Tubs		

Working Tools and Utensils

11	Scythes	1	Pair of Garden Shears
6	Rakes	1	Mallet and Pruning Chisel
5	Dutch Hoes	2	Mattocks
8	English Hoes	1	Flag Shovel
8	Forks	1	Edging Tool
3	Jets	2	Pair of Iron Reels with Lines
6	Watering Pots		
2	Tin Pipes for Watering Pines	2	Hand Saws
		1	Grindstone and Frame
1	House Engine	4	Rubstones
1	Brass Hand Engine	1	Cucumber cutter
2	Wooden Hand Engines [all for water]	91	Frames Glazed for Melons Pines and Cucumbers
3	Leather Pipes	35	Frames for the Fire Walls
1	Suction Pipe	21	Hand Glasses
1	Brass Pipe	9	Bell Glasses
1	Rose [for sprinkling]		Netting in five Parcels
2	Thermometers		A Number of Old Mats
2	Shovels	8	Common Wheel Barrows
4	Hammers	2	Water Barrows
1	Hook [Sickle]	3	Water Tubs
1	Hatchet	3	Stone Rollers
2	Iron Rollers	1	Large Fruit Basket
5	Boots for Horses to Roll the Garden with	8	Bushell Baskets
		3	Water Pails
8	Hand Baskets for Fruit		

INVENTORY, *Holkham MSS*

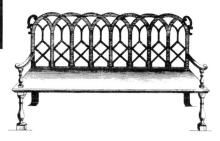

A gentleman's park is what I abhor. It is not beauty because it is not nature.

JOHN CONSTABLE

(left) Design for a garden seat. Charles Over, 1758.
(above) Captain Cook's monument and the Grenville Column, in the gardens of Stowe House, Buckinghamshire. J.C. Nattes, 1805.

View of the park from the terrace of Woburn Abbey, Bedfordshire, as proposed by Humphrey Repton.

YOU might draw, but I can't describe, the enchanting scenes of the park; it is a hill of three miles, but broke into all manner of beauty; such lawns, such woods, rills, cascades, and a thickness of verdure quite to the summit of the hill, and commanding such a vale of towns, and meadows, and woods extending quite to the Black Mountain in Wales, that I quite forgot my favourite Thames! Indeed, I prefer nothing to Hagley but Mount Edgecombe. There is extreme taste in the park: the seats are not the best, but there is not one absurdity. There is a ruined castle, built by Miller, that would get him his freedom even of Strawberry: it has the true rust of the Baron's Wars. Then there is a scene of a small lake, with cascades falling down such a Parnassus! with a circular temple on the distant eminence; and there is such a fairy dale, with more cascades gushing out of the rocks! and there is a hermitage, so exactly like those in Sadeler's prints, on the brow of a shady mountain, stealing peeps into the glorious world below! and there is such a pretty well under a wood, like the Samaritan woman's in a picture of Nicolo Poussin! and there is such a wood without the park, enjoying such a prospect! and there is such a mountain on t'other side of the park commanding such a prospect, that I wore out my eyes with gazing, my feet with climbing, and my tongue and my vocabulary with commending.

WALPOLE TO RICHARD BENTLEY, SEPTEMBER, 1753

IN England, when a new manner is universally adopted, in which no appearance of art is tolerated, our gardens differ very little from common fields, so closely is common nature copied in most of them ... and a stranger is often at a loss to know whether he is walking in a meadow, or in a pleasure ground, made and kept at very considerable expense. He sees nothing to amuse him, nothing to

excite his curiosity, nor any thing to keep up his attention.

At his first entrance, he is treated with the sight of a large green field, scattered over with a fair straggling trees, and verged with a confused border of little shrubs and flowers; upon further inspection, he finds a little serpentine path, turning in regular 'esses' amongst the shrubs of the border, upon which he is to go round, to look on one side at what he has already seen, the large green field ... From time to time he perceives a little seat or temple stuck up against a wall; he rejoices at the discovery, sits down, rests his wearied limbs, and then reels on again, cursing the line of beauty, till spent with fatigue, half roasted by the sun, for there is never any shade, and tired for want of entertainment, he resolves to see no more.

Vain resolution! there is but one path; he must either drag on to the end, or return back by the tedious way he came.

WILLIAM CHAMBERS, *Dissertation on Oriental Gardening*

THE KITCHEN-GARDEN AT TRENTHAM 1828

THEY were out when we came. I rushed to the *potager* – you know my weakness – and walked up and down between spinach and dahlias in ecstasy. This is in many ways a beautiful place and the *tenue*, the neatness, the training of flowers and fruit trees, gates, enclosures, hedges, are what in no other country is dreamt of; and then there is a repose, a *laisser aller*, a freedom, and a security in a *vie de château* that no other destiny offers one. I feel when I set out to

165

In the garden at Sedgwick Park, Sussex, 1901.

walk as if alone in the world – nothing but trees and birds; but then comes the enormous satisfaction of always finding a man dressing a hedge, or a woman in a gingham and a black bonnet on her knees picking up weeds, the natural gendarmerie of the country, and the most comfortable well-organized country.

HARRIET, COUNTESS GRANVILLE, TO HER SISTER, LADY CARLISLE, 1828

THE DUCHESS OF EDINBURGH IS BORED AT EASTWELL PARK 1884

YOU seem to enjoy your country life. I could also enjoy it under different circumstances though I find that inland English country seats are so exactly alike that I never find anything new in them to describe or admire: the same turf, the same lawns and trees, the everlasting evergreens, so charming in the South and so depressing during an English winter, the same endless parks with their elms and beeches and their meagre deer and idiotic sheep and lambs which get so dreadfully on my nerves just now with their bleating. Ravens and blackbirds, as stately and prim as the rest of the depressing scenery, picking up worms, and stiff beds of flowers in the so called pleasure grounds. No high waving grass with thousands of flowers, no real forests with valleys and streams, no gaily dressed peasants men and women returning from their field work and singing merrily, like one sees abroad.

THE DUCHESS OF EDINBURGH TO A FRIEND, EASTWELL PARK, KENT, APRIL, 1884.

MISS JEKYLL SPEAKS HER MIND 1899

IT is a curious thing that many people, even amongst those who profess to know something about gardening, when I show them something successful – the crowning reward of much care and labour – refuse to believe that any pains have been taken about it. They will ascribe it to chance, to the goodness of my soil, and even more commonly to some supposed occult influence of my own – to anything rather than the plain fact that I love it well enough to give it plenty of care and labour. They assume a tone of complimentary banter, kindly meant no doubt, but to me rather distasteful, to this effect: 'Oh, yes, of course, it will grow with you; anything will grow for you; you have only to look at a thing and it will grow.' I have to pump up a laboured smile and accept the remark with what grace I can, as a necessary civility to the stranger within my gates, but it seems to me evident that those who say things do not understand the love of a garden.

GERTRUDE JEKYLL, *Wood and Garden*

SUCCESS AT SISSINGHURST 1937

NEVER has Sissinghurst looked more lovely or been more appreciated. I must say, Farley has made the place look like a gentleman's garden, and you with your extraordinary taste have made it look like nobody's garden but your own. I think the secret of your gardening is simply that you have the courage to abolish ugly or unsuccessful flowers. Except for those beastly red-hot pokers which you have a weakness for, there is not an ugly flower in the whole place. Then I think, *si j'ose m'exprimer ainsi*, that the design is really rather good. I mean we have got what we wanted to get – a perfect proportion between the classic and the romantic, between the element of expectation and the element of surprise. Thus the main axes are terminated in a way to satisfy expectation, yet they are in themselves so tricky that they also cause surprise. But the point of the garden will not be apparent until the hedges have grown up, especially (most important of all) the holly hedge in the flower garden. But it is lovely, lovely, lovely – and you must be pleased with your work.

HAROLD NICOLSON TO VITA SACKVILLE-WEST, JUNE 1937

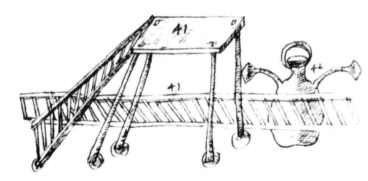

(right) Designs for water-closet at Felbrigg Hall, Norfolk. Robert Brettingham, 1794.

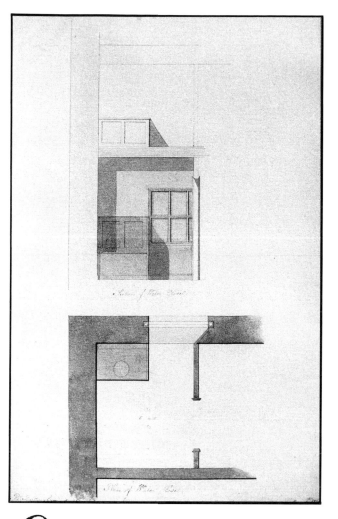

11
Plumbing,
Or
The
Lack
Of
It

*O*n the whole, the history of plumbing, and of technology generally in English country houses, has been one of installing gadgets which fail to work. It is a two-steps-forward one-step-back story. In medieval houses the privy or garderobe system was introduced as the great new hope for salubrious living. It was a system of shafts, dropping into pits, drains, or moats. But the walls of the shafts grew filthy, and drains, moats and houses stank after they had been occupied for a few weeks. In the sixteenth century there was a reaction in favour of the close-stool – a box containing a receptacle, which a servant could remove and empty at a convenient distance from the house.

In the late seventeenth century water-closets and plunge baths enjoyed a vogue among the very rich. But before the invention of the S-bend trap, water closets smelt. Earth closets came into favour in their places.

In the late eighteenth century water closets at last broke the technological barrier. At the same period, or a few decades later, tub baths and radiators appeared, along with hot water to service them. Unfortunately, the water was seldom hot. Open fires, and hip baths filled by servants carrying water in cans, were as effective, if not more so. All foreign visitors commented on the cold of English houses. Bathrooms did not really establish themselves adequately until the 1920s – and then only in some houses.

In the 1950s oil-fired central heating became the new toy of country-house owners. A picture or a few pieces of silver were sold to pay for its installation, and the boiler was shown to visitors with as much pride as a prize hunter. Then oil prices soared, and cold descended on the houses once again.

GLEDHOW HALL. LEEDS.

J. Kitson Junr. Esqr.

BATH-ROOM IN BURMANTOFT FAIENCE.

A bathroom in Burmantoft faience, installed at Gledhow Hall, near Leeds, c. 1885.

A
SERVANT
EXHORTED
C. 1460

SEE the privy house for easement be fair, sweet and clean
And that the boards thereupon be covered with cloth fair and green,
And the hole himself, look there no board be seen.
Thereon a fair cushion, the ordure no man to demean.
Look there be blanket, cotton, or linen to wipe the nether end
And ever when he calleth, wait ready and attend
With basin and ewer, and on your shoulder a towel, my friend.

JOHN RUSSELL, *Book of Nurture*

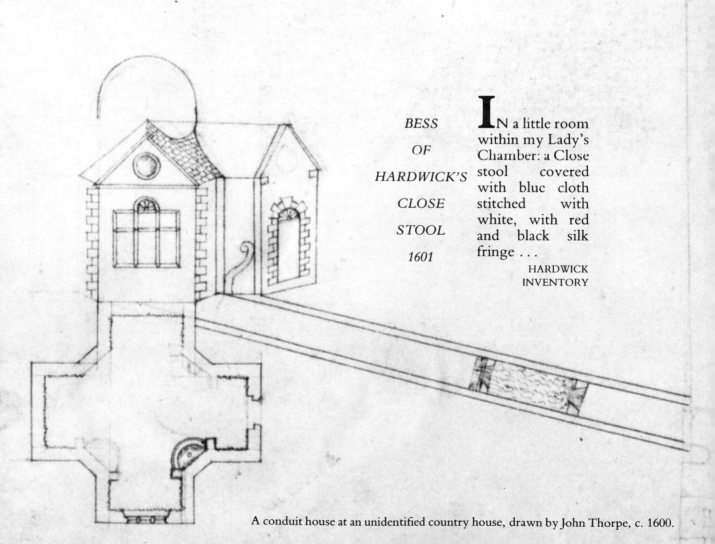

BESS
OF
HARDWICK'S
CLOSE
STOOL
1601

IN a little room within my Lady's Chamber: a Close stool covered with blue cloth stitched with white, with red and black silk fringe . . .

HARDWICK
INVENTORY

A conduit house at an unidentified country house, drawn by John Thorpe, c. 1600.

The plunge-bath at Stowe House, Buckinghamshire. J.C. Nattes, 1807.

A

BATH

FOR

THE

DEVON-

SHIRES:

CHATSWORTH

1697

THERE is a fine grotto, all stone pavement, roof and sides. This is designed to supply all the house with water besides several fancies to make diversion. Within this is a bathing room, the walls all with blue and white marble, the pavement mixed one stone white, another black, another of the red rance marble; the bath is one entire marble all white finely veined with blue and is made smooth, but had it been as finely polished as some, it would have been the finest marble that could be seen; it was as deep as one's middle on the outside and you went down steps into the bath big enough for two people; at the upper end are two cocks to let in one hot the other cold water, to attemper it as persons please; the windows are all private glass.

CELIA FIENNES, *Journeys*

DANGERS

OF

A

TOOTHBRUSH

1721

I must now mention a thing of an inferior kind, which perhaps my Love will not easily admit of, though I am fully satisfied of the truth of it . . .; which is, that using a brush to yr teeth and gums (as you constantly do) will certainly prove in time extremely injurious to them both, and especially to the last, which will be quite worn away by it; and I beg of ye for the future to use a sponge in its room.

SIR JOHN PHILIPPS, OF PICTON CASTLE, PEMBROKESHIRE, TO LADY PHILIPPS, 7 NOVEMBER, 1721

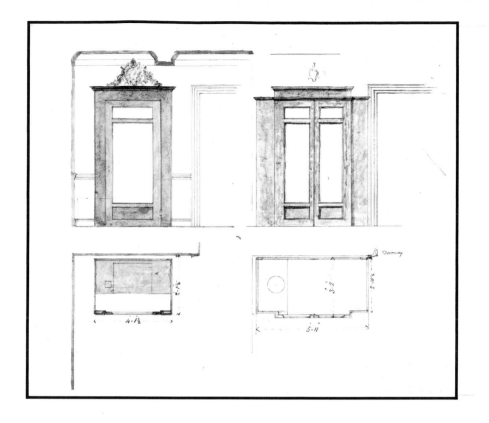

DUCAL WATER-CLOSETS AT CANNONS 1725

BETWEEN cabinet and his Grace's dressing room.
Marble pavement, marble lining and marble basin.
Japanned seat, fretwork ceiling with gilding, painting
by Scarptena

£251.29

In passage outside library leading to waiting room.
Marble basin to the water closet, plug, cock and handles

£12

Next her Grace's closet
Marble paving and skirting and marble basin.
Dutch tiles, wainscot seat, wainscot bath lined with
red, Japanned close stool, curtains.

£78:4:0

CANNONS INVENTORY

Designs for ducal water-closets to be concealed in cupboards at Stowe.

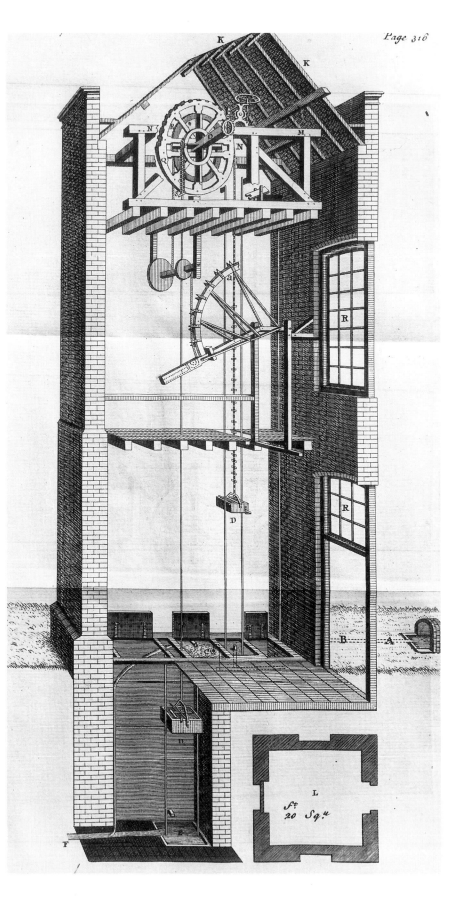

Page 316

MR WYNDHAM MAKES HIMSELF COMFORT-ABLE: AN EARTH-CLOSET AT FELBRIGG 1751

I think it the best place imaginable. Should not the inside be stuccoed, or how do you do it? how many holes? There must be one for a child; and I would have it as light as possible. There must be a good broad place to set a candle on, and a place to keep paper. I think the holes should be wide and rather oblong, and the seats broad and not quite level, and rather low before, but rising behind. Tho' the better the plainer, it should be neat.

WILLIAM WYNDHAM TO ROBERT FRIARY, 1751

'Mr Gerves's Multiplying Wheel Bucket Engine', installed to supply water to Chicheley House, Buckinghamshire, c. 1729.

BATHS

OF

THE

1860s

EVERY big country house boasted one or more large iron tanks encased in mahogany, evidently designed to do duty as baths and – judging from their size – designed to accommodate several people at once. At one end of these tanks was a brass dial on which were inscribed the words 'hot', 'cold' and 'waste', and a revolving handle manoeuvred an indicator into position opposite such of these inscriptions as a prospective bather might be attracted to ... A call on the hot water supply, however, did not meet with an effusive or even a warm response. A succession of sepulchral rumblings was succeeded by the appearance of a small geyser of rust-coloured water, heavily charged with dead earwigs and bluebottles. This continued for a couple of minutes or so and then entirely ceased. The only perceptible difference between the hot water and the cold lay in its colour and in the cargo of defunct life which the former bore on its bosom. Both were stone cold.

In the face of such uninviting conditions, it can readily be understood that these huge enamelled iron tanks were not popular as instruments of cleanliness. In fact, although Eastwell and Baron's Court, two big country houses in which much of my early youth was passed, each boasted two of such baths, I have never heard of any of the four being used for the purpose for which they were no doubt originally designed. As boys, my brother and I found the lower bath at Eastwell admirably suited to the trial trips of our toy boats; and at Barons Court, where we had no toy boats, it was our practice to use the ground floor bath as an occasional aquarium.

LORD ERNEST HAMILTON, *Old Days and New*

AN

AMERICAN

COMPLAINS

1869

IF there be a bathroom in an English house, it must answer for the whole household. If there be a lift, it stops at the dining-room floor, although coals and water have to be carried to the higher stories. If hot and cold water be laid on, it is only in certain select apartments. Ventilators are almost unknown, except, perhaps, that antiquated sort which are let into the windows. Heated air is considered unhealthy, and so the ladies and children sit before the grate-fires with shawls over their shoulders, and catch cold in order to prevent injuring their lungs. Gas is making its way into all English houses now, but is still forbidden to be used in sleeping apartments, although the smoke from even a wax candle is hardly preferable to the odour of the small amount of gas which can possibly escape. No stranger can live for a week in an English house and not be ill from exposure to the chilly halls and stairways, even if he succeed in making himself comfortable before the fire. The English wrap themselves up to cross the hall as though they were going out of doors. Refrigerators are comparatively a new invention here. Iced water is vetoed as injurious to the teeth. It is true that in England one generally has no trouble to keep cool; the trouble is ever to get warm.

STEPHEN FISKE, *American Photographs*

A

BATH

FOR

MR

LEES-

MILNE

THONOCK

HALL

LINCS

1947

PITCH dark when called by a dear old man who entered my bedroom and pulled back the heavy curtains. Rats' tails of grey fog swirled across the window panes. Tenderly this old retainer brought into the room a red blanket which he spread before the empty fire grate. Then he trundled a small tin hip-bath on to the red blanket. Then he brought a brass can of tepid water, enough to cover the bottom of the bath. The room must have been several degrees below zero. He might have been a ghost performing the customary function of a hundred years ago. But one hundred years ago there would have been a blazing fire in the grate.

JAMES LEES-MILNE, *Caves of Ice*

(right) Detail from the monument to Sir William and Lady Catherine Savage. Elmley Castle, Worcestershire, c. 1616.

12
Birth
&
Death

Many of the most dramatic or poignant incidents in country houses were connected with births or deaths, as at all levels of society. But they had an additional significance there, because of the worldly stakes involved. They ensured the continuance of a line or marked the transfer of property and the beginning of a new reign. They called for celebration. Christening parties tended to be of a relatively minor nature, however, perhaps because death in childhood was so common that it seemed to be tempting providence to make too much of a show. With a funeral one knew exactly where one was.

Country-house funerals could be formidable affairs. A public state funeral is the closest equivalent today. They were often preceded by the lying-in-state of the corpse, for the benefit of neighbours and tenantry who filed past by the hundred. The whole house could be shrouded in black, and hundreds of black-robed mourners formed a great funeral cortege from the house to the church. After the coffin had been lowered into the grave, or carried into the vault, the upper servants symbolically broke their staffs of office, and threw them after the coffin. Then came the funeral feast, at which up to a thousand people could gorge and get drunk in and around the house. The central feast took place in the great chamber, and was presided over by the chief mourner sitting under a black canopy.

The lavishness at funerals was generally on the decrease in the eighteenth and nineteenth centuries, although it survived at some great houses, as the description of the funeral of the Duchess of Rutland in 1825 makes clear.

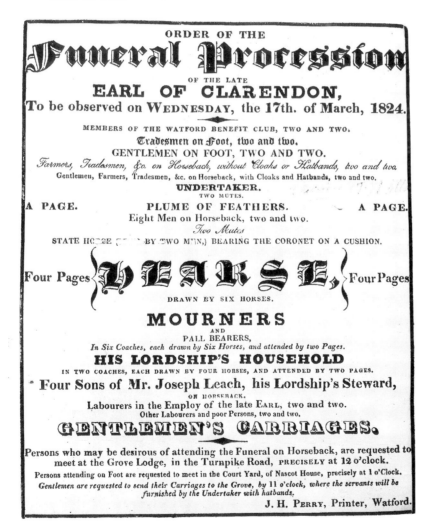

ORDER OF THE
Funeral Procession
OF THE LATE
EARL OF CLARENDON,
To be observed on WEDNESDAY, the 17th. of March, 1824.

MEMBERS OF THE WATFORD BENEFIT CLUB, TWO AND TWO.

Tradesmen on Foot, two and two.

GENTLEMEN ON FOOT, TWO AND TWO.

Farmers, Tradesmen, &c. on Horseback, without Cloaks or Hatbands, two and two.

Gentlemen, Farmers, Tradesmen, &c. on Horseback, with Cloaks and Hatbands, two and two.

UNDERTAKER.

TWO MUTES.

A PAGE.   PLUME OF FEATHERS.   A PAGE.

Eight Men on Horseback, two and two.

Two Mutes

STATE HORSE (LED BY TWO MEN,) BEARING THE CORONET ON A CUSHION.

Four Pages ⟩ HEARSE, ⟨ Four Pages

DRAWN BY SIX HORSES.

MOURNERS
AND
PALL BEARERS,
In Six Coaches, each drawn by Six Horses, and attended by two Pages.

HIS LORDSHIP'S HOUSEHOLD
IN TWO COACHES, EACH DRAWN BY FOUR HORSES, AND ATTENDED BY TWO PAGES.

Four Sons of Mr. Joseph Leach, his Lordship's Steward,
ON HORSEBACK.

Labourers in the Employ of the late EARL, two and two.

Other Labourers and poor Persons, two and two.

GENTLEMEN'S CARRIAGES.

Persons who may be desirous of attending the Funeral on Horseback, are requested to meet at the Grove Lodge, in the Turnpike Road, PRECISELY at 12 o'clock.

Persons attending on Foot are requested to meet in the Court Yard, of Nascot House, precisely at 1 o'Clock.

Gentlemen are requested to send their Carriages to the Grove, by 11 o'clock, where the servants will be furnished by the Undertaker with hatbands.

J. H. PERRY, Printer, Watford.

Order of the Funeral Procession of the Earl of Clarendon, 1824.
Col. Pl. XVIII (right) The christening of the child of Sir Henry and Lady Unton, c.1596.

WHICWOD

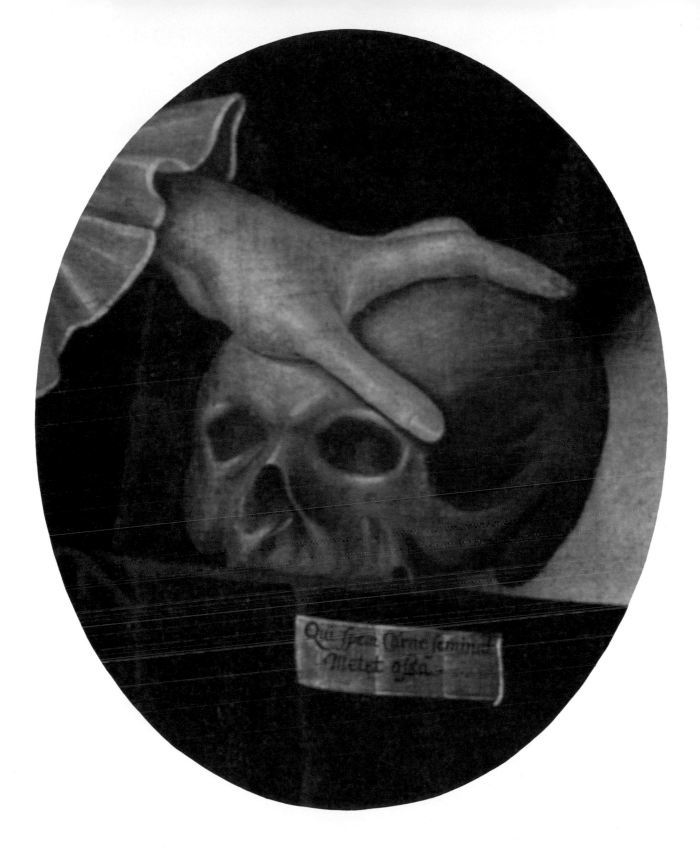

Col. Pl. XIX (top left) The Saltonstall family. David des Granges, 1636–7.

Col. Pl. XX (left) The Cholmondeley Sisters. Unidentified artist, c.1600.

Col. Pl. XXI Detail from the portrait of Sir Thomas Aston at the death-bed of his wife. John Souch, 1635.

Col. Pls. XXII and XXIII. Two portraits of babies by Joshua Reynolds: (top) Georgiana, Duchess of Devonshire, and her daughter Georgiana, later Countess of Carlisle, c.1784; (above) Caroline, Duchess of Marlborough, with her daughter, also Caroline, who became Viscountess Clifden, c.1764–5.

Food eaten at the funeral feast of Lady Katherine Howard, Framlingham Castle, 1465

MOURNING

FOR

LADY

KATHERINE

1465

2	great boars	48	partridges
12	great oxen	14	pheasants
40	sheep	7	peacocks
12	hogs	36	mallards
70	pigs	36	plovers
12	swans	800	eggs
80	geese	30	gal. milk
200	conyes [rabbits]	3	gal. honey
24	capons	32	barrels beer
140	chickens	3	pipes wine
30	ducks		

PASTON LETTERS

HOW

WILLIAM

WENTWORTH

GOT

HIS

BIRTH-

MARK

C. 1550

SIR William Gascoigne coming to hunt the buck in the park at Wentworth Woodhouse before my said father was born (as he told me) the buck at last was taken in the pond near the house by the hounds. Wherefore my father's mother, being then great with child of him, came with her mother in law to bid him welcome &c. Whereupon he, being of a wild wilful disposition, looked in my grand mother's face (for in truth I have heard discreet men say that he had a strange gift to conjecture beforehand many things that were to come) and swore a great oath that she was with child with a boy and earnestly swore he would with the tip of his finger only, dipped in the buck's blood, mark that boy for his own upon his mother's cheek; saying he was assured that it would be a boy and having a beard the red spot would not be seen, when he was a man. She refusing, he threatened to lay all his whole bloody hands upon her face, unless &c. Thereupon my grandmother, seeing no remedy, suffered him to touch her cheek with the tip of his finger dipped in blood, which mark, said my father to me, I here show unto thee. And opening the hairs of his beard, I there saw it plainly.

SIR WILLIAMS'S ACCOUNT OF THE PROVIDENCES
VOUCHSAFED HIS FAMILY, WRITTEN 1607

DAME MARGARET REMEMBERS HER FAMILY, 1639

EXTRACTS from the will of Dame Margaret Verney, of Claydon, 2 May, 1639, addressed to her son Ralph.

Give to your wife my diamond clasps, sheep head, and the rest of my odd diamonds and my sable muff and six of my new great smocks. If cook is with me give her some £3 and some of my worser gowns.

Give your father my gilt tankard and the case of silver-hafted knives, and desire him to leave them to your eldest son.
Bestow some £1 apiece of toys or black rings for my mother, my brothers and sister and their husbands and wives.

There are 4 very fine smocks in your father's little linen trunk and one of my four breadth Holland sheets for your own girl Peg.
Pay the undermaids, and poor, and Mr Aris next before the bigger sums.

Take your father's tablet picture yourself and give him Prince Henry's. They both lie in the red box, and I desire your father that he will not let any of my household linen be sold, but that it may go to you and your eldest son and I hope to his son too, only some of my broderie of my own making give to your sisters.
Now pray let none of my papers be seen; but do you burn them yourself.
All but my notes, and account and medicinable and cookery books, such keep.

Let me be buried in lead at Claydon next where your father proposes to lie himself, and let no stranger wind me, nor do not let me be stripped, but put me a clean smock over me, and let my face be hid and do you stay in the room and see me wound and laid in the first coffin, which must be wood if I do not die of any infectious disease, else I am so far from desiring it that I forbid you to come near me.

So the God of Heaven bless you all.

VERNEY PAPERS

178

EPITAPH ON THE MONUMENT OF SIR WILLIAM DYER AT COLMWORTH, 1641

MY dearest dust, could not thy hasty day
Afford thy drowsy patience leave to stay
One hour longer: so that we might either
Sit up, or go to bed together?
But since thy finished labor hath possest
Thy weary limbs with early rest,
Enjoy it sweetly: and thy widow bride
Shall soon repose her by thy slumbring side.
Whose business, now, is only to prepare
My nightly dress, and call to prayer:
Mine eyes wax heavy and the day grows cold.
Draw, draw ye closed curtains: and make room:
My dear, my dearest dust; I come, I come.

LADY CATHERINE DYER

PREPARING FOR A FUNERAL 1666

THE hall to be hanged with a breadth of black baize
The passage into my lady's bedchamber to be hanged with a breadth of baize
The great dining room, where the better sort of mourners are to be, to be hanged with a breadth of baize.
The body to be there.
The little dining room where the ladies and gentlewomen are to be [and]
The withdrawing room to the dining room, where the close mourners are to be, to be hanged with a breadth of baize
Over the hall porch a large escutcheon on a piece of baize
That some person be appointed to conduct some of the best sort of mourners & others of chief rank into the withdrawing room, where the chief mourner and his assistant with pennon and standard-bearers are to be. That the better sort of the next mourners, and others be brought into the dining room (where the corpse is) and that the inferior sort and servants be in the hall . . . That some special servants to bring in the banquet with wine and beer.

FUNERAL DIRECTIONS FOR SIR GERVASE CLIFTON, OF CLIFTON HALL, NOTTINGHAMSHIRE

I desire my body may be interred at Westminster Abbey near those two dear pledges gone before me but with as much privacy and as small expense as my executors shall find convenient. And I desire and appoint that my heart may be interred six foot underground on the south east side of the stone dial in my little garden at Moor Park.

SIR WILLIAM TEMPLE'S WILL

Matthew Russell lying in state in the Baron's Hall, Brancepeth Castle, Durham, 1822.

...**S**IR William's house was the rendezvous of a very immoral set of men. One of his strange exploits among other frolics, was having a coffin made of copper (which one of his mines that year had produced), and placed in the midst of his great hall, and instead of his making use of it as a monitor that might have made him ashamed and terrified at his past life, and induce him to make amends in future, it was filled with punch, and he and his comrades soon made themselves incapable of *any* sort of reflection; this was *often* repeated, and hurried him on to that awful moment he had so much reason to dread.

MRS DELANY *Autobiography*

THE

DEATH

OF

BILLY.

WILLIAM

JAMES

AGED

6

DIES

AT

IGHTHAM

COURT

IN

1750

April 20. After Dinner Dear Billy was taken with a Vomiting.

April 21. Mr Meadhurst applied a Blister to his head ... he was birth shaved all over his head.

April 22. Billy is a little better. Applied 2 Blisters to his Arms about half past two in ye afternoon, clap'd Pigeons to his feet at 9 at night.

April 24. Mr Leigh came this morning. Carried off the last of the Hop Poles. Dear Billy died at 25 mins. past 4 in ye afternoon.

April 26. Dear Billy was Interr'd in ye Vault, was carried by four old servants ... Mr Leigh and I went in ye coach, all ye Servants had gloves.

DIARY OF MRS ELIZABETH JAMES

DEATH COMES TO LORD LYTTELTON 1779

ONE night, when he was in bed, a white bird, with a voice like a woman's, – or else, a female figure with a bird on her hand, – appeared to him, and told him that he must die at a particular hour on a particular night. He related the circumstances to some of his friends, who encouraged him in treating it as a delusion. The fatal night arrived. He was then at a house (Pitt Place) near Epsom; and had appointed to meet a party on the downs next morning. His friends, without his knowledge, had put back the clock. 'I shall cheat the ghost yet,' he said. On getting into bed, he sent his servant down stairs for a spoon, having to take some medicine. When the servant returned, Lord Lyttelton was a corpse.

SAMUEL ROGERS, *Table Talk*

Lord Helmsley on his death-bed, 1881.

A

DUCHESS

HAS

A

PRIVATE

FUNERAL

BELVOIR

CASTLE

DECEMBER

1825

THE Duke of Rutland left the Castle at nine o'clock for the Rev. C.R. Thoroton's, at Bottesford, there to await the coming of the funeral cortege. The nobility and gentry who had intended sending carriages, found on enquiry, that, as it was strictly considered a private funeral, the attendance of their equipages would be dispensed with.

As the Castle clock struck eleven, a signal was given from one of the towers, and the procession set out in the following order:

The superintendent of the Duke's woods, plantations and pleasure grounds, and the bailiff of her grace's extensive farm,

At the head of one hundred and thirty-six of the Duke's principal tenants of the neighbourhood, two abreast, on horseback, dressed in black, with silk hatbands and gloves.

The undertaker, on horseback.

Two mutes, on horseback, carrying staves covered with black.

Six attendants on horseback.

Two mutes carrying staves.

Plume of feathers, with the escutcheon of the deceased, borne by a person on foot

Her grace's favourite white mare, caparisoned in black, led between the two grooms who usually attended her grace when she rode out.

Her grace's coronet, on a scarlet cushion, borne by the house-steward, on a black state horse properly decorated.

THE HEARSE,

Drawn by six black horses, driven by her grace's coachman and postilion, with the family's arms richly emblazoned, and four pages on each side on foot, bearing staves tipped with silver.

Three mourning coaches and six, and four mourning coaches and four, properly decorated with feathers and escutcheons, and two attending pages in mourning on foot to each coach.

The first coach contained the Earl of Carlisle, his two brothers, the hon Wm. and Henry Howard, and Andrew Drummond Esq.

Second coach, Lord Chas. S. Manners, Lord Robt Manners, Wm. Sloane Stanley, Esq., Rd. Norman, Esq., and W.F. French, Esq.

Third coach, physician, apothecary, Solicitors, and steward.

Fourth coach, six upper men servants.

Fifth coach, six other men servants.

Sixth coach, five upper women servants.

Seventh coach, five other women servants, and nurse.

The Duke's second coachman, and two grooms as outriders, attendant upon the late Duchess' own carriage (empty), drawn by six black horses; with coachman, postillion, and two footmen.

Ten other servants of the establishment, in deep mourning on horseback.

Numerous clergymen and gentlemen of the neighbourhood.

REV. IRWIN ELLER, *History of Belvoir Castle*

Monday 30 November 1874
Blenheim Palace
12.30 p.m.   Woodstock

Dear Mrs Jerome,

I have just time to write a line, to send by the London Dr to tell you that all has up to now thank God gone off very well with my darling Jennie. She had a fall on Tuesday walking with the shooters, & a rather imprudent & rough drive in a pony carriage brought on the pains on Saturday night. We tried to stop them, but it was no use. They went on all Sunday. Of course the Oxford physician cld not come. We telegraphed for the London man Dr Hope but he did not arrive till this morning. The country Dr is however a clever man, & the baby was safely born at 1.30 this morning after about 8 hrs labour. She suffered a good deal poor darling, but was vy plucky & had no chloroform. The boy is wonderfully pretty so everybody says dark eyes & hair & vy healthy considering its prematureness. My mother & Clementine have been everything to Jennie, & she cld not be more comfortable. We have just got a most excellent nurse & wet nurse coming down this afternoon, & please God all will go vy well with both. I telegraphed to Mr Jerome; I thought he wld like to hear. I am sure you will be delighted at this good news and dear Clara also I will write again tonight. Love to Clara.   Yrs affty
                                        RANDOLPH S. C.
I hope the baby things will come with all speed. We have to borrow some from the Woodstock Solicitor's wife.

LORD RANDOLPH CHURCHILL TO MRS LEONARD JEROME

Curls of Sir Winston Churchill, aged five, preserved at Blenheim Palace.

A

BOY

FOR

BLENHEIM

1895

AFTER an embarrassing inspection of my person, she [Francis Anne, Dowager Duchess of Marlborough – Consuelo's husband's grandmother] informed me that Lord Rosebery had reported favourably on me after our meeting in Madrid. She expressed great interest in our plans and made searching inquiries concerning the manner of life we intended to live, hoping, she said, to see Blenheim restored to its former glories and the prestige of the family upheld. I felt that this little lecture was intended to show me how it behoved me to behave. Then fixing her cold grey eyes upon me she continued, 'Your first duty is to have a child and it must be a son, because it would be intolerable to have that little upstart Winston become Duke.'

MEMOIRS OF CONSUELO, DUCHESS OF MARLBOROUGH

Ethel Buxton, aged 3 months. Drawn by her sister Ellen at Leytonstone House, Essex, 1864.

NOTES ON THE SOURCES

CHAPTER 1. ARRIVALS AND IMPRESSIONS

p. 13   H. Nicholas, *Memoirs of Sir Christopher Hatton* (London, Richard Bentley, 1847) p. 126.

p. 14   Daniel Defoe, *Tour Through Great Britain* (London, Peter Davies, 1927) II, p. 583.
6th Duke of Devonshire, *Handbook of Chatsworth and Hardwick* (London, 1844) pp. 111–12.

p. 15   William Howitt, *Visits to Remarkable Places* (London, 1840) p. 509.

p. 16   Robert Gathorne-Hardy, *Ottoline* (London, Faber and Faber, 1963) pp. 171–4.

p. 19   James Lees-Milne, *Ancestral Voices* (London, Chatto and Windus, 1975) pp. 171–2.

p. 21   Ben Jonson, *Poems* (ed. Ian Donaldson, London, Oxford University Press, 1975) pp. 87–91.

p. 23   William Camden, *Britannia* (translated Philemon Holland, 1610)
Letters of Horace Walpole (ed. Paget Toynbee, London, 1903–5) IV, p. 423
The Torrington Diaries (ed. C. Bruyn Andrews, London, Methuen, 1935) p. 30.
Journal of Princess (later Queen) Victoria, Royal Archives, Windsor.
Evelyn Waugh, *Diaries* (ed. M. Davie, London, Weidenfeld & Nicolson, 1976) p. 329.
Sacheverell Sitwell, *British Architects and Craftsmen* (London, Batsford, 1945) p. 29.
Nikolaus Pevsner, *Buildings of England: Derbyshire* (London, Penguin, 1953) p. 151.

p. 24   *Poetical Works of Alexander Pope* (Aldine Poets, London, Bell and Daldy, c. 1860) II, p. 192.
Letters of Walpole (see n. for p. 23) VIII, p. 193.
Prince Pückler-Muskau, *Tour in Germany, Holland and England* (London, 1832) IV, pp. 182–4.

p. 26   William Wordsworth, *Poems* (ed. T. Hutchinson, London, 1916) p. 477.
Constance Sitwell, *Bright Morning* (London, Jonathan Cape, 1942) p. 41.

p. 27   Henry James, *English Hours* (London, 1905) pp. 209–10.
Constance Sitwell, *Bright Morning* (op. cit.) p. 40.

p. 28   Deborah, Duchess of Devonshire, *The House: a portrait of Chatsworth* (London, Macmillan, 1982) p. 226.

CHAPTER 2. THE FAMILY

p. 31   William Howitt, *Visits* (see n. for p. 15) pp. 318–20.

p. 32   *Journal of the Furniture History Society* VII, (1971) 'The Hardwick Hall inventories', p. 32.

p. 33   F.P. and M.M. Verney (ed.), *Memoirs of the Verney Family* (London, Longmans Green, 1904) II, pp. 317–18.

p. 34   A. Jessopp (ed.), *Lives of the Norths* (London, George Bell, 1890) I, pp. 171–2.
Everard MSS, Essex County Record Office.

p. 35   *Haverfordwest and its Story* (L. Brigstocke, Haverfordwest, 1882) pp. 152–3.

p. 36   Maria Edgeworth, *Letters from England 1813–44* (ed. Christina Colvin, Oxford, Clarendon Press, 1971) pp. 162–3.
Malcolm Elwin (ed.), *The Autobiography and Journals of Benjamin Robert Haydon* (London, Macdonald, 1950) p. 417.

p. 37   Augustus J.C. Hare, *The Years with Mother* (ed. M. Barnes, London, Allen and Unwin, 1952) p. 186.

p. 38   Lees-Milne, *Ancestral Voices* (see n. for p. 19) pp. 105–6.

p. 40   E.F. Buxton, *Family Sketchbook* (ed. E.R.C. Creighton, London, Geoffrey Bles, 1964) p. 43.

p. 41   Earl of Selborne MSS.
Augusta Fane, *Chit-Chat* (London, Thornton Butterworth, 1926) pp. 46–7.

p. 42   Rosina Harrison, *Rose: My Life in Service* (London, Cassell, 1975) pp. 64–5.

p. 43   John Betjeman, *Summoned by Bells* (London, John Murray, 1960) pp. 99–101.

CHAPTER 3. GUESTS

p. 47   F.J. Furnivall (ed.), *The Babees Book*, etc. (Early English Text Society XXXII, 1868) pp. 373–4.
Historical Manuscripts Commission *Manuscripts of the Marquis of Salisbury*, (London, 1904) pp. 303–4.

p. 48   F.E. Halliday (ed.), *Richard Carew of Antony* (Andrew Melrose, London, 1953) p. 136

p. 49   *Lives of the Norths* (see n. for p. 34) III, pp. 170–1.
George Sherburn (ed.), *The Correspondence of Alexander Pope* (Oxford, Clarendon, 1956) II, p. 515
Ibid., IV, p. 185.

p. 51   Norman Ault (ed.), *Poems of Alexander Pope* VI (London, Methuen, 1964) p. 125.

p. 52   Earl of Ilchester (ed.), *Lord Hervey and his Friends* (London, John Murray, 1950) pp. 71–4.
R.E. Prothero (ed.), *Letters and Journals of Lord Byron* (London, John Murray, 1898) I, pp. 154–4.

p. 54   Pückler-Muskau, *Tour* (see n. for p. 24) III, p. 314.
John James, *Memoirs of a House Steward* (London, Bury, Holt & Co., 1949) p. 93.

p. 55   Edmund Gosse, *Life of Algernon Charles Swinburne* (London, Macmillan, 1917) pp. 95–6.
Henry James MSS, Houghton Library, Harvard University.

p. 56   Dorothy Henley, *Rosalind Howard, Countess of Carlisle* (London, Hogarth Press, 1958) pp. 42–3.

p. 57   B.E.C. Dugdale, *Arthur James Balfour* (London, Hutchinson, 1936) pp. 195–6.
Devonshire, *The House* (see n. for p. 28) p. 151.
John Jolliffe, *Raymond Asquith: Life and Letters* (London, Collins, 1980) pp. 151, 78–9.

p. 59   David Garnett, *Flowers of the Forest* (London, Chatto and Windus, 1955) pp. 108–9.
Michael Holroyd, *Lytton Strachey* (London, Heinemann, 1968) II, p. 205.

p. 60   Katherine Mansfield, *Collected Letters* (Oxford, Clarendon, 1984) p. 323.
Virginia Woolf, *Letters* (London, Hogarth Press, 1976) II, pp. 174, 197–8, 379.
Devonshire, *The House* (see n. for p. 28) p. 48.

p. 61   Evelyn Waugh, *Diaries* (ed. M. Davie, London, Weidenfeld & Nicolson, 1972) pp. 328–9.

p. 62   Harold Nicolson, *Diaries and Letters 1930–39* (London, Collins, 1966) p. 60.

CHAPTER 4. EATING AND DRINKING

p. 65   F.J. Furnivall (ed.), *The Babees Book, etc.* (Early English Text Society, XXXII, 1868) pp. 375–7.

p. 66   *The Countess of Kent's Choice Manual* (London, 1653) pp. 2, 8.
A. Macdonnel (ed.), *The Closet of Sir Kenelm Digby, Knight, opened* (London, 1910 reprint of the 1668 ed.) p. 62.
Robert May, *The Accomplisht Cook* (London, 3rd ed., 1671) pp. A7–8.

p. 69   Bradford MSS, Staffordshire County Record Office.

p.71   Henry J. Todd, *The History of Ashridge* (London, R. Gilbert, 1823) p. 54.
Stowe MSS, Huntington Library, California.
Consuelo Vanderbilt Balsan, *The Glitter and the Gold* (London, Heinemann, 1953) p. 68.
John Evelyn, *Acetaria: a Discourse of Sallets* (London, 1699), pp. 27, 31, 69.

p. 72   P. Quennell (ed.), *The Journal of Thomas Moore 1818–1941* (London, B.T. Batsford, 1964) p. 11.
The Works in Architecture of Robert and James Adam (London, 1773–9) I, pp. 8–9.
Irvin Eller, *History of Belvoir Castle* (London, 1841) p. 329.

p. 74   Osbert Sitwell (ed.), *Two Generations* (London, Macmillan, 1940) p. 129.
Fane, *Chit-Chat* (see n. for p. 41) p. 50.
Harold Nicolson, *Small Talk* (London, Constable, 1937) pp. 75–6.

p. 78   Harold Macmillan, *Winds of Change* (London, Macmillan, 1966) pp. 188–9.

CHAPTER 5. LOVE, LUST AND MARRIAGE

p. 81   John Aubrey, *Brief Lives* (ed. A. Powell, London, Cresset Press, 1949) pp. 372, 33.

p. 82   Ibid., p. 373.
R. Latham and W. Matthews (eds.), *The Diary of Samuel Pepys* VI (London, G. Bell and Sons, 1972) pp. 158–60, 175–6.

p. 85   Samuel Rogers, *Table Talk* (London, 1887) p. 235.
Letters of Byron (see n. for p. 52) II, p. 447.

p. 86   L.E.O. Charlton (ed.), *The Recollections of a Northumbrian Lady* (London, Jonathan Cape, 1949) p. 114.

p. 88   W.H. Mallock, *Memoirs of Life and Literature* (London, Chapman and Hall, 1920) pp. 116–17.

p. 89   Nancy Mitford (ed.), *The Stanleys of Alderley* (London, Chapman and Hall, 1939) pp. 10–11.

p. 90   Scawen Blunt MSS, Fitzwilliam Museum, Cambridge.

p. 92   Anita Leslie, *Edwardians in Love* (London, Hutchinson, 1972) p. 16.

CHAPTER 6. PARTIES

p. 95   L.C. Martin (ed.), *Poetical Works of Robert Herrick* (Oxford, Clarendon Press, 1956) pp. 101–2.

p. 96   *Memoirs of the Verney Family* (see n. for p. 33) II, p. 290.

p. 97   Alice Archer Houblon, *The Houblon Family* (London, Constable, 1907) II, p. 40.
J. Greig (ed.), *Diaries of a Duchess* (London, Hodder & Stoughton, 1926) pp. 102–3.

p. 98   E.J. Climenson (ed.), *Passages from the Diary of Mrs Philip Lybbe Powys* (London, Longmans Green, 1899) pp. 185–7.

p. 100 W.J. Smith (ed.), *The Grenville Papers* (London, John Murray, 1852) II, pp. 407–8.

p. 101 Walpole, *Letters* (see n. for p. 23) VII, p. 392.
Gentleman's Magazine, April, 1801, pp. 297–8.

p. 104 Constance Sitwell, *Bright Morning* (London, Jonathan Cape, 1942) pp. 44–6.
Dorothy Henley, *Rosalind Howard Countess of Carlisle* (London, Hogarth Press, 1958) pp. 48–50, 51–2.

p. 105 Cecil Beaton, *The Wandering Years* (London, Weidenfeld and Nicolson, 1961) pp. 250–2.

CHAPTER 7. ROYAL VISITS

p. 109 Froissart, *Chronicles* (tr. Thomas Johnes, London, 1855) I, pp. 102–3.

p. 110 John Nichols (ed.), *Progresses and Public Processions of Queen Elizabeth* (London, 2nd ed., 1823) III, pp. 101–2, 110–11.

p. 112 Ibid., III, p. 91.

p. 113 Chatsworth MSS.

p. 114 Lord Herbert (ed.), *Henry, Elizabeth and George* (London, Jonathan Cape, 1939) pp. 138–9.

p. 115 Mrs Philip Lybbe Powys (see n. for p. 98) pp. 217–18.

p. 116 Robert Huish, *Memoirs of George IV* (London, 1831) I, pp. 239–40.

p. 118 MS diary of Elizabeth George, in possession of Stowe School Library, from an original communication by Philip Blackett.

p. 119 Duke of Portland, *Men, Women and Things* (London, 1937) p. 305.

p. 120 Anon [Julian Osgood Field], *Uncensored Recollections* (London, Eveleigh Nash and Grayson, 1924) p. 330.

CHAPTER 8. SERVANTS

p. 123 Furnivall, *Babees Book* (see n. for p. 65) pp. 182–3.

p. 124 British Museum, Harleian MS 6815.

p. 126 V. Sackville-West (ed.), *The Diary of Lady Anne Clifford* (London, Wm. Heinemann, 1923) pp. lvii–lxi.

p. 128 Historical Manuscripts Commission. *Manuscripts of Lord Middleton* (London, H.M.S.O., 1911) pp. 576–7.
J.P. Cooper (ed.), *Wentworth Papers 1597–1628* (Royal Historical Society, Camden, Ser. IV, Vol. 12, 1973) p. 15.

p. 129 *Some Rules and Orders for the Government of the house of an Earle* (London, R. Triphook, 1921) pp. 44–5.

p. 130 Verney MSS, Buckinghamshire County Record Office.

p. 131 George Chandler, *Liverpool* (London, B.T. Batsford, 1967) pp. 149–50.

p. 132 Swinton Park (Cunliffe-Lister) MSS, Bradford Central Library.

p. 133 Stowe MSS, Huntington Library, California.
A.S. Turberville, *Welbeck Abbey and its Owners* (London, Faber and Faber, 1938) II, pp. 59–60.

p. 134 Jonathan Swift, *Directions to Servants and Miscellaneous Pieces, 1733–42* (Oxford, Basil Blackwell, 1959) pp. 18–19, 24.
Byron Letters (see n. for p. 52) II, p. 46.

p. 135 Thomas Cosnett, *The Footman's Directory* (London, 2nd ed., 1825) pp. 97–8.

p. 136 *Northumbrian Lady* (see n. for p. 86) pp. 177, 196.
Chit-Chat (see n. for p. 41) pp. 50–1.
James, *House-Steward* (see n. for p. 54) p. 97.
Printed sheet preserved at Hatfield House.

p. 138 Diana Cooper, *The Rainbow Comes and Goes* (London, Rupert Hart-Davis, 1958; Century, 1984), pp. 34–6.

p. 139 Typescript memories of Gerald Horne communicated by the late David Green.
David Freeman, *Tredegar House below Stairs* (Leaflet available at Tredegar House).

p. 140 Harrison, *Rose* (see n. for p. 42) pp. 121–2.

CHAPTER 9. ANIMALS

p. 145 John Chamberlain *Letters*
House of an Earle (see n. for p. 129) p. 25.
M.A. Lower (ed.), *Lives of William Cavendish, Duke of Newcastle, and of his wife, Margaret* (London, John Russell Smith, 1872) p. 58.

p. 146 Edward Lucie-Smith (ed.), *The Penguin Book of Elizabethan Verse* (Harmondsworth, Penguin, 1965) p. 152.

p. 147 B. Seeley, *A Description of Stowe* (Buckingham, 1783 ed.) pp. 8–9.

p. 149 Stowe MSS, Huntington Library, California.
G. Eland (ed.), *Purefoy Letters 1735–1753* (London, Sidgwick and Jackson, 1931) II, p. 407.

p. 150 *Hardwick Handbook* (see n. for p. 14) p. 211.
Boyd Alexander (ed.), *Life at Fonthill 1807–22* (London, Rupert Hart-Davis, 1957) p. 120.

CHAPTER 10. PARKS AND GARDENS

p. 153 Nichols, *Progresses* (see n. for p. 110) pp. 476–7.

p. 154 *Richard Carew of Antony* (see n. for p. 48) pp. 174–6.

p. 155 W. Lawson, *A New Orchard and Garden* (London, Cresset Press, 1927) pp. 63–5.

p. 158 Hugh MacDonald (ed.), *Poems of Andrew Marvell* (London, Routledge & Kegan Paul, 1952) pp. 89–90.

p. 159 Aubrey, *Brief Lives* (see n. for p. 81) p. 366.

p. 161 John Woolridge, *Systema Horticulturae* (London, 2nd ed., 1683) pp. 61–2.
John Evelyn, *Kalendarium Hortense* (London, 1664) p. 63.
John Evelyn, *Directions for the Gardiner at Sayes Court* (London, Nonesuch Press, 1932) pp. 98–101.

p. 162 Laurence Gleming and Alan Gore, *The English Garden* (London, Michael Joseph, 1979) pp. 128–9.

p. 163 Walpole at Hagley, *Walpole Letters* (see n. for p. 23) III, p. 186.
William Chambers, *A Dissertation on Oriental Gardening* (London, 1772) pp. 5–6.

p. 164 F. Leveson Gower (ed.), *Letters of Harriet Countess Granville 1810–45* (London, Longman Green, 1894) II, p. 35.

p. 165 R. B. Beckett (ed.) *John Constable's Correspondence* (Suffolk Records Society, 1962–8) p. 98.

p. 166 Royal Archives, Windsor.
Gertrude Jekyll, *Wood and Garden* (London, Longmans Green, 1890) p. 141.
Nicolson, *Diaries* (see n. for p. 62) pp. 301–2.

CHAPTER 11. PLUMBING, OR THE LACK OF IT

p. 169 Furnivall, *Babees Book* (see n. for p. 65) pp. 179–80.
Hardwick Inventory (see n. for p. 32) p. 32.

p. 170 Christopher Morris (ed.), *The Journeys of Celia Fiennes* (London, Cresset Press, 1947) p. 100.
Philipps MSS, National Library of Wales.

p. 171 Stowe MSS, Huntington Library, California.

p. 172 R.W. Ketton-Cremer, *Felbrigg: the Story of a House* (London, Rupert Hart-Davis, 1962) p. 135.

p. 173   Ernest Hamilton, *Old Days and New* (London,
               Hodder and Stoughton, 1924) p. 88.
          Stephen Fiske, *English Photographs* (London, 1869)
               pp. 196–7.
p. 174   James Lees-Milne, *Caves of Ice* (London, Chatto
               and Windus, 1983) p. 126.

CHAPTER 12. BIRTH AND DEATH

p. 177   J. Gardner (ed.), *The Paston Letters* (London, 1904)
               p. 177.
          Wentworth Papers (see n. for p. 128) p. 27.

p. 178   F.P. and M.M. Verney (eds.), *Memoirs of the
               Verney Family* (London, Longmans Green, 1904)
               I, pp. 224–5.
          British Museum, Add. MS 38141.
p. 181   Lady Llanover (ed.), *Autobiography and
               Correspondence of Mrs Delany* (1st series, London,
               1861) p. 66.
          Ightham Court MSS, Kent County Record Office.
p. 182   Rogers, *Table Talk* (see n. for p. 85) pp. 120–1.
p. 183   Eller, *Belvoir Castle* (see n. for p. 72) pp. 138–9.
p. 184   R.S. Churchill, *Winston S. Churchill* (London,
               Heinemann, 1966–   ) I, pp. 1–2.
p. 185   *The Glitter and the Gold* (see n. for p. 71) p. 57.

ACKNOWLEDGEMENTS

Quotations on pages 23 and 166, and illustrations on pages 56, 78, 117 and 118 are reproduced by gracious permission of Her Majesty the Queen. Thanks are due to Viscount Wimborne and Myles Thoroton Hildyard for help in getting photographs of pictures in their possession; to Frances Dimond, Peter Day and Olive Waller for assistance at the Royal Photograph Collection, Chatsworth and the *Country Life* Photographic Library; and to Clive Aslet, John Harris, Gervase Jackson-Stops, Susan Lasdun, Anne Hawker, Ann Walker, Greta Soggot, Celia Jones, Billa Harrod and Barbara Bagnall for assistance and encouragement of various kinds.

PHOTOGRAPHIC CREDITS

Endpapers (Ketteringham household: Lady Harrod). Page 1 (Baccelli servants) Lord Sackville; photo Courtauld Institute of Art. p3 (Sperlings taking tea) Neville Ollerenshaw. p5 (Manuscript) National Trust, Waddesdon Manor. p6 (View from Stowe) *Country Life*. p9 (Elveden tea party) Messrs. Sotheby's London. p10 (Blickling jug) National Trust, Blickling. p11 (Wisbech Castle) Wisbech and Fenland Museum; photo R.C. Wylie. p12 (painted screen) Victoria & Albert Museum, London. p13 (Longford Castle) Earl of Radnor. p14 (Belton House) National Trust; photo Graham Challifour. p15 (Wilton House) Earl of Pembroke. p17 (Under portico, Stowe) Buckinghamshire County Museum, Aylesbury. p20 (Newburgh priory) Captain V.W. Wombwell. p23 (Bess of Hardwick) National Trust; photo R. Wilsher. p25 (Badminton House) Duke of Beaufort; photo Royal Academy of Arts. p29 (Harden family) Abbot Hall Art Gallery, Kendal. p30 (Cave family) Lady Braye, Stanford Hall; photo Courtauld Institute of Art. p31 (Elizabeth Vernon) Duke of Buccleuch and Queensberry KT. p32 (Perseverance) National Trust. p33 (Trevelyan family) National Trust; photo Charles Waite. p35 (Catherine Allan) Abbot Hall Art Gallery, Kendal. p36 (Girl trying on garland) Victoria & Albert Museum. p37 (Blind man's buff) Victoria & Albert Museum. p38 (Capesthorne Hall) Sir Walter Bromley Davenport, Bart. p39 (Wootton House) Sir Walter Bromley Davenport, Bart. p40 (Buxtons of Northrepps) Mrs E.R.C. Creighton. p41 (Duchess of Marlborough) National Portrait Gallery, London. p42 (Lord Leconfield) Central Press Photos. p43 (Duke of Devonshire and children) Duke of Devonshire, Chatsworth; photo Macmillan. p44 (Mrs Ronald Greville) National Trust. p45 (Arthur Williams Wynn) Lady Fitzwilliam. p46 (Incident at Langton Lodge) Neville Ollerenshaw; photo Victor Gollancz. p50 (Henry Fox and friends) National Trust, Ickworth. p53 (Artist at Petworth) Tate Gallery, London. p54 (Edward Lear sketching) *Letters of Edward Lear* (ed. Lady Strachey, 1909), p.173. p56 (Blenheim shooting party) Royal Photograph Collection, Windsor. p58 (Group on ice) Earl of Cawdor; photo Anthony J. Lambert. p60 (Chaplin signature) Private collection; photo Weidenfeld & Nicolson. p62 (Madresfield group) Private collection. p63 (Wilden House) photo Weidenfeld & Nicolson. p64 (Luttrell Psalter) British Museum, London. p67 ('To make a pheasant') photo Weidenfeld & Nicolson. p70 (Silhouette) Victoria & Albert Museum, London. p70 (Table of Fowl) photo Weidenfeld & Nicolson. p73 (Tea party) Collection of Mr Paul Mellon. p75 (Carved Room, Petworth) Lord Egremont. p76 (Unidentified tea-party) Royal Photograph Collection, Windsor. p78 (Sunningdale Park) Royal Photograph Collection, Windsor. p79 (Duke of Clarence) Luton Museum; photo Anthony J. Lambert. p80 (Madame Baccelli) Lord Sackville; photo Courtauld Institute of Art. p81 (Aylesford Friary) Private Collection. p82 (Nostell dolls-house) Lord St Oswald, Nostell Priory. p84 (Girl at dressing table)

The Marquess of Salisbury. p86 (Lansdownes at Bowood) Lord Newton *Lord Lansdowne: a biography* (1929). p87 (Playing the flute) Neville Ollerenshaw; photo Victor Gollancz. p89 (Bicyclists, Paddockhurst) Clive Aslet. p91 (Bootle-Wilbrahams paying court) Lord Skelmersdale; photo Anthony J. Lambert. p93 (Nelson at Fonthill) *Gentleman's Magazine*, 1801. p94 (West Wycombe party) *The Tatler*. p97 (Wynnstay theatre) photo *Country Life*. p99 (Edgcumbe party) photo *Country Life*. pp100, 103 (Festivities at Stowe) Buckinghamshire County Museum, Aylesbury, p105 (Garden party at Tredegar) Newport District Council, Tredegar House. p107 (Princesses at Cragside) National Trust; photo *Country Life*. p108 (Thomas Williams) *Country Life*. p109 (Queen Elizabeth out hunting) photo Fotomas. p111 (Elvetham) Nichols Progresses. p112 (Charles II and pineapple) National Trust. p116 (Queen Victoria at Castle Howard) *Illustrated London News*; photo Mary Evans Picture Library. p117 (Prince of Wales at Elveden) Royal Photograph Collection, Windsor. p117 (Prince of Wales, Easton Neston) Royal Photograph Collection, Windsor. p118 (Duchess of Teck, Trafford Park) Royal Photograph Collection, Windsor. p119 (Prince Henry, Lyme Park) National Trust. p119 (Duke of York, Elveden) photo Christie, Manson and Woods. p120 (Lansdownes at Bowood) Lord Newton *Lord Lansdowne: a biography* (1929). p121 (Beckford's dwarf) Duke of Hamilton and Brandon; photo Bath Public Library. p123 (Gilling musicians) photo Peter Burton. p124 (Bradford table carpet) Victoria & Albert Museum, London. p129 (Al fresco meal) photo Fotomas. p130 (Pots and pans, Erddig) National Trust. p132 (Kitchen by William Kent) Victoria & Albert Museum. p133 (Nostell dolls-house kitchen) Lord St Oswald, Nostell Priory; photo Angelo Hornak. p134, 135 (Drummond family servants) Victoria & Albert Museum. p137 (Maid at Stowe) Buckinghamshire County Museum, Aylesbury. p138, 139 (Erddig servants) National Trust; photos John Bethell. p140 (Petworth laundry) National Trust; photo Peter Jerrome. p141 (Henry Moate) University Art Collection, Hull. p142 (Van at Polesden Lacey) National Trust. p143 (Cabbage Castle) Ian Anstruther. p144 (Lord Rothschild and zebras) BBC Hulton Picture Library. p145 (Francis Russell and dogs) Marquess of Tavistock and the Trustees of the Bedford Estates. p146 (Hutton Bonville hound) Myles Thoroton Hildyard, Flintham Hall. p147 (Lord Southampton's cat) Duke of Buccleuch and Queensberry, Boughton House. p147 (Beckford dog) Duke of Hamilton and Brandon. p148 (Deer at Averham) Mr and Mrs Guy Titley; (Ledston Hall) Private Collection. p149 (Horses in stable) photo *Country Life*. p150 (Pugs at Wilton) Earl of Pembroke; photo David Robson. p151 (Formal Garden) Royal Horticultural Society. p152 (View to the Park) *Country Life*. p155 (Wilton garden) Worcester College, Oxford; photo Courtauld Institute of Art. p157 (Denham Place) Yale Center for British Art, Paul Mellon Collection. p159 (Fountain) Stephen Switzer *Hydrostaticks and Hydraulics* (1729). p160 (Enstone grotto) Plot *Natural History of Oxfordshire*. p164 (Mason's Garden, Nuneham) Private collection. p163 (Repton view) Marquess of Tavistock and the Trustees of the Bedford Estates. p164 (Sedgwick Park) *Country Life*. p165 (Stowe) Buckinghamshire County Museum, Aylesbury. p167 (Felbrigg water-closet) National Trust. p168 (Gledhow bathroom) photo Weidenfeld & Nicolson. p169 (Conduit House) The Sir John Soane Museum, London. p170 (Stowe bath) Buckinghamshire County Museum, Aylesbury. p171 (Stowe water-closets) Huntington Library, San Marino, California. p172 (Chicheley engine) Stephen Switzer *Hydrostaticks and Hydraulics* (1729); photo R.I.B.A. p175 (Elmley Castle) BBC Hulton Picture Library. p180 (Brancepeth lying in state) Viscount Boyne. p184 (Lord Helmsley) Sir Martyn Beckett, Bart. p184 (Churchill curls) Blenheim Palace. p185 (Buxton baby) Mrs E.R.C. Creighton.

COLOUR CREDITS I (Sidney family) Viscount De L'Isle VC, KG., Penshurst Place. II (Beauchamp family) Private collection. III (Sneyds at Keele) Peter Garnier; photo J.M. Kolbert, University of Keele. IV (Sir Rowland Winn) Lord St Oswald, Nostell Priory. V (Brooke family) The Marquess of Bath, Longleat House. VI (Sperlings at dinner) Neville Ollerenshaw; photo Victor Gollancz. VII (St Fagan's) Private collection; photo National Gallery of Art, Washington. VIII (Cotehele dinner) Cornwall County Library. IX (Assembly at Wanstead House) Philadelphia Museum of Art. X (Tichborne servants) Mr John Loudon. XI–XIV (Hartwell gardens) Buckinghamshire County Museum, Aylesbury. XV (Killing flies) Neville Ollerenshaw; photo Victor Gollancz. XVI (Gothic pavilion, Painswick) Private collection. XVII (Chiswick bridge) Private collection. XVIII (Unton christening) National Portrait Gallery, London. XIX (Saltonstall family) Tate Gallery, London. XX (Cholmondeley Sisters) Tate Gallery, London. XXI (Sir Thomas Aston) Manchester City Art Gallery. XXII (Duchess of Devonshire) Trustees of the Chatsworth Settlement. XXIII (Duchess of Marlborough) Duke of Marlborough, Blenheim Palace.

INDEX OF HOUSES

Figures in italics refer to black-and-white illustrations by page numbers. Roman figures refer to colour illustrations.

Other Publications:

THE EPIC OF FLIGHT
THE GOOD COOK
THE SEAFARERS
THE ENCYCLOPEDIA OF COLLECTIBLES
THE GREAT CITIES
HOME REPAIR AND IMPROVEMENT
THE WORLD'S WILD PLACES
THE TIME-LIFE LIBRARY OF BOATING
HUMAN BEHAVIOR
THE ART OF SEWING
THE OLD WEST
THE EMERGENCE OF MAN
THE AMERICAN WILDERNESS
THE TIME-LIFE ENCYCLOPEDIA OF GARDENING
LIFE LIBRARY OF PHOTOGRAPHY
THIS FABULOUS CENTURY
FOODS OF THE WORLD
TIME-LIFE LIBRARY OF AMERICA
TIME-LIFE LIBRARY OF ART
GREAT AGES OF MAN
LIFE SCIENCE LIBRARY
THE LIFE HISTORY OF THE UNITED STATES
TIME READING PROGRAM
LIFE NATURE LIBRARY
LIFE WORLD LIBRARY
FAMILY LIBRARY:
   HOW THINGS WORK IN YOUR HOME
   THE TIME-LIFE BOOK OF THE FAMILY CAR
   THE TIME-LIFE FAMILY LEGAL GUIDE
   THE TIME-LIFE BOOK OF FAMILY FINANCE

On D-Day—June 6, 1944—soldiers of the
9th Canadian Infantry Brigade swarm ashore at
Bernières-sur-Mer, France. The Normandy
invasion, the greatest amphibious operation in
history, was the opening phase of Operation
Overlord, the Allies' master plan for the
liberation of German-occupied Europe.

TIME
LIFE ®
BOOKS

Other Publi

THE EPIC O
THE GOOD
THE SEAFA
THE ENCY
THE GREA
HOME R
THE WO
THE TIM
HUMAN
THE AR
THE O
THE EN
THE A
THE T
LIFE
THIS
FOO
TIM
TIM
GR
LIFE
TH
T
L
L

THE SECOND FRONT

WORLD WAR II · TIME-LIFE BOOKS · ALEXANDRIA, VIRGINIA

450
5/93

BY DOUGLAS BOTTING
AND THE EDITORS OF TIME-LIFE BOOKS

THE SECOND FRONT

Time-Life Books Inc.
is a wholly owned subsidiary of
TIME INCORPORATED

Founder: Henry R. Luce 1898-1967

Editor-in-Chief: Henry Anatole Grunwald
Chairman of the Board: Andrew Heiskell
President: James R. Shepley
Editorial Director: Ralph Graves
Vice Chairman: Arthur Temple

TIME-LIFE BOOKS INC.

Managing Editor: Jerry Korn
Executive Editor: David Maness
Assistant Managing Editors: Dale M. Brown
(planning), George Constable, George G. Daniels
(acting), Martin Mann, John Paul Porter
Art Director: Tom Suzuki
Chief of Research: David L. Harrison
Director of Photography: Robert G. Mason
Senior Text Editor: Diana Hirsh
Assistant Art Director: Arnold C. Holeywell
Assistant Chief of Research: Carolyn L. Sackett
Assistant Director of Photography: Dolores A. Littles

Chairman: Joan D. Manley
President: John D. McSweeney
Executive Vice Presidents: Carl G. Jaeger,
John Steven Maxwell, David J. Walsh
Vice Presidents: Nicholas Benton (public
relations), Nicholas J. C. Ingleton (Asia),
James L. Mercer (Europe/South Pacific),
Herbert Sorkin (production), Paul R. Stewart
(marketing), Peter G. Barnes, John L. Canova
Personnel Director: Beatrice T. Dobie
Consumer Affairs Director: Carol Flaumenhaft
Comptroller: George Artandi

WORLD WAR II

Editorial Staff for The Second Front
Editor: William K. Goolrick
Picture Editor/Designer: Raymond Ripper
Picture Editor: Robin Richman
Text Editors: Gerald Simons, Henry Woodhead
Staff Writers: Malachy J. Duffy, Brian McGinn,
Tyler Mathisen, Teresa M. C. R. Pruden
Chief Researcher: Frances G. Youssef
Researchers: Marion F. Briggs, Loretta Y. Britten,
Christine Bowie Dove, Oobie Gleysteen,
Pat Good, Chadwick Gregson
Art Assistant: Mary Louise Mooney
Editorial Assistant: Connie Strawbridge

Editorial Production
Production Editor: Douglas B. Graham
Operations Manager: Gennaro C. Esposito,
Gordon E. Buck (assistant)
Assistant Production Editor: Feliciano Madrid
Quality Control: Robert L. Young (director),
James J. Cox (assistant), Daniel J. McSweeney,
Michael G. Wight (associates)
Art Coordinator: Anne B. Landry
Copy Staff: Susan B. Galloway (chief),
Patricia Graber, Victoria Lee, Celia Beattie
Picture Department: Alvin L. Ferrell

Correspondents: Elisabeth Kraemer (Bonn);
Margot Hapgood, Dorothy Bacon, Lesley Coleman
(London); Susan Jonas, Lucy T. Voulgaris (New
York); Maria Vincenza Aloisi, Josephine du Brusle
(Paris); Ann Natanson (Rome). Valuable assistance
was also provided by: Judy Aspinall, Penny
Newman (London); Carolyn T. Chubet, Miriam
Hsia, Christina Lieberman (New York); M. T.
Hirschkoff (Paris); Mimi Murphy (Rome); Traudl
Lessing (Vienna).

The Author: DOUGLAS BOTTING was born in
London in 1934 and was educated at Oxford University. His interest in military affairs began with
service in the British Army; he enlisted as an infantry subaltern and served in the King's African Rifles
in East Africa. Subsequently he traveled widely as
writer and film maker on scientific and explora-
tory expeditions to Arabia, Africa, Amazonia and
Arctic Siberia. He has written several books on
history and travel, including three volumes for
TIME-LIFE BOOKS Wilderness Europe in The
World's Wild Places series, Rio de Janeiro in The
Great Cities series, and The Pirates in The Seafarers
series. He is working on a definitive study of the
aftermath of World War II in Germany.

The Consultant: COL. JOHN R. ELTING, USA
(Ret.), is a military historian and author of The
Battle of Bunker's Hill, The Battles of Saratoga and
Military History and Atlas of the Napoleonic Wars.
He edited Military Uniforms in America: The Era
of the American Revolution, 1755-1795 and Mili-
tary Uniforms in America: Years of Growth, 1796-
1851, and was associate editor of The West Point
Atlas of American Wars.

Library of Congress Cataloguing in Publication Data

Botting, Douglas.
 The second front.

 (World War II; v. 13)
 Bibliography: p.
 Includes index.
 1. Operation Overlord. 2. World War, 1939-1945—
Campaigns—France—Normandy. 3. Dieppe Raid, 1942.
4. France—History—German occupation, 1940-1945.
I. Time-Life Books. II. Title. III. Series.
D756.5.N6B6   940.54′21   78-3405
ISBN 0-8094-2500-9
ISBN 0-8094-2499-1 lib. bdg.

For information about any Time-Life book, please write:

Reader Information
Time-Life Books
541 North Fairbanks Court
Chicago, Illinois 60611

CONTENTS

HITLER'S ATLANTIC WALL

The Atlantic Wall—beach obstacles, hidden gun batteries and, behind the bomb-damaged sea wall, barbed-wire entanglements—guards a French coastal village.

"IMPREGNABLE FRONT" FOR FORTRESS EUROPE

Todt and Speer (below, with pointer) supervised construction of the Wall. Rommel (bottom, left) and Rundstedt were charged with its defense.

In December 1941, Adolf Hitler boasted to the world that his Third Reich controlled the entire west coast of Europe from the Arctic Ocean to the Bay of Biscay. "It is my unshakable decision," the Führer added, "to make this front impregnable against every enemy." To keep his vow, Hitler conceived of an awesome defense line—a broad band of concrete, steel, guns and troops that would follow the shoreline for 2,400 miles. He called it the Atlantic Wall. In the next two and a half years, it became an obsessive project for him. For the Allied invasion planners it became the most formidable defensive barrier of the War.

Hitler ordered the building of 15,000 permanent strong points, which were to be manned by 300,000 troops. The defense posts, many of which he designed himself, were built by the German agency for military public works, Organization Todt, under its namesake, Dr. Fritz Todt, and his successor, Reich Minister Albert Speer. Construction officially started early in 1942, with the heaviest concentration of defenses rising along the narrowest part of the English Channel, between the Netherlands and Le Havre in Normandy. For two years, a quarter of a million men worked night and day. They used more than a million tons of steel and poured more than 20 million cubic yards of concrete.

The Wall inspired confidence in practically every German. There were a few skeptics, of course. The top commander in the West, Field Marshal Gerd von Rundstedt, doubted that the Wall alone could stop an Allied attack. At first, Field Marshal Erwin Rommel, the former commander of the famous Afrika Korps, called the Wall a "figment of Hitler's 'cloud cuckoo land.'" But after he was appointed inspector of coastal defenses in the West, Rommel set out to strengthen and deepen the defense line. He implanted mine-tipped obstacles along open beaches and flooded great inland areas to impede airborne invaders. His many improvements gave added weight to the German Propaganda Ministry's confident claims for the Wall: "This is why an enemy attack, even the most powerful and furious possible to imagine, is bound to fail."

A powerful coastal gun, its muzzle being serviced by a German, points seaward from a concrete blockhouse. Cased shells stand beside the rotating turret.

French laborers prepare to pour concrete into wooden forms to make steel-reinforced bunker walls.

Weary Frenchmen hired by the Germans are marched off to excavate for a sea-front fortification.

Overage Germans worked on the Atlantic Wall.

French colonial workmen enjoy a rice break.

Walls of a giant U-boat pen, being built by thousands of conscripted laborers, rise at the port of Bordeaux in 1942. Each open bay had docks on both sides.

MIGHTY INSTALLATIONS BUILT BY SLAVE LABOR

The Atlantic Wall was constructed largely by slave labor. To make up for German manpower that had been drained off by the armed forces and war industries, prisoners of war and civilians who had been rounded up in occupied countries were brought to Organization Todt to work on the mighty coastal defenses. At the peak of construction in 1943, fully 90 per cent of the workers in Organization Todt were

conscripted foreigners. The rest included paid French volunteers, and German technicians and supervisors.

Under close guard and a great deal of pressure, the conscripts did backbreaking labor around the clock. On the heavily fortified Channel Islands, they toiled seven days a week, at least 12 hours a day, with a 10- to 30-minute break for lunch. Their rations were insufficient for such strenuous labor, and they were issued no work clothes. One Sunday a month they were given a half day off.

Most of the conscripts were put to work

on the largest and most elaborate of the Atlantic Wall installations. These were the ports containing U-boat bases, whose artillery and machine-gun nests were designed to defend the harbor as well as the submarines. Each of the biggest bases—in France at Brest, Lorient, Saint-Nazaire and La Pallice—was built by a work gang composed of up to 15,000 men. The gang was supposed to build a base—construction that would take three years under normal conditions—in six months. Some crews came close, and the men who faltered were simply replaced.

11

OBSERVATION TOWER WITH RADAR

SUPPLY BUNKER UNDER CONSTRUCTION

FOOD STORAGE BUNKER WITH REFRIGERATION

PERSONNEL BUNKERS

CREATING DEFENSES FOR SPECIAL FUNCTIONS

The German planners designed almost 700 standard units for the tens of thousands of individual defense works of the Atlantic Wall. Then, using selected units, they put together an emplacement tailor-made for each specific function. There were heavy coastal-gun sites and antiaircraft positions, artillery and machine-gun pillboxes, ammunition bunkers, multistory observation towers, communications posts and medical facilities. Huge supply bunkers with facilities for storing water and refrigerating food were built in compliance with Hitler's directive that the troops "must never be

HEAVY ARTILLERY EMPLACEMENT

OBSERVATION POST

A sampling of concrete defense structures, differing in functions (labels), displays the monolithic massiveness common to most Atlantic Wall strong points.

forced to surrender because of a shortage of ammunition, rations or water."

The centerpiece of most defense complexes was the gun emplacement. Weapons were housed beneath stepped overhangs that gave them maximum arcs of fire while preventing enemy shells from falling into the blockhouse. Many sites had air-conditioned magazines and conveyors to move shells to the guns.

The larger batteries had heavy concrete bunkers for gun crews. These accommodations generally housed from 10 to 150 men, who slept in double or triple tiers on steel-framed bunks that folded against the walls when not in use. Though space was at a premium, some complexes had recreation areas, libraries, well-equipped kitchens and mess halls. One bunker even had an officers' bar, complete with wood paneling and upholstered chairs.

A gun emplacement masquerades as a house with curtained windows and a balustrade along the roof.

An observation post (center) is painted to resemble

A German antitank gun pokes out of a bunker disguised as a modest villa in southwest France.

Disguised as the Strand Café, this seaside lookout

EXPERTS IN THE ART OF CAMOUFLAGE

In 1942 Lieut. General Rudolf Schmetzer, German Inspector of Land Defense West, laid down the principle that camouflage was as important as thick concrete. Heeding his dictum, local commanders spared no effort to hide or disguise their posi-

the dark-beamed, Norman-style residence at right.

post displays false windows and painted curtains.

The figure of a matron, painted in a bunker's false window, draws mock salutes from passing Germans.

tions. The Fifteenth Army, which was deployed along the Channel coast from Ostend, Belgium, to Caen in Normandy, even formed a special study group—consisting of a botanist, zoologist, geologist, engineer, tank expert, artilleryman and infantryman—to come up with new and better ways to make the army's bastions look like something else.

In towns all along the Atlantic Wall, defense works were carefully disguised as local buildings by means of false roofs, painted windows and dummy doors. Many observation posts were made to look like churches, complete with steeples. And the concrete façades of gun batteries carved into seaside cliffs were painted to match the rock formations.

The most common type of camouflage was more effective but much less esoteric: plain dirt. Since many of the defense positions were built underground for protection, the Germans simply covered them over with protective layers of earth, leaving openings only for guns and for observation purposes. And the defenders were much too shrewd to let raw earth betray an underground bunker or command post. Atop the positions they placed a cover of natural vegetation.

A German soldier on guard duty patrols a beach lined with tetrahedral antitank obstacles, a number of them supporting the rifles of his off-duty comrades.

A row of curved obstructions composed of metal rails protects a village on the French coast. These objects were designed by the Germans to snag tanks.

16

A pair of horses tow a formidable antitank barrier, known as a "Belgian Gate," into position. The gates were approximately nine feet high and nine feet wide.

THE CHANNEL COAST: "ZONE OF DEATH"

To defend the open beaches along the crucial Channel coast, Field Marshal Rommel spun out a steel spider web to entrap and destroy any foolhardy attackers. By June 1944 the Germans had barricaded the shoreline from Cherbourg to Calais with half a million assorted anti-invasion obstacles and more than four million mines planted in depth.

Great logs and steel beams were driven into the sand and tipped with mines or metal cutters to gut landing craft. Hedgehogs—twisted steel girders welded together—studded tidal flats. Concrete antitank obstacles lined the beaches.

Rommel, who designed many of the obstacles himself, warned the Allies against challenging this "zone of death." He also said, "The war will be won or lost on the beaches," and by the eve of D-Day, he had done his best to win it there.

The low tide exposes rows of mines and wooden stakes guarding a possible Allied landing site.

Field Marshal Rommel (front row, third from left) and other high German officers inspect antitank and anti-landing-craft obstacles on a Pas-de-Calais beach in

April 1944. Rommel expressed satisfaction with the defenses in this sector of the Atlantic Wall, but he was disappointed with those along the Normandy coast.

1

On the afternoon of June 4, 1940, as 338,000 soldiers were being evacuated from Dunkirk in the desperate effort to save the British Army from annihilation by the German blitzkrieg then steam-rolling across France, Prime Minister Winston Churchill made a stirring, but seemingly unlikely, promise to the House of Commons. "Britain will fight on," he thundered, "if necessary for years . . . if necessary alone. . . . We shall go back."

On that dark day for British fortunes, and in the darker ones to come, the prospect of Britain's Army recrossing the Channel and defeating Germany on the soil of Europe was remote indeed. At a time when Britain was gearing up its meager resources for a last-ditch defense to stave off an expected German invasion, an offensive of its own seemed out of the question. But on the day Churchill made his vow, a British planner in the War Office conceived the idea of a force of specially trained commandos to carry out guerrilla raids against the German Occupation forces across the English Channel. It was the modest beginning of an effort to strike back, an effort that would culminate four years later in the launching of a vast Allied armada and the opening, on the beaches of France, of a western front against Germany.

Less than three weeks after Dunkirk, the commandos struck. On June 23, the day after France signed her humiliating armistice with Germany and Hitler crowed that Britain had been "driven from the Continent forever," a party of 120 British Commandos raided Boulogne on the French coast and inflicted such damage as they could with 20 Tommy guns—half the number that Britain possessed at the time. The raid was not particularly successful. No prisoners were captured, little information was gained, and part of the Commando force, which on its return to England landed at another port than the one intended, suffered the humiliation of being arrested by military police and held for a short while as a party of deserters.

The Commandos had no illusions about the importance of the Boulogne raid. As one of their officers put it: "We went there merely to show the Hun we can go back any time we bloody well feel like it."

The Commado strikes continued, against far-ranging targets in France, Norway, Italy and Libya. Their objectives were always limited: to destroy enemy defenses or industrial plants or utilities, to capture prisoners and garner infor-

REHEARSALS FOR INVASION

mation—and generally to boost Allied morale. While they served to harass the Axis and to keep them constantly on the alert, the attacks did little to change the course of the War. The Commando raids were mere pinpricks in the hide of the Axis behemoth. It was the best that Britain could do.

Even though Churchill dreamed of an invasion of the Continent and British strategists had been studying that possibility since October 1940, there was no hope that Britian could launch an effective offensive so long as it was fighting a defensive war alone in the West. It needed friends—allies to fight on its side. Eventually it got them. In June 1941, Hitler turned his armies eastward and invaded Russia. As enormous battles raged, with the Germans penetrating deeper and deeper into the vast country across a broad front, Stalin began exhorting Churchill to open a second front at the earliest possible moment and thereby relieve his hard-pressed armies. Six months later, after the Japanese attack on Pearl Harbor in December 1941, the United States joined the war against the Axis, and Britain, Russia and America were now united in what came to be called the Grand Alliance. The opening of a second front no longer seemed so remote.

As interest in an invasion mounted late in 1941, the British organization that conducted the Commando raids, the Combined Operations Command, was given a new chief and a new direction. Captain the Lord Louis Mountbatten, a cousin of the King and a brilliant and forceful organizer who had been a destroyer commander at the start of the War, was put in charge. Under his dynamic leadership, Combined Operations became less an organization for pinprick raiding parties and more an embryo invasion headquarters.

Accordingly, the Commando raids became less important for the damage they inflicted and more and more valuable for gathering the experience and information necessary for planning a full-fledged invasion of Europe. No one knew exactly what was required, what snags might arise, what defenses would be encountered. It was essential to find out.

There was no lack of ideas. The planners at Combined Operations were wildly unorthodox young men, and in the first months of 1942 they dreamed up many fanciful schemes. The boldest and most far-fetched was to land and drive an armored column to Paris, shoot up the German Army headquarters at the Hotel Crillon, rekindle the flame on the Tomb of the Unknown Warrior, then drive back to the Channel for reembarkation to England.

Fortunately, a cooler but no less imaginative head prevailed. As his senior staff officer, Mountbatten had chosen a highly creative Royal Navy officer, 40-year-old Captain John Hughes-Hallett, who later became one of the outstanding planners of D-Day. It was Hughes-Hallett who devised perhaps the most brazenly impudent and successful Commando operation of the War—the Saint-Nazaire raid (pages 24-25), which took the Germans by surprise and knocked out the only dry dock on the Atlantic coast that was capable of servicing their newest and mightiest battleship, the Tirpitz. The destruction of the dry dock prevented the Tirpitz from venturing into the Atlantic and wreaking havoc on the Allied convoy routes.

The success of the Saint-Nazaire raid was misleading, however. It gave Hughes-Hallet and his Combined Operations planners the mistaken impression that it was feasible to attack other heavily fortified ports by direct assault, provided only that the defenders were taken by surprise.

In the meantime, the pressure on Britain and America to launch a second front had been mounting. The German armies had plunged even deeper into the Soviet Union, and Russian losses were appalling. Millions of soldiers, and as many civilians, had been killed in battle or had perished of starvation, cold and disease. Stalin demanded a major military diversion from the Western Allies. "A second front is essential," he said, "and therefore must be possible." A great public clamor for supporting the Russians arose in Britain, Canada and the United States. In British cities billboards and walls blossomed with the hand-painted injunction SECOND FRONT NOW.

In the judgment of American military chiefs, the Soviet Union was in such desperate straits that it might soon be knocked out of the War, freeing a mass of German soldiers and equipment for an invasion of Great Britain. To counteract an anticipated Russian collapse, and possibly to prevent it, General George C. Marshall, American Chief of Staff, ordered plans prepared for an emergency invasion of France. Two connected plans were drawn up by his protégé, Major General Dwight D. Eisenhower, and in April Marshall presented them to Churchill. The first plan, bearing the code name Operation *Sledgehammer*, called for landing some 12 divisions (10 of them British) in the autumn of 1942. The *Sledgehammer* force would establish a bridgehead and wait to be joined by a larger army—Operation *Roundup*—in the spring of 1943, when many more American troops would be available.

These plans drew strong but opposite reactions from British strategists. They were enthusiastic about *Roundup*, but they emphatically rejected *Sledgehammer*. The Germans were too strong, they argued, and the Allies too weak. There were not enough men and not yet enough materials for such a vast operation; there were not sufficient craft to carry them in or aircraft to cover them. Though America's capacity for war production was immense, the British argued, the U.S. was not yet geared for total war and its arsenals as yet were empty. The British were adamant that

there could be no second front in 1942, and they got the Americans to agree to a smaller invasion of North Africa in the autumn under General Eisenhower.

The idea of opening a second front had not been abandoned entirely. But instead of the real thing, there would be a dress rehearsal at a French port. At this stage of the War, both British and American strategists alike thought that any full-scale invasion of Europe, when it came, would have to aim at a port, and seize it intact, as the only way of getting supplies and reinforcements ashore quickly. With this in mind, a few weeks after the Saint-Nazaire raid the Anglo-American invasion planning group known as the Combined Commanders, headed by Eisenhower and General Sir Bernard Paget, sent Combined Operations a list of French ports and a polite request: "Please raid one of these ports in sufficient strength to persuade the enemy to react as if he were faced with actual invasion."

From the list of ports Mountbatten and his planners chose Dieppe, on the English Channel. Dieppe had several advantages over other possible targets. It was near enough to be reached by ship under cover of darkness, it was well within the operating range of RAF fighter planes, and its defenses were strong enough to ensure a major German reaction, from which the invasion planners hoped to learn much.

Specifically, the Dieppe raid would afford practice in handling an assault fleet off an enemy coast, in trying out new kinds of assault craft and equipment, in capturing and holding an enemy port. It would have the additional practical benefit of destroying German defenses, dock and rail installations, gasoline dumps and radar stations. And there would be the bonus of captured secret documents and prisoners. The raid had two strategic purposes as well—to force the Luftwaffe into a decisive air battle and to relieve German pressure on Russia by drawing troops and warplanes away from the Eastern Front.

For the main assault force, Combined Operations called upon the services of the 2nd Canadian Division, under the command of Major-General John Hamilton "Ham" Roberts, a respected artillery officer whose military career dated back to World War I. The Canadians had been based in England since 1939 and now, 150,000 men strong, they formed the backbone of the island's anti-invasion defenses while the British Army fought in the Middle East and South-

In this 1942 London Daily Mail cartoon, Prime Minister Winston Churchill is reminded of his long-standing promise to invade Europe by three "children," representing Britain's Army, Navy and Air Force. The cartoon reflected the growing clamor in England for the opening of a second front on the Continent to help relieve the Soviet Union in its desperate struggle against the Germans. The Soviet Ambassador to England demanded immediate action, saying, "There is no time to wait until the last button is sewn to the last uniform of the last soldier."

east Asia. During their two and a half years in England they had not seen any combat and they had gained a reputation as the most overexercised and underemployed army in the War. The Canadian government knew its men were frustrated and demoralized by inactivity and was pressuring the British government to send them into action at the earliest opportunity. Dieppe provided that opportunity.

The plan for the Dieppe raid, which bore the code name Operation *Jubilee,* evolved painfully, with many alterations, as spring gave way to summer. The attack was to be carried out on an 11-mile front, with Dieppe roughly in the center. The terrain was formidable. Two high headlands flanked the beach at the town, and beyond the headlands to either side rose unscalable chalk cliffs. Moreover, these natural defenses had been skillfully strengthened with artillery pillboxes, antiaircraft batteries and machine-gun nests. Combined Operations disregarded British intelligence estimates of the strength of the Dieppe defenses and judged that the German garrison in the area was no cause for concern. It consisted predominantly of raw recruits, older soldiers judged unfit for combat duty and Polish conscripts who had failed to qualify for their Army in 1939. But the terrain and the strength of its defenses more than made up for the garrison's shortcomings.

The final plan of attack called for landing six infantry battalions, one tank regiment, two Commando formations and various support units in five separate operations. On the outer flanks, several miles to either side of Dieppe, British Commando units would destroy two big coastal batteries, at the hamlets of Berneval and Varengeville, to prevent them from firing on the invasion fleet. Just to the east and west of the town, two Canadian regiments would knock out the German gun emplacements on the pair of headlands overlooking Dieppe.

Thus protected, the main assault force would land on the mile-long beach in front of the town. This force, consisting of two Canadian infantry regiments, would capture Dieppe and throw up a defensive perimeter around the Allied beachhead. Then tanks and foot soldiers would pass through the perimeter and attack a German airfield and the headquarters of the German 302nd Infantry Division, both within four miles of Dieppe. As soon as the port had been secured, another Commando unit would come in to seize the invasion barges that the Germans had stockpiled.

All in all, the plan was overambitious and hopelessly inflexible. In typescript it ran to 199 pages. It made no allowances for enemy interference in the attack, nor did it allow for individual initiative by the Canadian unit commanders—their every move was spelled out. Only the Commandos demanded—and got—the right to attack their assigned objective in any manner they saw fit.

The most grievous deficiencies in the plan were the most elementary ones. No overall commander was appointed; the naval forces and the landing parties would have coequal chiefs. There was to be no preliminary aerial bombardment and only brief naval shelling. Heavier bombardment had been ruled out partly because of the planners' concern for the safety of the townspeople, partly because of their fears that the resulting rubble would make the streets impassable to tanks, and partly because the Royal Navy could not spare any battleships and the RAF declined to contribute any bombers. Nor would any paratroopers be landed behind Dieppe to draw off some of the shore-front defenders; airborne attacks were considered too susceptible to cancellation due to adverse weather. Just as at Saint-Nazaire, surprise was supposed to win the day.

As final preparations for the Dieppe raid were made in August, the Allies' fortunes in Europe were at their lowest ebb, the Germans' at their fullest. Between the English Channel and the Black Sea, and between Norway and the islands of Greece, more than 400 million people had fallen under Hitler's rule. The German Afrika Korps under Field Marshal Erwin Rommel had defeated the British at Tobruk in Libya and was driving them eastward into Egypt. In the Atlantic, German U-boats were sinking merchant ships at a faster rate than replacements could be built. In the Far East, the all-conquering Japanese were threatening India, raising Allied fears that Japan might link up in the Middle East with its German and Italian allies and establish an Axis dominion over half the world.

The Dieppe raid, if all went as planned, would be one bright and inspiring light in the darkness.

Through the late hours of August 18, 1942, and the early hours of August 19, the Allied strike force steamed across the English Channel toward Dieppe. It was a beautiful,

A DARING STRIKE STAGED BY COMMANDOS AND AN ELDERLY DESTROYER

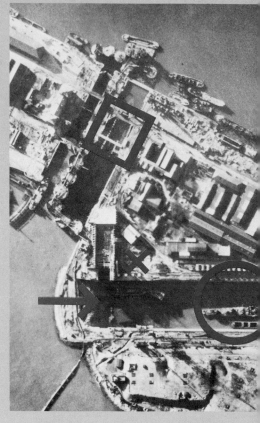

The Campbeltown, embedded in the gate of the great dry dock, is examined by Germans on the morning after the Saint-Nazaire raid. Even though the ship later blew up and destroyed the gate, German propagandists used this picture in stories calling the raid "new proof of England's military impotence."

Months after the raid, the remnants of the Campbeltown (circle) lie in the drained dry dock. The pump house (cross) and the old harbor entrance (rectangle) were wrecked by the British. Later, the Germans built a sand embankment to protect the dock's smashed gate (arrow), where the ship blew up.

Just after midnight on March 28, 1942, 630 British Commandos and sailors raced up the Loire estuary toward Saint-Nazaire aboard 18 small armed boats and one obsolete American Lend-Lease destroyer, the *Campbeltown*. Their mission was to wreck the only dry dock on the Atlantic coast big enough to handle Germany's huge battleship, the *Tirpitz*, thereby reducing her ability to stage devastating attacks on transatlantic convoys bound for the British Isles.

The raiders' main weapon of destruction was the *Campbeltown* herself; concealed above her fuel compartment were five tons of high explosives connected to delayed-action fuses. To confuse the German defenders, the British had disguised the destroyer as a German torpedo boat, cutting her funnels aslant and topping her masts with captured German battle flags.

The ship's disguise fooled the Germans just long enough. Although they spotted the floating time bomb more than a mile from her target, they waited until the old destroyer was approximately half a mile from the dry dock before firing. With machine-gun bullets and artillery shells battering her armored hull, the *Campbeltown* burst through an antitorpedo net, smashed into the huge dry-dock gate and stuck there at dead center *(arrow, above right)*, her bow crumpled by the impact. The men aboard set their time fuses and abandoned ship.

Meanwhile, combat units and demolition teams from the small boats were busily wrecking other port facilities, including the water pumps and operating equipment for the dry dock. The boats provided cover fire, and one of them released delayed-action torpedoes into a metal gate blocking the old entrance to the harbor. Caught in a deadly cross fire, 10 of the small boats were hit and began sinking. At 2:50 a.m., Naval Commander R. E. D. Ryder *(right)* gave the order to withdraw. The eight vessels that were still afloat managed to rescue only 271 men.

In spite of the heavy losses, the raid turned out to be a smashing success—though how smashing was not apparent at first. The following morning, while curious Germans *(above left)* poked around the *Campbeltown*, time fuses detonated her charges. A tremendous explosion ripped the destroyer in half and blew aside the dry-dock gate, and a great surge of water carried the vessel's aft section through the gap into the dock itself. The blast killed more than 200 Germans.

Two days later, as the German work details were cleaning up the wreckage, the delayed-action torpedoes exploded and destroyed the old harbor entrance.

Though the Germans spent 18 months and huge sums of money trying to repair the dry dock for the *Tirpitz*, the battleship remained in northern waters, unable to impede the shipment of Britain-bound American manpower and supplies.

Commander R. E. D. Ryder was awarded the Victoria Cross for his service as the Naval chief of the raid.

balmy summer night. The sea was calm, the wind quiet. For much of the voyage the moon shone down, illuminating the low silhouettes of 237 blacked-out Royal Navy ships—destroyers, troop carriers, tank landing craft, assault boats and antiaircraft barges traveling in parallel columns. For the members of the invasion force—nearly 5,000 Canadian infantrymen and tank crews, 1,100-odd British Commandos, 15 Free French soldiers, five expatriate German interpreters and a complement of 50 U.S. Rangers, the new American counterpart of the British Commandos—these were the last moments of peace and reflection.

The fleet passed easily through the German coastal minefield, which had been cleared hours earlier by 15 British minesweepers. Just before 3 a.m. the ships drew up about 12 miles from the coast, and their crews began to prepare the landing craft for the run to the shore. Everything was going exactly according to plan. Radio silence had been maintained; no enemy ships or planes had appeared. There seemed every chance that Operation Jubilee would hold on to its most crucial asset—surprise.

The troop ships lowered their landing craft into the water, and the men of the four preliminary assault forces clambered down into them. These forces—one each assigned to destroy the two outlying coastal batteries and to overrun the two coastal headland positions—were scheduled to land at 4:50 a.m., just before dawn. If the Berneval and Varengeville coastal batteries were not silenced, their big guns would be turned on the Jubilee fleet with full fury. If the headlands were not neutralized, the main assault force, scheduled to land on the Dieppe beach at 5:20 a.m., would fall prey to raking fire from both sides. To keep the element of surprise, the four assault teams would have to land at the same time. Any deviation in their schedule and they would pay the consequences of landing against enemy forces that would by then be fully alerted by the sounds of combat up or down the coast.

Soon after 3 a.m. the four flotillas of landing craft began to follow behind the gunboats guiding them to their respective beaches. For 37 minutes all went well. Then disaster struck. At 3:47 on the far left of the strung-out assault forces, men aboard the 23 landing craft of No. 3 Commando were suddenly startled to see the silhouette of a darkened ship dead ahead. Before the crews could take evasive action, a star shell shot into the sky, illuminating the black sea in its brilliant glow and revealing the unmistakable outline of a German convoy of five small cargo ships and three armed escorts steaming southwestward along the coast in the direction of Dieppe.

It was the cruelest luck imaginable—a few minutes earlier or later and the two flotillas would have passed each other unobserved in the darkness. But it need never have happened. Since 10:40 the previous evening the convoy had been observed on radar, first at Dover, and later at the Royal Navy headquarters in Portsmouth by a young Wren with a brother in No. 3 Commando. Two warnings had been radioed to the *Jubilee* fleet, but because of some technical breakdown on the headquarters ship, the destroyer H.M.S. *Calpe*, neither message had been received. For the lack of warning, the 460 men of No. 3 Commando were virtually helpless as the Germans opened fire. Most of the landing craft were unarmed and unarmored wooden boats, whose only defense was to speed off in all directions.

But the British gunboats accompanying this part of the invasion fleet put up a stiff fight. Jagged flickers of orange, marking the muzzle blast of their guns, erupted across the dark sea. A German ship exploded and burned on the water. The flames revealed another German ship sinking fast and three more retreating into the darkness. The British gunboat leading the Commando landing craft was stopped by a shell in its boilers. Some of the landing craft went down. Some turned back. Five on the left and a solitary one on the right held their course. As a coherent force No. 3 Commando had all but ceased to exist.

The roar and flash of gunfire caused confusion for miles around. The British destroyer escort, five miles away to the east, thought the battle was taking place on the land. The headquarters ship had no idea where the gunfire was coming from. German sentries in their lookouts on the cliffs raised the alarm, but some of their superiors thought the sea battle was a routine convoy interception and gave no order to stand to. At 4:15 a.m. the gunfire died down, then ceased. For the next half hour all was quiet on the water.

To the men on board the solitary landing craft now spearheading the Commando 3 attack, the quiet seemed ominous and unreal. To Lieutenant Henry Thomas Buckee,

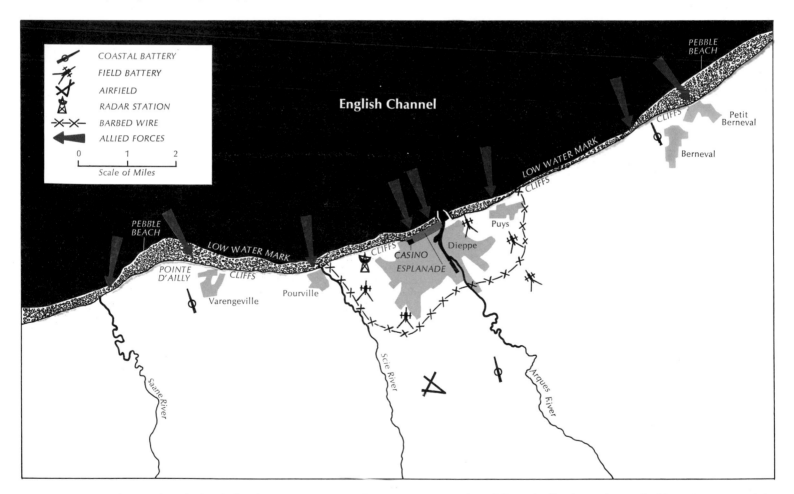

The biggest raid of the War, launched at daybreak on August 19, 1942, by some 6,000 British and Canadian troops, was a complex operation involving five assaults on the German-held French port of Dieppe and its outlying defenses. To permit the British fleet to approach Dieppe safely, Commandos attacked the long-range gun batteries at Berneval and Varengeville. Both of these two-pronged assaults prevented the enemy guns from firing on the fleet. To knock out guns that threatened the main assault on Dieppe itself, other units attacked batteries on top of the flanking headlands at Puys and Pourville. These attacks were bloody failures. When the main assault force hit the beach at Dieppe, the troops were mowed down by heavy fire from both headlands—as well as from shore-front machine-gun nests. Following a desperate morning-long battle, the raiders withdrew. Their casualties totaled 4,394 dead, wounded, missing and taken prisoner—more than two thirds of the whole force.

the landing craft commander, Major Peter Young, the officer in charge, and the five sailors and 19 soldiers with them, it seemed as if they were about to attack the armed might of German-occupied Europe completely on their own. They could see no sign of any other Allied soldiers or ships, not even the other stragglers from their own force. The men were on schedule, but they felt very vulnerable and alone as their boat drew close to the French cliffs and their objective, the Berneval gun battery that controlled the easterly sea approaches to Dieppe.

As the solitary landing craft came in below the cliffs to the east of Dieppe, Lieutenant Buckee said to Major Young:

"There you are, there's your beach."

"What do we do now?" the major asked.

"My orders are to land even if there's only one boat."

"Those are my orders too," Young agreed. "We are to land whatever happens, even if we have to swim."

At 4:45 a.m., five minutes early, the landing craft touched down at the edge of the secluded beach of Belleville, and the 20 Commandos raced up the rocky beach and into the mouth of a deep gully. It was the only exit from the beach, and the Germans had strung barbed wire up and down its flanks. The Commandos used the wire as climbing ropes and pulled themselves up the gully to the top of the cliff. Then they spread out around the gun battery and, using scrub brush for cover, opened fire. Outnumbered by more than 10 to 1, they could only hope to distract the 200-man German garrison from the main assault on Dieppe farther down the coast.

For about an hour and a half the Commandos pestered the battery. At one point the exasperated Germans swiveled a big 6-inch gun around and attempted to blast the Commandos out with artillery shells at a range of 150 yards. But the gun could not be depressed low enough to hit such a close target, and the shells roared harmlessly out over the French countryside. Eventually the Commandos' ammunition ran low, and Major Young's handful of men were forced to withdraw to the beach and reembark at 8:10 a.m. They did not lose a man.

The other landing craft of No. 3 Commando managed to reach their beach 20 minutes late. All the advantage of surprise was gone. They landed in broad daylight in the face of the determined fire of a fully alerted enemy. None

reached the Berneval battery. Many were gunned down in the boats, on the beach and in the gully beyond. Some hid in the nearby hamlet of Petit Berneval but were later betrayed by the villagers and rounded up. At the end of the morning 38 of those who had landed lay dead and 82 were prisoners. Among the dead was 19-year-old Ranger Lieutenant Edwin Loustalot. He was the first American soldier of the War to be killed on European soil.

At the opposite end of the landing area, 11 miles west of the Berneval battery, No. 4 Commando was right on time to make its assault against the other coastal battery, at Varengeville. This force was led imperturbably by Lieut. Colonel the Lord Lovat, chief of Clan Frazer, who went into battle dressed as if for a Highlands sporting expedition—in corduroy slacks and a gray sweater and packing a Winchester hunting rifle. His 252 Commandos landed in two groups on adjacent beaches and quickly mounted their pincer attack on the six-gun battery. The 112 defenders were overwhelmed by a bayonet and knife attack of such fury and efficiency that it left only four of the Germans alive. The Commandos blew up the six big guns and set fire to the battery installations. Then, at precisely 7:30, just as planned, they reembarked and went home, taking with them their wounded, the four German survivors and some new-laid eggs presented by an elderly Frenchwoman.

The British Commando attacks on the outer flanks had accomplished their objectives, preventing the big coastal batteries from bombarding the naval force assembled off Dieppe during the most crucial part of the raid. But the two other preliminary assaults, intended to secure the headlands flanking the beach at Dieppe, soon collapsed, dooming the main attack on the town itself.

To the east of Dieppe, the landing craft carrying the Royal Regiment of Canada became badly scattered as they began their run into the little resort beach at Puys. The Royals lost 17 precious minutes while their boats regrouped. During the delay a German soldier at Puys, awakened by the gunfire at Berneval to the east, had rushed to his gun and began firing into the night, rousing his comrades. By the time the Royals landed at Puys the Germans were waiting for them.

German fire raked the landing craft, clanging against the metal-sided wooden boats or piercing them entirely. The men sprawled, clung to the deck and watched blue and white tracer bullets rushing by overhead with a sharp sound like dry twigs snapping. Then the landing craft touched down, and their ramps were lowered and the men stood up. The butchery began.

Fewer than 100 Germans defended Puys against more than 650 Canadian invaders. But their guns, mounted in concrete pillboxes and fortified houses on the rugged headland, commanded the entire 200 yards of pebbly beach. First, German snipers singled out officers and signalmen and put bullets through their heads or their radio sets, thus depriving the Royals of both leadership and communications. Heavy machine guns, antitank and antiaircraft guns, mortars and rifle fire smashed the Royals at almost point-blank range. The beach was scourged with orange flame,

roaring shell bursts, flying shrapnel and showers of pebbles.

As the soldiers began jumping into the shallow water, they were cut to pieces, blown to bits, disemboweled, blinded, mangled and killed. Fewer than 20 men in the first wave reached the relative safety of the sea wall, some 50 yards from the boats. In minutes the beach was littered with the dead and dying. A blast of machine-gun fire cut off the legs of a sergeant, and as he fell the same burst severed his hand at the wrist. Along the water's edge the spume of the waves flopped blood-pink on the shore.

As the newly arrived landing craft lowered their ramps, their crouching human cargo was exposed to the direct aim of machine-gun fire from concrete pillboxes in the sea wall, and the men in the first rows were slaughtered. The men behind them were so shocked by the bloody spectacle that

Towering over the French coast three and a half miles to the west of Dieppe, the 80-foot-high lighthouse at Pointe d'Ailly guided the gunboats and landing craft of No. 4 Commando—one of four units that preceded the main invasion force—as the troops on board prepared their predawn attack on enemy gun emplacements. Even though the beacon was a help to the Commandos, one officer remarked that under its light," we felt like thieves in an alley when the policeman's torch shines."

they froze in the landing craft and had to be forced out at pistol point by Naval officers, who threatened to shoot them if they did not disembark. They ran into the withering fire, and within three minutes the Royal Regiment, the crack battalion of the Canadian Army Overseas, had virtually ceased to exist.

Some men did succeed in crossing the beach to the sea wall, moving miraculously through small gaps between the machine guns' field of fire. But the sea wall was 10 to 12 feet high, and the esplanade above it was wreathed with dense coils of barbed wire and swept with still more machine-gun bursts. It was suicidal to try to scale the wall but almost as dangerous to remain huddled below it, caught in constant enfilading fire. Before long the living and the dead formed a compact mass at the base of the wall.

Some men lay there, pretending to be dead, knowing that the slightest movement would bring gunfire down on them. Others were driven by rage and despair to acts of spectacular foolhardiness. One soldier went berserk and stood up in full view of the Germans, firing his Bren gun at them and screaming as he did so; he was still screaming when a hail of lead lifted him off his feet. A lone lieutenant charged a pillbox on the sea wall, heedlessly wading forward in a stream of bullets, and as he died he flung a grenade through the gun slit. Another officer attacked the headland all by himself, clawing his way up the high chalk cliff. As he climbed, Germans and Canadians alike stopped firing and watched in awe. He was about 80 feet up when his strength gave out and he clung to the cliff unable to move up or down. At that moment a single shot rang out across the almost silent beach, and the officer shuddered and fell backward into space.

A few men led charmed lives. Under constant heavy fire they went about their duties like sleepwalkers. One man, Corporal L. G. Ellis, managed to climb up a flight of stairs in the sea wall. He made his way inland, wandered about aimlessly, killed a sniper, dodged a shell, shot up Puys village, returned to the sea wall, ran down the beach, took off his clothes, waded through the sticky, blood-filmed water and the bobbing bodies, then swam safely out to sea.

Landing in the Royals' second wave, Lieut. Colonel Douglas Catto attempted to organize his ravaged battalion on the beach. Cutting through the coils of barbed wire on top of the sea wall, Catto and 20 men rushed up onto high ground beyond. The Germans at once unleashed a drenching fire that isolated Catto from his regiment.

On the beach, panic had broken out. When a landing craft tried to withdraw, it was stormed by hysterical soldiers who rose from the heaps of dead along the sea wall. In their efforts to climb aboard they overwhelmed the craft by the sheer weight of their numbers, as the sailors tried in vain to beat them off with the boat hooks. The craft, ramp down and doors jammed open, began to fill with water while German fire riddled most of the men on board. About 50 yards from the shore the sinking craft was hit by a shell and capsized. Some men clung to the upturned hull and were ultimately saved, but those who floundered in the water nearby were machine-gunned to death.

By 7 a.m. the end was near. The Germans emerged from their fortified gun emplacements on the cliffs and dropped stick grenades down on the Royals wriggling and ducking among the rocks below. Shortly after 8 a.m. the Germans saw a white handkerchief knotted to a rifle barrel being waved above the sea wall at the western end of the beach and ceased their fire. At 8:35 a.m. the men of the German garrison reported to their commander, General Conrad Haase: "Puys firmly in our hands; the enemy has lost about 500 men prisoners and dead."

Exactly 278 Canadians were taken captive, more than a third of them wounded. Lieut. Colonel Catto and his party were the last to surrender, at about 4:30 that afternoon. Of the 650 men who had actually landed at Puys, 67 returned to England that day. One of them was Corporal Ellis, who had spent two and a half hours swimming about before he was fished from the sea. The Royals had suffered 94.5 per cent casualties.

While the Royals were dying in droves, another Canadian regiment, the South Saskatchewan, was struggling to take the west headland overlooking the Dieppe beach. Unlike the Royals, the South Saskatchewans had landed at the little resort of Pourville, two miles to the west of Dieppe, nearly on time—and achieved almost total surprise. They rapidly overran Pourville and began their attack on the German installations in and around the fortified farm called Les Quatre Vents, or The Four Winds, on the headland.

Half an hour after the Sasks hit the beach, the follow-up battalion, the Queen's Own Cameron Highlanders of Canada, landed at Pourville with a bagpiper playing Scottish battle tunes—the sounds of his instrument were mistaken by some Canadians on shore for the squeaking wheels of German horse-drawn artillery. Some of the Camerons reinforced the South Sasks; others advanced inland toward the airfield at Saint Aubin, and after penetrating about a mile they laid low in a wood and waited for the Canadian tanks that were supposed to join them from the main landing at Dieppe. But no tanks came and eventually the outgunned Camerons fell back to the beach.

In and around Pourville, the Saskatchewans had bogged down in fruitless actions against stiffening German resistance. The farm, a radar station and an antiaircraft battery on the headland remained in German hands. Having failed to take their objectives in time, both the Sasks and the Camerons began a fighting retreat from Pourville to the beach. There, under increasing German fire, they watched for boats to come to evacuate them. They waited—and died—for one hour.

At 5:20 a.m., when the main attack on Dieppe got under way, the commanders aboard the headquarters ship *Calpe* had no inkling of the failure at Pourville or the calamity at Puys. General Roberts, commanding the ground forces, might have had time to cancel at least part of the assault had word reached him that the two headland landings had gone wrong. But he and Captain Hughes-Hallett, commanding the naval forces, were forced to operate in a vacuum until it was much too late to save the main force from pointless sacrifice in a campaign already lost.

The naval smoke screens, set up to conceal the ships from enemy gunners, also hid the joint commanders' view of the fighting on the beaches. Communications between the *Calpe* and the shore had broken down as radio operators were killed on the beaches and their radios destroyed. To confuse matters even more, the Germans transmitted deceptive messages, such as "Royal Regiment of Canada not landed." In sum, the commanders could not form any clear picture of the preliminary assaults. Not until nearly three hours after the first landings at Puys did the commanders receive trustworthy information that the Royals were in trouble. The pathetic message, much delayed in retransmission, read: "Is there any chance of getting us off?" By then there was little the commanders could do to change the course of events at Puys or anywhere else.

The plan for the main assault at Dieppe called for landing two regiments of Canadian infantry—the Royal Hamilton Light Infantry on the western half of the beach, the Essex Scottish on the eastern half. Their first mission was to knock out the German defenses so that the tanks of the Calgary Regiment could move on into the town.

As the landing craft carrying the 1,552 infantrymen and tank crews sped in toward Dieppe, the 4-inch guns of four British destroyers opened up with a 10-minute bombardment of the fortified beach-front buildings along the Boulevard de Verdun. At the same time, 50 cannon-firing Hurricanes swooped down in a brief low-level attack against the German defenses. To the men in the landing craft, the sea and air bombardment seemed outrageously inadequate, as indeed it was. When the boats had about 200 yards to go, three red flares burst in the air, signaling the end of the abbreviated bombardment. The ships' guns ceased firing. The Hurricanes flew away. Pinned down no longer, the Germans retaliated with a fearsome mortar barrage.

The Canadians bore up under German fire all the way to the beach. There they were pinned down, wounded and

Surrounded by battle-weary men, Lieut. Colonel the Lord Lovat, leader of No. 4 Commando, checks his casualty list after returning to Newhaven, England, from the disastrous Dieppe raid. Lord Lovat executed his attack with such precision and dash that only 12 of his 252 men were lost.

killed. The naval shelling had done little but set houses on fire. The cannon of the RAF Hurricanes had barely chipped the thick concrete of the German pillboxes.

The sea front was held by only a single company of enemy infantry, but the positions of the Germans were virtually unassailable. Soldiers were firing from the roofs and windows of the houses along the boulevard and from the casino on the beach. Other Germans poured down enfilading fire from the headlands and from machine-gun nests in the eastern cliffs.

These machine guns, unreported by British intelligence, cut broad swaths through the Essex Scottish, which landed almost below the eastern cliffs. Within 25 minutes of its landing, the regiment had lost 30 to 40 per cent of its men. In the next 45 minutes its casualties mounted to nearly 80 per cent. One group of about 15 Scots managed to cross the sea wall, blasting through the barbed wire on top. They raced across bullet-torn lawns, reached the houses beyond and fought their way to the docks. There they ran into impenetrable fire and were forced to fall back to the beach.

At the western end of the beach the Hamiltons fared a little better. Those nearest fought their way into the casino, whose front abutted the sea wall, and battled the defenders from room to room. In an hour the Canadians captured the lower floors of the casino, but the top floor remained in German hands throughout the morning. From the cover of this building, several small parties of Canadians dashed into the town. Two groups fought their way to a movie theater and then on to the Church of Saint-Rémy, but they were forced to withdraw.

The tanks of the Calgary Regiment, which had landed behind the assault forces, had even less luck in penetrating the Dieppe defenses. No matter what the crewmen tried, their tanks—27 of the new Churchill type that had never before been in action—could not break into the town. Several of these were put out of action shortly after landing. Fifteen climbed over the sea wall, but strong, concrete antitank barriers denied them entrance to the streets leading into Dieppe. As they rumbled about the esplanade, the tanks were easily picked off by German antitank guns. A few survivors returned to the beach, where they took up a hull-down position for a final fight.

All this time the commanders on board the *Calpe* had received no sure indication of how the main assault was faring. General Roberts did get a message saying that the Essex Scottish had fought their way into town. Thinking that meant the whole regiment and not just the few survivors who had done so, Roberts ordered part of his reserves, the French Canadians of the Fusiliers Mont-Royal, to land in support. He assumed he was exploiting success; in fact he was reinforcing failure.

At 7 a.m. the Mont-Royals went in. Nearly 200 men in bullet-riddled wooden boats were landed in the wrong place, on an isolated little beach below the west cliff, from where they could neither move nor take any part in the fighting. The rest of the Mont-Royals landed in the right place but met the fate of the regiments that had preceded them there. Most stayed pinned down in hollows on the rocky beach or behind the hulks of wrecked tanks. Only one group of Mont-Royals was able to scramble off the beach and penetrate the town. Led by Sergeant Pierre Dubuc, they fought their way as far as the docks. There their ammunition ran out and they were forced to surrender. They obeyed the Germans' orders to strip to their underclothes and line up against a wall. Then the nearly naked Mont-Royals overpowered their guard and fled through the streets back to the beach. Since they were without uniforms they were fired on by neither side.

At 8:30 a.m., General Roberts was informed that the casino had fallen into Canadian hands and that the western part of the beach was under Canadian control. Believing that the tanks were entering the town, he ordered in the last of his reserves, the Royal Marine Commandos. They moved forward under the cover of a smoke screen and supporting naval fire. But when they emerged from the smoke they saw before them a nightmarish panorama of burning landing craft, disabled tanks and dead and wounded soldiers amid erupting shells fired at point-blank range.

The Commando leader, Colonel J. P. Phillips, put on a pair of white gloves and, turning his back to the enemy, motioned to the following boats to turn back from the slaughter. Phillips continued to signal after everyone else on his craft was killed. Then he too fell. But most of the craft did turn back, escaping annihilation.

No objectives had been taken, and German resistance

was intensifying as reinforcements arrived. The 10th Panzer Division from Amiens was moving on Pourville, and German reinforcements were getting ready to rush the beaches. Time after time, British destroyers ran a gauntlet of shellfire to blast away at the German positions, one ship coming in so close that her stern touched the bottom as she turned. At one point in the action German officers wearing white dress uniforms could be seen through binoculars by the men on the beach. The officers had drinks in their hands and cigars in their mouths and were enjoying the victorious scene from a terrace on the west headland.

At 9 a.m. Captain Hughes-Hallett advised General Roberts that if the men on the beaches were to be evacuated, the decision would have to be made at once; it would take time to organize the rescue ships. The withdrawal was fixed for the earliest time possible, 11 a.m. That meant two more hours of hell for the men on the beaches.

Overhead the RAF got the battle it wanted. Its 74 Allied squadrons met the Luftwaffe, which flew in like hornets from bases as far away as Germany, Belgium and Holland. Over the beaches and the fleet the two air forces fought a massive battle. The RAF lost 106 planes to the Germans' 48.

The evacuation was a horror from the start. As the rescue ships' sirens screamed out their urgent summons, the soldiers on the Dieppe beaches struggled down to the water's edge in dazed little groups, many falling along the way. As their fire diminished, the Germans' intensified, and the survivors clustered helpless in the midst of an appalling barrage. The men in the tanks, sacrificing all hope of escape for themselves, kept up such covering fire as they could and prevented the Germans from storming the beach. An RAF Hurricane formation saved many soldiers by laying a smoke screen between them and German machine guns that were only 200 yards away.

But there was no withstanding the massed artillery bombardment, which by now had been reinforced by additional guns. Canadians died en masse at the water's edge. Many others died in the sea when their landing craft, overloaded with desperate men, capsized or were blown apart. In one overcrowded boat the Canadians shot their German prisoners and heaved the bodies overboard to lighten the sinking craft. All told, only 370 Canadians managed to escape the beach at Dieppe; 1,600 stayed there, 500 of them dead, the rest prisoners.

At the same time, the shattered troops who had tried unsuccessfully to take the west headland dominating the Dieppe beach were being evacuated from the beach at Pourville—with much the same harrowing results. Approximately 690 soldiers were killed or wounded. The living were forced to construct a parapet out of the bodies of the dead to cover their retreat. All together, 601 men were eventually extricated from Pourville.

At 12:20 the last attempts at evacuation were abandoned. Half an hour later, the *Calpe* sailed close to the shore at high speed to give short-range covering fire for any men who might still be alive on the beach. For the first time General Roberts was able to see the battlefield for himself. He could not make out any signs of life. At 1:08 p.m. he received his last message from the senior officer alive on shore: "Our people have surrendered." On that battered beach, the walking wounded began to drag their crippled comrades out of the water, saving them from drowning as the tide came in. Then they sat on the stones and wept.

Aboard the *Calpe*, a message from General Roberts was attached to the leg of a carrier pigeon and dispatched to the headquarters of the Canadian Army in England. "Very heavy losses in men and ships," read the message. "Did everything possible to get men off, but in order to get any home had to come to sad decision to abandon remainder. This was joint decision by Force Commanders. Obviously operation completely lacked surprise."

At 1:30 the remnants of the fleet and the remnants of the 2nd Canadian Division set course for England. "The journey back," a British Marine recorded afterward, "was one of utter misery. The mess deck was crowded with survivors, wounded lay around everywhere, a stench of mutilated humanity prevailed. I was in a state of utter shock. I lay on the deck and tried to gather my shattered wits together. I had no knowledge of what our role had been, I knew even less of what, if anything, we had achieved. I suppose someone, somewhere, was able to make a pattern of the day's events. I couldn't."

At 5:40 p.m. Field Marshal Gerd von Rundstedt, Commander in Chief of the German Army West, recorded in his diary: "No armed Englishman remains on the Continent."

In the ships taking them back across the Channel the shocked survivors fell into a deathlike sleep. Some were found still asleep in dark corners of their vessels 24 hours after their return to England. Five hospitals worked without a break for two days and two nights. In one operating room eight doctors at four tables did surgery for 40 hours nonstop. One doctor alone did 167 operations in a single night. "When some of the lads awakened from the ether," one survivor recalled, "they lived the battle all over again. The language was so cruel it was no wonder the nurses wore earplugs."

The Dieppe raid—a gallant, ill-planned rehearsal for the Second Front—was in almost every respect a disaster for the Allies. Of the 5,100 troops who actually landed, 3,648 failed to return. The Commandos, fighting on their own initiative, had fared well, suffering only 247 dead, wounded and prisoners. Not so the Canadians, who had been obliged to fight by the book; 907 were killed, and 1,946 taken prisoner, 568 of them wounded—virtually wiping out the 2nd Canadian Division. The Royal Navy lost a destroyer, 33 landing craft and 550 men. The RAF lost another 153 men. The German losses were light: 316 in the Army, 113 in the Navy, 162 in the Luftwaffe—a total of 591, of whom 297 had been killed.

The Dieppe raid was a great German victory. Marshal Henri Philippe Pétain and Pierre Laval, heads of the French Vichy government, were the first to congratulate the German High Command for the "rapid clearing of French soil."

Strategically, from the British point of view the assault was a total loss: it not only failed to cripple the Luftwaffe, it also failed to relieve German pressure on the Russian front. But it served some purposes. The action convinced Hitler that it was possible to repel an invasion at the water's edge. It deluded him into believing that the Allies' next invasion would be directed against a port and thus led him to neglect the defense of the open beaches. For the British, as Churchill later wrote of the raid, "it was a mine of experience." It taught the Second Front planners that no invasion could succeed if it was directed against a fortified port rather than open beaches. It proved that surprise was not so important or reliable as a massive and prolonged preliminary bombardment from sea and air, together with overwhelming close-fire support during the initial stages of the attack. It also showed that, once control of the air was established, a large fleet could be maintained off an enemy coast indefinitely; that tanks and signal parties should not be landed before beaches had been secured; and that attacks against heavily defended areas should be developed around the flanks rather than head on.

Many of these lessons were not new, but their importance was doubly underlined after Dieppe. So, too, was the need for a properly trained permanent naval force to operate landing craft, for properly organized headquarters ships, for special armored vehicles to protect the beach demolition squads, and for many other technical innovations in equipment and their use. Medical analysis of wounds pointed up the need for better designed landing craft to cut down on the number of casualties. "For every soldier who died at Dieppe," said Mountbatten later, "10 were saved on D-Day."

The Second Front planners took all of these lessons to heart, as several shrewd Germans expected they would.

"It would be an error," advised Field Marshal von Rundstedt in his summary of the Dieppe raid, "to believe that the enemy will mount his next operation in the same manner. . . . Next time he will do things differently."

AFTERMATH OF A TRAGIC RAID

In the aftermath of the disastrous Dieppe raid, wounded Canadian soldiers lie on the beach beside an abandoned tank, while a landing craft burns on the water.

STARTLING EVENTS IN DIEPPE

At 2 p.m. on August 19, 1942, the bewildered citizens of the port city of Dieppe, France, slowly emerged from their homes and stared about them. Their city was a shambles. Buildings had been gutted by shells, and streets were littered with roof tiles, shattered glass and fallen telephone lines. Hundreds of prisoners, bloodstained and pale, were being marched to collection points by German guards. On the beach lay battered tanks and wrecked landing craft. Bodies were everywhere—some hanging on barbed wire, many huddled under the sea wall.

What the stunned people of Dieppe were seeing was the aftermath of one of the biggest and boldest commando raids of the War, in which some 6,000 British and Canadian troops had stormed ashore at dawn along a broad front, and, after eight hours of fierce fighting, had withdrawn in bloody defeat. The population, warned by a BBC broadcast "to refrain from all action which might compromise its safety," had remained under cover throughout the raid.

More than 400 dead raiders were found right after the attackers withdrew, and within the next four days the sea washed up 475 more. The Germans buried the dead in a mass grave and permitted the townspeople to cover the mound with hundreds of wreaths and flowers. A few days after the burial, the Germans made an unexpected show of respect for their fallen enemies. The Wehrmacht Graves Commission sent coffins to Dieppe, and 500 soldiers reburied the dead in individual graves with full military honors.

Then the Germans made another surprising gesture: they rewarded the townspeople for taking no part in the raid. Hitler sent Dieppe a gift of 10 million francs and, more important, he announced that he was releasing French prisoners of war from Dieppe.

It happened that the Dieppe officials had only a sketchy list of local prisoners of war, so they asked the townspeople to supply them with the proper names and addresses—all that the Germans required for releasing a POW. The officials were not too fussy about verifying the names and addresses given them; they simply handed the long list over to the German authorities. Thus, in a happy epilogue to the tragic raid, hundreds of Frenchmen were allowed to go home—including many who had never set foot in Dieppe.

French POWs, freed by Hitler to reward Dieppe citizens for taking no part in the raid, wave joyously from a homeward-bound train covered with graffiti.

After the morning-long battle, townspeople of Dieppe sweep up the debris in front of a barbershop. By 4 p.m. nearly all of the stores were open again.

Wounded Canadians, rounded up by German soldiers, lie waiting on the roadside for transportation at Pourville, scene of bloody fighting west of Dieppe.

Under guard at a waterfront assembly point, Canadian prisoners await orders from the Germans. A few captives served as stretcher-bearers for the wounded.

Canadian prisoners march in a grim parade through Dieppe. Captives were searched, questioned and registered before being sent to POW camps in Germany.

HARSH TREATMENT FOR CAPTURED RAIDERS

In the hours after the raid, more than 2,000 captured Canadian and British troops were herded together in Dieppe. Some of the prisoners were dressed only in their underclothes and makeshift shoes made of rubber strips torn from their Mae West life jackets; these soldiers had been left behind during the raiders' desperate withdrawal, and had stripped off their uniforms and boots and swum out to sea, trying in vain to catch an outbound landing craft.

More than 500 prisoners were badly injured. One man with a huge abdominal wound struggled along holding back his intestines with his hands. However, despite their wounds and their defeat, many POWs marched in step with their heads high. They received treatment at a Dieppe hospital and, in a week, were sent to prison camps in Germany.

Unfortunately, a relic of the raid added to the sufferings of the imprisoned raiders. On the battle-torn beach, inside a waterproof package, a German officer found a copy of the British plan for the Dieppe operation. The plan contained orders that "wherever possible, prisoners' hands will be tied to prevent destruction of their documents." The Germans were infuriated by what they called these "Wild West measures." Then came a further provocation: the British raided one of the Channel Islands on October 4 and tied up several defenders. In retaliation, the Germans kept the Dieppe prisoners bound with ropes and handcuffs from 8 a.m. to 9 p.m. They pursued the practice for more than a year before relenting.

A Luftwaffe officer studies Allied equipment left on a landing craft. The square marker on the craft identified it to others heading shoreward during the raid.

Laden with captured gear, a German leaves a beach to the dead.

LESSONS LEARNED FROM THE SPOILS OF BATTLE

The Dieppe raid left behind an enormous and valuable booty. The Germans collected several landing craft, 28 Churchill tanks, one command car, 80 mortars, six self-propelled guns, 60 antitank rifles and some 1,500 small arms. They carefully studied all the captured matériel, but they were most interested in the 43-ton Churchills. These were the Allies' latest tanks, specially waterproofed to operate in six feet of water.

German technicians ran thorough tests on the Churchills and wrote detailed reports on the tanks' strengths and weaknesses. Months later, a British spy stole copies of the reports and forwarded them to London. The British welcomed the Germans' shrewd analysis of the tanks' defects and used it in designing later tanks.

The Germans' final assessment of the Dieppe raid was equally astute, if less palatable to the British. The German High Command called it an "amateur undertaking" that was "carried out in opposition to all good military sense."

A tank landing craft, one of several stranded on the beach at Dieppe, gives the Germans a rare opportunity to analyze the recent progress of British designers.

At a German base near Paris, General Sepp Dietrich, the noted tank corps leader, examines a captured Churchill, brought from Dieppe for study and display.

On the day after the raid, the camouflaged Dieppe casino, where room-to-room fighting raged for hours, stands as a battered reminder of the Germans' victory.

On the 12th of March, 1943, British Lieut. General Sir Frederick E. Morgan stepped into a crowded elevator at New Scotland Yard, London, on his way to a meeting at Combined Operations Headquarters, the amphibious command run by Admiral Mountbatten. The admiral himself jumped into the elevator at the last minute and greeted Morgan warmly. In spite of the crowd of people around them, Mountbatten congratulated Morgan on his appointment as Chief of Staff to the Supreme Allied Commander (Designate), or COSSAC for short—a title used to describe Morgan's whole operation. COSSAC was the planning embryo for the Supreme Headquarters of the Allied Expeditionary Force, or SHAEF, which in 1944 would command the long-awaited invasion of occupied Europe.

Thus Morgan learned for the first time of the daunting assignment that was to engage all his energies for the next year. He was an excellent choice for the post, having had solid experience in both invasion planning and invasion operation. In 1942 he had been a task-force commander in the invasion of North Africa, and he had just completed preliminary planning for the invasion of Sicily, which was to take place in July. Morgan was also a self-starter with extraordinary executive ability.

Morgan immediately established headquarters in Norfolk House, St. James' Square, in London. He gathered together a small but rapidly growing staff of British and American officers; COSSAC had to be a joint effort since neither Britain nor the United States had the resources to mount the invasion alone. The staff was already hard at work when, in April, General Sir Alan Brooke, Chief of the Imperial General Staff, handed Morgan his orders from the Combined Chiefs of Staff.

"There it is," Brooke said. "It won't work but you must bloody well make it."

Morgan's orders called for the planning of a large-scale invasion of the Continent, to be launched as early as possible in 1944. This immediately forced him and his staff to make a giant leap in military logic. Since it was impossible to plan an invasion without deciding first its ultimate goal, COSSAC set as the objective the defeat of Germany on German soil and drew up a master plan—later code-named *Overlord*—that estimated the enormous numbers of troops

2

A British general lays the groundwork for "Overlord"
"We must take a port with us"
Crisis over a shortage in landing craft
SHAEF and Eisenhower take command
The magnificent deceptions of Operation "Fortitude"
Paving the way with saturation bombing
The countdown for invasion
Alarming last-minute German troop movements
History's most important weather forecast
Ike says go

OVERTURES TO OVERLORD

and the immense quantities of matériel that would be needed at various stages in the campaign to reach that goal. In effect, COSSAC worked backward through *Overlord* to its initial assault phase, Operation *Neptune*.

The planning of the invasion, which preoccupied Morgan and COSSAC throughout 1943, was a mind-boggling enterprise. No useful precedent existed. Unlike the massive invasion of Sicily, which would begin with most of the troops and supplies within striking distance in North Africa, the assault on Western Europe had to be started virtually from scratch, and it depended on the speculative dates when manpower and matériel would become available in the huge quantities needed. Somehow the COSSAC planners would have to produce soldiers by the millions, along with the millions of tons of paraphernalia needed to keep them living, moving and fighting. All this and more the COSSAC staff would have to do under great pressure, for the Combined Chiefs soon fixed May 1, 1944, as D-Day.

Fortunately, the planners had a wealth of data with which to begin detailed work. The sea approaches, winds, tides, nature of the beaches, their exits and hinterlands, the pros and cons of every port and beach that might be captured, airfields or ground suitable for building airfields, enemy coastal defenses, strength of enemy troops, location of enemy naval forces, the capacity of the assault area for the build-up of invasion forces—information about all these aspects of the possible invasion areas had been assiduously gathered by previous planners, using secret agents, aerial photos, Commando landing parties, even seaside picture postcards collected from prewar British tourists. All that COSSAC now had to do was dig through the files.

Morgan and COSSAC discarded old preconceptions in their search for the best area for the invasion. They considered regions as unlikely as Portugal and Norway, Denmark's Jutland and the Netherlands' Frisia—even Dunkirk. It was not just beaches they were looking for. "The landing beaches were just one x in an algebraic expression that contained half the alphabet. What was wanted was a lodgement area into which we could blast ourselves and from which our main bodies, having suitably concentrated themselves within it, could erupt to develop the campaign eastwards," Morgan wrote later.

Various factors determined the choice. One of the most important considerations was the range of friendly fighter aircraft. The Allies could not count on getting a firm foothold on the beaches without total supremacy in the air above them. Air supremacy could be gained only with an overwhelming cover of fighter planes. Since these fighters were based in England, it followed that the farther from England the invasion forces landed, the less time the planes could spend in the air over the beaches before having to turn back to refuel. In practice this meant that the invasion area had to be somewhere between Cherbourg and Flushing in the Netherlands.

The need for harbors further narrowed down the choice. Once they had landed, the invaders could not count on extending their beachhead into a staging area unless the rate of build-up of troops and matériel was greater than the Germans' rate of reinforcement with reserves. The build-up therefore depended on securing an area with wide beaches and large ports nearby, through which men and supplies could be rapidly unloaded.

Only two places were really suitable for the invasion—the Pas-de-Calais coast and the Caen sector of the Normandy coast to the west (*map, page 46*). The Pas-de-Calais was the more obvious choice. It was nearer England, so the seaborne journey of the invasion army would be shorter and simpler and air cover more easily provided. Once landed there, moreover, the Allied armies could be on the most direct route to Germany.

But because the Pas-de-Calais coast was the most obvious choice, it was also the most heavily defended section of Hitler's Atlantic Wall. Topographically it was also unsuitable. The high cliffs, narrow beaches and restricted exits would make it difficult to maintain a build-up on the beaches, so the Allies would be forced to capture a port immediately. In that respect as well the Pas-de-Calais was less than perfect. The capacity of the local ports of Calais and Boulogne was so small that the Allies would have to extend their staging area eastward or westward toward the big ports of Antwerp in Belgium or Le Havre in France, a difficult task against the expected opposition from the Germans. Finally, the English south-coast ports opposite the Pas-de-Calais were themselves too small to accommodate the invasion armada.

The Normandy coast had none of these drawbacks. "The

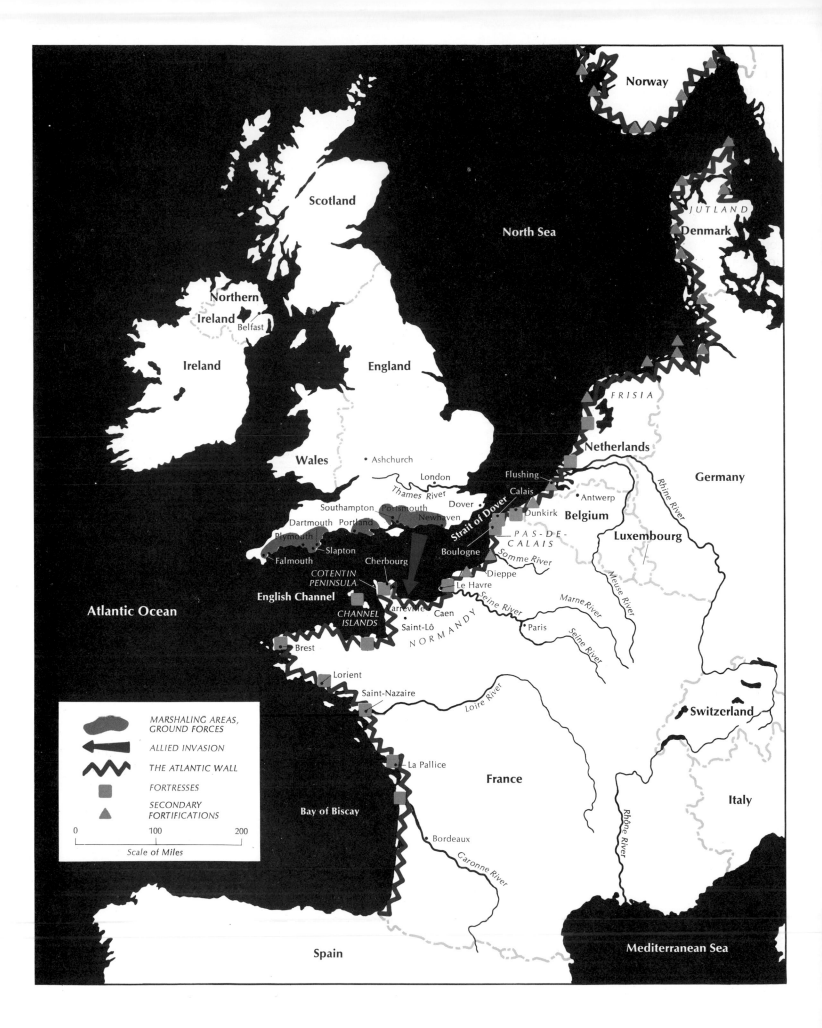

Caen sector is weakly held," COSSAC reported, "and the beaches are of high capacity and sheltered from the prevailing winds. Inland the terrain is suitable for airfield development and for the consolidation of the initial bridgeheads." Furthermore, the nearest major port, Cherbourg, was big enough to handle large amounts of matériel quickly. Normandy became the strike point.

The next problem was to determine the size of the assault. Since there were no existing guidelines for such an undertaking, the only thing to do was to make an arbitrary allocation of the forces that might be available at the time. However, the size of the invasion force was limited by the number of landing craft set aside for the assault. Morgan did not believe that enough craft would be available to transport more than three divisions on D-Day. He therefore proposed that the initial assault should be carried out along a 25-mile front by three seaborne divisions and two airborne divisions, with two additional seaborne divisions following up—a dangerously small force.

The English Channel and its weather were also factors to take into account. The Channel's big tides and extraordinary capacity for conjuring up storms often and on short notice had posed a serious problem in Britain's plans for small-scale, overnight Commando raids. Now the planners had to face the problems of using the Channel for a massive and prolonged amphibious operation.

COSSAC applied a lesson learned from the Dieppe raid: no major fortified port could be captured quickly by a frontal assault. Morgan set D-plus-14—14 days after D-Day—as the date for the capture of Cherbourg and calculated that it would take two or three months more to clear the mines and repair the damage left behind by the Germans. In the meantime, the invading troops would have to be supplied and reinforced on open beaches. But weather statistics showed that there were storms in the Channel every month of the year and that fair weather rarely lasted for more than four days at a stretch. It seemed that the only way to guarantee an uninterrupted flow of men and matériel to the Normandy front even in adverse weather was to provide sheltered water off the beaches. But how? The solution, worked out by British naval experts and construction engineers in 1943, proved to be one of the boldest and most original conceptions in military history: artificial harbors.

The basic idea of the artificial harbor had been dreamed up by Winston Churchill for a proposed invasion of Flanders in World War I. In 1917 he suggested building "a number of flat bottomed barges or caissons, made not of steel but of concrete, which would float when empty of water and thus could be towed across. On arrival the sea cocks would be opened and the caissons would settle on the bottom. By this means a torpedo- and weather-proof harbour would be created in the open sea."

Churchill's concept was brought to fruition by Hughes-Hallett, the driving force behind the raids on Saint-Nazaire and Dieppe, now a commodore and the senior Naval officer at COSSAC headquarters. In the summer of 1943, when the question of ports was raised at COSSAC, Hughes-Hallett remarked: "Well, all I can say is, if we can't capture a port we must take one with us." He believed that a large area of sheltered water could be created by sinking a line of ships in shoal waters off the invasion beaches. His scheme gave hope to the COSSAC planners. It was, they felt, the key to the whole operation.

The Combined Chiefs agreed to build two artificial harbors, later code-named Mulberry A (for the Americans) and Mulberry B (for the British)—together capable of handling 12,000 tons of stores and 2,500 vehicles a day. Since the harbors would have to be ready by May 1, 1944, only eight months were left for their design and construction.

A team consisting of the leading consultant engineers and naval contractors in Britain worked around the clock to solve the complex design problems of the Mulberries. The principal difficulty was the breakwater. Hughes-Hallett's sunken blockships alone would be inadequate. One bright idea was to create an artificial breakwater with an underwater wall of air bubbles, a method that was eventually rejected as being impractical on the scale demanded. The final plan incorporated the proposals of both Churchill and Hughes-Hallett: floating piers, caissons and blockships were all integral to the design.

More than 200 steel-and-concrete caissons were constructed; the largest, each as big as a five-story building, were 200 feet long, 55 feet wide and 60 feet high and weighed 6,000 tons. There were 23 floating pierheads, 10

On June 1, 1944, five days before D-Day, most of the million-odd German troops stationed in France and the Netherlands were dispersed along the Atlantic Wall, a 2,400-mile coastal barrier (saw-toothed line) of powerful fortresses (gray squares), lesser fortifications (gray triangles), innumerable machine-gun nests and long stretchers of formidable terrain. Most of the 3.5 million Allied troops in Britain were concentrated in southern England, in marshaling areas (shading) around the major embarkation ports. Across the English Channel, in the strongest sector of the Atlantic Wall, some 20 German divisions manned the French coast between two fortresses—the ports of Cherbourg, on the Cotentin Peninsula in Normandy, and Calais, well to the northeast. The Pas-de-Calais area, the closest to England and the likeliest invasion target, bristled with the mightiest defenses of all. But the Allies had their invasion site picked: a 59-mile stretch of the Normandy coastline west of Caen.

miles of steel roadway, 93 steel-and-concrete floats, each 200 feet long, 25 feet high and 2,000 tons in weight, and 74 cargo boats and obsolete warships to be used as blockships. To tow these vast and unwieldly parts from their moorings in creeks and inlets around the British coast to their final, exact position off an enemy shore on the far side of a treacherous sea would require every heavy-duty tug in Britain and America.

The staff of COSSAC applied another lesson from the Dieppe raid in its planning: the need for armored support as soon as the infantry had landed. General Brooke reckoned that without armor the Atlantic Wall could not be breached except at an unacceptable cost in soldiers' lives. So in March 1943 he turned the 79th British Armored Division into an experimental formation with the task of developing special armor for the invasion. The division commander was Major-General Sir Percy C. S. Hobart, a veteran of World War I and one of the great pioneer tank theoreticians, whose early ideas had been adapted by the Germans in the creation of their panzer formations.

Hobart realized that the tanks used at Dieppe had never reached their objective because most of the demolition engineers who were to have cleared the way through obstructions had been killed almost as soon as they landed. His solution was to construct tanks that could do their own demolition work. Hobart and his staff eventually produced an amazing variety of specialized armored vehicles (pages 172-181), the most important of which were devices that enabled a 33-ton Sherman tank to take to the water and swim ashore under its own power.

Yet another lesson COSSAC learned from Dieppe was the need for stronger and closer fire support for the first wave of assault troops. Clearly, neither bombing nor naval shelling could totally silence the German defenders, many of whom would be back in action soon after the bombardment ceased. To prevent assault troops from being dangerously exposed to point-blank enemy fire as they closed in on the beaches, it was essential to fill what General Paget, Commander in Chief, Home Forces, aptly called "the gap between the barrage and the bayonet." COSSAC proposed that assault infantry should be accompanied by floating artillery—guns, mortars and rocket batteries mounted in landing craft and gunboats. Later General Sir Bernard L.

Montgomery, ground commander for the invasion, proposed that some tanks on landing craft following close behind the leading infantry should provide support while they waited to land. By using both these measures, the Overlord planners hoped to saturate the German defenses with close-range fire up to the moment of landing.

Of all the technological devices thought up for Overlord, none gave COSSAC greater anxiety than the specialized landing craft. At first sight, the problem seemed to be one of production. General Morgan pointed out to the Combined Chiefs in August 1943 that the allocation of landing craft for Overlord was inadequate. But the shortage continued and actually became more acute, driving Churchill to exclaim in exasperation, "the destinies of two great empires seemed to be tied up in some goddammed things called LSTs." American production was stepped up until it could be stepped up no more, and in Britain one quarter of all the steel for new ships went into landing-craft production. But it was not sufficient.

In the end the Allies had to resort to the drastic action of postponing D-Day for a month in order to allow shipyards more time to increase stocks of landing craft. In fact, however, the postponement of the greatest amphibious assault in history need never have happened. The shortage of landing craft was not so much a failure of production as of allocation. On May 1, 1944, the original D-Day, Admiral Ernest J. King had at his disposal as chief of U.S. Naval Operations some 31,123 landing craft, while a mere 2,493 were assigned to Overlord. King was stockpiling landing craft for island fighting in the Pacific, and eventually General Marshall had to order him to share the wealth.

The landing-craft problem brought to a head the tensions underlying the Allies' differing approaches to the strategy and politics of Overlord. Though the British had good cause for complaining about the shortage of landing craft, the Americans, for their part, viewed the British protestations as a reflection of a deep-down lack of commitment to any invasion of France in 1944. The British had never been in favor of the Americans' strategy of a straight stab into the heart of Germany. Their preference was for encirclement and slow strangulation—an approach that had involved the Allies in Mediterranean fighting that a large number of

Americans thought was peripheral to the main objectives of the War. After the invasion of Italy in September of 1943, Churchill proposed extending the Mediterranean campaign into the Balkans. While President Roosevelt was insisting that *Overlord* should have overriding priority in the assignment of forces in Europe, Churchill proposed allocating only six tenths to *Overlord,* three tenths to Italy and one tenth to the Balkans.

Many Americans, slowly growing aware of the labyrinthine complexity of European politics, began to feel that there was more to the British obsession with the Mediterranean and the Balkans then met the eye. They felt that the British were tailoring their wartime conduct to suit their postwar interests in the Mediterranean. They read into the British attitude toward *Overlord* a profoundly sinister intention: to delay the defeat of Germany so as to exhaust the U.S.S.R. and leave Britain the dominant power in Europe.

In fact, as General Morgan remarked about *Overlord,* "there were undoubtedly those who would not be heart-

broken if the whole business were called off. There were other ways of winning the war." Russian victories on the Eastern Front meant that a second front to help the Russians was no longer the military or moral necessity it had formerly seemed to be. A powerful element, led by Air Chief Marshal Sir Arthur Harris, the head of the British Bomber Command, believed that Germany could be bombed into submission at less cost in money and manpower. It would just take longer. But Roosevelt wanted to win the War in 1944.

The British also entertained suspicions of the Americans. They doubted the Americans' tactical ability to carry out an invasion of the Continent and, later, their strategic capacity to do so. In 1943 General Morgan at COSSAC felt obliged to wonder why the Americans were so slow in delivering the landing craft, troops and matériel to solidify his plans for the invasion. "Were we really only taking part in a gigantic cover plan or hoax," he later recalled asking himself, "with the object of hoaxing, among others, ourselves?" With the United States so deeply committed to the war in the Pacific, and with Admiral King and other commanders arguing that the Pacific theater was of primary importance, the fate of *Overlord* always hung in the balance of global strategic priorities. Were the Americans procrastinating about *Overlord?* General Morgan had grounds to think so. Why, as late as November 1943, had various top U.S. commanders received no directives regarding their part in the invasion? Why, as November turned into December, was there not even a Supreme Commander to take charge? Were not the Americans furthering their interests in the Pacific at the expense of the liberation of Europe?

The biggest issue separating the British and the Americans was the matter of the ultimate goal of *Overlord.* "We tried in vain," Morgan later wrote, "to obtain some statement of a long term political object. The objective admittedly was Berlin, but an object and an objective are two different things." Was the object the destruction of Germany or the creation of a new Germany? Was it occupation or was it withdrawal?

The disagreement was political: essentially, the British argued that the Americans were abandoning Central Europe and the Balkans to the Soviet Union, while the Americans insisted that *Overlord*'s only concern should be military victory. The U.S., by virtue of its superior resources in men

British Lieut. General Sir Frederick E. Morgan, wearing a SHAEF shoulder patch on his uniform as one of the Supreme Headquarters' three deputy chiefs of staff, laid the initial groundwork for Operation Overlord in his earlier position as the Chief of Staff to the Supreme Allied Commander (COSSAC) between April and December of 1943. Morgan's successor, General Eisenhower, later wrote of him, "He had in the months preceding my arrival accomplished a mass of detailed planning, accumulation of data, and gathering of supply that made D-Day possible."

and matériel, had become the dominant partner of the alliance, so the American view prevailed. But Churchill and other British leaders were never reconciled to it.

Until May of 1943 it seemed highly unlikely that the actual build-up for *Overlord* would meet COSSAC's projected schedule. Only small numbers of U.S. troops and small quantities of American supplies had been reaching Britain under a year-old Second Front logistics program called Operation *Bolero (pages 64-77)*. It took time for the United States to gear up industrially for total war and to recruit an army, and the U-boat toll on the Atlantic convoy crossings put a brake on the rate of build-up. But by May 1943 there had been a dramatic turnaround in the Battle of the Atlantic. U-boat losses rose and Allied shipping losses fell; meanwhile American shipyard output broke all records. The Allied leaders gave the go-ahead for a cross-Channel invasion in the spring of 1944.

By late autumn of 1943, the build-up in Britain was accelerating at an almost unmanageable rate. The target—1.5 million American servicemen in Britain by May 1944 and another million by February 1945—came within reach. At the same time, the British were fast building their own army to a total of 1.75 milllion; they also expected to have 175,000 Commonwealth forces and 40,000 troops from France, Norway, Belgium, Holland, Poland and Czechoslovakia. Thus, an army of about 3.5 million men would eventually be gathered in Britain, together with all the planes, ships, guns, tanks, trucks, ammunition, fuel, rations, clothing, medicines and other supplies required to sustain a force of that size. By early 1944 Britain was top-heavy with troops and matériel. "It was claimed facetiously at the time," General Eisenhower wrote later, "that only the great number of barrage balloons floating constantly in British skies kept the islands from sinking under the seas."

To the U.S. Army officers charged with organizing the supply build-up, Britain posed some surprising problems. An Army transportation chief declared that the country was "so cramped and small, the railroad equipment so tiny, the roads so small and crooked, and methods so entirely different" that American operating methods would have to be totally transformed. Most of the ports were antiquated and inadequate. The dock workers were few and elderly (at Liverpool the average age of the dockers was 52), and restricted by archaic labor practices (union rules in Belfast, for example, made it advantageous to both employer and employee to discharge vessels as slowly as possible). Many of the winding roads of the English countryside and the narrow high streets of the towns were impassable for bulky military convoys. The railways were short of rolling stock and tunnels were too narrow for tanks on flatcars.

Complicating matters was the fact that the capacity of the ports was already strained. American imports for *Overlord*

A British war worker manufactures strips of aluminum foil for deceptive operations executed during the predaylight hours of D-Day morning. Since 1943, when the British began dropping the foil simply to jam enemy radar reception, they had learned the exact frequency of German radar from equipment captured in a Commando raid on Bruneval, France. Using this information, they cut the aluminum strips at precise lengths that would produce the same effect on German radar screens as an airplane. The foil, dropped in controlled patterns in a line toward the Pas-de-Calais area, helped to convince the Germans that a huge force of Allied aircraft was heading there, protecting an enormous invasion fleet.

represented only one tenth of the 25 million tons of freight that flowed through British ports each year to meet the country's civil and military needs. As the build-up reached a crescendo in the spring of 1944, Britain's limited port facilities and storage space reached the crisis point. An enormous backlog of cargo piled up in New York, and the danger grew that the invasion forces would not be properly supplied even in the midst of plenty. Churchill finally solved the problem by cutting Britain's own imports to allow room for the *Overlord* build-up.

Supplying the invasion forces was not entirely an American responsibility. Britain, despite its impoverishment and the overwhelming demands of its civilian population and armed forces, contributed greatly to the U.S. forces in a form of reverse Lend-Lease. The Quartermaster Corps of the U.S. Army in Britain acquired 63 per cent of its supplies from the British, the Corps of Engineers 58 per cent, the medical service 49 per cent and the Air Force 21 per cent, including 1,100 aircraft, mostly small transport and courier planes. As a whole, what the Americans called ETOUSA (European Theater of Operations, United States) received 31 per cent of all its supplies from Britain.

British and American authorities had at first believed that the huge influx of American servicemen into Britain would lead to disastrous cultural conflicts. There were strains, but the officials' worse fears proved to be unfounded. Considering the circumstances, the American invasion of Britain was in the main a friendly and harmonious affair *(pages 106-119)*. The British and the Americans saw in each other a new culture and a new way of life, though neither side was entirely convinced that it liked what it saw. To many of the British, the Americans were brash, bad mannered, tiresomely energetic and unpleasantly addicted to chewing gum and talking boisterously about the Brooklyn Dodgers baseball team. But for British girls at least, American boys were second only to German bombs as the most memorable experience of World War II.

By the autumn of 1943, a quiet crisis had gripped COSSAC and indeed the entire Allied military establishment in England: *Overlord* planning could not be jelled until someone was appointed to the post of Supreme Commander of the invasion forces. For a long time it had been assumed that the Supreme Commander would be a British general, and Churchill had already promised the job to General Brooke, the Chief of the Imperial General Staff. But it had gradually become clear that the majority of the force for *Overlord* would not be British but American and that the Supreme Commander should, therefore, be an American.

At first the consensus was that the American Chief of Staff, General Marshall, would be given the job. But Marshall was too valuable to President Roosevelt in Washington. For a time Roosevelt could not decide. At one point he proposed that Marshall should hold both jobs, but the British objected, on the reasonable grounds that Marshall would then be too powerful. Asked in October who the Supreme Commander was to be, Roosevelt said he had not made up his mind.

But if it was not to be Marshall, there was only one logical choice: General Dwight D. Eisenhower. Eisenhower had worked out the original invasion plan for the 1943 Operation *Roundup*; he had commanded three previous invasions in the European theater (North Africa, Sicily, Italy); he was a leader equally popular in both the American and British camps.

In December Roosevelt finally announced that Eisenhower was the man. COSSAC gave way to SHAEF (Supreme Headquarters of the Allied Expeditionary Force), and the embryo invasion headquarters became a full-fledged operational headquarters assigned to carry the war to the Germans without further delay.

General Eisenhower arrived in London to take up his duties in mid-January, 1944. In March the rapidly expanding SHAEF organization was moved from the old COSSAC headquarters in Norfolk House to a large encampment in Bushey Park near Henry VIII's old palace at Hampton Court by the Thames River in Middlesex. Here all the diverse departments of this huge and complex organization could be unified into a tented township that eventually held some 750 officers and 6,000 men. Eisenhower himself moved to a secluded home nearby, called Telegraph House, in an exclusive and leafy suburb on Kingston Hill. He did not care overmuch for big-city surroundings, and he eschewed the distracting social life of the capital. He had to. Few military men had ever assumed a burden as awesome as his.

To ease the burden, Eisenhower gathered around him a

galaxy of proven and talented military leaders. In selecting his top subordinates, he picked an extraordinary group of men who had already played decisive war roles. The man chosen as Deputy Supreme Commander was Air Chief Marshal Sir Arthur Tedder, who had been head of the RAF in the Middle East and the Allied air forces in the Mediterranean. The commander in chief of the Allied Naval Expeditionary Force was Admiral Sir Bertram H. Ramsay, who had planned the North Africa invasion and organized the brilliant rescue of the British Expeditionary Force from Dunkirk in 1940.

The commander of the Allied Expeditionary Air Force (comprising the RAF Second Tactical Air Force and the U.S. Ninth Air Force) was Air Chief Marshal Sir Trafford Leigh-Mallory, a tough and uncompromising airman who had commanded the famous 12 Group in the Battle of Britain, the air operations in the Dieppe raid and the RAF Fighter Command. Lieut. General Walter Bedell Smith, who had been Eisenhower's chief of staff throughout the North Africa and Mediterranean campaigns, was retained as his chief of staff for *Overlord,* while General Morgan, whose intimate knowledge of *Overlord* planning was irreplaceable, became deputy chief of staff.

For the all-important position of ground commander of the Allied armies during the initial assault and the establishment of the beachhead, Eisenhower wanted General Sir Harold R. L. G. Alexander, whom he regarded as an outstanding strategist. But Alexander could not be spared from his command of the Allied armies in Italy, and the job went to General Montgomery, whose Eighth Army the year before had decisively defeated Rommel's Afrika Korps. Montgomery's appointment pleased the British public and the British soldiers, who looked on him as a national hero, but it dismayed a number of senior American commanders, who found the man abrasive and egocentric.

Soon after Eisenhower's arrival in England, the Supreme Commander and his senior commanders reached agreement on a number of fundamental modifications of the original COSSAC plan. The three divisions provided by the old plan for the initial assault were simply not enough. There would be five divisions, and they would attack on a 50-mile front instead of the original 25-mile one. The new front reached from the mouth of the Orne River, near the important city of Caen, westward to Varreville on the east coast of the Cotentin Peninsula, with its vitally needed port of Cherbourg. However, the beaches near Varreville were cut off from the interior by high cliffs, river valleys and lagoons flooded by the Germans; these would surely become a death trap to seaborne forces landing there without additional support. It would therefore be necessary to take the American airborne division earmarked originally for the capture of Caen and drop it on the Cotentin Peninsula instead, along with an extra airborne division not called for in the COSSAC plan.

Leigh-Mallory protested passionately against these airborne operations; he believed strongly (but, as it turned out, wrongly) that the powerful German antiaircraft defenses and the widespread marshes and waterways of the peninsula would inflict losses of more than 70 per cent among the aircraft and paratroopers involved. But Eisenhower, however, convinced that the support of airborne troops was essential, overruled him.

To allow the production of landing craft, D-Day had been put back from May to the first week of June. The postponement was a mixed blessing: it gave time for more strategic bombing of Germany and for more training of the assault forces, but it also gave Field Marshal Rommel, commander of Army Group B and the northwestern French coast, more time for strengthening Hitler's Atlantic Wall.

Thanks to the various Allied intelligence-gathering agencies, SHAEF knew almost as much as Rommel about the Atlantic Wall and the deployment of German units that would have some effect on the mission. In January 1944, the same month that saw Eisenhower taking up his duties, Rommel had been given command of the two armies, the Seventh and the Fifteenth, whose infantry and artillery held the invasion coast between Antwerp and the Loire River. But Hitler had imposed an elaborate chain of command designed to maintain his control over the troops by limiting his commanders' power. As far as the invasion front was concerned, it was unclear—both to Rommel and to SHAEF—who would control what forces. To be sure, the coastal artillery and defense of naval ports were definitely the responsibility of the Navy, while antiaircraft guns were the Luftwaffe's. But Rommel, even though he was Hitler's favorite general and a master of tank warfare, had only nominal control over most of the panzer forces; their deployment was entrusted to a headquarters known as Panzer Group West, under General Leo Geyr von Schweppenburg.

Geyr's views on the proper use of armor to repel the invasion differed sharply from those of Rommel. A row had broken out between the two commanders. It was not resolved until March, when Rommel appealed to the Führer and asked that all armored and motorized units be placed directly under his command.

Hitler's answer was a compromise. Of the seven available armored divisions in Western Europe, three (the 2nd, 21st and 116th) were assigned to Rommel as Army Group B tactical reserves. The remaining four (the 1st SS, 12th SS, 17th SS Panzer Grenadier and Panzer Lehr) were assigned to Supreme Headquarters, OKW; they would comprise a central strategic reserve that could not be moved without OKW's authority—that is, without Hitler's approval. This compromise achieved nothing and was to have a calamitous result for the Germans on D-Day. OB West, headquarters for all German forces in Western Europe, lacked the authority to deploy or assign to Rommel the Strategic Reserves. Of the three armored divisions actually under Rommel's command, only one, the 21st Panzer, was anywhere near the invasion area on D-Day.

Rommel realized that he could not rely on panzer support, and he knew that the Allies could establish mastery of the air over any invasion beach they chose. Under the circumstances he had no choice but to rely on the Atlantic Wall and its static defenses to repel any Allied invasion. So he launched an all-out campaign to strengthen the Wall by whatever means came to hand. His orders to his commanders said: "In the short time left before the great offensive starts, we must succeed in bringing all defenses to such a standard that they will hold up against the strongest attacks. The enemy must be annihilated before he reaches our main battlefield. We must stop him in the water, not only delaying him but destroying all his equipment while it is still afloat." Every soldier and every weapon was packed into the Atlantic Wall or held in very close reserve behind it. "The high water line," Rommel insisted, "must be the main fighting line."

Rommel's aim was to create a defensive belt around the entire coast, but mainly on the Fifteenth Army sector be-tween Antwerp and the Orne River in Normandy and on the Seventh Army sector of Normandy west of the Orne. All through the spring of 1944 Rommel traveled up and down the Atlantic coast checking the construction work, encouraging the men. Lack of time, labor and materials prevented the completion of the Wall according to Rommel's final plan. Even so, by the end of May he had transformed the Wall into a formidable obstacle.

The staff officers at SHAEF were informed of Rommel's progress almost daily by Allied intelligence and reconnaissance flights, and they were profoundly disturbed when they learned that the invasion coast of Normandy between high water and low water was beginning to bristle with long parallel lines of special devices designed to impale or capsize assault landing craft—hedgehogs, tetrahedrons, dragons' teeth, curved rails and sharpened stakes tipped with mines. These obstacles threatened to wreak havoc among the initial assault waves, and they forced a number of

Off-duty soldiers play their accordions atop a camouflaged bunker of the Atlantic Wall. About 100 accordions were distributed by Field Marshal Rommel to boost the troops' morale and to reward them for passing a rigorous inspection of the Wall's gun emplacements and beach obstacles.

very important changes in SHAEF's plans for the assault.

It was now clear that in order to see their way through the obstacles, the invaders must land in daylight—not, as some planners had suggested, under cover of darkness. It was also clear that squads of special demolition engineers would now have to land very shortly after the first wave. Montgomery had intended the landings to be made at high tide, but this was now impossible because many of the landing craft would be wrecked on obstacles invisible just below the surface. On the other hand, if the landings were made at low tide to give the demolition squads maximum time to clear the obstacles before the tide covered them, the assault troops would have to cross a broad stretch of beach under heavy fire before they could reach the shelter of the dunes or the sea wall. Either way would mean heavy casualties.

Montgomery's solution was a hedge. He permitted the Americans to take their chances with a landing just after low tide, but he ordered his British and Canadian assault troops to land on a rising tide, when the main belt of obstacles was still above the water. For the British, at least, this would reduce the hazards to the landing craft and still give the engineers enough time to accomplish their job. But it would still leave the infantrymen exposed to enemy fire before their own support fire could be brought to bear. Montgomery therefore decided to revolutionize the technique of amphibious invasion by sending in armor in the vanguard of the assault. The floating Sherman tanks would now land in the first wave, other specialized tanks developed by Hobart would land in the second wave and the infantry in the third. Other tactical innovations were developed, but none were nearly as important as SHAEF's strategic efforts to take the enemy by surprise.

"Fortifications of concrete and steel, armed with modern fire power and fully manned by trained, resolute men, could only be overcome by surprise," Churchill later wrote. Only if Hitler was kept guessing as to the place, time, weight and aims of the invasion could the assault hope to achieve success. To coordinate various secret deceptive operations, Churchill established a central agency, the London Controlling Section (LCS), headed by two Englishmen, Colonel John Bevan and Lieut. Colonel Sir Ronald Wingate (a cousin of Lawrence of Arabia and of Orde Wingate of the

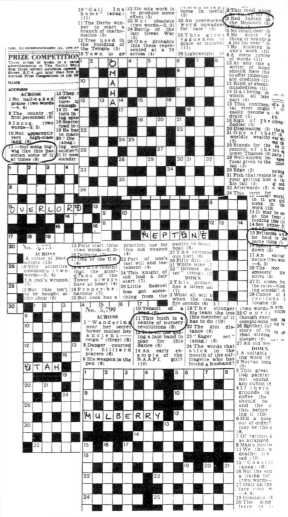

SOME PUZZLING COINCIDENCES

During the five weeks prior to D-Day, five crossword puzzles in London's *Daily Telegraph* horrified the SHAEF generals. Each contained a secret code word directly related to the impending invasion of Normandy: "Utah," "Omaha," "Mulberry," "Neptune" and "Overlord." The appearance of "Overlord" convinced the invasion planners that security had been breached.

Scotland Yard detectives questioned the puzzle compiler, Leonard Dawe. They discovered that he was an unassuming physics teacher who composed crosswords as a hobby. Dawe was convincingly bewildered by the interrogation, and the investigators finally drew the conclusion that it was all an amazing coincidence.

Burma campaign). In the words of an American member of the LCS, Colonel William H. Baumer: "Their object was to make Hitler run about like a blue arsed fly." Strategically, the deception campaign waged by the LCS and its associated intelligence agencies was either the first or the second most important factor in the outcome of D-Day, the other being Allied air supremacy.

The LCS leaked thousands of pieces of false information to the Germans through every intelligence outlet available—double agents, fake wireless transmissions, fictitious armies, the Resistance, calculated indiscretions. The aim of the campaign was twofold: first, to convince the Germans that the invasion would be at a different place and on a different date from the real one so they would not reinforce their defenses in the real invasion area with troops drawn from other fronts; and second, to delay their reaction to the Normandy landings by disrupting their communications, intelligence, supply and administrative systems.

Of all the multifarious activities surrounding D-Day, none was more extraordinary than the final deception program that was worked out by the LCS with the approval of the Joint Chiefs of Staff. It was in essence a credible war plan, drawn up at the highest political and strategic level. There were six principal deception plans, 36 subordinate ones and many more related stratagems. All around the perimeter of Europe thousands of guerrilla operations and Allied actions, rumors, feints, threats, raids and acts of sabotage were put into effect to bewilder the Germans and to keep their troops dispersed.

The deception plan most directly affecting the Normandy invasion was code-named *Fortitude*. The overall purpose of *Fortitude* was to tie down 90 German divisions, with all their air and naval support, in areas a safe distance from Normandy. One part of the plan was intended to bottle up 27 divisions in Scandinavia by making OKW believe that the Allies were about to make a diversionary landing in Norway. A deception organization, with a handful of men and women, was assigned to create a fictitious British Fourth Army of more than a quarter of a million men with headquarters under Edinburgh Castle. By April 1944 this ghost army was swamping German intelligence monitors with an endless stream of fake messages from fake divisions and corps, such as "80 Division requests 1,800 pairs of

Kandahar ski bindings" and "VII Corps requires the promised demonstrators in the Bilgeri method of climbing rock faces." British agents in Norway, with help from the Russians, compounded the deception so successfully that the 27 German divisions stationed in Norway were held there instead of being sent southward.

The key plan of *Fortitude* was calculated first to make the Germans believe that the invasion would take place in the Pas-de-Calais and then to make them believe, on D-Day itself, that the Normandy landings were merely a feint. Every possible trick was employed to make it seem that the invasion forces gathering in Britain were weighted toward southeastern England and pointed at Calais: British agents in neutral capitals even went around buying up all existing stocks of Michelin maps of the Pas-de-Calais. A fake army group of 50 divisions and a million men under the command of Lieut. General George S. Patton was established in southeastern England.

In fact Montgomery's 21st Army Group *was* assembling in the south of England—together with American troops that would form Bradley's 12th Army Group after the beachhead was secure. To Montgomery's group the Allies added a fictitious second, the First U.S. Army Group (FUSAG), consisting of the Canadian First Army, the American Third Army and 50 divisions that would come in directly from the United States. Though some of the 50 divisions in America were imaginary, the American Third Army and the Canadian First Army actually did exist and would eventually land in France. The trick was to persuade the Germans that they belonged to Patton's FUSAG and would form the main invasion force in the Pas-de-Calais on D-Day.

So while Montgomery's real army group was secretly assembling in southwestern England, Patton's nonexistent one appeared to be openly assembling in southeastern England. Fake landing craft, fabricated at Shepperton Film Studios near London, were moored in the Thames and other rivers in southeast England with laundry hanging realistically from their rigging. Fake ammunition dumps, hospitals, field kitchens, troop camps, guns and planes made of canvas and scaffolding crowded the fields, along with more than a brigade of inflated rubber tanks. Britain's leading architect, Sir Basil Spence, professor of architecture at the

Royal Academy, designed and constructed an enormous fake oil dock occupying three square miles of the foreshore at Dover, complete with jetties, storage tanks, pipelines, powerhouses and antiaircraft guns.

FUSAG was accepted as a real army by OKW and appeared in the official German listing of Allied forces. By May 1944 the Germans believed that there were 92 to 97 divisions assembling in Britain instead of the 35 that really were there; and though they were still uncertain when and where this huge force was going to land, they firmly favored the Pas-de-Calais. Captured documents showed that OKW had disposed its forces in accordance with the Allies' subversive intentions. An intercepted report revealed that Hitler's advisers continued to swallow the *Fortitude* deceptions and continued to believe that the invasion would hit the Pas-de-Calais, probably in July.

Of the Allies' real intentions the Germans learned precious little. The British and American counterintelligence agencies prevented the Germans from learning the secrets of *Neptune*. In Britain more than 100 German spies had been bribed or intimidated into transmitting erroneous information to Germany, forming an important element of the Allied deception campaign. The Germans' conventional sources of information had also failed them. Few Luftwaffe aircraft were able to penetrate the invasion assembly areas in southern England and return home safely, and Rommel complained in his weekly intelligence report for May 21 that "there are *no* results of air reconnaissance of the island for the entire period."

By contrast, Eisenhower on the eve of D-Day was the best informed military commander in history. He knew the enemy's order of battle, strength, defenses, supply, communications, morale, plans. The Germans could hardly conceal the movement of a tank from the reconnaissance aircraft or the prying eyes of the Resistance. Intelligence-gathering operations dealing with the Normandy invasion beaches started by COSSAC were intensified to an around-the-clock vigil under SHAEF. Swimmers, frogmen, Commandos and sea-level photo planes *(opposite)* constantly monitored the state of the beaches and the German defenses for the Inter-Services Topographical Unit at Oxford. In May 1944 alone, French agents sent to London 700 radio reports and 3,000 written dispatches on German military positions. By 1944 Admiral Ramsay had a continuous sea-level panoramic photostrip of the coastal invasion area made up of uncounted individual photos spliced together.

In mid-April the Allied intelligence-gathering network received shocking news. Aerial photos of the Orne valley revealed that the Germans were putting up antiglider obstacles in precisely the fields where the British were planning to land gliders on D-Day. Then air reconnaissance and agents' reports revealed intensive enemy ground activity in Normandy. The 21st Panzer Division was moved from Brittany to Caen, almost opposite the Second British Army invasion beaches, and the Panzer Lehr Division was moved to the area of Chartres–Le Mans, only a day from Caen.

The Allies' fears that their intentions were known to the Germans after all were increased when an infantry division and a parachute regiment were moved to the drop zones of the American airborne divisions at the base of the Cotentin Peninsula, and reports from agents indicated that the 17th SS Panzer Grenadier Division was getting ready to move north to Normandy from Poitiers.

In fact, these moves were not the result of the Germans' intelligence but of Hitler's intuition. On May 2, after a string of less successful guesses, Hitler had decided that there would be a strong Allied thrust in Normandy despite the fact that his staff continued to advise him that invasion would come in the Pas-de-Calais. He ordered reinforcements moved up to counter the attack. The SHAEF planners had to make rapid readjustments, among them altering the landing zones and objectives of the American 82nd Airborne Division. Facing the Allies in or near the invasion area, the Germans now had six infantry divisions and two panzer divisions, with two more panzer divisions 24 hours' march away. Normandy at the end of May was thus much more strongly held than it was only a few weeks before.

In the meantime, intense Allied aerial activity was cutting down the defense capability of the Germans. By the spring of 1944, Allied strategic bombing had so reduced German aircraft production that the Luftwaffe was reluctant to contest Allied sweeps over Germany. In April the Strategic Air Forces turned their attention to Germany's dwindling oil supply, and within a month they had cut oil production by 20 per cent. Marshaling yards, bridges and rail centers were

A CLOSE-UP PORTRAIT OF THE INVASION COAST

To prepare for the invasion, Allied reconnaissance planes flew hundreds of low-level sorties over the coast of Normandy, photographing the shoreline in minute detail. The photos were rushed to Oxford University, where the Inter-Services Topographical Unit had assembled a corps of draftsmen, geologists, photographic technicians and geographers. The corps carefully pieced together thousands of individual photos, forming a continuous sea-level panorama of the coast. The portrait was so accurate and detailed that the invasion warships could lay their guns according to grids superimposed on it.

The results so impressed General Eisenhower that he ordered 40,000 sets printed for tactical study by all of the assault units. To fill the enormous order, an air shuttle flew 730 miles of paper and 10 tons of chemicals from the U.S. every two days until the printing was finished.

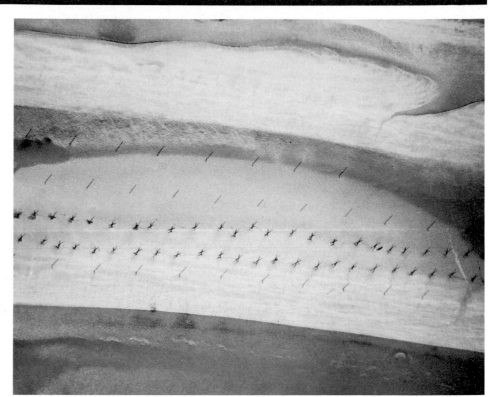

Every obstacle in this aerial photograph was transferred onto giant maps for tactical planning.

Guided by low-level reconnaissance photographs of the Bernières-sur-Mer coast, landing-craft crews accurately put British troops ashore here on D-Day.

Based on aerial photos, a scale model of the Queen and Roger Beaches at Sword gave officers due to land there an in-depth sense of the problems ahead.

pounded by heavy bombers and attacked with rockets by fighter planes. Throughout the entire aerial campaign the Allies' deception strategy was maintained, and for every bomb that was dropped over the Normandy invasion area, two were dropped elsewhere in the northern part of France. By the eve of D-Day, the Germans' ability to react to the invasion had been crippled by tactical destruction of German communication systems, bridges, rail centers and rail lines leading to Normandy.

By May the great army that was to breach the Atlantic Wall was one of the most thoroughly trained assault forces ever to go into battle. Throughout the early part of 1944 all units had studied and practiced the highly specialized skills of their trade. Tank crews had learned how to handle amphibious tanks in the open sea; glider pilots had learned how to crash-land their craft behind German lines in the dark; demolition teams had learned how to dismantle mined contraptions of concrete and steel in a rising tide; infantrymen had been trained for amphibious operations; landing-craft crews had learned how to set down troops in the right place and at the right time on an open beach held by a powerful enemy. Most important, various branches of the service had to learn how to cooperate with one another—spotter planes with battleships, bomber planes with infantry, Army and Navy engineers with each other.

The SHAEF commanders stipulated that on D-Day every individual soldier should know exactly what specific task he had to accomplish against a specific objective. Exhaustive maneuvers were held, and great pains were taken to make the assault exercises resemble the real thing as closely as possible. An exact replica of the worrisome German battery near Merville was constructed in a secret field in Berkshire so that British paratroops and glider troops could rehearse their precision nighttime attack on the D-Day target. American Rangers practiced cliff assaults with London fire-brigade ladders mounted on amphibious trucks, or DUK-Ws.

After the last maneuvers in May, the soldiers returned to their marshaling areas. Final supplies were issued for the voyage, and the units were broken down into boatloads to await the final move to the ships. Then there was nothing to do but wait. Some units had to wait for a month. The soldiers were briefed for D-Day in the last week in May.

Each man was carefully instructed in his unit's task with the help of aerial photos, models, maps and sketches. RAF glider pilots and aircrews were briefed by means of a special film that tracked across a scale model of the exact terrain over which they would fly on their route to the drop zones. Projected through a blue filter, the film gave a good representation of moonlight conditions.

It was a dangerous time for security. Though the troops had not been told the place names of their assault areas, they knew a great deal, and if only a few men were indiscreet, German intelligence could piece together a correct overall picture. General Morgan had warned: "If the enemy obtains as much as forty-eight hours warning of the location of the assault area, the chances of success are small and any longer warning spells certain defeat."

SHAEF was thus forced to impose strict security arrangements on both troops and civilians. On April 1 all unauthorized visitors were banned from coastal zones 10 miles wide in the areas where the assault forces were being concentrated. On April 17 the British government took the unprecedented step of restricting the diplomatic privileges of all nations, forbidding diplomats and diplomatic couriers to enter or leave England and censoring hitherto immune diplomatic correspondence. All mail by British forces involved in *Overlord* was strictly censored, and on May 25 transatlantic telephone, radio and cable facilities were denied to American personnel and a 10-day delay was imposed on their mail to the States.

In the last week of May the troops were sealed in their camps behind barbed wire and armed guards. They were not allowed to mail letters or even to say goodbye to their families or girl friends. One Royal Engineer who broke out of his camp returned to his unit the night before embarkation and—much to the amusement of his comrades—was sent to invade France under close arrest. For the handful of officers who knew the complete *Overlord* plan, a new system of security classification known as Bigot was introduced; documents stamped Bigot were even more confidential than those stamped Top Secret. Even this was not foolproof. In a U.S. Army mail-sorting office in Chicago a half-opened packet from England was found to contain Bigot papers, and a complete Bigot list of radio transmission frequencies and ciphers for use in the invasion was found in a briefcase left in a taxicab at Waterloo Station in London.

The complete plan for *Overlord* was set forth in one last briefing three weeks before D-Day. The Supreme Commander and his deputy commanders and other chiefs gathered in the circular model room of the old St. Paul's School, in Hammersmith, London, to outline the plan for the King of England, the Prime Minister and the commanders of the units that would be involved, with the aid of a map as broad as a city street. King George VI sat on a hard narrow school bench in the front row, with Churchill on his right and Eisenhower on his left. "As we took those uncompromisingly hard and narrow seats," wrote American Rear Admiral Morton L. Deyo, "the room was hushed and the tension palpable. The first to rise and break the silence was the Supreme Commander himself. It had been said that his smile was worth twenty divisions. That day it was worth more. He spoke for ten minutes. Before the warmth of his quiet confidence the mists of doubt dissolved. When he had finished the tension had gone. Not often has one man been called upon to accept so great a burden of responsibility. But here was one at peace with his soul."

Montgomery got up to explain the plan of battle for the initial assault phase of *Overlord,* Operation *Neptune.* The ships and landing craft of the Allied Naval Expeditionary Force under the command of Admiral Ramsay would begin transporting the armies across the Channel to France on D-minus-1. Ramsay's immense naval armada was divided in two: an Eastern Task Force for the three British beaches code-named Gold, Juno and Sword, and a Western Task Force for the two American beaches code-named Omaha and Utah. Shortly after midnight, while the armada was approaching the 59-mile invasion front, two aerial fleets, one British and one American, would begin dropping parachutists and glider troops behind the German coastal defenses, and by daybreak on D-Day, the British 6th Airborne Division would have secured the eastern flank of the bridgehead, the American 82nd and 101st Airborne Divisions the western flank.

Montgomery now went on to the next phase. Shortly after dawn, following a massive preliminary aerial and naval bombardment of the German shore defenses, five seaborne assault divisions would begin landing on five beaches lying between the flanks held by the airborne divisions—three divisions of the British Second Army under General Sir Miles Dempsey on the British invasion sector between the Orne River and Port-en-Bessin, and two divisions of the American First Army under General Bradley on Omaha and Utah Beaches in the American sector between Port-en-Bessin and Varreville on the Cotentin Peninsula.

The British and American ground forces were to secure their separate beachheads on D-Day, then on D-plus-1 to link up the beachheads, and on D-plus-2 to D-plus-9 to expand northwest, west and south to form a staging area in which to build up strength for a breakout toward Paris and the Rhine. In order to achieve this initial aim it would be necessary, first, for the British to hold the left flank around Caen against German panzer counterattacks; second, for the British and Americans in the center to secure the plateau far enough inland to protect the artificial Mulberry harbors from direct German artillery fire; and third, for the Americans on the right to seal off the base of the Cotentin Peninsula and move on the port of Cherbourg, so vital for the long-term unloading of troops and matériel.

The build-up of men and supplies on the beaches and inland would be accomplished with complete air supremacy. The Allied Expeditionary Air Force of Air Chief Marshal Leigh-Mallory had at its disposal 3,467 heavy bombers and 1,645 medium, light and torpedo bombers, plus 5,409 fighters. All these would provide a continuous air umbrella over the invasion area and would range far and wide to interdict German movement both on land and in the air.

The plan had been worked out in meticulous detail. Nothing had been left to chance. Speaking of the importance of the troops' frame of mind, Montgomery said in conclusion: "We shall have to send the soldiers into this party 'seeing red.' They must see red. We must get them completely on their toes, having absolute faith in the plan; and imbued with infectious optimism and offensive eagerness. Nothing must stop them. Nothing. If we send them into battle in this way—then we shall succeed."

But there could not be any control over one sovereign factor—the weather. There were only three days in each two-week period of June when the right conditions of both light and tide prevailed—when low tide and first light more or less coincided. If the additional requirement of a late-

rising full moon for the airborne night drop was taken into account, the number of days when the invasion could take place was reduced to three a month.

On those three days, yet another set of requirements had to be met: to ensure the safe handling of the landing craft, onshore winds should not exceed 8 to 12 mph and offshore winds 13 to 18 mph; to increase the firing accuracy of the bombarding ships, visibility should not be less than three miles; to enable the bomber squadrons and the transports carrying airborne forces to find their targets accurately, there should be no more than six tenths cloud cover and the cloud base should not be below 3,000 feet; to prevent paratroopers from being widely scattered in the drop, the land wind should be less than 20 mph; there should be no ground fog or heavy mist and no prolonged high winds in the Channel in the days before D-Day.

Meteorological records showed that the odds against the occurrence of such ideal weather in early summer were 50 or 60 to 1. But the forward momentum of the D-Day machinery was such that the operation could not be postponed for more than a day or two once it had been set in motion. For this reason, perhaps, no one at SHAEF had seriously contemplated the possibility that weather conditions might put a stop to the whole tremendous venture. When, at the beginning of June, that possibility stared everyone in the face, the countdown to *Overlord* entered its most nerve-racking phase.

On May 8, Eisenhower set D-Day for June 5, with the 6th and 7th as suitable alternatives. For the rest of the month of May southern England and the Channel basked in beautiful summer sunshine and barely a breeze ruffled the surface of the Channel. It was perfect invasion weather. On May 29 the SHAEF Meteorologic Committee, a team of British and American weathermen headed by a dour Scot, RAF Group-Captain J. M. Stagg, made a guardedly optimistic long-range forecast of the weather for the first days of June. On the basis of that forecast, the D-Day machine was set in motion.

All over England men and vehicles were put on the move from the sealed camps to the waiting ships. Tanks and trucks, bearing the white star that was the symbol of liberation, rumbled toward the south-coast ports in convoys up to 100 miles long. Marching regiments of men in full com-

bat kit filed down the narrow streets to the quays at harbors all over southern England. They tramped past the air-raid shelters, the sandbagged doorways and the boarded-up seafront shops, down the drab warworn streets of the tired English towns. As they marched a vast communal excitement began to fill the air, and people came out to line the streets and cheer them on and wave and cry. No one, including the soldiers, knew exactly where the soldiers were going. But everyone in England realized that this was the start of a great event in history. Everyone knew that this was the opening of the Second Front, the vindication of the bitter years of defeat and deprivation, the final expression of a single collective international will.

By June 3 all the assault troops—some 170,000 of them—were aboard. On the ships they were briefed again with maps and aerial photos of the beach sections they were destined for, although security was still so strict that they remained in ignorance of the place names. They practiced embarkation drill, sorted out weapons and stores and waited in a state of mounting tension for the word to go. Already some of the warships and Mulberry blockships that had the farthest to sail had set off from distant ports in Scotland and northern Ireland. Eisenhower cabled General Marshall: "We have almost an even chance of having pretty fair conditions . . . only marked deterioration would discourage our plans." By that very evening the "marked deterioration" was already heading *Overlord*'s way.

At 9:30 p.m. on June 3 Group-Captain Stagg painted a gloomy weather picture at a meeting of the Supreme Commander and his commanders in chief in the library at Southwick House near Portsmouth—the elegant Regency mansion that served as Admiral Ramsay's headquarters and as SHAEF's advance command post. Stagg said that the unexpected breakup of the long period of settled weather was due to the collapse of a high-pressure system over the Azores. The weather forecast for the British Isles and northeast Atlantic was "very disturbed and complex," he informed the commanders.

It was, in fact, the worst weather picture for that time of year in 40 or 50 years. "A series of three depressions were strung out across the Atlantic from north Scotland toward Newfoundland," noted Stagg. There would be strong winds in the Channel until June 7, he predicted, with ten tenths

Douglas A-20 attack bombers of the American Ninth Air Force stage a preinvasion raid on German defenses at Pointe du Hoc, a tiny peninsula jutting out from Normandy's checkerboard of fields and hedgerows. In the five weeks preceding D-Day, this command alone flew approximately 53,800 sorties against the enemy's coastal defenses and communication targets and dropped a total of about 30,700 tons of bombs.

cloud down to 500 or 1,000 feet. Under such weather conditions neither the sea bombardment nor the airborne assaults could take place. Eisenhower and his commanders decided to delay their decision until 4:15 the next morning, Sunday, June 4, but in the meantime gave orders to the flotillas that had the farthest to go to set sail.

The next 24 hours was a time of enormous strain for Eisenhower. The whole vast edifice of *Overlord* now rested on the expertise of a British meteorologic team and their assessment of a vague complex of pressure systems and cold fronts hundreds of miles away.

At 15 minutes past 4 o'clock on Sunday morning the commanders met again. The tension in the room was overpowering. Stagg confirmed his previous forecast. Admiral Ramsay was prepared to go ahead, though he did not like the prospect. So was General Montgomery. But Air Chief Marshal Leigh-Mallory said that his bombers could not operate in the heavy cloud that was forecast, and Air Chief Marshal Tedder agreed with him.

General Eisenhower said that since the Allied ground forces had no overwhelming superiority over the Germans, *Overlord* was not a sound operation without Allied air supremacy and could not be risked if that supremacy was taken away by the weather. He therefore postponed D-Day by one day. Further sailings of the invasion fleet were called off, and convoys already at sea were turned back. "When we went out into the quiet and still, almost cloudless morning," Stagg wrote in his diary, "the enormity of the decision we had just heard was borne in upon us." But he added: "There was still an element of doubt in what we had done."

At 11 a.m. the Admiralty issued a gale warning for the Irish Sea. All through Sunday the storm grew in fury, driving white breakers onto the beaches of Normandy. The bombarding warships that had sailed from the distant ports in Scotland and northern Ireland battered their way back to port through rough water in the Irish Sea. Part of one force was halfway to France before it was turned back by a seaplane. In the crowded harbors of southern England the

barrage balloons danced on their wires, the landing craft tossed at their anchors and the multitude of soldiers, many of whom had been packed on board for three or four days, waited seasick and anxious.

When the commanders met again at 9:30 that Sunday evening of June 4, the wind was still blowing hard, and it was raining out of an overcast sky. The commanders sat informally in easy chairs and couches in the long oak-paneled library, now used as a senior officers' mess. They stared at Stagg solemnly. It was, they all knew, a desperate moment. The invasion could not really be postponed for another 24 hours—the tide would be at its lowest point, the troops could not be kept cooped up and exposed on the decks of the landing craft any longer.

If D-Day had to be postponed, it would have to be postponed by two weeks, and then there would not be any moonlight for the airdrops. But such a postponement would cause untold chaos to the movement of troops and matériel. Follow-up units were already moving into marshaling camps evacuated by the assault units that had embarked on the ships, and it was virtually impossible to reverse the movement without jamming the *Overlord* machinery. The men had been briefed; if they were disembarked, there would be a tremendous risk to security as well as morale. There was further risk: Stalin had been promised that the Second Front would be opened in the first week in June and

RAF Group-Captain J. M. Stagg, the gloomy Scot whose last-minute forecast of a break in the bad weather launched the invasion, was none too happy with the demands of his job as chief meteorologist to SHAEF. He was frequently asked to predict weather five days in advance. This feat was impossible, he said gloomily, for "all the meteorological brains of the U.S. and British (and any other) weather services put together."

had timed his big summer offensive on the Eastern Front to coincide with it.

"The inescapable consequences of postponement," Eisenhower wrote afterward, "were almost too bitter to contemplate." It made little difference that a girl in the London office of Associated Press had accidentally and unwittingly sent out a flash on the teletype machine: "URGENT A.P. NYK FLASH EISENHOWER'S HQ ANNOUNCE ALLIED LANDINGS IN FRANCE." Though this news was broadcast in America and Moscow before it was killed, it had no bearing on Eisenhower's dilemma Sunday evening. Only the weather could decide. He therefore listened intently to Group-Captain Stagg, and what Stagg said surprised him.

"Gentlemen," said Stagg, "since I presented the forecast last evening some rapid and unexpected developments have occurred over the north Atlantic." A cold front was coming through faster and farther south than expected, he explained. After it had passed through the Channel area there would be a brief period of improvement starting on the afternoon of Monday, June 5, and lasting till late on the evening of Tuesday, June 6. At that time the weather would again become unsettled.

Stagg was offering the commanders the unexpected gift of a hole in the weather—and hole just big enough for the initial assault force to pass through.

A prolonged silence greeted Stagg's statement. There was the danger that though the short break in the weather might allow the first few assault waves to land, the bad weather due to follow could delay the build-up and leave the assault waves isolated onshore and an easy prey for the Germans.

General Eisenhower turned toward Montgomery and put the question to him: "Do you see any reason why we should not go on Tuesday?"

"No," Montgomery answered. "I would say—Go."

"The question is," Eisenhower said, "just how long can you hang this operation out on the end of a limb and let it hang there."

The decision of whether to launch or to abort the Second Front was for the Supreme Commander to make, and he had to make it alone.

At 9:45 he announced that decision: "I don't like it but there it is . . . I don't see how we can possibly do anything else. I am quite positive we must give the order."

Outside the door at the end of the meeting, Eisenhower came over to Stagg. "Well, Stagg," he said, "we're putting it on again. For heaven's sake hold the weather to what you told us and don't bring any more bad news." Then he smiled broadly and went out.

And yet, the final, irrevocable decision to launch the assault had to be delayed for one last weather report at the commanders' meeting scheduled for 4:15 on Monday morning, the 5th of June. "Our little camp was shaking and shuddering under a wind of hurricane proportions," Eisenhower wrote of that time, "and the accompanying rain seemed to be travelling in horizontal streaks. It seemed impossible in such conditions that there was any reason for even discussing the situation."

The meeting convened. "Gentlemen," Stagg began, "no substantial change has taken place since last time but as I see it the little that has changed is in the direction of optimism." He said that the fair-weather interval would extend through all southern England during the night and would probably last into the afternoon of Tuesday. Stagg subsequently wrote: "Immediately after I had finished the tension seemed to evaporate and the Supreme Commander and his colleagues became as new men. General Eisenhower had sat, turned sideways, facing me, taut and tense. Now a broad smile broke over his face."

"OK," Eisenhower said finally. "We'll go."

With those words the die was cast. The signal was flashed to the fleet: "PROCEED WITH OPERATION NEPTUNE."

Dawn was breaking as the commanders made their way to their tents and quarters, and the woods were loud with the song of birds. The planners, having done all they could, went to bed. The Second Front now belonged to the men who would do the fighting.

THE BIG BUILD-UP

U.S. P-51 fighters, their wing tips removed to provide clearance, are trucked through Liverpool on their way to an air base to be prepared for invasion duties.

"THE GREATEST MILITARY BASE OF ALL TIME"

A message pinned to a church door in a town evacuated for the GIs asks them to treat the building with the same respect shown it by the villagers.

In April 1942, when the Allies decided to invade Europe from England, the U.S. War Department set in motion an unprecedented plan, called Operation *Bolero,* to build up a million-man American force in the British Isles. The American Army's SOS (Services of Supply) was charged with the herculean task of arranging for the troops' transportation to Britain, the establishment of their camps and training grounds, and the building of additional airfields and storage facilities. Immediately SOS officers went to work in concert with British military men and civilian agencies.

The transatlantic shipments got off to a slow start in May, adding only 24,682 troops to the 11,962 already based in the British Isles, and the build-up lagged during the winter of 1942-1943, when 153,000 GIs were diverted to support the Allied invasion of North Africa. But thereafter, American troop landings in Britain rose sharply, to a monthly peak of 216,699 in April 1944. Meanwhile, cargo shipments peaked at nearly 500,000 tons a month, so overtaxing Britain's venerable ports and small labor force that the influx of war matériel had to be curtailed. All together, in little more than two years there arrived in Britain 1.5 million servicemen and five million tons of invasion supplies and equipment, including 8,000 airplanes, 1,000 locomotives and 20,000 railroad cars.

The Americans were quartered in 398,666 prefabricated huts, in 279,204 tented camps and in 111,590 British buildings of all kinds, ranging from thatched cottages in the countryside and warehouses in industrial towns to fashionable hotels in London's bustling West End. Hundreds of square miles of Britain—from the moors of Scotland to farmland along the southwest coast—were crowded with American supply depots, ammunition dumps, repair shops, truck and tank parks, camps and air bases. By the eve of the invasion in June 1944, after the expenditure of 400 million man-hours of labor and $644 million for new construction alone, Operation *Bolero* had transformed England into what General Eisenhower called "the greatest operating military base of all time."

Long rows of steel bays, each one holding 32 tons of artillery shells, flank an English country road concealed by trees from German reconnaissance planes.

Preparing to move, a citizen of Slapton takes down a portrait of Queen Victoria. Residents were reimbursed by the British government for moving expenses.

MANEUVERS HELD IN QUAINT COUNTRY VILLAGES

As invasion preparations speeded up in the autumn of 1943, American officers toured the English countryside looking for terrain that resembled Normandy so that the GIs could stage maneuvers under realistic conditions. One area chosen for a series of crucial maneuvers lay in southwest England. It consisted of 26 square miles of varied terrain surrounding Slapton Sands, a steeply sloping beach, and included a cluster of picturesque Devonshire villages that dated back several centuries.

Because the troops would be using live ammunition, the 3,000 inhabitants of the area were evacuated, and historic buildings were clearly marked with white tape, warning the troops not to fire on them. Between exercises on the beaches, soldiers practiced house-to-house fighting in the towns, swarming around empty pubs, post offices, schools and shops.

Two months after D-Day, the local inhabitants were permitted to return home. They found every window shattered and the old church in Slapton village badly damaged by an errant artillery shell. The townspeople complained to their government but received only partial compensation for the damage.

A white-coated Slapton butcher helps a moving man carry his chopping block out to a van. All businesses and households were cleared out within six weeks.

A dog gazes down an empty street of an evacuated Devonshire town. The British Women's Volunteer Service found temporary homes for most evacuees.

Acting as casualties, soldiers lie on a Cornwall beach, waiting for medics and landing-craft crews to evacuate them.

Preparing for soggy terrain in Normandy, men of the 8th Infantry Division cross a swamp on an infantry footbridge.

Burdened with battle gear, members of an airborne infantry unit scale fences and embankments in an attack drill designed to test their speed and stamina.

FINAL DRILLS FOR THE ASSAULT

At the start of invasion drills in January of 1944, each branch of the U.S. Army staged separate maneuvers to practice its own specialty in simulated combat. Then all of the branches—infantry, engineers, signal corps, tanks—joined Naval units in large-scale maneuvers that were designed to improve their teamwork and timing in Normandy-like amphibious operations.

Two huge joint maneuvers climaxed the arduous preparations. In one of these exercises, known as *Fabius,* selected American units spent two weeks training with British and Canadian forces. The majority of the Americans took part in *Tiger,* an exhausting nine-day operation. Both big maneuvers were marred by traffic jams and confusion, but the troops had little time left to smooth out the rough edges. It was May, and D-Day was only a month away.

In a gun park at Ashchurch village in southern England, 105mm howitzers are tended by GI maintenance men, who regularly cleaned the barrels and then

American fighter planes and bombers wait for their preflight servicing by busy Air Force mechanics.

A peaceful farmer walks his horse past invasion-bound half-tracks in the Ashchurch ordnance depot.

re-covered the muzzles to prevent corrosion.

A SUPERABUNDANCE OF EVERYTHING

As early as 1942, when only a trickle of armaments was reaching Britain, the Allied invasion planners realized that their toughest problem would be to find room in the tight little isles to stash the huge quantities of war matériel that American factories were beginning to produce. The U.S. Services of Supply promptly gave highest priority to a program of establishing adequate storage facilities. Gradually, the SOS officers acquired or built 73.5 million square feet of storage space, and they laid 170 miles of railroad trunk lines to route the goods to dozens of collection points.

The depot program proved to be the most successful part of the big build-up.

It provided the U.S. Ordnance alone with enough room to stockpile 320,000 different kinds of items, some of them as large as 10-ton wreckers. It set up ammunition dumps wherever unused space could be found—including public parks. It located farmers' fields and the green lawns of baronial estates that could be used as parking and storage space for 450,000 tons of ammunition and 50,000 vehicles.

By the eve of the invasion, the 1.5 million U.S. troops were supremely confident that they had more than enough supplies and equipment for the task ahead. They even had tons of chewing gum to combat seasickness on the voyage to France. But some supplies reminded them that the invasion would be no picnic: 124,000 hospital beds and, stacked high in a corner of a camp in Dorchester, uncounted coffins.

73

U.S. supplies and equipment, stored prodigally in depots all over the British Isles, include (clockwise from top left) stacks of construction lumber, barrels of motor

oil, sections of prefabricated Nissen huts, bundles of brooms, boxes of dried eggs and tiers of pontoons to form the bridges that would span France's rivers.

Neat ranks and files of American armored vehicles stretch across an English plain as far as the eye can see. The half-tracks (right), used to transport combat troops

and to drag artillery pieces, and the Sherman tanks were a small fraction of the 50,000 military vehicles shipped to Great Britain for the invasion of Normandy.

SUPREME COMMANDER

*Presiding as Allied Supreme Commander, General Eisenhower (center)
plans the invasion with his Anglo-American staff: (from left) Lieut.
General Omar N. Bradley, Admiral Sir Bertram Ramsay, Air Chief Marshal
Sir Arthur Tedder, General Sir Bernard Montgomery, Air Chief Marshal
Sir Trafford Leigh-Mallory and Lieut. General Walter Bedell Smith.*

Roosevelt's message (below) to Stalin names Eisenhower as commander of the invasion force, whose personnel wore a flaming sword insignia (above) symbolizing the liberation of Europe. U.S. Chief of Staff George C. Marshall drafted the message and sent it to Eisenhower as a souvenir.

A GIFTED TEAM WORKER FOR A PRESSURE POST

On Christmas Eve of 1943, after operating without a leader for nearly a year, the Allied forces assembling in Britain learned who was to have the momentous task of completing their preparations for the invasion of France and launching the assault. That day in Washington, President Roosevelt announced over the radio that the chief of the Supreme Headquarters of the Allied Expeditionary Force (SHAEF) was to be General Dwight D. Eisenhower.

Two years earlier, Eisenhower had been so little known, even in America, that a newspaper had called him "Lt. Col. D. D. Ersenbeing"; now, he was so famous that King George VI of England requested his autograph for a relative. Eisenhower's swift rise—first to commander of the North Africa invasion and then to chief of U.S. troops in the European theater—was due primarily to his ability to weld leaders with assertive personalities and differing national interests into a winning team. That talent had impressed German spies and they noted it in their reports. But some Allied observers considered Eisenhower unqualified for his new job. They pointed out that he had never personally commanded troops in battle and they accused him of being indecisive and overly conciliatory—more an arbitrator than a dynamic leader. Eisenhower's consideration for the British prompted several U.S. officers to grumble, "Ike is the best commander the British have." Alert to the charge, Eisenhower stopped carrying his swagger stick—an old habit that his critics might have condemned as too British.

Eisenhower assumed his manifold new duties in England on January 15, 1944. His most crucial and time-consuming work was discussing problems of strategy, tactics and supply with members of his high-powered American and British staff. But—contrary to his critics' beliefs—he never flinched at making the tough decisions. It was Eisenhower who decided to use paratroopers in Normandy despite predictions of 70 per cent casualties. And on June 5, when some SHAEF officers argued that the Normandy operation should be postponed because of bad weather, Eisenhower ordered the assault anyway.

On duty in England, Ike inspects Winston Churchill's "siren suit"—a garment the Prime Minister designed to permit air raid wardens to dress in a hurry.

Always short on time, the busy Supreme Commander checks his watch in his London office a week after taking charge of SHAEF.

At SHAEF's Southwick House headquarters near Portsmouth, Eisenhower gave the final go-ahead for the invasion in the library.

At an American air base, Eisenhower goes over invasion plans with Major General Lewis H. Brereton and Lieut. General Carl Spaatz (center) of the Air Force

LONG DAYS OF TAXING DUTIES

As Supreme Commander, General Eisenhower followed a man-killing schedule of routine duties and special assignments. He spent hours at SHAEF meetings and many hours more poring over his leather-bound logbook, which contained top-secret cables, intelligence reports and staff summaries. He received diplomats, attended business lunches with Churchill at least two times every week, and made frequent trips to examine new weapons and to review combat units.

Ike felt that the most important part of his job was visiting the troops. "It pays big dividends in terms of morale," he explained, "and morale is supreme on the battlefield." He set for himself a nearly impossible goal: to speak to every unit of troops that would take part in the invasion. Once he gave so many speeches that at the end of the day he was hoarse. Almost always, he spoke without written notes and finished to cheers of "Good ol' Ike!"

Attending graduation exercises at the Royal Military Academy, the Supreme Commander reviews the newly commissioned officers.

A stickler for military courtesy, Eisenhower returns the salutes of airmen (right) while visiting the British Second Tactical Air Force base.

Visiting U.S. troops at target practice, Eisenhower and Churchill try
out new Winchester carbines while SHAEF Lieut. General Omar N. Bradley
loads his weapon. Though the GIs fired at a range of 200 yards, the VIPs
got handicaps: Bradley's target was set up 75 yards away, Eisenhower's 50
yards, Churchill's 25 yards. They fired 45 shots and scored only 29 hits.

Flashing his famous grin, Eisenhower inspects the Quincy, an American
cruiser, in Belfast, Ireland. The Quincy later joined the warships that
bombarded the coast of Normandy in preparation for the troop landings.

In the Wiltshire countryside, Ike watches tank maneuvers of the U.S. 3rd Armored Division. Later, he steered an amphibious Sherman tank during its test run.

Ike examines aerial photographs of the damage done by Allied bombers to soften up enemy defenses.

The Supreme Commander tries the controls of a Marauder. The bombs on the plane represent missions.

Our landings in the Cherbourg — Havre area have failed to gain a satisfactory foothold and I have withdrawn the troops. (withdrawn.) This particular operation My decision to attack at this time and place was based upon the best information available, The troops, the air and the Navy did all that Bravery and devotion to duty could do. If any blame or fault attaches to the attempt it is mine alone.

July 5

n this accidentally misdated note scrawled by Eisenhower before D-Day, he assumes full responsibility for the decision to launch the invasion. The message, to be made public in the event the landings failed, proved unnecessary. Eisenhower later gave the note to one of his aides.

Paratroopers of the U.S. 101st Airborne Division, their faces camouflaged with night paint, chat informally with Eisenhower before departing from their base near Newbury to attack heavily fortified positions in Normandy. Ike, worried about the paratroopers' perilous assignments, spent part of the evening moving among them, listening to their jokes and stories.

3

In the gray predawn light of June 5, while the airborne troops who would spearhead the D-Day invasion were still asleep, the ground forces were already starting their slow seaborne journey to Normandy. Nearly 5,000 ships of all kinds—battleships and cruisers, frigates and sloops, tank landing craft and gunboats, troop transports and assault boats, repair ships, hospital ships, ammunition ships, ships to lay smoke screens, to direct aircraft and to be sunk as tide breakers off the Normandy coast—put out to sea that blustery morning. From the overcrowded harbors of the English south coast, from as far west as Falmouth and as far east as Felixstowe, the components of the greatest fleet that ever sailed butted through wind and swell toward the assembly point, Area Z, off the southern tip of the Isle of Wight.

No one who saw this panoply of overwhelming might could doubt that the Allies would triumph in the battle to come. An English Coastguardsman in his lookout high up on the Dorset cliffs at Saint Alban's Head watched in disbelief as more than a thousand ships streamed by. Below him were soldiers and tanks in landing craft; above were barrage balloons; on the horizon were flotillas of landing craft to the east and lines of battleships to the west and a whole fleet silhouetted against the white cliffs of the Isle of Wight to the south. When the last of the ships had disappeared southward over the horizon, the Coastguardsman turned for home. "A lot of men are going to die tonight," he told his wife. "We should pray for them."

The armada drove on through a moderate sea, with the wind blowing 16 to 20 miles per hour. Aboard the bouncing, heavily laden vessels, many soldiers and sailors were prostrated with seasickness. But the men did little complaining. On the decks and in the holds they cleaned their weapons, received briefings and learned for the first time exactly where they were going to land. Afterward, they spent most of their time "standing about looking out to sea, talking now and then and thinking," reported BBC war correspondent Robin Duff, who was aboard a U.S. troop transport. "When they spoke they were self-conscious. There was a tenseness and a sense of good humor and good fellowship that were impossible to translate into words."

The armada plowed forward, its ships flashing signals to one another. The troop transports were preceded by minesweepers, which cleared 10 lanes through the Germans'

THE AIRBORNE ASSAULT

mid-Channel minefield. The fleet was protected against German U-boats and torpedo boats by Navy and Air Force patrols and by a day-and-night umbrella of fighter planes. The ships took up their final order of battle as the sun began to dip in the sky. By 8 p.m. the leading minesweepers were off the Normandy coast at Cap Barfleur. At 10 p.m. the crewmen could pick out houses on the dark shore. Not a single German gun had been fired.

That afternoon, as the seaborne armada built up at its assembly point, the men of the Allied airborne forces spent their final hours in England in compulsory rest. Their last letter home had been written, their last briefing attended, their last check made, their parachutes fitted, their heavy equipment loaded on the planes and gliders that were to take them to Normandy to open the Second Front. Late in the afternoon, in sealed camps all over southern England, they lined up for their last hot meal. Then the paratroopers, British and American alike, loaded themselves up with 85 to 100 pounds of gear to meet every imaginable contingency.

As the evening light began to fade, nearly 20,000 men of the British 6th Airborne Division and the U.S. 82nd and 101st Airborne Divisions were driven out to 22 scattered airfields, where almost 1,200 transport aircraft (mainly C-47 Dakotas) and more than 700 gliders were assembled for the greatest airborne assault in history. General Eisenhower drove out to watch some units of the 101st prepare to take off from their base near Newbury. Ike's old friend and aide, Captain Harry Butcher, later wrote: "We saw hundreds of paratroopers, with blackened and grotesque faces, packing up for the big hop and jump. Ike wandered through them, stepping over packs, guns, and a variety of equipment such as only paratroops can devise, chinning with this and that one." Going the rounds at other airfields, British Air Marshal Leigh-Mallory found the troops "grim and not frightfully gay," but he had no doubt of their determination to do the job. Last-minute prayer services were held at every base.

Between 10 p.m. and midnight on June 5, paratroopers at English airfields stubbed out their cigarettes, drained their mugs of coffee or tea and took their seats in the aircraft. "Now the whole field is shaking with the roar of motors," wrote Private First Class David K. Webster of the American 506th Parachute Infantry. "Our tail swings around. We

wheel about and head up the runway. My legs are weak and my throat is dry and I can only talk in a stuttering whisper. With a soft rush we leave the ground."

Transport planes, bombers and gliders began to fill the night sky, their red and green navigation lights blinking fitfully. An American paratrooper peered out the open door of his transport; "I could hardly see the sky for the planes," he said later "—there just was not room for more." For hours the stream of aircraft droned above the darkened towns and fields of southern England, and sleeping people were awakened by the throaty rumble of the mighty air armada as it passed overhead.

Aboard the leading British planes flew the pathfinders who would mark the way for the main airborne forces. In addition to the normal heavy load, each man carried a 60-pound kit bag attached to his leg containing lights and beacons with which to define the glider landing zones (LZs) and paratroopers' drop zones (DZs). The pathfinders were scheduled to drop at 15 minutes past midnight. At the same time, the first British combat forces, in six gliders, would go into action. These were five platoons of the 2nd Battalion Oxfordshire and Buckinghamshire Light Infantry (known as "the Ox and Bucks") and a company of Royal Engineers. They had been assigned the task of capturing the bridges of the Caen Canal and Orne River, which guarded the eastern flank of the invasion beachhead.

The gliders carrying the Ox and Bucks ran into gusty wind on reaching the English Channel, and they began to pitch and yaw on the ends of their towropes. They were flying through ragged clouds, and at times the pilots could see nothing but the taillights of the towplanes and the rain spattering on the cockpit windows. But occasionally the clouds parted to reveal a scudding full moon and, far below, the dark, stormy Channel, flecked with the white arrowhead wakes of innumerable ships. The seaborne armies were right on schedule for their landings, to begin at 6:30.

Soon after midnight, the British pathfinders and glider troops saw below them the white, curving shore of France and two ribbons of water mirrored in the moonlight—the Orne River and the Caen Canal. At 12:18 a.m. the six aircraft carrying the pathfinders came over their targets beyond the east bank of the Orne. The first planeload of paratroopers jumped into space. At the same time, 5,000 feet above the mouth of the river, the leading glider pilot cast off his towrope and lifted up the glider's nose to reduce speed. The roar of the wind on the hull died down, and in the eerie silence the craft glided smoothly through the darkness toward enemy territory. The copilot opened the forward door and cold air streamed in. The leading glider leveled out from the dive, then made a 90° turn to the right.

Peering out into the darkness, Major John Howard, commanding the six-glider attack on the bridges, glimpsed for a second the dimly gleaming ribbon of the canal. His glider straightened up for the final approach to the canal bridge. At 3,000 feet the pilot dived steeply and the land rose up; fields and trees were rushing past below at 90 miles an hour. "Hold tight!" the pilot shouted. The platoon linked arms, lifted their feet off the floor and sat locked together, waiting for the impact of the soil of German-occupied France.

As the first airborne invaders were descending on their targets, the German defenders below remained supremely confident that no such thing could happen. The weather was too poor for an invasion. It was windy, cloudy and drizzly, with poor visibility and a rough sea. The weather —and the conviction that everything depended on it— obsessed the 58 German divisions west of the Rhine. By the evening of June 5, the weather was so marvelously bad that

men guarding the northwest coast of France looked forward to a quiet night off after weeks of constant alert.

In Cherbourg, Rear Admiral Walther Hennecke, Naval Commander Normandy, had already received a reassuring signal from the head of his meteorological station at Cap de la Hague at the tip of the Cotentin Peninsula. "Rough sea, poor visibility, force 5 to 6 wind, rain likely to get heavier." Assuming that the weather was too bad for even the usual air raids, the admiral had canceled the customary torpedo-boat patrols for that night. Major General Max Pemsel, chief of staff at Seventh Army headquarters in Le Mans, had received the same forecast from the meteorological section at Naval Group Headquarters in Paris. He came to the conclusion that the invaders could not come that night and, therefore, that they would not come for several weeks—not until the next favorable combination of tide and moon. He so informed Colonel General Friedrich Dollmann, commanding the Seventh Army, and Dollmann ordered his divisional and regimental commanders to leave their units and attend a *Kriegspiel,* a staff war game, in Rennes at 10 a.m. on June 6. The subject of the exercise: "Enemy landings in Normandy, preceded by parachute drops."

To get to the *Kriegspiel* on time, the Seventh Army commanders whose positions would be assaulted by the American airborne forces had left their posts before the first

American planes approached the Normandy coast. One of the last to depart was Major General Wilhelm Falley, commanding the 91st Air Landing Division located near Sainte-Mère-Eglise. As he set off, Falley told his chief of operations, "Nothing's going to happen in this lousy weather."

Field Marshal Rommel, whose Army Group B defended the coasts of France and the Netherlands, was out of touch. That morning he had left his headquarters at La Roche-Guyon between Paris and Le Havre and had started for his home at Herrlingen on the Danube in Germany. June 6 was his wife Lucie's birthday. He intended to celebrate with her, then drive on to Berchtesgaden to ask Hitler to transfer two armored divisions to Normandy. Rommel had labored tirelessly for months to improve his defenses, and he meant to make them invulnerable before any invasion came.

Rommel's superiors spent June 5 dealing with routine problems. Hitler was only concerned that day with Portuguese tungsten imports, diesel truck construction and a fecal examination by his doctor. At Berchtesgaden in Upper Bavaria, OKW—the Supreme Headquarters of the German Armed Forces—kept busy with normal staff work. "OKW had not the slightest idea that the decisive event of the war was upon them," later wrote the deputy chief of operations at Supreme Headquarters, General Walter Warlimont.

And yet on June 5, OB West—the Paris-based headquarters of all German ground forces in Western Europe—was in possession of evidence that the invasion was on its way. The headquarters had been warned in advance by a double agent working in the French Resistance movement.

According to the spy, the British Special Operations Executive, the agency in charge of underground activities throughout occupied Europe, had arranged with the Resistance to carry out extensive sabotage operations to coincide with D-Day. To alert the Resistance, the French-language service of the BBC would quote two lines from Paul Verlaine's poem "Autumn Song." The first line—"The long sobbing of the violins of autumn"—would be broadcast to indicate that the invasion date had been tentatively set. The second line—"Wound my heart with monotonous languor"—would mean that the attack was to begin within 48 hours and that sabotage instructions would follow in code.

Acting on the spy's tip-off, OB West arranged for all BBC transmissions to France to be monitored by the signal center of the Fifteenth Army at Tourcoing, on the Belgian border. On June 1 and 2, the BBC transmitted—and the German monitors received—the first line of the Verlaine poem. Then at 9:15 p.m. on the 5th of June, during a broadcast of many meaningless phrases such as "The doctor buries all of his patients," the signal center heard the vital second line of the poem.

The officer in charge quickly passed on the D-Day warning to his superiors. Within two hours the information had reached Supreme Headquarters at Berchtesgaden, the Commander in Chief West in Paris, Rommel's headquarters and the headquarters of the three big units that made up his Army Group B: the Seventh Army, the Fifteenth Army and the Netherlands Forces.

Incredibly, nothing happened. The warning was not relayed to any of the German troops guarding the invasion coast. In Normandy the Seventh Army's 84th Corps and the divisions of that corps were ignorant of the Allied plans until the invasion hit their coastal positions. Rommel was not recalled from Herrlingen.

The blame for this failure lay with the Commander in Chief West, Field Marshal von Rundstedt. That aged and inflexible officer did not believe that the invasion could take place in such foul weather, and he did not believe that the Allies would be so stupid as to announce their plans on the BBC in advance. In short, he did not believe the report of his own military intelligence, which had previously sounded false alarms, and for hours he did nothing to prepare his armies to meet the invasion.

The commanders in Normandy began finding out about the danger from local reports. One of the first to be informed was Admiral Hennecke, ensconced in his villa overlooking the sea at Cherbourg. Around midnight, the admiral was entertaining a group of musicians who had given a concert for the men at the Naval base. One of Hennecke's guests, a young woman, had seated herself at the piano and was playing Schumann's *Papillons* when the music was interrupted by a lieutenant. He reported to the admiral, "Very heavy air raids on towns and roads in the coastal area." Hennecke went down to his underground command post. The duty officer passed him reports from several observation posts. "Loud engine noise of approaching bomber

Getting ready for their drop into Normandy, soldiers of the British 6th Airborne wrestle an antitank gun up the ramp into a Horsa glider. The invaluable Horsa, which could carry some 7,000 pounds of cargo, brought in more than 20 per cent of the matériel airfreighted to Normandy.

formations . . . light reconnaissance aircraft penetrating over a broad front . . . target markers being dropped behind the front." The admiral was not alarmed—just puzzled. Something was happening, but he was not sure what it was.

The planes whose presence overhead had been reported to Hennecke were more than 1,000 RAF bombers, beginning all-night attacks to soften up German coastal defenses in preparation for the morning seaborne landings. Soon the admiral's uncertainty, and the confusion of German radar operators all along the northern coast of France, would be compounded by a ruse.

The Allied invasion planners, realizing that their airdrops would tip the Germans off to the invasion area, had carefully prepared a series of deceptive D-Day maneuvers, part of Operation *Fortitude*. Several plans were designed to convince the Germans that the activity in Normandy was merely a diversion for a much larger assault on the Pas-de-Calais area, well to the northeast.

The deceptive operations got under way at about the same time that airborne landings commenced in Normandy. To make the airdrops look like a feint, RAF bombers began dropping hundreds of life-size dummies by parachute all over Normandy. To mask the approach of the invasion fleet, powerful radio transmitters in England began jamming German radar stations along the Normandy coast. To point out the Pas-de-Calais as the Allies' objective, RAF bombers began flying hundreds of sorties throughout that area, and German-language broadcasts from England began ordering Luftwaffe planes away from Normandy to defend the Pas-de-Calais. Meanwhile, acting on coded instructions, the French Resistance began sabotaging German communications centers all over France.

The main feature of Operation *Fortitude* on D-Day was a massive electronic conjuring trick. Two small groups of British motor launches headed across the Channel toward the Pas-de-Calais. Each boat towed two 29-foot-long balloons, one floating in the air overhead and the other bobbing behind tethered to a raft. Each balloon was fitted with a nine-foot reflector that produced a radar echo resembling that of a 10,000-ton troop transport. Above the launches, two squadrons of RAF bombers flew in precise patterns, dropping strips of aluminum foil to simulate more planes on radar screens. Aluminum foil had been previously dropped

in bombing raids primarily to jam the German fighter control apparatus; this time, the bombers' precise flight pattern, together with the scattering of foil cut to a special length and shape, created the radar image of a huge air fleet. German radar stations—those that were not knocked out by jamming or bombing—soon began reporting an enormous sea and air armada bound for the Pas-de-Calais.

With all but a few Luftwaffe fighters now heading for the Pas-de-Calais, the Allies owned the air over Normandy. The 1,000 RAF bombers pounding the invasion coast had to contend with nothing but wind, bad weather and antiaircraft fire; their uninterrupted all-night sorties would drop nearly 6,000 tons of bombs on German coastal defenses

Saddled with 100 pounds of supplies and equipment, an American paratrooper adjusts his parachute before departing for Normandy. Each paratrooper was a walking arsenal: he carried two fragmentation grenades, one smoke grenade, one antitank mine and one antitank Gammon bomb made of plastic explosives in a cloth bag. He also had at least one personal weapon—rifle, carbine, pistol or submachine gun plus ammunition. Other gear included a pocketknife, flashlight, razor, spoon, maps, compass, first-aid kit, rations, entrenching tool, main and reserve parachutes, gas mask, jump knife, helmet and spare clothing.

between Cherbourg and Le Havre. To German troops on duty along the coast, the night was alive with enemy planes and the crump of their bombs. The soldiers could not understand why their Luftwaffe fighters did not rise to challenge the enemy.

On the bridge over the Caen Canal at Bénouville, Private Helmut Römer, a young German on sentry duty, heard bombs exploding in the direction of Caen and antiaircraft guns pounding in the region of Troarn. Suddenly he saw the dim shape of an aircraft swooping silently toward him at treetop height. At first he thought it was a bomber with its engines dead, and he watched transfixed as it hit the ground with a tremendous crash, careered across the tiny field on the far side of the canal, knocked over a cow and came to a splintering halt with its crumpled nose in a barbed-wire barrier less than 50 yards from the far end of the bridge. It was not a bomber, it was a huge glider, and for a moment no sound came from it.

Then Private Römer heard English voices calling their platoon's rallying signal: "Able-Able." Almost at once, another glider crash-landed 10 yards behind the first, then a third only 15 yards farther away. "Baker-Baker," called the Englishmen in the second glider, and the soldiers in the third replied, "Charlie-Charlie."

The Englishmen came rushing from their gliders, and one of them hurled a phosphorus grenade against the pillbox on the bridge. A machine gun in the pillbox opened fire but was immediately silenced by another English soldier who popped a grenade through the gunport. Römer had no time to call out the guard or even his own platoon. Some Germans appeared and began manning the trenches on the near side of the canal, but they could not stop the English invaders charging toward them across the bridge, firing as they ran. Römer flung himself into the trenches on the western side of the bridge. The British soon broke into the trenches and the Germans—Römer among them—ran off.

Thanks to the glider pilots' precise landings, the three platoons led by Major Howard secured the Caen Canal bridge less than 10 minutes after the first glider landed (page 99). Howard's other three gliders, attacking the Orne River bridge, did not land so accurately but were just as successful; the first platoon rushed to the attack and found that the German defenders had already fled. Thus, within

minutes the glider-borne strike force of the 6th Airborne had secured the first objectives of the invasion—the two bridges carrying the main road leading inland from the beachhead on the eastern flank of the 59-mile invasion front. The force's radio operator sent out his report using two code words for the bridges to announce their capture: "Ham and jam." The platoons settled into defensive positions to await reinforcements. Not far away, pathfinders for the 6th Airborne were setting out navigation lights and radar beacons to mark the paratroopers' drop zones east of the bridges and north of the village of Ranville.

The second wave of the 6th Airborne roared over the coast at 12:50, and some 2,000 paratroopers of the 5th Paratroop Brigade began their drop over the DZs marked by the pathfinders on the outskirts of Ranville. Guy Byam, a reporter for the BBC, jumped with the paratroopers and later recorded his impressions for broadcast: "Out, out, out fast into the cool night air, out, out, out over France." His parachute opened, and in about 10 seconds, "I find myself in the middle of a cornfield. I look around and even with a compass I can't be sure where I am—overhead hundreds of parachutes and containers are coming down. The whole sky is a fantastic chimera of lights and flak, and one plane gets hit and disintegrates wholesale in the sky, sprinkling a myriad of burning pieces all over the sky."

The paratroopers came down in a strong wind and many of them drifted wide of their DZs. The scattered men were rallied by the mellow calls of English hunting horns, and the reassembled units set about their assignments without delay. One battalion hurried off to reinforce the soldiers at the bridges. A second went to secure the eastern approaches to the bridges. The third battalion went to work clearing the landing zone for the third wave of the 6th Airborne, due to land by glider at 3:20 with the divisional headquarters and the brigade's heavy equipment—the all-important antitank guns, heavy mortars, machine guns and jeeps.

Then, shouting their war cry, "Tallyho," the paratroopers left the LZ and drove enemy infantrymen of the 21st Panzer Division out of Ranville—the first village in France to be liberated from German rule. As the invaders slipped by in the streets below, townspeople whispered from bedroom windows. *"Bonjour!"* Inevitably, the paratroopers caused some confusion. "We are the British Army of Liberation," a lieutenant announced to the matron of a maternity home near Ranville. "What!" exclaimed the matron, glancing in bewilderment at the lieutenant and his tiny party of nine disheveled young men. "All of you?"

At 3:30, as planned, 68 gliders of the 5th Parachute Brigade came in for their landings at the Ranville LZ. Some of them crashed into heavy poles implanted by the Germans to prevent such landings (pages 100-101). Two gliders collided and were destroyed. One slammed through a cottage and came out the other side carrying a bed. But 50 gliders landed accurately, on time and with only light casualties.

Cursing and cheering, the men struggled out of their gliders onto the plowed field. One soldier sang out, "I told yer we wouldn't 'ave to swim." Then, hacking their way into broken gliders, the men salvaged a number of jeeps and 10 of their 18 precious antitank guns. In small groups they

stumbled toward the dark outline of their rendezvous point, the square-towered Norman church in Ranville. At the edge of the field, the groups were halted by their advanced guard, who challenged them with the call "V for" and let them pass when they gave the countersign "Victory."

Beyond the landing zone, on a road near the Ranville church, everything was in a state of confusion. A hot little skirmish was being fought as the soldiers assembled and formed a column. Somewhere nearby German voices were heard; a burst of submachine-gun fire silenced them. Then some British soldiers, who had taken shelter in a ditch, protested an order to get back on the road. Above the clamor the familiar booming voice of the commander of the 6th Airborne Division could be heard: "Don't you dare argue with me! Get on, I say, get on."

Major-General Richard Gale, who had just landed with the main glider force, established order and got the column

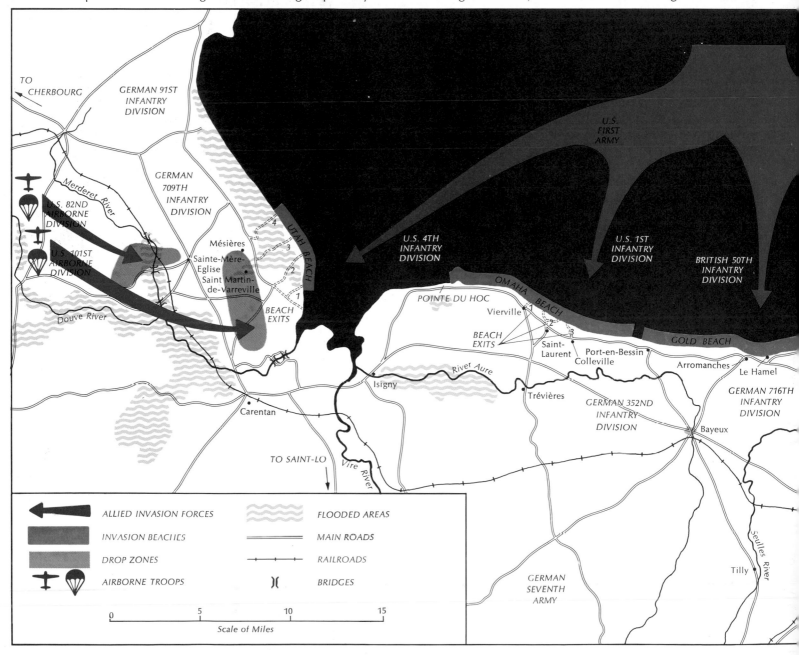

TO CHERBOURG

GERMAN 91ST INFANTRY DIVISION

U.S. FIRST ARMY

Merderet River

GERMAN 709TH INFANTRY DIVISION

U.S. 82ND AIRBORNE DIVISION

U.S. 101ST AIRBORNE DIVISION

Mésières

Sainte-Mère-Eglise

Saint Martin-de-Varreville

UTAH BEACH

U.S. 4TH INFANTRY DIVISION

U.S. 1ST INFANTRY DIVISION

BRITISH 50TH INFANTRY DIVISION

Douve River

BEACH EXITS

POINTE DU HOC

Vierville

OMAHA BEACH

BEACH EXITS

Saint-Laurent

Port-en-Bessin

Colleville

GOLD BEACH

Arromanches

Le Hamel

Carentan

River Aure

Isigny

Trévières

GERMAN 352ND INFANTRY DIVISION

Bayeux

GERMAN 716TH INFANTRY DIVISION

TO SAINT-LO

Vire River

Seulles River

ALLIED INVASION FORCES   FLOODED AREAS

INVASION BEACHES   MAIN ROADS

DROP ZONES   RAILROADS

AIRBORNE TROOPS   )(BRIDGES

Tilly

GERMAN SEVENTH ARMY

0   5   10   15

Scale of Miles

moving toward his preselected headquarters, a château in Ranville. Gale, a flamboyant six-footer described by an associate as "a bit of a buccaneer," set out on foot but soon called to his aide-de-camp for a handsome chestnut horse that he had found grazing in the landing zone. He mounted and completed the trip on horseback.

At the château, Gale drove the troops hard; there was much to do and little time to do it in. The men implanted their antitank guns, dug trenches, fought skirmishes, rounded up stragglers. Dawn was just two hours away. Then the Germans would come—the heavy tanks and crack troops of the 21st Panzer Division. Gale and his troops would have the difficult task of keeping the enemy from attacking the invasion beaches to the northwest.

Meanwhile, some six miles to the east, Gale's 3rd Parachute Brigade was running into trouble. Two of the brigade's three battalions were assigned to blow up the five

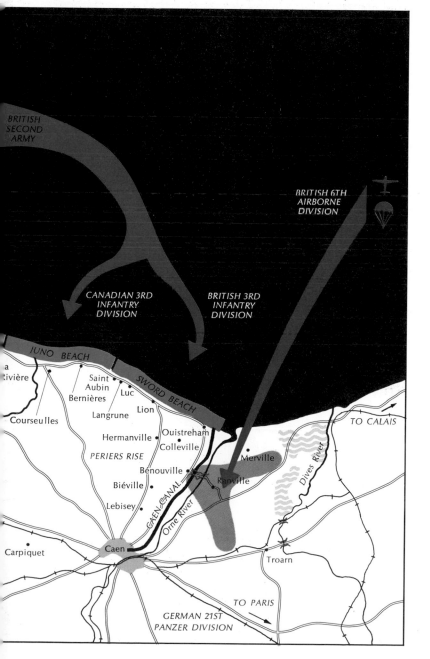

bridges across the Dives River and to occupy the high ground between the Dives and the Orne, thereby establishing a defensive position on the eastern flank of the invasion. There they expected to meet a counterattack by German panzers from the direction of Caen. But several of their drop zones had been inaccurately marked by the pathfinders. Many of the transport pilots found it hard to tell the Dives from the Orne and came in too fast and too high. Inexperienced pilots disobeyed orders and began dodging antiaircraft fire, tossing the overladen paratroopers about, delaying their jumps. The result was that the men were scattered over a wide area.

Even those who managed to jump over their appointed DZs were carried off course by the high wind. Hundreds of paratroopers came down in the swamps of the Dives and many died there. Some of them floated to earth many miles off course and took three or four days to rejoin their units. Several landed so far behind enemy lines that they were obliged to fight alongside members of the French Resistance for months before linking up with the British Army.

The paratroopers made the best of a bad situation. Singly and in small groups, challenged and sniped at by Germans, embraced by excited French civilians who loaded them with brandy, bread, strawberries and fresh milk, the men joined their skeleton units and set off for their objectives. They blew up four of their five target bridges over the Dives with little difficulty. But the fifth and most important bridge— the southernmost one at Troarn, which carried the main road from Caen to Rouen—would have remained intact but for the verve of a nine-man demolition team.

Landing about five miles from the bridge, the soldiers commandeered a medical-corps jeep and trailer and roared off to Troarn, only to crash into a barbed-wire barricade at the edge of the town. After struggling for 20 minutes to cut themselves free, they raced into Troarn and swerved up the main street with headlights on and their guns returning a barrage of German fire. Finally, they reached the bridge and swiftly blew it up. They then abandoned the jeep and made their way cross-country to their headquarters. The destruction of this bridge and the other four was to delay the expected German counterattack by several vital hours.

The last and toughest mission of the British airborne division had been assigned to the 9th Parachute Battalion,

The assault phase of Operation Overlord began shortly after midnight on June 6, 1944, when three Allied airborne divisions—the British 6th, U.S. 82nd and U.S. 101st—landed near predetermined drop zones (shaded areas) in Normandy. Their objective was to secure vital inland targets in preparation for the amphibious assault. Between 6:30 and 7:35 a.m., leading elements of five U.S., British and Canadian divisions hit invasion beaches whose code names would go down in history: Utah, Omaha, Gold, Juno and Sword. Though the Allies established beachheads and seized many of their targets in each sector, they met with stiff resistance from the German forces—deployed as shown—and were prevented from taking their most important D-Day objective, the city of Caen.

under 29-year-old Lieut. Colonel Terence Otway. The 650 men of the battalion were to storm the seemingly impregnable German battery at Merville, whose outer defenses consisted of a minefield, a barbed-wire entanglement 15 feet across and an antitank ditch. If they got that far, they would face a ring of machine-gun nests manned by more than 130 soldiers, and they would have to assault the heavy guns housed in a blockhouse with heavy steel doors and concrete walls six feet thick.

Nothing had been left to chance. Before Otway's attack, 100 RAF Lancasters were to drop enormous bombs on the position, and during the assault three gliders full of troops were supposed to crash-land on top of the battery to help out. If the attack failed, a British warship would shell the battery at dawn. But it was absolutely essential for Otway and his men to succeed, for the battery commanded the left flank of the British landing beaches. The battery would wreak havoc on the seaborne invaders if its four big guns were still in working order at daybreak.

Otway's mission seemed to be doomed even before he landed. The Lancasters dropped their two-ton bombs a half mile wide of the Merville battery, killing some cows and flattening the village of Gonneville-sur-Mer. On the way over, the five gliders carrying Otway's antitank guns and jeeps broke their towropes and crashed into the sea. And the battalion's parachute drop was nearly as calamitous. As the transport planes came over the French coast, the pilots began swerving violently to escape the flak. The parachutists, lined up for their jumps, were thrown to the floor in struggling heaps.

"Hold your course, you bloody fool!" Otway shouted out to his pilot.

"We've been hit in the tail!" a crewman yelled back.

"You can still fly straight, can't you?" Otway retorted. When his turn came to jump he handed a half-empty bottle of Scotch to the RAF dispatcher. "You're going to need this," he said, and then threw himself into space.

As Otway descended tracer bullets tore through his parachute, and he saw that he was falling straight toward a farmhouse that he instantly recognized from intelligence reports as a German headquarters. Otway bumped into the house at 15 miles an hour, and as he landed in a garden a German stuck his head out of an upstairs window and fired a pistol at him. One of Otway's men threw a brick at the German, and the head ducked back inside. Then Germans began pouring out of the front door, and Otway and two other men ran for their lives.

As Otway prowled around in the dark, he realized that he had a disaster on his hands. His battalion, instead of being concentrated on a field one mile long and a half mile wide, was widely scattered. It later turned out that his men had landed over 50 square miles of Normandy. About half of them had dropped into the swamps of the Dives, some as far as 30 miles away. Many had drowned. Otway himself saw one paratrooper up to his shoulders in mud, struggling and crying out as he sank inexorably and vanished from view beneath the slimy surface of a bog. "The drop's a bloody chaos," said Otway's second-in-command. "There's hardly anyone here."

Gradually, Otway assembled 155 men. About 400 were missing. The mortars, antitank guns, jeeps, heavy assault equipment and mine detectors were lost; the engineers and doctors were not to be seen. Otway had only one machine gun and scarcely enough explosives to blow up the German guns. But at 2:57 he gave up waiting for more troops and marched off with the men he had.

Nearly an hour later, they reached the outskirts of the Merville battery and got ready for the attack. Then the battalion suffered more bad luck: at 4:30, when two of the gliders that were supposed to crash-land on the battery appeared overhead, Otway's men could not find the flares to signal that they were present and ready for the carefully synchronized assault. One glider soared over the battery 100 feet up, then turned away and landed in a field four miles off. The other, set ablaze by tracer shells from the battery, crash-landed without casualties in an orchard 200 yards from Otway's position. The third glider never appeared; it had broken its towrope shortly after takeoff and had come down safely in England.

In desperation Otway gave the order to attack. The paratroopers moved through the minefield along a trail marked earlier by pathfinders. They blew two gaps in the barbed wire, charged through and swarmed across the antitank ditch. Then they attacked furiously in two groups. One group engaged the German machine gunners in savage hand-to-hand fighting in the trench network. The other group headed for the guns, fighting to within 30 yards of the steel doors in the concrete blockhouse. Two of the doors were open, and the paratroopers emptied their guns into the interior. Then they raced inside and grappled with the gun crews. The Germans battled fiercely but they were soon overwhelmed.

Otway's men blew up the guns in the blockhouse and then took a toll of their casualties. Around the battery lay more than 175 dead and wounded, 65 of them British. Of the 155 paratroopers Otway had led into battle some 20

minutes earlier, only 80 were now fit to march besides him.

Someone found a flare and fired a signal, announcing the destruction of the guns to a spotter aircraft circling overhead. The plane relayed the signal to the Royal Navy just 15 minutes before its big guns were scheduled to shell the position. Then Otway's signals officer took a carrier pigeon out of his blouse and sent it winging back across the Channel—above the approaching armada and below the incoming waves of bombers—with news that the major objective of the British 6th Airborne Division had been achieved.

At a quarter past midnight on D-Day, at almost the same

Three British gliders, commanded by Major John Howard (inset), lie within 50 yards of one another after a near-perfect landing that led to the capture of the Caen Canal bridge (partly visible at upper right). Air Chief Marshal Leigh-Mallory called the feat the War's finest piece of airmanship.

moment that the British pathfinders were landing on the eastern flank of the invasion beachhead, the American 82nd and 101st Airborne Divisions were dropping their pathfinders on the western flank of the beachhead 50 miles away. The pathfinders marked four DZs and one LZ with lights and radar beacons. One hour later, the main American paratroop force crossed the coastline in a huge aerial armada of some 800 planes.

The chief objectives of the American airborne divisions were to secure the west flank of the invasion beachhead and to spread inland across the neck of the Cotentin Peninsula, cutting off the port of Cherbourg so it could be captured once the Allied invasion forces had built up their strength. These tasks were vastly complicated by the terrain. The airborne target areas were all flooded, either by nature or by the Germans. Behind Utah Beach lay a long, mile-wide lagoon crossed by four narrow causeways. Ten miles farther inland, the Merderet and Douve River valleys, which were also airborne objectives, had been allowed to fill with water by the German forces.

Unless the causeways leading off Utah could be secured by airborne troops, the seaborne forces might be trapped on the beach under German guns. And unless the bridges across the Merderet were secured, a large part of the American invasion force might be bottled up between the lagoon and the flooded rivers, dangerously exposed to German counterattacks from the north, west and south.

From the outset, the American airborne operations were more confused than the British ones. The planes of the transport fleet, flying in formations of nine behind a screen of fighter planes, drifted apart in haze and clouds as they neared the French coast from the west. By the time the scattered formations broke out of the cloud banks over Normandy, many planes were too far off course to start looking for the pathfinders' drop zones—most of which, it later turned out, had been marked in the wrong places. To make matters worse, many pilots who came under German antiaircraft fire began dodging the flak bursts, heaving their passengers about and forcing them to jump in wild disarray.

For all these reasons, more than three quarters of the 6,500 men in each division were widely scattered and took no meaningful part in the action that occurred in their sectors. Thousands of paratroopers were simply lost. Individually and in small groups, they wandered about in fields cut up by impenetrable hedgerows and hiked along country roads between farming villages, fighting brisk skirmishes with German patrols along the way. And yet the drifters' erratic movements inadvertently helped some American units to win crucial engagements; they kept the Germans as bewildered as they were themselves.

The 101st Airborne, assigned to take the causeway exits behind Utah Beach and to throw up a defensive perimeter on the American southern flank, had to land with pinpoint accuracy to avoid falling in the mile-wide lagoon or in the 82nd Airborne's territory along the flooded Merderet valley a few miles inland. But the 101st's drops were a shambles. The paratroopers came down over an area 25 miles long and 15 miles wide, with a few stray groups even farther away. The division commander, Major General Maxwell

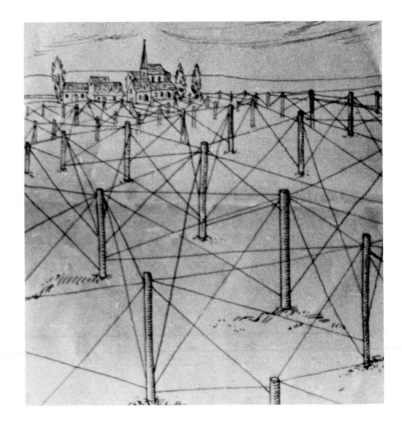

Field Marshal Rommel's own design (right) shows the tall, thick poles—known as "Rommel's asparagus"—that he ordered implanted in inland fields so that "enemy aircraft and gliders will break up while landing." The wires were designed to be connected to shells, which were never installed, and only 10 percent of his proposed 50 million stakes were in place by D-Day. But the wreckage of a Waco glider (far right) in a Normandy field is testimony to the effectiveness of these obstacles.

Taylor, landed all alone in a field and scouted around for half an hour before he found the first of his men, a private. In sheer relief the general and the private embraced like long-lost brothers.

The 101st paratroopers assembled as best they could in flattish terrain that offered few landmarks to guide them. Every man in the division had been issued a small metal toy that made a cricket-like click-clack sound when snapped between the thumb and the forefinger, and everywhere in fields and marshes lost soldiers were using the gadgets to signal their presence. The sharp signals also betrayed many men to German snipers. (For this reason the 82nd Airborne, which had suffered heavy losses using the sound makers in Sicily and Italy, had abandoned the devices and was using instead the whispered password "Flash" and the countersign "Thunder.") Gradually, the small groups of 101st Airborne men got larger. But by dawn General Taylor would have at his disposal only one sixth of his men. (A day later about half of the division was still missing.)

Nevertheless, several makeshift units of a dozen to 100 men began to function effectively. Troops of the 502nd and 506th Parachute Infantry Regiments seized two of the causeways leading across the long lagoon. On the Americans' southern flank, men of the 501st Parachute Infantry ran into stiff opposition from the Germans but managed to fling up a line of shaky defenses against counterattacks from the direction of Carentan. These and later objectives were attained less by plan than by good luck and extraordinary personal initiative.

Lieut. Colonel Robert G. Cole, commander of the 3rd Battalion of the 502nd Regiment, was the mainspring in a successful action that typified the fighting. Cole landed practically by himself just to the west of his drop zone, in 82nd Airborne territory, and he wandered still farther off course before he was informed at a farmhouse on the edge of the town of Sainte-Mère-Eglise that he was heading in the wrong direction.

With a handful of his paratroopers and some stray 82nd Airborne men, Cole hiked east toward his battalion's objective, the German gun battery at Saint Martin-de-Varreville. Click-clacking their crickets along the way, he and his men built up a little force of about 75 assorted paratroopers. They bumped into a small enemy convoy of vehicles, killed several Germans and took 10 prisoners. Then, on reaching the coastal battery, Cole was astonished to discover that the position had long since been abandoned—the result of several bombing missions that had damaged the fire-control setup and forced the Germans to remove the guns. So Cole marched his group of men approximately a mile to the southeast and captured the inland end of Exit 3 from Utah Beach. There the paratroopers lay in wait, and when an enemy force came toward them from the beach, Cole's men shot down 50 to 75 Germans.

About a mile due west of Cole's position, in the general area of the 1st Battalion of the 502nd Regiment, one enlisted man put on a remarkable display of reckless courage. Staff Sergeant Harrison Summers was a member of a small group of paratroopers who were advancing toward the western edge of the town of Mésières. In front of them lay a row of stone houses that served as the barracks for German

coast artillerymen; the position had been given the designation "WXYZ" by American intelligence. Summers' battalion commander, Lieut. Colonel Patrick Cassidy, told him to move up and wipe out WXYZ.

The sergeant rounded up 15 paratroopers; he had never worked with any of them before and did not even know their names. The men showed a distinct lack of enthusiasm for the attack, so Summers set out alone, hoping the others would follow him. Eventually a few did.

Summers sprinted for the first building, kicked open the door and dashed inside with his submachine gun blazing. Four German soldiers fell dead and the rest fled through the back door. Then, covered by his reluctant detachment from a ditch along the road, Summers bolted into the next house. It was empty.

Smashing his way into the third house, Summers mowed down six more Germans. Inside the fourth house he killed another six men.

Summers was joined by Private John F. Camien. Armed only with the Tommy gun and a carbine, Summers and Camien went from house to house, each taking a turn attacking with the Tommy gun while the other covered him with the carbine. Between them they gunned down 30 more Germans in the next few houses.

Then they came to a big building at the end of the line. It was the Germans' mess hall. Incredibly, 15 enemy soldiers were eating breakfast oblivious to Summers' private war outside. Summers burst through the door and cut down all 15 as they rose from the table.

In a few minutes of actual combat, Staff Sergeant Summers had personally accounted for more than 50 enemy dead. He was later awarded a battlefield commission and a Distinguished Service Cross for his action at WXYZ.

West of the 101st Airborne sector, the men of Major General Matthew Ridgway's 82nd Airborne Division encountered worse troubles but eked out no less vital successes. Most of the division made terrible drops. Two of the three regiments discovered to their horror that the flooding of the Merderet and Douve River valleys was far more extensive than they had anticipated; great tracts that looked like solid land in reconnaissance photographs, and that were described as safe landing areas by American intelligence, were in fact overgrown with tall grasses that hid flooded terrain. Some paratroopers drowned, dragged down into the muck and water by their 100-pound loads of gear. Many more men wallowed around aimlessly and learned where they were only by blundering upon the elevated roadbed of a railroad that ran from Caen to Cherbourg. By the time that they extricated themselves from the morass, they were too late to carry out their missions—to blow up the bridges over the Douve and to establish a defensive line to the west of the Merderet.

Farther east lay the 82nd Airborne's primary objective, the thriving crossroads town of Sainte-Mère-Eglise, whose capture General Ridgway had assigned to the 505th Parachute Infantry Regiment. To the German garrison holding the town, the American airdrop seemed to be a small, quick failure. About 30 paratroopers landed right in town, which was lit up by the lurid glare of a fire set by preattack bombers. One trooper landed in the main square and was immediately captured. Another fell on the church steeple and hung there from his parachute pretending to be dead for two and a half hours before he was cut down and taken prisoner. Two men plummeted through the roof of a burning house and died instantly when the mortar shells they carried exploded. One German soldier confronted some French civilians and, pointing to the body of a paratrooper hanging from a tree, shouted triumphantly, "All *kaput!*"

But the 505th was far from *kaput;* most of the regiment had landed in a compact area outside of town and quickly organized to attack Sainte-Mère-Eglise and establish defense lines to the north and south. The assault on the town was assigned to the 3rd Battalion, under Lieut. Colonel Edward Krause, who started out with 108 men. Banking heavily on speed, Krause wasted no time on a cautious house-to-house search. To keep his men from accidentally shooting each other in the dark, he ordered them to use only knives, bayonets and grenades; anyone who fired a gun would clearly be marked as an enemy.

The Germans were caught off balance after their effortless early victory in town. The little fighting they did took place on the outskirts. The mayor of the town, Alexander Renaud, violated the German curfew and went to find out what was going on. He found a lone American paratrooper who had landed in a pond and he pulled him out by his

Rifles at the ready, American soldiers of the 82nd Airborne Division prepare to rout out German snipers in battle-scarred Sainte-Mère-Eglise. The town, a vital communications hub, was taken by the paratroopers on the 6th of June and held against German counterattack for two days.

parachute. Then Mayor Renaud slipped back into town and watched for developments at his front window. In the first light of dawn, he saw that the Germans were gone and that American soldiers were strolling about.

The liberation of Sainte-Mère-Eglise had been that easy. In fact, it had been too easy. The real battle for the town started three hours later, when the Germans counterattacked in regimental strength. The Americans had to fight hard all day, but they kept the town and with it command of the vital main road between Cherbourg and Carentan. The capture of Sainte-Mère-Eglise, together with the successes of the 101st Airborne, meant that the Americans had accomplished most of their major missions.

All through the dark morning hours of June 6, while thousands of Allied paratroopers were scrambling toward their Normandy objectives and while thousands of Allied ships were closing in on the Normandy coast, the German commanders failed to take concerted action. Their disastrous indecision was due partly to the fact that they had been taken by surprise and partly to their own incompetence. But to a large degree, the Germans were befuddled by the Allies' brilliant plans of deception.

The main part of Operation *Fortitude*—the two small groups of balloon-toting motor launches—was an unquali-fied success. Shielded from enemy reconnaissance planes by a curtain of RAF fighters, the launches proceeded sedately toward the Pas-de-Calais. All night long, the image of an immense invasion armada covered German radar screens in the area; the radar operators did not learn of the deception until dawn, when the launches headed back to England and the ghost fleet suddenly disappeared from their screens. Meanwhile, the real invasion fleet was steadily sailing toward Normandy, but for hours it was masked by the intense radio jamming that, with the heavy Allied aerial bombardment, knocked out all but 18 of the 92 radar stations along the Normandy coast. Even after the 18 radar crews spotted the fleet, their hectic reports seemed far less convincing than the many seemingly solid reports of the ghost invasion fleet aimed at the Pas-de-Calais.

The other *Fortitude* operations worked exactly according to plan. The dummy parachutists dropped in Normandy persuaded German commanders to disregard reports of real paratroopers nearby. All through the early morning hours, Allied bombers continued plastering the Pas-de-Calais—and drawing Luftwaffe fighters away from Normandy. Many of the German pilots were misdirected by the British operator who was broadcasting from England on Luftwaffe frequencies. The German ground controllers soon noticed that the British operator mispronounced German words, and

they warned their pilots, "Don't be led astray by the enemy." But the warnings did no good; pilots continued to follow the spurious orders—along with wrong orders from their real controllers. At one point, an exasperated German controller swore into the microphone. At this, the British operator deftly told the Luftwaffe pilots, "The Englishman is now swearing!" In despair, the German controller shouted, "It is not the Englishman who is swearing, it is *me!*"

Confused by this barrage of deception, the German generals did little all night long, while they waited for the murky situation to clarify. Even after a few commanders began to sense that the real invasion was beginning in Normandy, they could not persuade their superiors to share their alarm much less to speed reinforcements.

The hour after midnight, when the chaotic airborne landings were at their most vulnerable, passed calmly in nearly all important headquarters throughout Normandy. General Erich Marcks, in his 84th Corps Headquarters at Saint-Lô, about 20 miles from the coast, was perhaps the first key officer to realize that the threat to Normandy was genuine and urgent. An officer on Marcks' staff later recalled that "at 0111—unforgettable moment—the field telephone rang. Something important was coming through; while listening to it the General stood up stiffly, his hands gripping the edge of the table." The message being read to him told of British operations: "Enemy parachutes drop east of the Orne estuary. Main area Breville-Ranville and the north edge of the Bavent forest. Countermeasures are in progress." Then Marcks was informed by an aide of unusual air activity in and around Cotentin Peninsula—the area of the American airdrops.

Putting together the two alarms, Marcks acted swiftly. He flashed a command to the 352nd Infantry Division west of Bayeux: "State of readiness 2." Marcks also called back the divisional commanders who were on their way to the *Kriegspiel* in Rennes. General Falley of the 91st Air Landing Division, who had departed too late to get far, returned in a

hurry and soon ran into a group of American paratroopers. They opened fire, and Falley's car crashed. As the general reached for his pistol, the Americans shot him dead.

At 2:15 a.m., General Pemsel, the Seventh Army chief of staff, telephoned his commander, General Dollman. "General," he said, "I believe this is the real invasion. Will you come over immediately?"

At about the same time, Rommel's chief of staff, General Hans Speidel, was awakened with reports of the paratroop landings. Speidel was skeptical, concluding only that a few men might have been air-dropped to link up with the French Resistance; nevertheless, he telephoned Rundstedt at OB West in Paris. Soon thereafter Speidel was called by Pemsel, who said: "Engine noise audible from sea on east coast of Cotentin. Admiral, Channel Coast, reports ships located by radar off Cherbourg." All of this, Pemsel said, pointed to a major operation. Speidel still was dubious but he dutifully relayed Pemsel's report to Rundstedt. At 2:40 a.m. Pemsel was informed that Rundstedt did not consider this scattered Normandy activity to be a major operation. In any case, the Seventh Army was ordered put on the highest state of alert.

By 2:55, after Rundstedt had pondered Pemsel's report of enemy ships, he told his OB West operations officer, General Bodo Zimmerman, to telephone Hitler at Berchtesgaden to let the Führer know what was happening. Rundstedt was beginning to think that a major attack was in progress. But would the main blow hit Normandy or the Pas-de-Calais?

By 4:15, when American landing craft were setting out on their long run to Omaha Beach, the field marshal had finally made up his mind. He announced that the airborne landings were "definitely the opening phase of a sea landing to be expected at dawn." A quarter of an hour later he issued a command that required Hitler's approval; he ordered the available Strategic Reserves—two crack German armored divisions, the 12th SS Hitler Youth and the Panzer Lehr—to move up to the Normandy coast at once.

Had Rundstedt's order deploying the Strategic Reserves

been implemented even at that late hour, a prompt German counterattack in strength might have pushed the Allied invasion back into the sea. But Rundstedt's order was not implemented. His message to Supreme Headquarters in East Prussia requesting approval of his order was ignored for two vital hours while Colonel General Alfred Jodl, Hitler's chief of operations staff, who had to act on it first, was allowed to go on sleeping. Nor did anyone awaken the Führer, who had only recently retired to bed with a sleeping draft; his Naval aide-de-camp, Admiral Karl Jesko von Puttkamer, feared "that if I woke him at this time he might start one of his endless nervous scenes which often led to the wildest decisions." And no one disturbed Field Marshal Rommel at his home in Herrlingen until shortly after 6 a.m.

At about 6:30, as the Allied seaborne landings were beginning, Jodl finally woke up. He was furious to learn of Rundstedt's "arbitrary employment" of the Strategic Reserves without Hitler's approval. Jodl maintained that it was wrong to commit the Strategic Reserves before the Allies' intentions were known; the airborne landings in Normandy, he said, might be a trick to divert German attention from what appeared to be a much larger assault aimed at the Pas-de-Calais. Jodl countermanded Rundstedt's order deploying the Strategic Reserves.

Jodl's command marked one of the decisive moments of the War. It meant—as Rundstedt's operations officer, General Zimmerman, later declared—that "the first critical day was lost! The success of the invasion was already decided!"

In Normandy dawn was coming. The survivors of the British 6th Airborne lay quiet in their positions between the banks of the Dives and the Orne. They turned their blackened faces to the south and the east, toward the advancing enemy. At Ranville the last antitank guns were manhandled into place. On the grounds of General Gale's château headquarters, the paratroopers carved out their last trenches with plastic explosives. The general, who had left for a quick inspection of the captured bridges, came bowling back in his jeep. As he strode inside, Gale was overheard muttering to himself, quoting lines from Shakespeare spoken by King Henry V before the battle of Agincourt: "And gentlemen in England now a'bed / Shall think themselves accursed they were not here."

Some 50 miles to the West, the men of the 101st Airborne were still fighting scattered skirmishes beside hedgerows and along the coastal roads. In and around Sainte-Mère-Eglise, the isolated regiment of the 82nd Airborne was preparing to defend the town against counterattack. But many American paratroopers heard nothing more important than the kick start of a German motorbike and the occasional crack of a sniper's rifle in the distance.

Then, in the faint first light of dawn, the British paratroopers and later the American paratroopers heard a new sound. The entire 50-mile invasion front was rocked by a rumbling, concussive roar as the guns of Allied warships opened up a continuous bombardment of the German coastal defenses and artillery batteries. At Ranville, the earth trembled and women screamed. Huge 15-inch shells were roaring their way overhead heading for targets 10 miles inland. At the Caen Canal, a British soldier exclaimed, "Cor, what next? They're firing jeeps!"

At German strong point W5 above Utah Beach, naval shells rained down incessantly in a deafening barrage. They blew up the minefields, filled the trenches with sand, battered the concrete bunkers and covered the Germans inside with fine white dust. The soldiers lay helpless with their hands pressed over their ears.

Suddenly a soldier cried, "Ships!" Second Lieutenant Arthur Jahnke, the strong-point commander, grabbed his telescope and, peering through the gray haze, saw innumerable black hulks—like the silhouettes used in lectures on enemy ship identification. Jahnke gasped at the sight. The sea was full of ships and the air was full of barrage balloons.

Unlike their High Command, the German soldiers along the beaches of Normandy had no doubt about what was happening. The day of invasion had come.

YANKS IN BRITAIN

American servicemen, based in Britain for the long-awaited invasion of France, amble past Buckingham Palace on a sightseeing tour through fogbound London.

THE GI OCCUPATION OF ENGLAND

In a show of Allied solidarity, children in a crowd of English civilians wave American and British flags during an American military parade in London.

Dear old England's not the same,
The dread invasion, well it came.
But no, it's not the beastly Hun,
The G-- D--- Yankee Army's come.

This rude anti-American verse, from a wartime British ballad titled "Lament of a Limey Lass," embarrassed many proper Englishmen, who had no desire to offend their allies. Yet the verse—and the others on the following pages—contained more than a kernel of truth. By May 1944, Britain had been inundated by some 1.5 million U.S. soldiers brought over for the invasion. They were billeted in more than 100,000 British buildings in some 1,100 locations, mainly—the Scots were relieved to note—in southern England. The Yanks were frightfully brash by British standards, and without a by-your-leave they turned staid London into the boisterous GI capital of the world. "On some streets," said American war correspondent Ernie Pyle, "an Englishman stood out as incongruously as he would in North Platte, Nebraska."

Even on their best behavior the Yanks caused tensions. An American private earned nearly five times more than his British counterpart, and he spent his pay freely (and often successfully) on British women. British soldiers considered this unfair competition, and their resentment was presently captured by a Cockney comedian who coined a phrase that swept the country. There were only three things wrong with the Yanks, he said: they were "overpaid, oversexed and over here."

But the problems caused by the collision of two cultures proved to be much less serious than the Allied commanders had feared. Most Englishmen genuinely liked the Americans and welcomed them into their homes. They appreciated the Americans' generosity in handing out candy bars and chewing gum to sweets-starved British youngsters. They enjoyed the free-and-easy air that the Americans brought to British pubs, dance halls and quiet country towns. The infectious gaiety of the GIs was "as good as tonic," one Englishman said, and "for a while the people forgot about the war."

U.S. airmen and a British woman pose unsubtly for a publicity picture, flaunting favors from a British party thrown to promote Anglo-American relations.

In front of a country pub, GIs cultivate a taste for British beer. At first some American soldiers found the brew so tasteless that they added salt for flavor.

A LIBERAL EDUCATION IN FOREIGN FOLKWAYS

They moan about our lukewarm beer—
Think beer's like water over here,
And after drinking three or four
We find them lying on the floor.

Flat, warm British beer was only one of many local peculiarities that the Americans taught themselves to put up with—if not to like. They learned to drive on the left side of the road and to eat fish and chips out of last week's newspaper. They also learned British English: e.g., that a copper was a penny, not a policeman, that a vest was not an outer garment but an undershirt. And the GI billeted in a boardinghouse learned not to laugh when his landlady promised to "knock him up"—i.e., waken him—in the morning.

The GIs never did learn to like the British wartime diet of mutton, boiled kidneys, Brussels sprouts, tea, and coffee that tasted like mud. This fare depressed the Americans so much that steaks, bananas, tomatoes and other solid American food had to be imported from the States. A GI sergeant later said, "I think the first shipment of peanut butter saved our lives."

An English hostess introduces a visiting American soldier to a British institution: afternoon tea.

An adventuresome GI tries his hand at darts, which was new to most Yanks. The soldiers' interest in the classic British pub game was heightened by betting.

At Tussaud's, GIs and WACs admire wax figures of famous Americans.

A Yeoman warder points out sections of interest in the Tower of London.

Queen Elizabeth of England plays hostess to U.S. sailors at a London club.

At Stonehenge in southern England, American servicemen take a lesson in local prehistory from a British guide during a break in their training maneuvers.

SEEING THE SIGHTS IN A WAR ZONE

They swarm in every train and bus,
There isn't room for both of us.
We walk to let them have our seats,
Then get run over by their jeeps.

Off-duty GI sightseers overcrowded all of the British transportation facilities as they spread out through the country individu-

ally, in small groups or on large, organized tours. Some of them visited quaint old English towns. A few made pilgrimages in search of ancestral homes or the haunts of famous English authors. Swarms of GIs visited London landmarks—and were often admitted first, to the dismay of British tourists already waiting in line. In London, Madame Tussaud's Wax Museum was the Americans' favorite, and to repay their patronage the museum added to the exhibit the figures of 14 U.S. Presidents, Generals

Eisenhower and MacArthur, and Admiral Harold Stark *(top left)*.

Some GIs were insensitive to Britain's historical sites. One sergeant, unimpressed by Scarborough Castle, an imposing ruin overlooking the sea, told a British family that "it was a waste of a marvelous site for a hotel" and ought to be pulled down. But every American was moved by one tour set up by the Army to introduce newly arrived GIs to the realities of war: they were taken to see Britain's bomb-ravaged areas.

"Don't forget, Beryl—the response is 'Hiya, fellers!' and a sort of nonchalant wave of the hand."

"They won't let on who the camp is for."

"Those guys just don't know there's a war on!"

"TAXI!"

"Dear Momma, in England they drive on the left side of the road . . ."

"Doris sends her love and has asked me to play 'Deep in the Heart of Texas' as a reminder of them all at Shepherd's Bush."

"DOING ANYTHING TONIGHT, BABY ?"

"Making it look like home"

STRUBE in *Daily Express*

During the War, British cartoons on the subject of ubiquitous American GIs ranged in tone from good-natured joshing to barely suppressed bitterness.

JAUNDICED VIEWS OF THE BOISTEROUS ALLIES

Yanks say they've come to shoot and fight,
It's true they fight . . . yes—when
they're tight.
I must admit their shooting's fine,
They shoot a damn good Yankee line.

To British cartoonists, the GI seemed more interested in winning a woman than in winning the War. However, the newspaper editors culled cartoons that seemed offensively anti-American. It was just as well, for some that got printed were biting enough. One cartoon (left, bottom right) attacked the Yanks' un-British aggressiveness: U.S.

airmen forced down in Germany hail a cab and start operating just as if they own the place. In another cartoon that was unkind to the soldiers of both nations (top, left), British overseas troops, listening to a BBC program, hear an English girl ask the disc jockey to play an American song for her conveniently located GI boyfriend.

London's Rainbow Corner, the largest American service club in England, attracted thousands of fun-seeking GIs and also brigades of Piccadilly prostitutes.

COURTSHIP AMERICAN STYLE

And you should see them try to dance,
They find a partner—start to prance.
When we're half dead, they stop and smile,
How'm I doin', Honey Chile?

Many an English "Honey Chile" wanted to go out with GIs and engage in a form of athletic dancing they called jitterbugging. The young couples did this terpsichore to the music of visiting USO bands: Cab Calloway's, Artie Shaw's and Glen Miller's.

They did it in crowded British pubs, American Red Cross clubs and especially in London's GI club, Rainbow Corner, near Piccadilly Circus.

But what the GIs really liked to do best was make time with British women. They flattered their dates incessantly and plied them with nylon stockings, bottles of perfume and scented soap—wartime luxuries that were obtainable in England only at the American post exchanges. "We felt like queens," recalled one English woman. The GIs were notoriously vigorous in pressing their suit. When a new panty appeared on the market it naturally inspired the popular joke: "One yank and they're off!"

The results of the American-British affairs became conspicuous. So many British women were put in a family way that clinics and welfare organizations found it difficult to keep accurate statistics. Uncounted GIs pestered their commanders for permission to marry, and thousands actually applied for marriage licenses (70,000 British women eventually went to the U.S. as war brides). But whether an affair was serious or casual, it came to a sudden pause when the camps were sealed and the GIs were denied communication with their women. D-Day was about to begin.

116

Inside Rainbow Corner, GIs found a dance hall, game room, library, jukeboxes, barbershop, lounges, an American snack bar and attractive British volunteers.

A GI and his date embrace in London's Hyde Park, one of many public places where American soldiers and their British girl friends tried to find a little privacy.

And then he leaves you broken-hearted,
The camp has moved—your love departed.
You wait for mail that doesn't come,
Then realize you're awfully dumb.

This message scrawled on a tent was left behind by a GI, gone off with his unit to invade Normandy.

119

THE INVASION ARMADA

At an English port, a motorized artillery unit bound for Normandy rolls up ramps into cavernous landing ships. The invasion fleet was ready days ahead of time.

UNLEASHING THE COILED SPRING

By June 1, 1944, at ports and beaches all around the British Isles, the more than 170,000 soldiers of the assault wave and the 5,000 ships of the D-Day armada were braced for the invasion of Normandy. To the Allied Supreme Commander, General Eisenhower, the mighty expedition was like a "great human spring, coiled for the moment when its energy should be released and it would vault the English Channel in the greatest amphibious assault ever attempted."

In fact that moment lasted three days, starting on June 3, when the first ships pulled out of their ports. By nightfall on June 5 the fleet had assembled 13 miles southeast of the Isle of Wight for the journey across the Channel. Minesweepers led the armada, followed by warships, freighters, landing vessels, swarms of tugs and, among the troop transports, converted yachts and luxury liners.

For the soldiers on board, the choppy voyage was tense and interminable. Seasick men groaned at railside while belowdecks troops with strong stomachs enjoyed hearty preinvasion feasts that included roast beef, steak, chicken à la king, peas, plum pudding and ice cream. Some of the men tried in vain to read or sleep; others visited chaplains or wrote last letters home. To dispel somber thoughts, soldiers improvised sports and other types of entertainments. On one ship, men of the 3rd Canadian Division put on a talent show. On H.M.S. *Ben Machree*, U.S. Rangers strung heavy ropes from the masts and amused themselves by swinging across the deck.

The waiting came to an end shortly before dawn on June 6, when the first troops scrambled down cargo-net ladders into landing craft and began the 8- to 11.5-mile run to the beaches. Troops huddled underneath blankets to get out of the cold spray. Many soldiers were now so seasick that they filled their issued vomit bags and began using their steel combat helmets. As the men bobbed about miserably in their assault craft, one of the officers said, "I'll bet they'll be glad to hit the beach." His companion, looking toward the bristling shore, replied: "The poor sons of bitches, they're lucky to be where they are."

Members of the RAF fill barrage balloons with helium before turning them over to the Navy to protect D-Day convoys from German air attack.

A landing craft loaded with Canadian infantrymen plows through heavy seas toward a horizon almost totally obscured by other ships of the invasion fleet.

Killing time aboard ship en route to Normandy, soldiers relax, ready grenades, play shuffleboard and card games, and even study French from pocket dictionaries.

Troops on an invasion barge squeeze in between trucks, cranes and command cars. All told, the fleet ferried 20,111 vehicles to France for the D-Day operation.

In the predawn darkness of D-Day, a Royal Navy cruiser blasts German coastal guns and fortifications. The warships that provided covering fire for the amphibious assault were stationed from three to 14 miles offshore. The long-range guns began their attack two hours before the landings.

Framed by two Americans in steel helmets and life jackets, infantrymen wade through the chest-high surf between landing craft, closing in on Omaha Beach at H-Hour, 6:30 a.m. The skippers of many landing craft were unable to see through the heavy smoke of the bombardment, and they failed to go aground on their assigned sector of the beach.

4

In salvo after salvo, the American and British warships in the Bay of the Seine pounded away at the German fortifications along the 59-mile stretch of Normandy shore. Orange fire from the gun muzzles of fighting ships flashed in the dawn. The battleships and cruisers were standing about six miles out, the smaller, more agile destroyers were less than four miles offshore; and the thunder of their fire rolled up and down the coastline.

Adding to the barrage, thousands of Allied fighters and bombers, flying in over the bay in wave after endless wave, strafed and bombed beaches code-named Utah and Omaha, Gold, Juno and Sword.

As the shells from the battleships and cruisers roared overhead, the spray-soaked and seasick U.S. assault troops surged toward shore. The Americans were leading off the seaborne attack with landings by the 4th Division at Utah, the westernmost of the D-Day beaches, and by the 1st Division at Omaha, the next target beach down the twisting coastline. They would hit the beaches, coded into sections (e.g., Easy) and subsections (e.g., Red and Green), at 6:30, H-Hour, one hour after low tide, when the obstacles would be exposed and easier for the engineers to demolish. Farther east on the British beaches, where the tide came in later, H-Hour at Gold, Juno and Sword was set for 7:30.

In the clumsy U.S. landing craft plunging and bucking through choppy seas toward the Normandy shore, soldiers heard the reassuring drone of the bombers and the snarl of the fighters, and through holes in the low cloud cover they caught glimpses of massed formations of warplanes. From the distant shoreline came the rumble of exploding bombs. These sights and sounds gave hope to the men about to face the defenses of the Atlantic Wall. It seemed inconceivable to them that either the enemy or his weapons could survive such a monumental bombardment.

Over Utah Beach, 269 Marauder medium bombers of the U.S. Ninth Air Force, flying low beneath the clouds, took visual aim on seven German defenses on the beach and dropped 4,404 two-hundred-fifty-pound bombs on them.

At one of these defenses, German strong point W5 on the dunes at the southern end of the beach, Second Lieutenant Arthur Jahnke and his men huddled in their shelters as the American bombs hit the dunes and buried them in sand. The lieutenant had barely dug himself out when a

AMERICAN LANDINGS

destroyer moved out of a line of U.S. warships and began shelling the strong point with murderously accurate salvos. Jahnke's world exploded and flew apart, and when the bombardment moved inland, he found that many of his men were dead and that his guns, flamethrowers and telephone switchboard were all destroyed. Against the landing craft already streaming shoreward in a long line abreast, Jahnke's shattered strong point could muster only two machine guns, one mortar and the soldiers' rifles. Half stunned by the bombardment, the survivors took up their positions. Behind the first wave of landing craft they could see many others speeding toward the shallows. The Germans of W5 waited for the storm to break.

Among the American assault troops was the oldest man and the only general to land on the beach in any of the initial waves on D-Day. Fifty-seven-year-old Brigadier General Theodore Roosevelt, assistant division commander with the U.S. 4th Division, was an extraordinary soldier by any standard. Eldest son of President Teddy Roosevelt, and a cousin of Franklin D. Roosevelt, the general had already participated in landings in North Africa, Sicily and Corsica. A small, wrinkled man with a fibrillating heart, an arthritic shoulder and a raucous voice, General Roosevelt was renowned for his courage under fire and his easy-going, affectionate relations with his men. Though too old for amphibious combat, Roosevelt had persuaded General Bradley, the commander of the U.S. First Army, to let him take part in the D-Day landings "to steady the boys." Armed with only a pistol and a walking stick, the little general had a reassuring effect on the scared and seasick young soldiers of the first assault wave, and he was to be an inspiration to everyone under fire that morning.

The first wave of 20 landing craft approached the southern end of Utah Beach at full speed. To the men of the 4th Division the straight, featureless shore was almost invisible under the clouds of smoke and sand raised by the naval barrage. When the first wave was only 300 to 400 yards from the beach, the assault company commanders fired smoke signals into the air, and instantly the support craft raised their fire from the beach. There was a brief period of uncanny quiet. At 6:31, almost exactly on H-Hour, 10 landing craft lowered their ramps and the 300 men of the 2nd

Battalion of the 8th Infantry Regiment—the first amphibious assault troops to land in France on D-Day—walked off into the waist-deep water and waded through 100 yards of the surf to the dry sand beyond. A few minutes later the 10 landing craft carrying the 1st Battalion of the 8th Infantry Regiment touched down to the right. The tide was a long way out, and in front of the soldiers lay a stretch of firm, gently shelving yellow sands 500 yards wide, strewn with beach obstacles and surmounted by a 100-yard belt of low dunes. The men were elated. They brandished their rifles in the air and shouted to one another. To the surprise of everyone, there was little response from the Germans.

There were several reasons for the sparse opposition. Many of the Germans had been killed and their guns destroyed by the preliminary bombardment, and the survivors were too numbed and demoralized to man their posts when the Americans landed. And the Americans, to their good fortune, had landed in the wrong place. The smoke and dust of the naval bombardment had obscured landmarks on the shore, and a strong lateral current running off the beach had forced the boats off course. Instead of landing at their intended site, where the Germans happened to have two powerful batteries, the assault boats came ashore some 2,000 yards farther south, in an area where the enemy defenses were much weaker.

Moreover, 28 duplex-drive (DD), 33-ton Sherman tanks floated ashore in their inflatable canvas covers with the first waves. The Germans had not expected armor to rise out of the sea against them. When Lieutenant Jahnke first saw the tanks, they seemed like immense floating boxes several meters high, drifting slowly toward the land. Only when they climbed out of the water and moved up the beach, deflating their canvas covers and revealing their turrets and guns, did the horrified Jahnke recognize them for what they were.

The tanks opened fire on strong point W5. They knocked out one machine-gun nest and a mortar. A German lance corporal named Friedrich, in an old French tank, shot up a landing craft of Army engineers and kept the American infantry pinned down at the waterline with his machine gun. Then his tank was hit in the turret, with a sound like a church bell cracking. As a last resort Jahnke decided to launch a secret weapon against the advancing American tanks: remote-controlled, unmanned miniature tanks about

three feet high and capable of carrying 200 pounds of dynamite a distance of 600 yards before being detonated by radio. But the bombardment had upset the delicate electronic circuitry of the Goliaths, as they were known, and they could not be directed near their targets. The little tanks crawled about aimlessly and then lay still on the shore. The Americans found the tanks amusing oddities, but when a group of them wedged a hand grenade in one it blew up like a bomb and tore them to pieces.

To the invaders the lightness of the German opposition was gratifying but the configuration of the beach was puzzling. Where were they exactly? Their maps and plans did not check with what they saw. General Roosevelt, who made a reconnaissance of the rear beach area, was the first to find out their true position and quickly helped the two assault battalion commanders improvise an attack plan to conform with the terrain confronting them.

To the Americans the W5 strong point, which guarded the beach road running inland to the village of Sainte-Marie-du-Mont, was the most troublesome of the German defenses on Utah. Led by General Roosevelt, they launched a 600-man charge across the beach toward the strong point. Crouched in the lee of the antitank wall at the back of the beach, they blew holes in the wall to let the tanks through. To Lieutenant Jahnke the next few minutes were like a dream. Out of the corner of his eye he was aware of the flash of a shell nearby. He felt a blow in the small of his back, and then passed out. When he recovered consciousness he found he was buried under sand and someone was tugging at his legs. Suddenly he was pulled out into the air and light. He looked up and saw that his rescuer was an American soldier.

Wounded, bloody and dusty, Jahnke was taken behind a tank for interrogation. It did not last long. From a grass-covered hill 10 miles away, a German battery began a counterbombardment of Utah Beach. The Americans flung themselves down into the hollows in the sand or against the sides of their tanks as the shells landed among them and shot up great spouts of sand and metal. Jahnke was hit by a piece of shrapnel that tore open his side; his American guard crawled up to him and gave him a cigarette and a gauze dressing from his first-aid kit.

Jahnke was smoking his cigarette, in a state of some shock, when he was ordered to get up. An American general was standing opposite him. Jahnke raised his hand to his bare head in salute. The general half raised his hand to salute him back, then changed his mind. He lowered his hand and gave an order that Jahnke did not understand. Then the young German lieutenant was led away from the war, down the beach to a waiting landing craft and captivity in England.

After he ordered Jahnke to the rear, General Roosevelt stomped up and down, oblivious to the shellfire, his cane in his hand, waving a map as if he were looking for land to buy. He had a tough decision to make. He could divert all succeeding waves of the 4th Division to this new, relatively calm stretch of beach. But only one road led inland. Thirty thousand men and 3,500 vehicles were scheduled to land at Utah during the day. If the road could not be kept open, the beach would become hopelessly glutted with men and machines—easy prey for a German counterattack. Roosevelt could, on the other hand, march his troops up the beach to the original assault area. But there the exit road inland was fiercely defended by German strong points. Troops landing there, according to plan, were being cut to pieces by enemy fire.

Roosevelt conferred briefly with his battalion commanders and made his decision. He would try to capitalize on the felicitous error and commence the invasion of France from the wrong place. He would, in his own words, "start the war from here."

Roosevelt's gamble paid off. His rapid move inland deepened the beachhead and cleared the area for the fresh assault waves piling up on the shore. (On July 12, just after General Eisenhower appointed him commanding general of the 90th Division, General Roosevelt suffered a heart attack and died. He was buried at Sainte-Mère-Eglise, just six miles from Utah Beach, and was posthumously awarded the Medal of Honor.)

By the time that the Germans were able to adjust their fire to the more southerly beach, the landings on Utah Beach had gathered uncheckable momentum. Four hundred men from the Naval-demolition and Army-engineer teams had come in on the heels of the assault waves and within an hour had blown up the German beach obstacles and bull-

In this aerial view of Utah Beach, American infantrymen swarm ashore during the first minutes of the invasion. On the beach (bottom), men sprawl in the sand, some already dead or wounded, while others wade in through the surf. The two large vessels at top right, some 300 yards offshore, are LCTs that have just unloaded the tanks seen nearing the shore in an irregular line. The other vessel is a troop-carrying LCI.

dozed a route through them for landing craft to follow.

By 9 a.m. the leading regiment, the 8th Infantry, and the tanks had broken through the Atlantic Wall on a two-mile front between the sea and the lagoons at the back of the dunes. By 10 a.m. the main body of the follow-up regiment was landing with so little trouble it seemed almost like routine training. An endless stream of men, tanks, guns, vehicles and supplies poured onto Utah from the sea. There was little opposition at this end of the beach. The distant German guns kept up a sporadic fire, but they did not loosen the American grip on the beachhead. Noticing that the German guns seemed to be ranging on the barrage balloons that protected the landing craft, one landing-craft commander ordered his balloons cut loose, and as they floated out to sea they were pursued by salvos from the puzzled German artillery. After that, all of the other balloons were released.

Some of the assault troops at Utah, instead of immediately driving straight inland, swung north and south along the beach to attack the positions that should have been occupied in the initial landing. The Americans desperately needed more routes off the beach, and during the morning they got them. One by one the strong points guarding roads inland, north and south of the original beachhead, fell to the assault troops, and by the end of the morning three exits from the beach were in American hands.

Still, progress was painfully slow. The Germans had made good use of the terrain behind the sand dunes of Utah. There they had flooded a stretch of meadowland usually kept dry for cultivation, thus confining the American flow of men and matériel to the three causeways that traversed the marshy ground. As the Americans pushed westward and southwestward over the causeways, aiming to link up with the hard-pressed 101st and 82nd Airborne forces then struggling to capture key coastal villages, German shells knocked out vehicles, creating massive traffic jams and slowing the American surge to a crawl. But American casualties remained remarkably light. By the end of the day, only 197 soldiers who landed on Utah had been killed or wounded; 60 were missing, presumed drowned.

Just southeast of Utah, a much fiercer battle was under way on the wild, four-mile-long crescent beach between the towns of Vierville-sur-Mer and Colleville-sur-Mer. What happened there early on June 6, 1944, made Omaha one of the immortal names of American military history, as valiant and as terrible as Guadalcanal, Tarawa and Iwo Jima. On Omaha Beach was fought the bloodiest and the most desperate battle of D-Day. It was there that the Germans came nearest to throwing the invaders back into the sea.

Omaha Beach was not a good place for an amphibious assault. At either end it was dominated by sheer cliffs 100 feet high. The beach, 300 yards across at low tide, shelved gently up to a steep bank of coarse pebbles, impassable to vehicles in most places. The pebble bank was backed by a combination of sand dunes and sea wall, also impassable to vehicles.

Behind the dunes lay a level shelf of sand, marsh and coarse high grass. From there the ground sloped up to a farmland plateau 150 feet high. Only four exits led inland from Omaha Beach—three were cart tracks, the fourth a paved roadway; all wound through deep, thickly wooded

The ill-starred infantrymen of A Company, 116th Regiment, 29th Division gathered for a group picture at Fort Meade, Maryland, in 1941. Three years later, within 10 minutes of their D-Day landing on Omaha Beach, an estimated 96 per cent of the company's 197 men were killed or wounded—one of the highest casualty rates of the Normandy invasion. Particularly hard hit was a group of 35 men from the small town (total population 3,800) of Bedford, Virginia. Twenty of them perished.

ravines in the plateau (usually referred to as "draws" in American military reports because of their resemblance to the dry watercourses of the American West). Each track led to one or another of the stout little stone villages on the Isigny–Port-en-Bessin coast road, which ran along the cultivated edge of the high plateau approximately one mile inland. The westernmost track led to Vierville, the easternmost to Colleville, the two in the middle to Saint-Laurent-sur-Mer. Fortified by the Germans, each village blocked the Americans' only routes off Omaha.

The Germans had made the geography of Omaha even more difficult for the Americans. The beach between the low and the high watermark had been thickly planted with mined obstacles: upright iron frames called Belgian Gates, a 10-foot-deep line of heavy wooden stakes angled toward the sea and steel hedgehogs angled to stave in the bottoms of landing craft. Thus the troops of the first waves, who landed at low tide, would have to advance on foot up a beach that offered no cover from fire other than the mined obstacles until they reached the relative shelter of the pebble bank at the top of the beach.

Immediately above the pebble bank the Germans had constructed a thick barricade of coiled barbed wire. Beyond this, the flat shelf of sand and marsh between the beach and the escarpment beneath the high plateau was heavily mined and crosscut with antitank ditches. The Germans had sited their weapons so that no inch of Omaha Beach was left uncovered by fire. From the cliffs at either end of the beach, high-velocity 75mm and 88mm guns, protected by concrete walls three feet thick, could pour flanking fire over the entire beach. Defensive strong points were sited on the slope above the whole stretch of the beach, especially near the entrance to the draws.

Each strong point was a complex system of pillboxes, gun casemates, mortar pits, firing trenches and open positions for light pieces of artillery and antitank guns, surrounded by wire and minefields and connected to one another and to underground bunkers and magazines by tunnels and deep trenches. The machine gun was the basic weapon of the German emplacements at Omaha Beach, but the defenders could also bring to bear multibarreled rocket launchers, obsolete French tanks sunk flush with the ground and heavy infantry mortars in concrete pits.

The German defenses at Omaha were among the worst encountered by the Americans in the entire War. And the beach defenses were only the first line. The string of villages behind Omaha formed a second line of defense. The flooded valley of the River Aure, about four miles farther inland, formed a third line, which the Americans would have to traverse if they were to avoid being bottled up in the narrow coastal strip. The Americans would never have dreamed of landing at Omaha if there had been anywhere else to land. But along the 20-mile stretch of coast between Utah and the British beaches there was nowhere else—only sheer cliffs and rocky offshore reefs.

Along with the unfriendly terrain and formidable defenses, a sudden shift of German troops had worsened the prospects of the invaders. Up until a week before D-Day, the Americans had not been particularly worried about the quality of the Omaha defenders. Their intelligence reports indicated that the beach lay within a 45-mile stretch of coastline held by the 716th Infantry Division—a nonmobile

outfit equipped only for a static role, low in morale, 50 per cent of them foreign conscripts, mostly Polish or Russian. Only 800 to 1,000 men actually manned the beach defenses against the 34,000 Americans who were to land there on D-Day. Those were promising odds. But in the week preceding D-Day Allied intelligence confirmed that the crack German 352nd Infantry Division, a mobile unit battle-hardened on the Eastern Front, had moved up from Saint-Lô to stiffen the crust of the coastal sector that included Omaha Beach. This information was received too late to pass on to the American assault troops already on their way to the area. They went into action believing that Omaha was weakly manned, even if strongly fortified.

To make matters worse, the Americans committed costly errors in their D-Day planning. The commander of the American task force, Rear Admiral Alan G. Kirk, rejected the advice of Admiral Sir Bertram H. Ramsay, the overall Allied Naval Commander in Chief, to anchor the American transports within eight miles of the shore. Anxious to keep his transports out of range of German coastal batteries, Admiral Kirk instead anchored them 11 to 12 miles offshore—where the wind-whipped seas were running far too rough for the clumsy landing craft.

Furthermore, the U.S. Army ignored lessons learned by the Canadians during the Dieppe raid—the need to avoid frontal attacks on fortified objectives and the need for close armored support for infantry in the first minutes of a landing. The American commanders also rejected as unproven the specialized armor—the mine-clearing tanks, the flame-thrower tanks and the pillbox-busting tanks—developed by the 79th British Armored Division to deal with beach obstacles and fortifications while under fire. And though some floating DD tanks were allocated for the Omaha assault, they were too few in number and were cast afloat too far from the shore. The unfortunate soldiers of the 1st Division, one of the Army's toughest and most experienced outfits, were in effect required to carry out a frontal assault on a fortified position with little but light weapons to help them. And the engineers were expected to clear gaps, dismantle obstacles, demolish roadblocks and lift mines by hand while defenseless and under fire. Under such circumstances it is not surprising that Omaha threatened for a while to develop into an even greater tragedy than Dieppe.

The plan for the Omaha landing called for two regimental combat teams in the initial assault: the 116th Infantry Regiment on the right between Vierville and Saint-Laurent, the 16th Regiment on the left between Saint-Laurent and Colleville. As soon as the teams had gained a foothold on Omaha, the remainder of the 1st and the 29th Divisions of the U.S. V Corps would land. The 29th would clear the area between the coast and the River Aure as far west as the Vire estuary, while the 1st Division would wheel left to link up with the British Second Army at Port-en-Bessin and then drive south to secure a bridgehead over the Aure to the east of Trévières. By nightfall on D-Day the V Corps hoped to have established a beachhead 16 miles wide and six miles deep. Such was the plan.

Almost from the moment of their descent into the sea nearly 12 miles offshore, the troops of the early assault waves ran into trouble. Ten landing craft carrying more than 300 men were swamped by the steep waves, some within a few minutes after launching. Others remained afloat only because their occupants bailed water furiously with their steel helmets. The artillery, transported in DUK-Ws, went wholesale to the bottom. Another tragedy occurred 6,000 yards from the shore when 29 DD tanks were launched from their LCTs to make their own way to the eastern side of Omaha Beach. These tanks could operate in only relatively calm and protected waters, and very quickly their inflated canvas covers began to collapse in the choppy seas. The tanks sank like stones.

Some crewmen managed to escape through the hatches, and they thrashed about in the waves, choking on the salt water. Others sank inside the tanks. Of the 29 tanks, only two reached the shore. Three others, their flotation bags deflated, were beached from an LCT whose damaged ramp could not be lowered at sea. Thus the 16th Infantry landed with almost no armor support. The remaining 32 DD tanks, destined for the 116th Infantry flank on the western sector of Omaha, were not launched because the Army officer in charge wisely considered the sea too rough. He decided to go in and beach them instead.

For those whose landing craft stayed afloat, the approach to the beaches was absolute misery, and for many the only note of encouragement in an otherwise dismal dawn was the booming sound of the battleships flailing away at the enemy shoreline. Novelist and war reporter Ernest Hemingway, who was on board a landing craft bound for Omaha, later described the scene: "As the LCVP rose to the crest of a wave, you saw the line of low, silhouetted cruisers and the two big battlewagons lying broadside to the shore. You saw the heat-bright flashes of their guns and the brown smoke that pushed out against the wind and then blew away.

"Those of our troops who were not wax grey with seasickness, fighting it off, trying to hold onto themselves before they had to grab for the steel side of the boat, were watching the *Texas* with looks of surprise and happiness.

"There would be a flash like a blast furnace from the 14 inch guns of the *Texas*, that would lick far out from the ship. Then the yellow brown smoke would cloud out and, with the smoke still rolling, the concussion and the report would

On a shell-battered landing craft off Omaha Beach, a medic gives a blood transfusion to an American crewman wounded too severely to be transferred to a hospital ship. Scattered on the deck around them are fragments from the kapok jackets of other crewmen killed by a shell blast.

hit us, jarring the men's helmets. It struck your ear like a punch with a heavy, dry glove.

"Then up on the green rise of a hill that now showed clearly as we moved in would spout two tall black fountains of earth and smoke.

"'Look what they're doing to those Germans,' I leaned forward to hear a GI say above the roar of the motor, 'I guess there won't be a man alive there,' he said happily.

"That is the only thing I remember hearing a GI say all that morning."

The men were deceived by the aerial and naval bombardment. The low cloud cover, the dust and the smoke made it impossible to pinpoint targets on the beach. Few bombs or shells fell near German positions, and the salvos from the rocket craft burst in the water short of the beach. The German batteries and strong points came to life as soon as the bombardment lifted, and as the first wave of American assault troops ran in to the shore, they met increasingly heavy fire from enemy guns and artillery. Over the last quarter of a mile it was clear to everyone that enemy fortifications had not been knocked out.

At defensive strong point WN62, located among the sand dunes beside the track that led to Colleville, the German soldier manning the observation post watched carefully as

On Utah Beach after the battle, U.S. Navy demolition experts dismantle German dynamite-laden, radio-controlled dwarf tanks, not one of which had managed to reach its target. This was not the first failure for the minitanks. They had been used against the Allied landing at Anzio, Italy, in February 1944, and 14 had been destroyed by Allied gunners in one day.

the first line of landing craft from the awesome invasion fleet neared the waterline directly in front of him. Lance Corporal Hein Severloh, 21, a farmer from Metzingen, had his fingers curled around the trigger of his machine gun. In the trench on the slope to the left, three more machine guns were manned by the men from the strong-point garrison. In front of the strong point was the mortar pit. Behind the observation post were two more mortar positions. The infantry were dug in forward. Inside the bunker the commander of the site, a Lieutenant Frerking, was on the telephone giving firing instructions to the battery officer at Houteville, five miles inland, where the regiment's 105mm howitzers were positioned. "Wait for the order to fire," he finished. They waited in silence.

The tide had ebbed a long way out and not yet begun to turn. The landing craft sped toward the shore, then lurched to a halt on the sandbars a little beyond the beach. The range was 400 yards.

"Target Dora," Lieutenant Frerking shouted into his telephone, "Fire!"

At 6:30, as their landing craft touched down, the American soldiers heard a prolonged tattoo of machine-gun bullets beating on the ramps, and when the ramps were lowered they saw the surf in front of them whipped by a hail of bullets. Lance Corporal Severloh had squeezed off a long burst that traversed the advancing Americans from one end of the line to the other. An instant later, the howitzer shells from the 1st Battery at Houteville came screaming over, exploding in showers of sand on the beach.

The six boats of Company A of the 116th Infantry tried to land in a cauldron of fire delivered by the German strong point guarding the Vierville exit and by the gun emplacement on the bluff at the western end of the beach. One landing craft foundered 1,000 yards out. Another craft, hit by four shells, disintegrated. The other four boats grounded on a sandbar 30 yards short of the nearest beach obstacles and several hundred yards short of the sea wall, their nearest effective cover. Then the ramps were lowered and the men leaped into water up to six feet deep.

"As the first men jumped," runs the official report of A Company, "they crumpled and flopped into the water. Then order was lost. It seemed to the men that the only way to get ashore was to dive head first in and swim clear of the fire that was striking the boats. But, as they hit the water, their heavy equipment dragged them down and soon they were struggling to keep afloat. Some were hit in the water and wounded. Some drowned then and there. . . . But some moved safely through the bullet-fire to the sand and then, finding they could not hold there, went back into the water and used it as cover, only their heads sticking out. Those who survived kept moving forward with the tide, sheltering at times behind under-water obstacles and in this way they finally made their landings.

"Within ten minutes of the ramps being lowered, A Company had become inert, leaderless and almost incapable of action. Every officer and sergeant had been killed or wounded. . . . It had become a struggle for survival and rescue. The men in the water pushed wounded men ashore, and those who had reached the sands crawled back into the water pulling others to land to save them from drowning, in many cases only to see the rescued men wounded again or to be hit themselves. Within 20 minutes of striking the beach A Company had ceased to be an assault company and had become a forlorn little rescue party bent upon survival and the saving of lives."

The assault on Omaha Beach was a shambles. The Army and Navy engineers who had the crucial task of clearing and marking boat lanes through the beach obstacles suffered appallingly. German shells detonated the explosives packed tightly on the landing-craft decks, blowing the engineers to pieces. Few of the surviving teams landed in the right places, and as a result several of them had no tank or infantry support. Burdened with equipment and explosives, they made easy targets as they struggled ashore, and much of their equipment, especially the buoys and poles for marking the cleared lanes, was lost. Some of the obstacles could not be destroyed because the rising tides had covered them, others because infantrymen were taking shelter behind them. One blew up prematurely when its charges were set off by mortar shells, killing engineers and nearby infantry. In half an hour the engineers could clear only six gaps through the obstacles and just one of those could be marked. In their heroic effort during this bloody day, they suffered 41 per cent casualties.

Meanwhile, the assault troops were being mowed down

at the water's edge or pinned down behind the sea wall or pebble bank at the top of the beach. Some of their personal weapons, and many of their support weapons—bazookas, flamethrowers, mortars—were lost in the chaotic landing. When the subsequent waves came in, German fire was tornadic, and the new arrivals simply contributed to the chaos, augmenting the heaps of dead and the huddles of living soldiers. The losses in the first hour of the assault, particularly opposite the Vierville exit, were awesome.

As the tide crept remorselessly in, the press of men became more concentrated, and along the pebble bank the bodies of the living and the dead eventually formed a solid, motionless belt seven yards wide. Too exhausted and too shocked to move, their units scattered or broken, many of their officers and noncoms killed or wounded, uncertain of their bearings, unsure of where to go or what to do in the face of the unrelenting German fire that hammered around them, the bewildered troops were slow to rally and even slower to move off the beach and advance inland. Succeeding waves of men, support weapons and transport were arriving now, but as there was only one marked channel through the obstacles, some boats blew up when they hit mined stakes underwater, or they were impaled on steel obstacles, where they foundered or became easy targets for the German guns, which blew them out of the water.

Ernest Hemingway, in his landing craft, came into the eastern end of Omaha. The battle was at its height; Hemingway noticed that the tanks were still on the beach. "Just then," he wrote, "one of the tanks flared up and started to burn with thick black smoke and yellow flames. Farther down the beach, another tank started burning. Along the line of the beach, they were crouched like big yellow toads along the high water line. As I stood up, watching, two more started to burn. The first ones were pouring out grey smoke now, and the wind was blowing it flat along the beach. As I stood up, trying to see if there was anyone in beyond the high water line of tanks, one of the burning tanks blew up with a flash in the streaming grey smoke.

"On the beach on the left . . . the first, second, third, fourth and fifth waves lay where they had fallen, looking like so many heavily laden bundles on the flat pebbly stretch between the sea and the first cover. To the right, there was an open stretch where the beach exit led up a wooded valley from the sea. It was here that the Germans hoped to get something very good and later we saw them get it.

"I saw three tanks coming along the beach, barely moving, they were advancing so slowly. The Germans let them cross the open space where the valley opened onto the beach, and it was absolutely flat, with a perfect field of fire. Then I saw a little fountain of water jut up, just over and beyond the lead tank. Then smoke broke out of the leading tank on the side away from us, and I saw two men dive out of the turret and land on their hands and knees on the stones of the beach. They were close enough so that I could see their faces, but no more men came out as the tank started to blaze up and burn fiercely."

On the bridge of the U.S.S. *Augusta* 12.5 miles offshore, General Bradley, commander of the U.S. First Army and overall commander of the American landings on D-Day, watched and waited anxiously. A desperately worried man, he had heard almost no news of the Utah landings, and the few signals he had received from Omaha indicated an impending disaster: wrecked landing craft, burning vehicles, exploding ammunition and continuous German shelling. By 9:00 a.m. the situation looked so bad that Bradley considered abandoning Omaha and transferring the follow-up waves to the British beaches on the Allies' left. Shortly afterward he sent an urgent message to SHAEF, asking permission to use that alternative. This message did not reach SHAEF until so late that it was no longer relevant.

In the midst of all this confusion a few small, isolated groups began to move out of the lee to the pebble bank, and with infinite pains they found a way over the marshy flat behind the beach and up the bluff to the plateau. Several units of the 1st Battalion, 116th Infantry had been set down farther to the east than intended. There the beach was less heavily defended and was obscured from German view by the smoke of vegetation set on fire by the naval bombardment; under cover of this screen they were able to rush off the beach and work their way through the barbed wire and minefields and up the ridge to Vierville, almost half a mile inland. They were joined by a company of the 1st Battalion, which had also landed too far east and had probed an unmined gap between the German strong points.

THE RANGERS' ATTACK ON A CLIFFTOP BATTERY

Early on D-Day morning, 225 Americans of the 2nd Ranger Battalion landed below the cliff at Pointe du Hoc, three miles west of Omaha Beach. Their mission was to scale the 100-foot-high precipice and destroy a coastal battery that Allied intelligence said contained six 155mm German howitzers. These powerful guns had to be prevented from wreaking havoc on the Americans landing at Omaha and the fleet offshore.

The Rangers, defying enemy fire pouring down from above, used rocket guns to shoot grapnels with ropes attached to them into the cliff face. Then they started climbing hand over hand up the face. One by one, they were picked off by German snipers and fell into space. One wounded Ranger slid down his rope, careening off rocks, before he lost his grip. It was, a buddy said later, "a lifetime before his body hit the beach." Other men managed to struggle into crevices in the cliffside.

But more and more Rangers reached the clifftop, and soon they routed the enemy. Only then did they learn—with dismay and outrage—that the howitzers were not in the battery. The Rangers found them hidden a mile inland and destroyed them.

The Rangers paid dearly for their herculean attempt to silence the nonexistent battery. At the end of the day, after the unit had fought off three German counterattacks, only 90 out of the 225 Rangers who had started the climb up the cliff were still able to bear arms.

Rangers occupy a former fortification at Pointe du Hoc, as German defenders are taken captive. The draped flag serves as a marker to prevent Allied shelling.

Before midmorning there were 200 Americans in Vierville—just enough to drive off a German counterattack designed to overrun what was left of the troops pinned down on the beach by the formidable German strong points.

Farther to the east, parts of the 2nd and 3rd Battalions of the 116th Infantry also landed under cover of the unintended smoke screen of burning grass near the draw at Les Moulins. The smoke there was so thick that some troops, in order to reach the crest of the beach, had to put on their gas masks. Others made little progress until they discovered a minefield that had been detonated by the bombardment, and several groups from both battalions were able to work their way over the bluff toward Saint-Laurent before the Germans closed in with shellfire.

On the left flank of Omaha Beach part of the 16th Infantry had been similarly assisted by navigational errors that had set them down half a mile or more east of their planned objectives. They thus side-stepped the formidable German strong points still guarding the entrance to the Colleville draw, which the decimated first wave was to have stormed, and instead found a way up the steep but weakly defended gully in the cliffs that bound Omaha Beach at its eastern end. By 9:30 a.m. they had breached the German defenses at this point and were moving steadily eastward along the top of the cliffs toward Port-en-Bessin, where they were supposed to link up with the British invasion force.

On their right, men of the 1st and 2nd Battalions of the 16th had enjoyed no such good fortune. Most of them had been chopped to pieces by the guns of the Colleville draw. Some lay motionless beneath the crest of the beach, pinned down by the German fire.

A courageous lieutenant and a wounded sergeant eventually got the men up and moving. Standing up under fire, the lieutenant and the sergeant walked over to inspect the barbed-wire entanglement above the pebble bank, then walked back and looked down at the men, hands on hips. "Are you going to lay there and get killed," the lieutenant asked, "or get up and do something about it?" No one moved. So the lieutenant and the sergeant went back to the wire, still under fire, and blew a gap through it themselves. This rallied the men, and in single file they followed their officer over the ridge along a narrow, mined track where a false step meant death or injury. Many were the false steps, and the wounded lay where they fell, for fear of setting off other mines, while the rest of the column stepped over them and moved on. Through this dangerous gap, which claimed many casualties, 300 men eventually passed through the German defenses en route toward Colleville.

The bulk of the American troops were nevertheless still stuck on the beach when at 9:50 a.m., on board his headquarters ship, Major General Clarence R. Huebner, commander of the 1st Division, received a message from them: "There are too many vehicles on the beach; send combat troops. 30 LCTs waiting off shore; cannot come in because of shelling. Troops dug in on beaches, still under heavy fire." If Huebner's troops did not break out from the beach quickly, further reinforcements from the German 352nd Division might tip the balance and overrun the American positions. Huebner took drastic measures at once. He interrupted the meticulous flow of material to the beach and ordered the follow-up regiment, the 18th Infantry, to go in and more DD tanks to be put straight down on the beach. At the same time he called on the Navy to punch out the German strong points and batteries even at the risk of hitting his own men.

On board the battleship *Texas*, Rear Admiral C. F. Bryant, acting on Huebner's request, exhorted gun crews on his ships over the radio: "Get on them, men! Get on them! They're raising hell with the men on the beach, and we can't have any more of that! We must stop it!" The destroyers swept in close to the beach, some coming into waters so shoal that only a few inches separated keel and bottom. All morning they fired, and well into the afternoon. Their sterns occasionally touched the sandy bottom as they came in and turned to deliver their salvos. Their fire was almost the only artillery support most of the troops saw that day, and it filled the gap caused by the loss of many of the DD tanks and the DUK-Ws carrying the Army guns.

By 11 a.m. the battle was beginning to go in the Americans' favor. Colonel George A. Taylor, commanding the 16th Infantry, yelled across the beach: "Two kinds of people are staying on this beach, the dead and those who are going to die. Now let's get the hell out of here!" He then led his troops forward to attack the German positions. At 1:30 p.m. General Bradley on board the *Augusta* received a report from V Corps: "Troops formerly pinned down on beaches Easy Red, Easy Green, Fox Red now advancing up heights beyond beaches." Overwhelming reinforcements of men and matériel began to wear the German defenders down. At the main exits fresh troops and new tanks captured the German strong points weakened by bombardment from the destroyers, and the engineers were clearing the minefields. But the Americans still had to advance inland and deepen their front before the day was won.

As it turned out, they were assisted by the German 84th Corps' lack of detailed information about the Omaha engagement. Communications had been broken by the bombardment, and the paltry information that General Marcks, the 84th Corps commander, received from the invasion front indicated that his troops in the British sector were more hard pressed than the 352nd Division at Omaha. The armored reserves that might have made all the difference to the outcome at Omaha were consequently pitched against the British, who in the meantime had landed on the beaches code-named Gold, Juno and Sword. At 1:35 p.m. General Marcks was erroneously informed by the 352nd Division's chief of staff that the invasion had been thrown back into the sea, and Rommel's headquarters were therefore informed that "the situation in the area of 352nd Division is now restored."

The available 352nd Division reserves were squandered during the course of the day on repeated counterattacks against three companies of U.S. Rangers, around 200 men in all, who at 7:00 a.m., in a bold stroke, had scaled the 100-foot sheer cliffs at the Pointe du Hoc (page 139) and had captured the German battery whose big guns, it was thought, would have commanded both the Utah and Omaha fleet anchorages. The guns, some damaged by the bombardment, were found to be unmanned and were put out of action by a Ranger patrol of two men. But the Rangers, hard pressed for the rest of the day, successfully held out against German forces that otherwise might have inflicted serious reversals on the main American assault force at Omaha.

Ninety minutes after landing on Omaha's left bank, the follow-up regiment, the 18th Infantry, reached the seaward edge of Colleville to reinforce some companies of the 16th Infantry that were fighting a house-to-house battle in the village. It was late afternoon before vehicles could move off the beach, and not until the evening did a few tanks and howitzers arrive in Colleville to support the infantry. Shortly before nightfall the resolute troops of the U.S. 1st Division penetrated the Germans' second line of defense along the Colleville–Saint-Laurent road, pushing their front line to the south and east of the coast road and extending their beachhead to between one and one and a half miles inland—a remarkable achievement for men who had been so badly drubbed in the morning. A short way down that coast road to the west, two infantry regiments and an artillery battalion of the 29th Division, after clearing Vierville, hung on grimly to the outskirts of Saint-Laurent.

By dark, V Corps held a beachhead six miles long and not even two miles deep. Its hold was precarious. The minefields were not completely cleared; German mortars and artillery still harassed the beach; there was a grave shortage of tanks and guns and the troops were in a seriously weakened condition after a bloody and exhausting day in which they had sustained some 3,000 casualties.

Whether the Americans were at Omaha to stay depended on what the German defenders could throw against them in the night and in the days to follow. And that, in turn, depended on the fortunes of the British battling it out on Gold, Juno and Sword.

ORDEAL AT OMAHA

A GI, his form blurred by photographer Robert Capa's movement, crawls under fire toward Omaha Beach. Poking up at rear are German antiboat obstacles.

These 10 historic D-Day pictures, taken at Omaha Beach by LIFE photographer Robert Capa, survived an accident that destroyed many more.

STALKING DEATH WITH A CAMERA

"If your pictures aren't good," Robert Capa often used to say, "you're not close enough." Certainly Capa got close enough to the action on June 6, 1944. The veteran combat photographer, who had covered the Spanish Civil War and the World War II campaigns in North Africa and Italy for LIFE, was in the first wave to head for the Easy Red sector of Omaha Beach.

At 6:31 a.m., when Capa left his landing craft with a rifle company of the 16th Infantry Division, he knew that he was risking his life. But he did not have death on his mind. He was thinking "very much of getting the best pictures of the day." His first impression was that "my beautiful France looked sordid and uninviting." The Germans' invasion obstacles had turned the pleasant shoreline into "the ugliest beach in the whole world." To reach the sand, he and the riflemen had to traverse some 100 yards of tidal flats in the face of machine-gun fire. As the bullets "tore holes in the water" around him, Capa kept shooting pictures furiously. He headed for the protection of a burned-out amphibious tank and reached it "between floating bodies." Then as the tide came in, he made it to the beach and threw himself on the sand.

Now began a savage mortar bombardment that pinned down the Americans. Capa felt "a new kind of fear shaking my body from toe to hair, and twisting my face." He attempted to reload his camera, but could not, his hands were trembling so. "I did not think and I didn't decide it," he wrote later. He stood up and he ran toward an incoming landing craft. "I knew that I was running away. I tried to turn, but couldn't face the beach." As he climbed on board, he felt an explosion. "The skipper was crying. His assistant had been blown up all over him, and he was a mess." Capa turned and took one more photograph of the beach. He had made 106 pictures in all.

His three rolls of film were rushed to LIFE's London office for processing. There a darkroom technician, eager for glimpses of the landing, dried the film too fast. The excessive heat melted the emulsion and ruined all but 10 frames.

Slogging through the surf past a fallen comrade, a company of American riflemen struggles toward the beach between bursts of enemy machine-gun fire.

Stopped by deadly fire from bluffs overlooking the beach, invaders in the first wave take shelter behind German barriers and a disabled American tank.

Men in the first wave trade fire with the enemy from behind a jumble of long logs implanted in the sand to prevent invasion craft from reaching the beach.

Pinned down by enemy gunfire at H-Hour-plus-1, riflemen in the second wave huddle behind German obstacles. By 9:30 a.m. the Americans had won a foothold.

5

The Americans who had landed on Utah and Omaha Beaches had been pinned down and shot up for a whole hour on D-Day before the first British soldiers set foot on their invasion beaches to the east—Gold, Juno and Sword, in that order. The difference in the H-Hours was only the beginning; the British were going to do things differently all day long. They had to.

British strategy had been dictated by a powerful threat that the Americans did not have to face: German tanks. By the end of D-Day, the British Second Army under General Miles Dempsey would have to clash with at least one panzer division, the crack 21st, in order to achieve its two primary objectives, the capture of the city of Caen and the securing of the eastern flank of the Allied invasion front. This meant that Dempsey's 75,000 British and Canadian troops had to move inland far and fast in order to set up defenses deep enough to contain the expected assaults by masses of counterattacking German tanks. The beachhead would be none too safe even if it extended 20 miles into France by nightfall, but General Montgomery, the chief strategist for the British, believed that his troops should push inland as far as possible.

To make reasonably sure that the Second Army was not detained on the beaches, Montgomery had arranged for the 137 warships with the British invasion fleet to lay down a pulverizing two-hour preliminary bombardment, starting 20 minutes before the American shelling and lasting 80 minutes longer. Moreover, Montgomery had the British transports positioned three or four miles closer to the coast than the U.S. vessels to give the troops a shorter ride shoreward. The Americans had set their H-Hour at 6:30 because the tide was near its lowest point, exposing the Germans' underwater invasion obstacles. But Montgomery and Dempsey had set theirs at 7:30, not only to ensure the longer bombardment but also to enable the landing craft to ride in with the tide and place the men higher up on the beach.

At about 6:15, after 45 minutes of thunderous naval shelling, the first wave of landing craft set out for the shore four or five miles away. The seas were rough, and many men became seasick. But visibility was good, and the troops, crowded together shoulder to shoulder, could see up ahead beaches that were entirely different from the American ones. Nowhere on their 24 miles of beaches from Ouistre-

BRITISH BEACHHEADS

ham west to Le Hamel were there natural terrain features as formidable as the high bluffs overlooking Omaha or the flooded lagoon behind Utah. The British faced only low beaches, a sea wall close by, small summer resorts and ugly villas *(page 156)* along the coast road, and beyond, flat, open country—good tank terrain. It seemed a civilized scene to the soldiers who watched its details materialize before them. But the tankmen saw nothing. They were buttoned up and ready to go in their Churchills, Shermans and specialized tanks *(pages 172-181),* including those equipped to swim ashore at the head of the first wave.

Awaiting the assault along the shoreline, the German defenders braced for action. Their forces consisted of 10 beachside companies of infantry, 50 mortar teams, 500 machine guns and 90 artillery pieces. Behind the beaches, in defensive positions four to six miles deep, stood another 14 companies of infantry and 22 batteries with more than 100 guns. And behind them waited another five infantry battalions and more gun batteries.

As the Germans swung into action, landing craft a few hundred yards from the shore began catching shells and machine-gun fire. But the British and Canadians sat still under the barrage, steeled by at least one motive the U.S. Army lacked: revenge. They were the avengers of Dunkirk and Dieppe, and now was the time to repay the Germans.

Shortly before 7:30 the gates of the landing craft clanged open, and the soldiers in their hobnailed boots clanked down the ramps into the surf. For a time after that the British attacks bore less resemblance to a crucial military action than to a traveling road show. From aboard rocket barges and close-in destroyers, loudspeakers blared forth two songs of the day, "Roll Out the Barrel" and "We Don't Know Where We're Going." Some of the Commando units, which were assigned the difficult task of filling the gaps between the Infantry beachheads, were led ashore by bagpipers playing martial Highland airs. Australian newsman Alan Moorehead, covering the invasion for the London *Daily Express,* said that "the whole scene looked at from this distance was toy-like and unreal. It lacked the element of danger or excitement, even of movement."

The landings were easier than the British had dared hope, certainly much easier than those on Omaha. But they were not really easy. Landing craft struck mines and foundered, or

were shelled into floating wrecks. Shells set tanks on fire in their LCTs at sea. Many men were killed aboard landing craft. The bodies could not be taken back to England—they would delay the reembarkation schedule—so the landing-craft crewmen heaved them overboard, weighted down with any heavy objects they could spare.

On the shore, tanks lumbering up the beaches ran over screaming wounded men. Soldiers hurt at the water's edge were dragged up the beach by their comrades, who feared that they would otherwise be drowned in the still-incoming tide. The infantrymen on the tide-narrowed beaches had only to run about 100 yards to reach the German positions or the shelter of the sea wall. But in several German pillboxes and bunkers, the defenders recovered quickly from the nerve-shattering bombardment, and they kept the invaders pinned down on the beach longer than the demanding British timetable allowed.

The French seaside villages made a strange battlefield. Weeping civilians appeared at garden gates to pour wine for the advancing soldiers. In the rubble of Saint-Aubin-sur-Mer, Commando mortar men wheeled their weapon around in a purloined ice-cream cart, while in a Ouistreham café a Frenchman in pajamas danced about crying joyously, "It is the day! The day of liberation!" And the weird tanks that the soldiers called Funnies were everywhere: flail tanks beating lanes through minefields; Churchills armed with huge mortars, blasting gaps in the sea wall to let other tanks and trucks inland; floating tanks swimming ashore, casting off their flotation gear at the water's edge and immediately going into action, crashing through barbed-wire thickets and knocking out bunkers with point-blank fire.

Death on the British beaches was a random harvest rather than the grim reaping of Omaha. How a soldier fared often depended on where he landed. Some units came ashore in undefended areas. Others landed near positions whose defenders instantly surrendered; some Germans came over the dunes with suitcases already packed. But British units that were set down before resolute defenders or caught in murderous crossfires suffered greatly. Men arriving in the second wave found scattered concentrations of bodies lying where they had fallen, their blood clotting the sand.

In a few vital areas, the British and Canadians were held up on the beaches for an hour and more. But generally they maintained the initiative and carried the fight to the Germans in the streets of the villages and in the open fields beyond. One by one, most of the units with inland objectives fought their way off the beaches and began advancing on or close to their assigned schedules.

All through the morning landings, the key German commanders were virtually out of touch with the front; their communications had been so severely damaged by aerial bombardment, naval shelling and French Resistance sabotage that Seventh Army headquarters did not learn of the first British landings until 8:45 a.m., an hour and 20 minutes after they occurred, and it did not receive first word of the American landings at Utah until 11 a.m. In Germany itself, at nearly every headquarters, generals knew by midmorning —at the very moment the news of the invasion was breaking in the Allied countries—that something was up in Normandy, but the size and objectives of the operation were unclear to them throughout the day. Far away at OKW, the Supreme Headquarters in Germany, the prevailing opinion was that the Normandy attack was a feint for a larger strike at the Pas-de-Calais. For this reason, OKW Chief of Operations Staff Jodl, who carried out Hitler's orders while the Führer was sleeping nearby, refused to release the strategic panzer reserves despite urgent appeals from Field Marshal von Rundstedt, Commander in Chief, OB West, Paris.

British crewmen make final checks on their midget submarines before heading to Normandy on June 2, 1944. The two 57-foot vessels positioned themselves off the invasion coast on the 4th of June. At daybreak on D-Day the submarines surfaced and transmitted radio and sonar signals that accurately guided the British fleet to its appointed anchorage.

At La Roche-Guyon, to the west of Paris, the Army Group B headquarters of Field Marshal Rommel desperately telephoned the same request, but was told by OKW: "The landing operation in Normandy will certainly not be the only attempted major landing by the Allies. A second attack must be expected definitely in the Pas-de-Calais and therefore the withdrawal of troops from that sector to assist in Normandy cannot be allowed." When Rommel's staff officers protested, OKW sharply informed them that they "had no data whatever on which to base any judgment."

Rommel himself, at home in Herrlingen in southern Germany, had been told at 6:30 a.m. of the airborne activity in Normandy and was not unduly alarmed. But shortly after 10 a.m. his chief of staff, General Speidel, phoned to tell him that some sort of amphibious invasion was also taking place there. This news hit Rommel hard. "How stupid of me," he said quietly as he hung up the phone. "The call had changed him," his wife Lucie later said, "there was a terrible tension." Rommel was, said his aide, Captain Helmuth Lang, "terribly depressed," and the field marshal canceled the planned meeting with Hitler at Berchtesgaden. Rommel prepared to leave for his headquarters at 1 p.m.

Finally, at around 10 a.m.—by which time all of the 1,600 German tanks in northwestern France were fueled up and awaiting orders to move toward the British beachhead—Hitler woke up. In his pajamas he listened to a briefing by his adjutants. Then he sent for Jodl and OKW Commander in Chief Wilhelm Keitel. It was his view, the Führer said, that Jodl was right and that the Strategic Reserves should not be committed to Normandy until the battle picture clarified.

Then, before bathing and dressing, Hitler told Jodl to issue orders starting the bombardment of London with Germany's secret weapon: the long-range V-1 rockets. Some 60 launching sites were being built, most of them in the Pas-de-Calais area, and nearly 12,000 of the huge flying bombs had been stockpiled in northern France, Belgium and Germany. Jodl issued the appropriate code word, "Junkroom." (In fact, by the time the V-1 campaign actually began on the night of June 12, only seven launching sites were operative; the rest had been damaged by Allied bombing raids or delayed by shortages of equipment and matériel.)

The Führer did not hold his usual noontime conference with his generals. Instead he entertained the new Hungarian Premier, Döme Sztójay, at Klessheim Castle near Salzburg, an hour's drive from OKW headquarters in Berchtesgaden. Reports continued to come in from Normandy, and Hitler told his deputy chief of operations, General Warlimont, that he would think about the situation during lunch. After his usual vegetarian meal, the Führer emerged and announced his decision: Rundstedt could bring up the two elite panzer divisions of the Strategic Reserves, the 12th SS Hitler Youth from south of Rouen and the Panzer Lehr from near Chartres. (It would be 4 p.m. before the two divisions received their marching orders.)

Meanwhile, all through the echelons from OKW on down, the German fighting forces were suffering severely from the elaborate chain of command that Hitler had installed to keep tight personal control over his armies. No frontline general had clear authority to act on his own initiative, nor did any general know which of several superior headquarters would issue him orders. And no general in Normandy was more disastrously shackled than the commander of the vital division that anchored the whole German line. He was General Edgar Feuchtinger, and his 21st Panzer Division, a veteran force that had served with distinction in North Africa, would be chiefly responsible for defending the primary British objective, Caen.

In the dark morning hours of D-Day, Feuchtinger could be certain of only two things. First, he knew that British paratroopers were landing a few miles from his territory along the Orne River and that his panzers, nearest the scene, should act at once. But second, he knew that without orders from Army Group B he could not move his tanks. As he later wrote, "I could do nothing immediately but warn my men to be ready. I waited impatiently all that night for some instructions. But not a single order from a higher formation was received by me."

Finally, at 6:30 a.m. Feuchtinger acted on his own: "I ordered my tanks to attack the British 6 Airborne." Then, at 7:00, "I received by first intimation that a higher command did still exist. I was told by Army Group B that I was now under the command of 7 Army." But two hours later, "I was informed that I would receive any future orders from 84th Infantry Corps." It was not until 10 a.m. that "I was given my first operational instructions. I was ordered to stop the move of my tanks against the Allied Airborne troops, and turn west and aid the forces protecting Caen."

Feuchtinger followed his orders from 84th Corps and tried to disengage his panzers from combat with the British 6th Airborne. This was no easy maneuver under the best of circumstances, and the tanks, which had to cross from east to west over the Orne, were impeded by rocket-firing fighter-bombers and streams of refugees. Finally, late in the afternoon, most of the panzers broke free of traffic and advanced in two long columns. Despite all their problems, Feuchtinger's tank crews would give the British all the fight they could handle in the most important battle of D-Day.

Before the struggle for Caen developed, many battles were fought to a decision all along the British beaches. With few exceptions, the Germans fought courageously. But they had little knowledge of what was going on around them and, for all their elaborate fixed positions, they enjoyed only a slight advantage fighting in the flat and open terrain. They were widely dispersed, their attackers sharply concentrated, and they could only hope to hold fast in islands of resistance until mobile reinforcements came to their aid.

Gold Beach, on the British right, near the Americans on Omaha, was assigned to two British units, the 50th Division and the 8th Armored Brigade, with tanks in the van. The main defenses facing them were two well-fortified villages at either end of Gold: Le Hamel in the west, nine miles from Omaha, and La Rivière in the east at the juncture of Juno Beach. The attack on Le Hamel was led by the 231st Brigade, whose mission was to capture the town of Bayeux and to link up with the Americans at Port-en-Bessin.

On landing near Le Hamel, one battalion of the 231st ran

Tanks of the 27th British Armored Brigade splash ashore from a landing craft near the village of Hermanville on Sword Beach. The unit spent one hour battling to break out of the beach, during which 50 per cent of its tanks and bulldozers were disabled by mines, obstacles and enemy guns.

into stiff defenses and was held up until midafternoon by troops of the same 352nd German Division that was inflicting such heavy casualties on the Americans at Omaha. But a second battalion landed out of range of the Le Hamel guns, overran the defenders on its front in 40 minutes and headed inland. Later in the day, this battalion seized the high ground overlooking Arromanches, the anchorage point for Mulberry B, one of the two immense artificial harbors that were to be built along the beachhead.

At the other end of Gold Beach, one battalion of the 69th Brigade was forced to fight for La Rivière street by street. But another battalion had little difficulty in piercing the defenses and routing the enemy. By 9:30 the brigade owned the high ground one mile inland, and by 12:30 the rest of the 50th Division had landed on Gold and was assembling inland on a beachhead that now measured three miles wide and two and a half miles deep. All afternoon various British units pressed forward to the south, and by evening they were in the outskirts of Bayeux, whose German defenders were already withdrawing. Three miles away, other units reached the road from Bayeux to Caen.

The results of the day's action on Gold were a mixed bag. By cutting the Bayeux–Caen road, the British had put themselves in a good position to prevent German tanks from reaching the vulnerable Americans on Omaha. But they had failed to link up with the Americans; the battalion that had captured Arromanches was stalled there, seven miles away from the appointed rendezvous point, Port-en-Bessin.

To the left of Gold, on Juno Beach, the principal assault force was the 3rd Canadian Division. The Canadians were supposed to make the deepest penetrations of the day, join in the attack on Caen and capture the strategically important airfield at Carpiquet 11 miles inland. Their front was four miles wide, bracketing the small fishing port of Courselles on their right and the seaside resort village of Saint-Aubin-sur-Mer on their left at the juncture of Sword Beach.

At Courseulles the Canadians ran into serious problems even before they landed. They were scheduled to come in at 7:35 a.m., late enough so that the rising tide would float their landing craft over jagged offshore reefs, but the choppy seas delayed them a critical half hour longer, leaving the demolition teams little time to clear the mined anti-invasion

obstacles before the incoming tide covered them. It also gave the Germans plenty of time to recover from the naval bombardment and to prepare a hot welcome. On the way in, 90 of 306 landing craft were knocked out by the mined obstacles or German shells. But the Canadians still swarmed ashore, attacked furiously and refused to be stopped.

The 7th Canadian Brigade landed at Courseulles at 8 a.m. with close armored support from floating tanks swimming ashore from 800 yards out. The bolt assault overwhelmed or outflanked the German strong points, and two battalions—the Royal Winnipeg Rifles and the Regina Rifles—quickly moved inland. But the rising tide had reduced the beach to a narrow strip so crowded with tanks, trucks and guns that a reserve battalion took 90 minutes to get through. By the time the reserves left the beach, the Winnipegs and the Reginas had plunged several miles inland.

To the east of Courseulles, at the village of Bernières-sur-Mer, the 8th Canadian Brigade got into trouble by landing ahead of its tanks, forcing the soldiers to fight without fire support at the most critical moment of their assault. The battalion on the right, the Queen's Own Rifles, was carried to within 100 yards of the sea wall; in the short stretch that remained, half of one company was killed by enfilading enemy fire. The German strong points kept blasting away until the Rifles took them by storm with the support of point-blank fire from a gunship close inshore. Even then, pockets of Germans held out grimly, tying up three battalions of a follow-up brigade until 3 p.m.

Farther east, around Saint-Aubin-sur-Mer, brutal and complex battles raged all day. The Canadians' left-flank battalion, the French-Canadian Régiment de la Chaudière, had to fight for nearly three hours without tank assistance before the determined German defenses could be silenced. At nearby Langrune-sur-Mer, a British Commando unit was bogged down in a bitter fight in the streets and gardens against enemy troops that could be ousted from blocks of fortified houses only after large-scale demolition.

All in all, D-Day action on Juno was a success. The Canadians almost—but not quite—reached their outermost objective; they were within sight of Caen and established on the fringes of both Bayeux and the Carpiquet airfield when darkness halted operations. Other Canadian units had linked up on the right with British troops on Gold Beach, forming a solid beachhead 12 miles wide and at least six miles deep. But the Canadians on the left were still separated from Sword Beach by two and a half miles of enemy-held territory, and several Canadian battalions that had lost valuable time on the beaches could not make it up once they had fought their way into the clear.

Yet the real danger lay farther to the east on Sword Beach. Somewhere behind the beach lurked the tanks of the 21st Panzer Division. Sword was the one place where things had to go right, and all day long the issue was in doubt.

The principal units assigned to take Sword Beach were the 3rd British Infantry Division and two redoubtable Commando brigades *(pages 162-171),* the 1st and the 4th. The most important objective—the key to the whole Allied invasion—had been assigned to the British 3rd in concert with troops of the 3rd Canadian Division from Gold Beach. They were to capture Caen, which dominated a plateau about seven miles from the shore and permitted access to good tank country all the way to Paris.

The British 3rd, held up by offshore reefs and a tricky tide,

landed on Sword a little late and ran into fully prepared shoreline defenders. It took an hour for the British to win the beach and even longer to unsnarl a massive traffic jam of tanks and trucks that had piled up during the battle.

As the troops started inland, they watched for signs of General Feuchtinger's 21st Panzer Division, whose exact location had not been established by Allied aerial reconnaissance. They did not know that tanks of the 21st had been operating against the British 6th Airborne since dawn, or that other elements of the 21st were scattered in a big arc around Caen. But they knew enough to proceed cautiously. Feuchtinger's division was known to have 16,000 men, 40 mobile assault guns, four motorized infantry battalions and an antitank battalion with 24 guns. But the real danger lay in the 21st's 146 tanks—most of them powerful Mark IVs. The last thing the British wanted was a brawl with those tanks; it might leave them too weak to fight off an attack by the 12th SS Panzer Division, which British intelligence expected to arrive from the Rouen area on D-Day afternoon.

Accompanied by Churchill and Sherman tanks, the 1st South Lancashire Regiment of the 8th Brigade spearheaded

At the corner of Hollywood and Vine, Los Angelenos pore over newspaper accounts of the invasion, announced by Eisenhower while they were asleep. Across the continent in New York City, crowds prayed in the streets for victory. Said Mayor Fiorello La Guardia, "It is the most exciting moment in our lives."

On D-Day morning at a castle near his Berchtesgaden headquarters, Adolf Hitler studies a map while Colonel General Alfred Jodl points out the Allied beachheads in Normandy. The Führer, who had been conferring with Hungarian Premier Döme Sztójay (seated, far left) and Foreign Minister Joachim von Ribbentrop (top left), was so unsettled by the news that he permitted this rare photograph showing him wearing spectacles. Hitler recovered quickly and—to give the impression that he had allowed the invasion in order to trap the Allied army —remarked: "Those Dummkopfe, thank God they have finally made a landing."

the 3rd Division's drive inland. By 9:30 these forces had taken the village of Hermanville, a mile and a half from Sword Beach on the shortest road to Caen. But their drive petered out less than a mile down the road, where they ran into guns of the 21st Panzer's antitank battalion, which were set up on a slope the British called Periers Rise. The South Lancs missed their chance to make a bold strike. Instead of plowing past the antitank guns and some infantry defenders, they dug in below Periers Rise and waited for the 185th Brigade, which was supposed to carry the attack into Caen.

But the 185th had been delayed. Its King's Shropshire Light Infantry battalion (or KSLI) was to lead the way from Hermanville to Caen riding on the backs of the 65 tanks of the Staffordshire Yeomanry. The plan misfired. At the appointed hour, 11 a.m., the 600 men of the KSLI, led by Lieut. Colonel F. J. Maurice, were waiting for the tanks at the appointed rendezvous, an orchard near Hermanville. But the tanks were stuck in the traffic jam on the beach.

Finally Colonel Maurice got tired of waiting and made a daring decision: he would order his troops to start out for Caen on foot and trust that the tanks would catch up soon.

At 12:30, the KSLI set off on its lonely, hazardous march, hiking along in spread-out formation, ready to disperse in case of attack. It was a lovely sunny afternoon. Swallows swooped over the grass, bees buzzed in the flowers along the hedgerows and the yellow corn stood high in the fields.

By about 2 o'clock, when Maurice's men finally started their attack up Periers Rise, the first tanks had finally emerged from the traffic jam on the beach, and 20 Shermans were on hand to join the assault. Almost at once, the tanks and the infantry came under heavy fire from German positions blocking the road to Caen. All but three of the Germans' 24 antitank guns had been removed and thrown into the fighting farther west, but those three were nearly enough: they knocked out nine of the Shermans. Eventually the surviving Shermans and a KSLI company overwhelmed the last German strong point from the rear.

While other units of the 185th Brigade took up defensive positions on Periers Rise, Maurice pressed on toward Caen with his KSLI, his tanks and some antitank guns. By 4 p.m. they were moving through the village of Biéville. They were

now only three miles from the northern outskirts of Caen and had high hopes of capturing the city by nightfall.

Those hopes were quickly dashed. About 90 tanks of the 21st Panzer Division had finally broken free of refugee traffic south of Caen—and the first contingent, a strong battle group of about 40 Mark IVs and a battalion of infantry, circled the city and reached the village of Lebisey dead ahead of Maurice and the KSLI.

The leader of the battle group was Colonel Hermann von Oppeln-Bronikowski, and at Lebisey he was met by his commander, General Feuchtinger, and by a distinguished visitor, General Marcks, whose 84th Corps had controlled the 21st Panzers since 10 a.m. To see the battlefront for himself, Marcks had traveled 40 miles from his headquarters at Saint-Lô, and he had reached a sobering conclusion. "Oppeln," he told the colonel, "the future of Germany may very well rest on your shoulders. If we don't throw the British back into sea we shall have lost the war."

Marcks pointed out a serious flaw in the British lines. From Lebisey, a gap several miles wide reached all the way to the coast between Langrune and Lion-sur-Mer. Fierce fighting had been going on around those seaside resorts all day long, and various invading units had failed to clear out the German defenders. If those defenders could be reinforced, the Germans might be able to maintain a wedge three miles wide between the British and the Canadians and, eventually, begin to roll up the beachheads in both directions. As the first step in the counterattack, Marcks and Feuchtinger sent Oppeln-Bronikowski plunging into the gap with his powerful battle group.

The 40 Mark IVs had traveled little more than a mile when they bumped into Colonel Maurice's forces just outside of Biéville. In the opening phase of the first big tank battle of the invasion, the Shermans of the Staffordshire Yeomanry knocked out two Mark IVs, and antitank guns stopped two more. The Germans then veered off into the woods to the west. When they emerged, British pursuers knocked out another six tanks. At this point, the enemy forces disengaged, each going its separate way.

As the battered panzers resumed their drive toward the sea, Maurice's infantry and tanks pressed on toward Caen.

The leading company of the KSLI was only two miles away when it ran into intense enemy fire from a wooded ridge in front of Lebisey. Maurice judged that the German position was too strong to attack without reinforcements. No one had arrived to help, and the other two battalions of the 185th Brigade were strung out along the road to his rear. Reluctantly, Maurice halted his bold push on Caen. He pulled back slightly toward Biéville and dug in there for the night. It would be weeks before any British units surpassed Maurice's high-water mark on the road to Caen.

Meanwhile, at about 7 p.m., Oppeln-Bronikowski and the remnants of his battle group reached Periers Rise and learned to their dismay that it was heavily manned by the British. The panzers' right wing was stopped cold by antitank guns, which knocked out at least seven more Mark IVs. But the German left—a half-dozen tanks supported by a company of infantrymen—slipped through the British lines and drove on to the north. At around 8 p.m. this little force actually succeeded in reaching the coast at Luc-sur-Mer, halfway between Langrune and Lion. There the Germans waited, confident that General Feuchtinger would reinforce them with more tanks as soon as possible.

That was precisely what Feuchtinger had in mind, and he dispatched the rest of his available Mark IVs—perhaps 50 tanks. This battle group was trying to slip past the British defenders on Periers when a tremendous coincidence disrupted their promising counterattack.

Suddenly the sky was filled with planes, and before the Germans' eyes fresh airborne forces swooped past on their way to reinforce the British 6th Airborne along the Orne River a few miles to the east. What the Germans were seeing was the biggest glider force to go into action in Normandy: 250 gliders, towed by 250 transport planes and guarded by a great flight of fighter planes. Aboard the gliders were two infantry battalions of the 6th Air Landing Brigade, the 6th Airborne's artillery, light tanks and reconnaissance regiments. The gliders held a steady course through German antiaircraft fire while the Spitfire and Mustang fighters plunged down to rake the German batteries with cannon and machine-gun fire.

As the gliders neared the Orne, they cast off their tow

cables and slipped silently over the trees and rooftops to their landing zones. At the same time, 600 canisters of supplies and ammunition were dropped by parachute from the transport planes. At one stroke, this massive reinforcement doubled the strength of the besieged and exhausted 6th Airborne, which had been in action nonstop for approximately 20 hours.

To the German tank crews, the enemy planes and gliders seemed to be a huge bridge reaching across the whole horizon. "We looked up," said a lieutenant of the panzer infantry, "and there they were just above us. Noiselessly, those giant wooden boxes sailed in over our heads. We lay on our backs and fired, and fired into those gliders, until we could not work the bolts of our rifles anymore. But with such masses, it seemed to make little difference."

The Germans lost heart. To General Feuchtinger on the outskirts of Caen, it seemed that the great airborne force was landing directly in the path of his northbound tanks. His division had saved Caen for a while, but at a terrible cost; he would end the day with a total loss of 76 out of 146 tanks. Knowing he had done all he could until the reserve panzer divisions arrived, Feuchtinger called off his counterattack toward the coast and reported his failure to Seventh Army headquarters. The Seventh Army report to other commands said simply: "Attack by the 21st Panzer Division rendered useless by heavily concentrated airborne troops."

For the Germans, D-Day ended as it had begun—in confusion or delusion or both. General Marcks of the 84th Corps believed that the American landings on Omaha Beach had been smashed. General Dollmann and his Seventh Army staff thought that the American seaborne landings, whose strength and objectives they could not comprehend, were a sideshow that could easily be dealt with at leisure, and that the British landings were a separate, serious threat against which they should instantly commit all available reserves. OKW in Germany was still waiting for the other shoe to drop—the expected Allied strike at the Pas-de-Calais. Rommel, who had predicted that the War would be won or lost on the beaches, suspected that it had already been lost. In spite of the heavy losses suffered by Feuchtinger's 21st

Panzer Division, higher headquarters kept sending him orders to wipe out the invasion beachhead at once.

For the Allies, D-Day had brought a tremendous victory. The much vaunted Atlantic Wall had been breached: seaborne troops had passed through it and secured ground well beyond it; airborne troops behind it, isolated and vulnerable, had held fast. The Allies' mastery of the air was complete: their strategic and tactical air forces had flown 10,585 D-Day sorties; the Luftwaffe had flown 319, and most of those had been shot down or driven off.

The whole vast, complex assault phase of *Overlord* had worked. So effective was the deception program of Operation *Fortitude* that while the German High Command looked toward the Pas-de-Calais, the Allies had landed 152,000 troops and hundreds of tanks in Normandy without receiving a single massed counterattack or suffering anywhere near the serious casualties that even the most optimistic Allied commander had expected. SHAEF's official secret prediction had been for 10,000 dead in the initial assault. In fact, no more than 2,500 men had lost their lives, and total casualties—including wounded, missing and prisoners—were probably fewer than 12,000, of whom 6,600 were American, 3,500 British and 1,000 Canadian.

The Allied commanders were elated, but they were far from complacent. Their beachhead was small, their front thinly held. The American seaborne forces had not yet linked up with the 82nd Airborne, though only a mile now separated them. The Utah beachhead was isolated, the penetration beyond Omaha was tenuous. A seven-mile gap still separated the British and the Americans, and the 3rd British Division was still three miles away from the 3rd Canadian Division. Worst of all, Caen remained in the hands of the Germans, and without Caen as an anchor the whole invasion front was afloat.

On D-plus-1, and for many days thereafter, the battle to expand the Allied beachhead would continue. But another crucial battle was already beginning—the battle to reinforce the bloody invasion beaches. Everything now depended on whether the Allies could land troops and supplies faster than the Germans could bring up their tank divisions from the east.

BRITAIN'S SHOCK TROOPS

Spearheading the British drive inland from Sword Beach, the 1st Commando Brigade advances, under cover of a British tank, past shell-damaged houses.

A PAIR OF BRIGADES IN DUBIOUS BATTLE

Two Commando brigades, both crack units but destined to meet with very different luck, headed shoreward on D-Day morning charged with two of the British Army's most crucial missions. One unit was Brigadier the Lord Lovat's 2,000-man 1st Brigade; it was to land at the eastern edge of Sword Beach. The other Commando force, bound for the juncture of Sword and Juno Beaches, was made up of about 1,000 men from Brigadier B. W. Leicester's 4th Brigade. Trained to hit hard and fast, these units were assigned tasks considered too difficult for the infantry.

Lovat's men, ordered to link up with the 6th Airborne units that had come by parachute and glider during the night, put on a display of casual daring, as befitted their long experience in Commando raids. They wore green berets, disdaining steel helmets. Their bagpiper played as the landing craft came in under heavy fire. Two noncoms sat in full view and shouted mocking advice to the German gunners: "Put your sights up, Jerry," and "Down a little."

On the beach, Lovat found first-wave units of British infantrymen pinned down by enemy fire. His Commandos advanced through the infantry lines and knocked out the German machine guns. To reinforce the paratroopers on schedule, Lovat had to cover six miles in only three-and-a-half hours, and he was determined to be there on time.

Meanwhile, the men of the 4th Brigade, whose mission was to plug the five-mile gap between the Sword and Juno beachheads, had run into trouble even before reaching the shore at Saint Aubin. The preinvasion bombardment had completely missed the beach defenses there, and German mortar shells inflicted heavy casualties on the incoming landing craft. Once ashore, the Commandos' luck was even worse. A German strong point blocked their advance and prevented them from closing the gap. Then a battalion of enemy infantrymen plunged through the opening and reinforced the German positions near Saint Aubin. It was not until the following day that the 4th Brigade, with the blockbusting aid of a Sherman tank, finally overran the strong point and consolidated the two beachheads.

A Commando unit, equipped for speed with light weapons and bicycles, prepares to race inland from a beach congested with tanks and trucks.

Commando snipers, one of them disguised in torn camouflage netting and the other wearing a rain cape, receive instructions from a 1st Brigade officer (right).

Fighting in a haze of gun smoke, 4th Brigade Commandos take cover from German mortar fire on a roadside at Saint Aubin. After two days of savage combat in

the area, the 500-man unit had lost 217 officers and men, including 50 Commandos who were rescued from the water and involuntarily returned to England.

Advancing at last, 4th Brigade Commandos tramp through a village between Sword and Juno Beaches.

To speed their advance, 1st Brigade Commandos use a horse and wagon to lug their gear forward.

Villagers inform 4th Brigade Commandos of

German units deployed near Saint Aubin. A Frenchman also helped the 1st Brigade Commandos, sabotaging power lines to German positions at Ouistreham.

BLAZING A TRAIL BY BICYCLE AND FARM CART

While the hard-luck 4th Brigade was fighting for survival near Saint Aubin, the 1st Brigade was striving valiantly to avoid a fight. In order to reach the 6th Airborne units in time, Lord Lovat could not afford to engage the Germans unless they insisted on impeding his advance.

Following a route carefully selected to avoid main roads and major strong points, the Commandos raced along hedgerows, cut through barbed wire and crossed an antitank ditch using scaling ladders. Confronted with a minefield, they carefully picked their way through it rather than wasting precious time on a long detour. While Commando mortar teams kept the enemy blinded with smoke bombs, the reconnaissance units sped ahead of the main body on lightweight bicycles.

As they advanced, the Commandos im-

provised cleverly to make up for their lack of artillery support. One enterprising officer flagged down a passing British tank, whose obliging crew shelled a pillbox that was blocking the way.

Though the 1st Brigade obeyed orders to avoid the enemy, it left an impressive trail of ruin along its six-mile route. Before the Commandos reached the gliders of the 6th Airborne Division, they knocked out four strong points and destroyed a battery of four field guns.

The Commandos dig in among crash-landed gliders of the airborne troops.

MISSION ACCOMPLISHED, WITH BAGPIPES SKIRLING

Soon after noon on D-Day, Lord Lovat and the men of the 1st Brigade were closing in on the Orne River bridges where they were to link up with the 6th Airborne Division. By then, the paratroopers were in desperate need of reinforcements. The men had been fighting continuously for more than 12 hours; their ammunition was almost exhausted and their casualties were mounting under an unrelenting German mortar barrage. Before too long the paratroopers heard the skirl of bagpipes in the distance and they knew that the Commandos had broken through.

At about 1 p.m. the Commandos came into view and Lovat's bagpipes squealed out the tune of "Blue Bonnets over the Border." The paratroopers raised a cheer and, ignoring German sniper fire, rushed out from cover to greet the Commandos. For a moment the paratroopers mingled boisterously with the Commandos. Then both units went back to fighting again.

Lord Lovat strode up to the paratroop colonel in charge. With a glance at his wrist watch he said nonchalantly, "I'm sorry that we are a couple of minutes late."

On guard in the shadow of a giant Horsa glider, Commandos of the 1st Brigade man their Bren gun and scan the area with binoculars for signs of German troops.

THOSE WONDROUS TANKS

The most spectacular of the British specialized tanks, a Churchill "Crocodile," throws flames 120 yards, using 400 gallons of napalm stored in its trailer.

HOBART'S MENAGERIE OF MECHANICAL MONSTERS

Before taking over the tank program, Hobart was in the Home Guard: the regular Army had forced him to retire because of his eccentric ideas.

At H-Hour all along the British invasion beaches, weird attack vehicles that looked like canvas-covered bathtubs swam ashore *(right)*. Then they lowered their canvas flotation collars and revealed their true identity as fully armed Sherman tanks. The German defenders were flabbergasted, and one of the tank drivers later said, "I still remember very vividly some of the machinegunners standing up in their posts looking at us with their mouths wide open."

The floating tank, or DD (duplex drive), was only one of an amazing variety of specialized armored vehicles, called "Funnies," that crawled over the supposedly impenetrable Atlantic Wall at Normandy. The British also had modified Sherman and Churchill tanks that exploded mines and laid roadways, as well as some that shot flames. The need for such vehicles had been dramatized by the disastrous British defeat at Dieppe, in which tanks that were supposed to cover advancing infantry failed to break through German obstacles and left soldiers exposed to enemy fire.

The man who developed the Funnies and trained their crews was Major-General Percy C. S. Hobart, a prickly genius personally selected by Churchill to modernize Britain's tank program. As commander of the 79th Armored Division, Hobart and his staff designed, built and tested more than a dozen specialized modifications. Then he saw to it that enough were modified to serve the Allies' D-Day needs.

British General Montgomery, the field commander of all the invasion forces, ordered the Funnies to be distributed among his British, Canadian and American forces. But the Americans accepted only a few swimming DDs; they declined the rest of the Funnies—a decision they later regretted, especially during their bloody struggles on Omaha Beach. For the Funnies did save countless British lives. General Eisenhower wrote after D-Day: "The comparatively light casualties which we sustained on all the beaches except Omaha were in large measure due to the success of the novel mechanical contrivances which were employed. . . . It is doubtful if the assault forces could have firmly established themselves without the assistance of these weapons."

THE INVALUABLE DD: A TANK THAT COULD SWIM

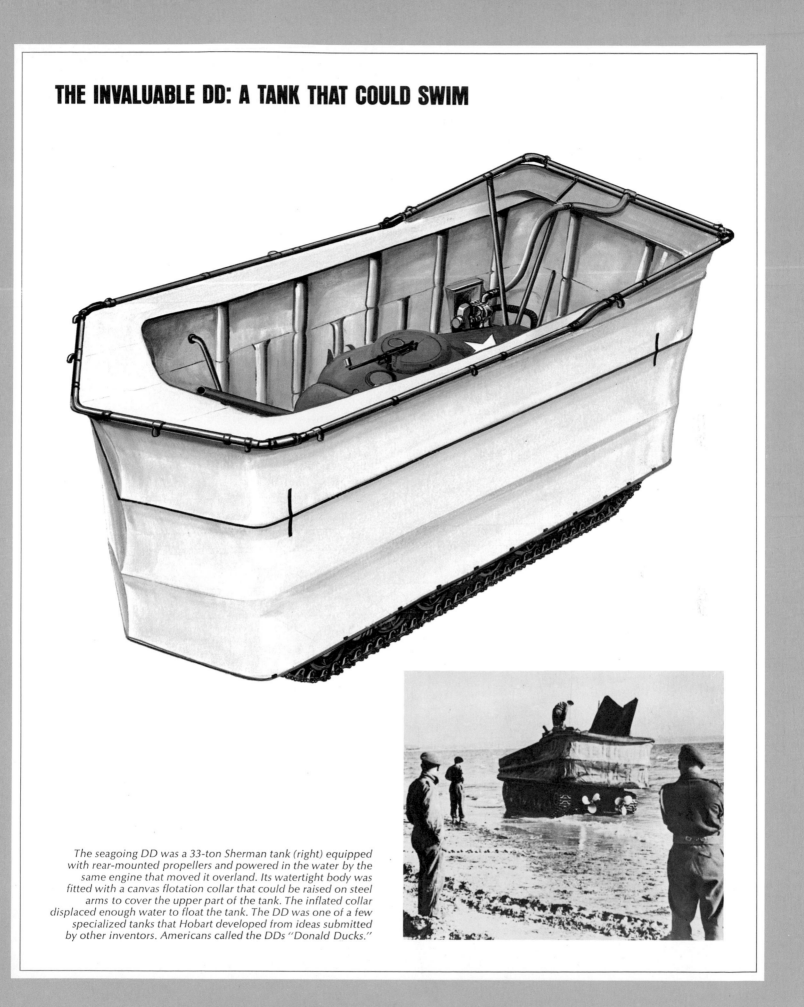

The seagoing DD was a 33-ton Sherman tank (right) equipped with rear-mounted propellers and powered in the water by the same engine that moved it overland. Its watertight body was fitted with a canvas flotation collar that could be raised on steel arms to cover the upper part of the tank. The inflated collar displaced enough water to float the tank. The DD was one of a few specialized tanks that Hobart developed from ideas submitted by other inventors. Americans called the DDs "Donald Ducks."

CLEARING MINES WITH A BATTERY OF FLYING CHAINS

The Sherman flail tank—nicknamed the "Crab" by the British—was designed to clear paths through minefields for the infantry. The flails were massive chains attached to a 10-foot-wide metal drum that was mounted on the front end of the tank. As the tank trundled forward at one and a half miles per hour, its drum was rotated at high speed, slamming the chains against the ground and detonating any mines buried in its path.

A CHURCHILL TANK THAT FIRED "FLYING DUSTBINS"

The Churchill AVRE (Armored Vehicle Royal Engineers) was used to destroy enemy strongholds, and to protect and transport demolition teams. It had a short-barreled mortar mounted on the turret in place of the usual long gun. The 290mm mortar fired a 40-pound projectile—called a "Flying Dustbin" because of its square shape—that could demolish most enemy pillboxes and barriers. The tank could fire two or three rounds a minute.

177

A TOW SERVICE FOR CRIPPLED TANKS

For all their versatility, the Funnies were just as susceptible to breakdowns and enemy fire as their regular cousins. Tanks disabled on the battlefield often blocked advances. To remove crippled tanks, Hobart equipped some Churchills with winches, pulleys and towing equipment at front and back. A crewman from the rescuing tank—known as an Armored Recovery Vehicle (ARV)—attached the towing apparatus to the disabled tank (inset), which was then coaxed, lifted and pulled out of the way.

ROLLING OUT THE CARPET

The "Bobbin" was a Churchill equipped with a giant spool, on which was rolled a 110-yard-long carpet of coir—a coarse material made from the husks of coconuts. This carpet, stiffened by bamboo rods, was unrolled in front of the advancing Bobbin, permitting it and other vehicles to traverse soft, slippery clay. The carpet was first pulled down from the spool and guided by hand until it was caught under the tank treads. Then the forward movement of the tank pulled down more of the carpet. The spool could be lowered (inset) when the tank was on level ground.

A MOVABLE ROADWAY AND BRIDGE

The Armored Ramp Carrier—dubbed "ARK"—was a turretless Churchill tank whose flat superstructure supported two runways. Attached by hinges at both ends of each runaway were adjustable ramps. When an ARK reached a sea wall too high to climb, it would push its nose against the wall and lower its rear runways, thus forming a roadway on which other tanks could climb over the wall. ARKs also took up positions in the middle of ditches and streams and, by lowering both sets of ramps, created bridges for other vehicles to cross.

BIGGER BRIDGES FOR BIGGER OBSTACLES

Whenever ARKs (left) proved to be too small to overcome an obstacle, Churchill AVREs equipped with small box girder bridges took over. The 30-foot bridge, mounted on the front of the tank and held in position by cables, was lowered by a hand-operated winch at the rear. To position the bridge for use, the tankmen lowered it to within a few feet of the supports it would rest on. Then they set small charges that cut the cables, and the bridge fell into place. The bridge could support a 40-ton load.

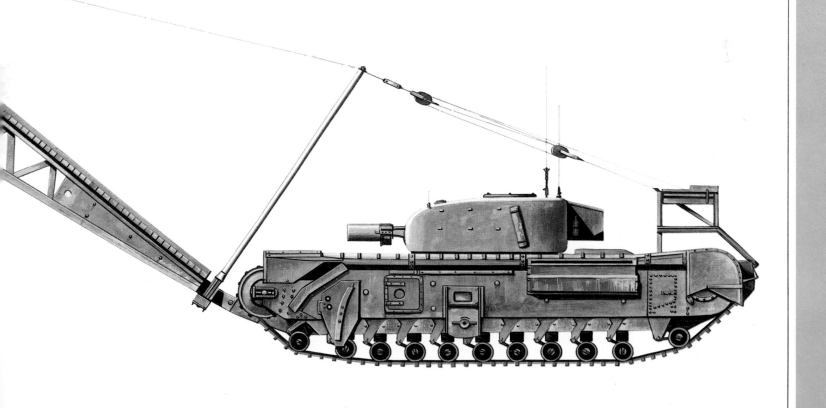

6

The Allies spent the night of D-Day clinging to their patches of Normandy coastline. Although the Germans mounted no serious thrusts at the beachheads, the invaders got little rest during the hours of darkness. On the beaches they labored to clear away the wreckage, preparing for the incoming flood of men and machines scheduled to resume at first light. Farther inland, infantry patrols padded through orchards and farmyards, alert to enemy movement. Those GIs or Tommies lucky enough to catch a few winks awoke stiff and cold in their foxholes, beside their field guns and tanks, to find the sun rising in a brilliant blue sky, across which buzzed swarms of fighter planes.

At the village of Saint-Aubin-sur-Mer, just behind Sword Beach, Lieut. Colonel James L. Moulton and his men of No. 48 Commando arose to clean up the mess around them. "It was a shocking sight," Colonel Moulton wrote later. "Many corpses, some of them badly dismembered, were lying among the rest of the debris of the assault: wrecked and burnt out tanks, equipment and stores of every sort, scattered on the beach or drifted up along the water's edge; wrecked landing craft broached-to on the beach or in the sea among the beach obstacles. . . . Among all this, several French women were walking about, picking up what tinned food they could find—incredibly they had small children with them, who gazed with indifferent curiosity on the shattered corpses, the broken equipment and the scattered tins of food."

But the Allies had little time to pause and contemplate the death and destruction on the beaches. Their task now was to keep the Germans on the run. General Montgomery, the Allied ground commander, arrived off the invasion beaches on board H.M.S. *Faulknor* early on the morning of June 7. In shipboard meetings with General Bradley, the American First Army commander, and General Dempsey, the British Second Army commander, Montgomery stressed the importance of maintaining the Allied initiative, of shoving the Germans still farther inland to protect the beaches during the vital influx of fresh fighting men, their weapons and supplies. It was also essential, Montgomery told his commanders, to link up the bridgeheads so the Germans could not drive wedges through the gaps between them.

For the moment Montgomery issued no new orders. Operation *Overlord* continued according to plan. The two

THE FIGHTING INLAND

Allied armies would strive to complete their D-Day objectives. The Americans were to capture Carentan, thus linking up their Utah and Omaha beachheads, and then thrust across the neck of the Cotentin Peninsula to isolate the port of Cherbourg as a preliminary to its capture. The British were to continue their battles for Bayeux and Caen, deepen their bridgehead southward across the Caen–Bayeux road and, on their right flank, link up with the American V Corps at Port-en-Bessin.

But on June 7 it was clear to the Allies that this was easier said than done. Air reconnaissance showed that German armored reserves were moving up on Caen and resistance was stiffening there. And the Americans were still in trouble on Omaha. German resistance there was so strong that the 29th Division found it almost impossible to expand its beachhead westward, and the beach itself was still under fire by mortars and shells and so cluttered with wreckage that stores could be unloaded only in a few places.

Inland, on the Cotentin Peninsula, the situation was precarious. All through the night General Ridgway's scattered and isolated 82nd Airborne Division—still short of 60 per cent of its infantry and 90 per cent of its artillery—had borne the brunt of the German counterattacks across the Merderet River, one of which had been stopped only 400 yards short of Ridgway's command post. Dawn found the Americans in desperate straits and almost out of ammunition. As the day wore on, however, the picture improved. By noon the 82nd had been reinforced with glider infantry and supply drops and had linked up with the seaborne forces from Utah, where the beach was firmly in U.S. hands.

Although the Germans kept trying, they could not break through the American line along the Merderet. By nightfall the VII Corps at Utah held a bridgehead eight miles deep and nine miles long.

By then even the situation at Omaha had improved. The savage fighting of D-Day had drained the morale of the German defenders, and there were no available resources to reinforce them. The Americans of the V Corps were able to force their way to the River Aure, about four miles south of Omaha Beach, and establish a bridgehead across it. The worse was over, though nobody knew it yet.

While the Americans were struggling to expand their beachheads, their allies to the east defused a German counterattack aimed at the gap between the British and Canadian forces north of Caen. The attack was to be launched with two panzer divisions, the 12th SS and the 21st, which between them had 160 tanks and five battalions of infantry. General Kurt Meyer, commander of the 12th SS, thought this was a force large enough for the assault. General Feuchtinger, commanding the 21st, did not agree with Meyer. Feuchtinger, who had lost nearly half his tanks on D-Day, wanted to wait until both units were joined by a third division, the Panzer Lehr, then on its way to Caen from near Chartres, over 100 miles away. Field Marshal Rommel, who had arrived back at his headquarters, ended the disagreement with an order to launch the attack immediately, aiming at the coast through the gap between the 3rd Canadian and 3rd British Divisions.

But the British and Canadians struck first. The British hit the 21st at Lebisey, north of Caen, while the 12th SS was distracted by a Canadian push toward the Carpiquet airfield west of the city. Meyer was forced to commit nearly all his forces against the Canadians, and though he was able to drive them back with heavy casualties, he was left with only 17 tanks and one infantry battallion to carry out the original attack down the gap that led to the sea. Before he could even start, the Allies had closed the gap.

The Germans were so heavily involved in their struggle to hold Caen against the 3rd British and 3rd Canadian Divisions that they could do very little to check the advance of the 50th British Division northwest of Caen. Consequently, most of the Caen–Bayeux road fell into British and Canadian hands, and on June 8, Bayeux was captured by the British— the first important town in France to be liberated from German occupation.

The German intelligence officer at the 84th Corps headquarters bunker in Saint-Lô, Major Friedrich Hayn, was told of this loss by a German woman auxiliary on the Bayeux telephone exchange:

"Herr Major, British tanks are now passing the Soldiers' Club," she coolly informed him. "They are right in the middle of the town. . . . I'm the last one here."

Then she added: "Now the Tommies are driving past the building outside. You can hear for yourself, Herr Major."

She held the telephone out the window and the intelligence officer in Saint-Lô heard the clanking of the enemy tanks. It was unbelievable.

The tanks belonged to a squadron led by Lieut. Colonel Stanley Christopherson. "We were the first troops into the town," the colonel recalled. "We were given a most enthusiastic and spontaneous reception by the inhabitants who demonstrated their joy by throwing flowers at the tanks and distributing cider and food among the men.

"One enemy machine gun post concealed in a house held out in the south of the town, which caused the building to catch fire as a result of our gunfire. After a very short space the clanging of a bell heralded the arrival of the Bayeux fire brigade, manned by a full team all wearing shiny helmets. Regardless of the machine gun fire, they held up the battle, entered the house, extinguished the fire, and brought out the German machine gun section."

Unlike other towns in Normandy, Bayeux had suffered no war damage. The shops were full of Calvados and wine; there were evening gowns for sale in the shop marked haute couture. The Lion d'Or, an old inn, was open for business as usual, and correspondent Alan Moorehead was astonished to discover that he could have lunch there. "The proprietress was a round little woman dressed in black," he wrote, "and she accepted our arrival with aplomb. We watched the lunch arrive. Soup, omelettes, steak, vegetables, cheese. The wine was a dry Sauterne, 15 shillings a bottle. The Armagnac was a genuine Armagnac."

With the capture of Bayeux the liberation of France had truly begun. "While we ate," said Moorehead, "there was a commotion in the square outside. A crowd came yelling up the Rue St. Jean, driving an old man in front of them. His shirt was torn off to the waist. There was blood running down his face, his eyes were wide with fright. Every now or then a man or a woman would run forward to beat him or scratch him. They did this viciously, with an evident sense of gratifying some pent up desire for revenge. It was difficult to get much sense out of the crowd. They merely shouted, 'Collaborateur.' Presently more victims were brought out and beaten in the square in front of the hotel. It was the first of many such incidents we were going to see through France and Belgium."

The invasion had not simply liberated a few Frenchmen on the Normandy coast: it had fired Frenchmen every-

U.S. gliders sit in a patchwork of Normandy fields after landing two miles south of Sainte-Mère-Eglise on June 7 with infantry, artillery and vehicles— reinforcements for the isolated and hard-pressed 82nd Airborne troops. C-47 tow ships circle over the landing zone on their way back to England.

184

where. Fearful of massive German reprisals, Eisenhower on D-Day had asked the civilian population of France not to rise against the German Occupation authorities. This appeal was largely ignored. The Resistance emerged en masse and in strength, and France was soon in a state of open rebellion. Sabotage spread through the factories. Guerrillas blew bridges and ammunition dumps, cut telephone lines and harassed German road convoys. The French railway network used by the Germans for supplying and reinforcing their armies in the west was devastated. On D-Day night alone there were 950 interruptions on the railways; after D-Day every train leaving Marseilles for Lyons was derailed at least once. All lines to the busy junctions of Troyes, Lille and Tourcoing were cut within a night or two after D-Day and were kept cut until the end of the month. The main line between Toulouse and Paris was cut 800 times in June.

Normandy villagers welcome an advancing British unit. The invasion brought local inhabitants hardships as well as freedom. Many villages were destroyed, food distribution was disrupted and for a few months after D-Day life was harder than it had been during the German Occupation.

While the French were crippling German transport on the ground, the British and Americans were doing the same from the air. On D-Day, OKW had ordered up reinforcements from the south—the 2nd SS Panzer from Toulouse, the 17th SS from the Loire Valley, the 77th Infantry from Saint Malo, the 3rd Parachute from Brest and battle groups from three other divisions in Brittany. The 2nd SS in Toulouse was so hampered by air strikes on the railway that it could not entrain its tanks for 11 days.

Rundstedt reported that Allied planes controlled not only the battlefield but also the approach route, to a depth of more than 100 miles. The warning cry "Low flying aircraft!" was constantly heard down the marching troop columns. A staff officer of an SS division recalled his journey to the Normandy front on June 7:

"Our motorized columns were coiling along the road toward the invasion beaches. Then something happened that left us in a daze. Spurts of fire flecked along the column and splashes of dust staccatoed the road. Everyone was piling out of the vehicles and scuttling for the neighboring fields. Several vehicles were already in flames. This attack ceased as suddenly as it had crashed upon us fifteen minutes before. The men started drifting back to the column again, pale and shaky and wondering how they had survived this fiery rain of bullets.

"The march column was now completely disrupted and every man was on his own, to pull out of this blazing column as best he could. And it was none too soon, because an hour later the whole thing started all over again, only much worse this time. When this attack was over, the length of the road was strewn with splintered antitank guns (the pride of our Division), flaming motors and charred implements of war.

"The march was called off and all vehicles that were left were hidden in the dense bushes or in barns. No one dared show himself out in the open any more. Now the men started looking at each other. This was different from what we thought it would be like."

General Fritz Bayerlein, who had been chief of staff of Rommel's Afrika Korps, was himself attacked from the air as the 260 tanks of his crack Panzer Lehr struggled to reach the front after having been ordered up from Chartres. With Bayerlein in the staff car was his driver, Corporal Kartheus,

and his orderly officer, Captain Alexander Hartdegen. Hartdegen described what happened at dawn on June 8:

"We were bowling along the road when we saw three fighter bombers in the dawn sky. They had evidently spotted us, for they were streaking along the straight road at low altitude, straight at us. The brakes screeched. As a dozen times earlier that day, General Bayerlein let himself drop into the roadside ditch out of the moving car. I caught sight of a concrete culvert, raced toward it, and dived into the pitch-dark pipe head first. Kartheus also managed to get out of the car just before the aircraft cannon spat out their first shells. In an instant the BMW staff car was ablaze. The next plane streaked right along the ditch, opening up at us as it dived. The 20mm shells burst immediately in front of my concrete pipe. The corporal had just called out to Bayerlein: 'Crawl away from the car, Herr General, get away from it'—then he was silent."

Hartdegen was saved by the concrete culvert, but Corporal Kartheus lay dead in the ditch. Bayerlein suffered only a few cuts and shrapnel wounds, but the staff car was a smouldering pile of scrap metal on the road.

"Ten such attacks in succession," commented Hartdegen, "are a real foretaste of hell."

Incidents like these taught the Germans to move only at night. No motor vehicles were allowed within a radius of 500 yards of any military headquarters by day, and all tracks and tire marks had to be painstakingly obliterated. Tanks and other vehicles had to stay still and hidden in the shade of the dense, leafy woods.

The paralysis of German troop and tank movements caused by Allied air strikes and Resistance sabotage meant that the Allies were gaining the advantage in the crucial battle of the build-up—even though high winds, shelling and congestion on the beaches had put them 50 per cent behind schedule in unloading men and matériel. In those days just after the landings, work was proceeding on the two Mulberry harbors, but they would not be functional until D-plus-12. Blockships sunk as temporary breakwaters off the beaches provided some shelter for landing craft, but it was not until the Allies decided to run the ships right up on the beach to unload—waiting for the next high tide to float them off if necessary—that the disembarkation of men, vehicles and supplies could begin to catch up. As seen on the beaches, the logistics of *Overlord* were staggering.

"Almost as though on conveyor belts, a regular steady stream of DUK-Ws was moving," a BBC announcer reported from the British beaches. "Hundreds of them, they went out empty from the shore, changed from wheel drive to propeller a few yards out, and made tracks, or rather wakes, for the merchantmen lying out to sea. They were coming inshore, reversing the process, and driving their piled cargoes of crates, tires, petrol, shells, up the coast roads to the depots . . . 2,000 tons they brought in on this small sector alone yesterday, and it will be nearer 3,000 tons today. That's only the DUK-Ws, mind you; there are LCTs, Rhino ferries, and innumerable other craft piling in supplies for our armies ashore. The beaches are alive with vehicles and men. There's a stream of traffic coming off the craft and going away up the roads and into the interior. As you come in towards the beaches, it's rather like driving in on the roads towards an industrial town; it's like a great, enormous industrial area—a remarkable sight."

From the crowded beaches endless columns of men and vehicles moved inland. "I think that one of the things I shall never forget," an RAF officer, Wing Commander L. A. Nickolls, recalled of the days immediately following the invasion, "is the sight of the British infantry, plodding steadily up those dusty French roads towards the front, single file,

heads bent down against the heavy weight of all the kit piled on their backs, armed to the teeth; they were plodding on, slowly and doggedly towards the front with the sweat running down their faces and their enamel drinking mugs dangling at their hips; never looking back and hardly ever looking to the side—just straight in front and down a little on to the roughness of the road; while the jeeps and the lorries and the tanks and all the other traffic went crowding by, smothering them in great billows and clouds of dust which they never even deigned to notice. That was a sight that somehow caught at your heart."

Although the Allies were clearly winning the battle of the build-up, they had failed to expand their bridgehead as swiftly as the *Overlord* strategists had hoped. By June 10 the Americans of the VII Corps were locked in an inch-by-inch struggle to cut the neck of the Cotentin Peninsula. To the east the Germans clung doggedly to the key road center of Carentan—an Allied D-Day objective—and thus maintained a dangerous gap between the V and VII Corps. On the eastern flank of the Normandy bridgehead, the British and Canadians were still frustrated in their attempts to take Caen and its vital system of roads, some of which led to Paris, only 120 miles away.

Amazingly, the German High Command continued to believe that the Normandy landings were a diversionary

In their first postinvasion meeting on D-plus-4, British General Bernard Montgomery (left), commander of all Allied ground forces in France, and Lieut. General Omar Bradley, U.S. First Army commander, discuss troop movements in a quiet field near Port-en-Bessin.

feint. The Allies maintained their deception program after D-Day, convincing the Germans that a large force under General Patton—whom they considered to be a tank commander second only to their own brilliant General Heinz Guderian—would form the main body of the real invasion in the Pas-de-Calais. The intention of the Allied forces in Normandy, Hitler believed, was to turn northeast across the Seine, link up with the presumed main force near Calais and make a concerted drive on Germany by the shortest possible route. It was thus of paramount importance to the Germans to hold the eastern flank of the Allies' bridgehead and, at all costs, to prevent the British and Canadians from breaking out across the Orne to the Seine. And to hold the eastern flank, they would have to hold Caen. The Germans therefore opposed the British and Canadian advance with all the means at their disposal.

On the 10th of June, Montgomery launched a pincer attack against Caen. Since he had had no success in attacking Caen directly from the beachhead north of the city, he decided to try to encircle the place. He would send the 51st Division and 4th Armored Brigade on a southward sweep from their sectors east of the Orne; these forces would link up with the famous 7th Armored Division, the Desert Rats, which would make a sweeping arc from left to right, south of the city through the town of Villers Bocage.

But before the British drive on the left flank could get under way, it was thwarted by an attack by the 21st Panzer Division. And the 7th Armored almost met disaster in their counterclockwise sweep around Caen. They had roared through Villers Bocage in their new light and swift Cromwell tanks and, finding a long stretch of empty road before them, were storming toward their objective southeast of Caen. Suddenly they met a unit of SS heavy tanks—four Tigers concealed in positions on either side of the road. The odds were heavily in favor of the Desert Rats, but the German company commander, Lieutenant Michel Wittman, was a formidable foe, a tank killer with 119 victories to his credit on the Russian front.

From hiding, Wittman opened fire at the leading British tank with his 88mm gun. The vehicle burst into flames and shuddered to a halt, blocking the entire British column. Then, as the Cromwells deployed to attack, Wittman rolled his 50-ton Tiger out from cover and moved down the stalled line of British vehicles, firing as he went. The thin-skinned British personnel carriers and the unprotected half-tracks exploded in geysers of flame and metal. Armor-piercing rounds from the few British tanks that tried to shoot back bounced like peas off the Tiger's thick steel plate.

A second company of Tigers, with eight tanks, now joined the fray, and in less than 10 minutes the leading brigade of the 7th Armored Division was nothing but scrap metal: 25 tanks, 14 half-tracks and personnel carriers. The Tigers plowed on into Villers Bocage, where the British soldiers, supported by a handful of tanks, were holed up with bazookas in houses. The Tigers shot up the houses and harried the British tanks, but the big panzers had outrun their infantry support. In the close quarters of the village, Tommies with bazookas began knocking out the Tigers, including the one operated by Wittman, who had to abandon it. Finally, the Germans were forced to retreat. But 12 of their tanks had smashed the spearhead of an armored division and stalled the whole attack. Again, the campaign for Caen bogged down in a grim slogging match between tanks.

Montgomery later claimed that events had gone exactly according to his master plan. His plan, he maintained, was to draw the main strength of the Germans against the British and Canadians in the east so that the American First Army could more easily gain territory and break out in the west. "In the Caen sector," Montgomery wrote, "the acquisition of ground was not so pressing; the need *there* was by hard fighting to make the enemy commit his reserves."

If this was so, it appears to have been news to Eisenhower, who became increasingly impatient at the lack of progress on the British front, as did some senior British air chiefs, who were anxious to capture and use important German airfields east of Caen.

Over the next month the Germans around Caen fought with determination, skill and strength. The hardened veterans from Montgomery's old Eighth Army were used to the sweeping freedom of the North African desert and took a while to adapt to the strangely cramped and inhibiting conditions imposed on tank fighting by the Bocage country with its maze of hedgerows. But they held on. So did the 6th Airborne, which stood firm on the east bank of the Orne against persistant German counterattacks. South of Bayeux the 50th British expanded their bridgehead inland, aiming for a line beyond Villers Bocage. But for the moment the fighting at Caen was a standoff.

For men new to battle, the front was a bizarre place and rarely matched their preconceptions of a battlefield. It was a place full of incongruities. Few soldiers—few generals, even—really understood what was going on around them. Woodrow Wyatt, who was with the British Liberation Army, was impressed not by the violence at the front line but by the absence of it.

"When the battle was stationary for a while I often drove down to visit the forward units," Wyatt wrote later. "The approach was always the same. The quick change from the hubbub and noise of the jumbled convoys in the back areas to roads deserted save for an occasional civilian walking very slowly. A few cattle in the fields grazing among the dead and swollen bodies of their fellows, but no farmworkers. A complete silence—not even the sound of birds, a sense of being in an unreal world with no life, so that even the people in the villages timidly looking out of their shell-damaged houses don't seem alive. There is no reality because no one is doing his normal job. Even the war does not exist—until you see a notice 'You are in the sight of the enemy now' and a little further on 'Drive slowly'—dust causes shells,' and then a few steel helmeted soldiers cautiously poking their heads out of slit trenches to see who is going by. . . . The opening exchange of courtesies wasn't the weather but 'How many times have you been shot up today?' followed by a visit to the latest shell or mortar holes, much as one might go and see how the sweet peas were coming on in a country garden."

Perhaps the greatest burden of the battle fell on the German tank crews, many of whom were relegated to a strange new role in the thrust-and-parry fighting that was characteristic of the battle to defend Caen and contain the western flank of the Allies. Low on fuel and ammunition, pinned down and practically immobilized by the Allied fighter-bombers and naval shellfire, the panzers dug in, hull down, among the dense hedgerows of the Bocage area. Their crews led lives more suited to U-boat men waiting for a kill than to the erstwhile practitioners of blitzkrieg and mobile armored warfare. The use of crack offensive units in a static defense was a novel event in World War II.

The Panzer Lehr tanks defending the German perimeter around Caen became simply armored antitank guns. Each tank was the nucleus of an infantry unit, for without it no position could be either taken or held. A small squadron of perhaps four Mark IV tanks, with crews of five infantrymen hanging all over the outside, would move off for "outpost duty." With their tanks concealed in well-reconnoitered sunken lanes, orchards and hayricks, the tank crews would busy themselves for hours camouflaging. The tanks were festooned with branches cut from a hedge until not an inch of turret could be seen. Then the crew would obliterate their tracks by painstakingly straightening each flattened blade of grass or stalk of corn. Then they would board their tanks and take up their duties as a forward antitank screen against the British armored spearheads. Only under the cover of darkness could they emerge again for a breath of fresh air and a stretch. All day they would be on lookout, peering intently at the landscape ahead of them through their binoculars.

It was like living in a tomb—a tomb that served as gun position, arsenal, barrack, toilet, galley and radio post. The first two days were bearable. After that it was unsufferable. There was no hot food. The men, cooped up in the steamy, tiny space of the tank interior, soon got on one another's nerves. With no water to wash in they soon became intolerably smelly. In the daylight hours they would have to relieve themselves in empty shell cases. Under such circumstances an enemy attack was almost welcome.

So it was for the crew of a Mark IV stationed outside of Tilly, a village eight miles to the west of Caen. At 2 o'clock in the afternoon on the third day of outpost duty, the tank driver suddenly shouted:

"Alarm! Tommies!"

The crew immediately came awake.

"Ten Tommies with a manhandled antitank gun. They're crossing the field now. They're taking up position."

"High explosives," the skipper ordered calmly.

"Four hundred meters."

"Fire!"

The 75mm shell burst in front of the antitank gun. Of the 10 British soldiers, only three were still on their feet; they ran toward an apple tree with low, spreading branches.

American infantrymen advance through the streets of battle-scarred Carentan, won from the Germans on the 12th of June. The capture of the crossroads town consolidated the Allied beachheads, which freed the U.S. V Corps and VII Corps to attack toward the port city of Cherbourg.

"Turret eleven o'clock."

"High explosives."

"Four hundred and twenty meters."

"Fire!"

The shellburst shredded the top of the tree.

"Fire!"

The trunk of the tree was smashed.

"Fire!"

The tree was destroyed. The Tommies were torn to pieces by shrapnel. The Mark IV stayed where it was, waiting.

It was a brutal moment, but less brutal than some. The combat troops grew accustomed to encountering the daily horror, but they rarely became used to the horror itself.

Colonel Ralph Ingersoll found himself in the square of a small inland village. "The sight that fascinated me most," he later wrote, "was a corpse of a German soldier in a roadway near the corner. It had been run over by so many tracked vehicles that it was ironed flat like a figure in a comic strip—really—absolutely flat, the arms of its grey uniform at right angles to its pressed and flattened coat. Its black boots and the legs that were in them were just as flat and thin as if they had been cut from a sheet of dirty cardboard."

The dead were everywhere, but the dead were easier to stand than the dying. "The thing I hated," a Canadian soldier recalled, "was when they'd call up a carrier with a flame thrower to burn out one of their pillboxes. I can still

turn sort of green when I think of it. I remember once there was this pillbox, and we could hear the guys inside yelling. We didn't know what they were yelling and I told the sergeant maybe they wanted to surrender but the door was jammed. I said it might have taken a hit and buckled and they couldn't get out. But the sergeant yelled to the guy with the flame thrower to turn on the heat, and you should have heard those Germans in that pillbox screaming. God, it was awful."

It was in this atmosphere of casual brutality that the British and Germans traded advances and retreats in their bloody fight for Caen. The Americans, meanwhile, were making intermittent gains in the west. After their relatively eventless landing on Utah, the men of the VII Corps had run into increasing German resistance in their push toward Cherbourg and had been finally halted at Montebourg on the main Cherbourg road.

The soldiers of the V Corps, on the other hand, after having suffered so heavily at Omaha, had picked themselves up and dusted themselves off and with remarkable resilience had penetrated deep beyond the German defensive line along the River Aure. By June 10, the V Corps had linked up with the British on their left flank at Port-en-Bessin. By the 11th the V Corps had advanced south of Omaha to capture Caumont—10 miles inland—and had drawn level with the British who were battling for possession of Tilly on the road to Villers Bocage. Farther west, they had moved inland to capture Isigny and were threatening to link up with the VII Corps on their right.

Rommel's pressing priority now was to stop them from crossing the Vire estuary and giving the Allies a continuous bridgehead. The key to this engagement was the town of Carentan, which lay on the main road to Cherbourg.

During the 10th of June the 502nd Regiment, 101st Airborne Division, advanced on Carentan down a long, exposed causeway north of the town. This causeway, some six to nine feet above the level of the marshes on either side, was utterly devoid of cover, providing a perfect field of fire for German snipers and machine gunners hidden in the thickets and hedgerows of the high ground at the edge of the marshes. Strung out in single file down the length of the causeway, crouching and crowding, the regiment advanced toward Carentan with great difficulty, suffering heavy losses from the withering fire that was pouring down upon them.

After enduring endless hours on this lethal causeway, I Company of the 3rd Battalion was bombed and strafed by two German planes at dusk of that June day; within a few seconds it lost 30 men dead or wounded. A curious thing then occurred. I Company was finishing several days of hard fighting. Its soldiers had been drenched, shelled, sniped at, strafed and bombed. Many of them had slept only briefly. And now they succumbed to combat fatigue, a malady born of heavy and prolonged action that had also begun to infect other Allied units all over the Normandy front by this stage of the campaign.

The men of I Company had thrown themselves to the ground to escape the air attack, and now they lay there in a kind of bewitched torpor. They had almost no interest in what had happened and no curiosity about who had been killed or wounded. The officer in charge found that no matter how hard he tried he could not keep them awake. Some were asleep within two or three minutes of the strafing, and he found it impossible to tell which of his men were asleep and which of them were wounded. Some had rolled down the embankment of the causeway and lay half in the marsh. Believing that these were the wounded, he went down to them but found they had simply fallen into the water in their sleep and had not even wakened as they hit the icy water. Others lay on the ground completely soaked through, sleeping the sleep of utter spiritual exhaustion. For the next four hours they took no part in the battalion's attack.

The next day, the weary and depleted 502nd went into reserve, and another 101st Airborne regiment, the 506th, resumed the advance down the causeway to Carentan. At the same time, the 101st's 327th Glider Infantry attacked the town from the east. On June 12 the two American pincers gradually closed on Carentan. U.S. troops entered the town and found little opposition. The Germans, almost out of ammunition, had retreated, leaving behind a small and ineffectual rear guard. The fall of Carentan enabled the V and VII Corps to join up; the Allies now had an unbroken lodgment about 10 miles deep by about 60 miles wide. It was yet another step down the grinding road that would lead to the heart of France and on to Germany itself.

As the German line buckled under American pressure,

Hitler issued one of his standfast orders that had cost the Germans so much in the war on the Eastern Front: "There can be no question of fighting a rearguard action, nor of retiring to a new line of resistance. Every man shall fight and fall where he stands." But there were not even enough men for that. German reserves had been delayed and mauled en route to the front by Allied air strikes. There were only two bicycle battalions available to reinforce the defenses and stem the breakout of the V Corps from Omaha. The crack 352nd Division, which had opposed the Americans on the beach, was cut to shreds and, according to the 84th Corps, had "small combat value." With the panzer divisions locked in a wasting battle with the British Second Army, Hitler's entire army group was strained and off balance.

On June 12, Rommel informed Keitel, chief of OKW, that he proposed to switch his point of attack to the Cotentin Peninsula, in order to avert the danger of Cherbourg, before launching a major attack between the Orne and the Vire. But he could not even achieve this. He was forced to continue using his panzer divisions to hold Caen and had to content himself with cordoning off the Allied bridgehead to prevent a major breakout. But as the British kept up the pressure on Caen, and the Americans on Saint-Lô, the German line came to a breaking point.

Rommel had always counted on defeating the Allies on the coast. The Germans thus had no defense in depth. Reserves arrived late and were committed to action piecemeal so that offensive units were soon reduced to static defense. Neither the Luftwaffe nor the German Navy was in any position to interrupt the Allies' reinforcement by sea and movement by land. On June 17, Rommel and Rundstedt met with Hitler to discuss the Germans' plight.

The meeting took place at Margival near Soissons in northeast France in the bombproof bunker constructed in 1940 as Hitler's headquarters for the invasion of England. The meeting lasted from 9 a.m. until 4 p.m., with a break for lunch (at which Hitler bolted down a heaping plate of rice and vegetables—after it had been tasted for him to make sure it was not poisoned). According to Rommel's chief of staff, General Speidel, Hitler "looked pale and sleepless, playing nervously with his spectacles and an array of colored pencils which he held between his fingers. He sat, hunched upon a stool, while the Field-Marshals stood."

Rommel and Rundstedt had asked to hold the meeting for two reasons. They wanted to let Hitler know that they considered the situation on the Normandy front hopeless, and they wanted Hitler to make a visit to the front, to see the situation for himself and to encourage his troops by a personal appearance.

The meeting did not go well. Rundstedt told Hitler that no effective German counteroffensive could be launched so long as the Allies enjoyed total supremacy in the air. Rommel, who had been up all night inspecting the front, was tired and touchy and became increasingly blunt with the Führer as the day wore on. He told Hitler that he wanted to withdraw the Caen front to the Orne River so he could disengage his panzers and let them reorganize. As Rommel warmed to his argument, he became more and more outspoken. He told the Führer that he believed the Italian front would fall, the Russian front would fall and the Western Front would fall, and that there would be nothing to stop the Allies from sweeping into Germany. He proposed the unthinkable to Hitler—end the War.

Hitler told him not to worry about the future course of the War but to look to his front. Withdrawal was inconceivable; capitulation was unmentionable. The course of the War was about to change, Hitler informed them. New wonder weapons would see to that. V-1 flying bombs, already in service, were about to be launched against London in such large quantities that they would ensure the collapse of Britain. The Luftwaffe was about to introduce their first jet fighters into the War, and they would soon sweep Allied aircraft from the skies.

As the disconsolate Rundstedt and Rommel made their way back to their doomed troops and their lost causes, one of Hitler's wonder weapons, a V-1 destined for England, did a U-turn over the Channel coast and flew back across France. Immediately above Hitler's headquarters at Margival, its engine cut out and a few seconds later the errant war head exploded near the *Führerbunker*. Hitler, safely secreted under many feet of protective concrete, was unhurt. But he wasted no time. He canceled his visit to the Normandy front. He leaped into his car and was driven to his airplane. He never returned to France, and before long it would not matter. There the walls of his fortress Europe were slowly but inexorably crumbling.

NEW WORK ON THE BEACHES

At the end of D-Day, amid the ruins of battle on Omaha Beach, Normandy fishermen stare thoughtfully at American dead, assembled for transport to England.

BUILD-UP TIME IN NORMANDY

General Eisenhower (lower right) and three American commanders disembark from an amphibious vehicle to survey the Normandy build-up.

On June 7, the day after D-Day, the invasion entered its second critical phase on the Normandy beaches. Even as the Allied dead were being gathered for shipment to England and the French civilians were struggling to return to normalcy, great flotillas of ships began pouring ashore more men and matériel from England. The task of the new units was to reinforce the D-Day assault troops, who were fighting to link up the individual beachheads and to expand their front inland. By D-plus-24, hundreds of thousands of soldiers and vehicles and 570,000 tons of supplies had to be landed on beaches that had never before seen cargoes larger than the catch of local fishing boats.

That June afternoon, a motley convoy of antiquated ships arrived offshore. The ships were to be sunk as part of two giant artificial harbors designed to increase the flow of supplies by creating an area of sheltered water with piers on which to land vehicles and bulk cargo difficult to land on the open beaches. To supply the 25 divisions that would arrive in the next 20 days, these ports, code-named Mulberries, would have to handle 6,000 tons of supplies daily by D-plus-5, 9,000 tons by D-plus-12, 12,000 tons by D-plus-18.

By the evening of D-plus-10, the massive movement of men and tonnage from England had shifted into high gear, and though the two artificial harbors were still incomplete, some 183,000 tons of supplies and 81,000 vehicles had already been landed in Normandy. Despite the fact that troops were arriving an average of two days behind schedule, some 557,000 soldiers had landed and were hurrying into combat. Hordes of landing craft, freighters and outboard Rhino ferries had transformed Omaha Beach and Gold Beach into major ports.

Supreme Commander Eisenhower set foot on French soil on D-plus-6. Ike was delighted with the progress of the invasion. Though the British were still battling to capture Caen, American troops were at that very moment driving into the streets of Carentan, eight miles inland, opening a vital main road and linking British and American forces in the interior. The Second Front was secure.

Oblivious of the ships and trucks laden with supplies around them, French children play in a tidal pool on Gold Beach, which was taken by the British.

Protected by barrage balloons, Omaha Beach swarms with ships and trucks funneling supplies inland to support the American troops, some of whom were pushing toward the vital port of Cherbourg. By D-plus-24, almost 180,000 tons of supplies and 50,000 vehicles had landed at Omaha.

Troops of the U.S. 2nd Division land on Omaha Beach on D-plus-1 and begin their trek inland to fight for the crucial high ground of Cerisy Forest, 12 miles to the south. On the way, the infantrymen captured the town of Trévières on D-plus-4. Then they took the forest with little difficulty.

A concrete caisson, one of 213 used in the artificial harbors, is pushed into place off Omaha Beach.

A "LITTLE RIPPLE" IN THE FLOOD OF SUPPLIES

In the days after the landings, work forged ahead on the assembly of the two artificial harbors, Mulberry A for the Americans at Saint-Laurent and Mulberry B for the British at Arromanches. "The whole project was majestic," Churchill said, and indeed it was. In a period of approximately eight months some 20,000 British workmen had fashioned two million tons of steel and concrete into 600-odd sections that were towed piecemeal across the Channel by more than 100 tugs and assembled into two enormous floating ports.

At 4:30 in the afternoon on D-plus-10, an LST landing craft dropped its ramp onto the first completed pier runway of Mulberry A. Two days later, 24,412 tons of supplies and ammunition rolled ashore from the two Mulberries.

But then the capricious Channel weather intervened. On the morning of D-plus-13, gale-force winds and heavy surf began to pound the Normandy coast, driving landing craft against the piers and tearing sections of the piers from their moorings and crashing them against each other. By daybreak on D-plus-16, Mulberry A was a useless mass of twisted wreckage. Mulberry B, protected by a reef, suffered considerable but not disastrous damage.

Yet so powerful was the momentum of the build-up that the great storm caused, in Eisenhower's words, "little more than a ripple" in the flow of Allied supplies. When unloading resumed on D-plus-17, the British Mulberry, repaired and reinforced with salvageable parts from Mulberry A, went back into business, and the Americans landed 16,400 tons on the open beaches. By August 1, the armies that had established the Second Front were strong enough to break out of their Normandy beachhead and begin the liberation of the rest of France.

Sixty-foot-high caissons, sunk in place in 30 feet of water by opening intake valves at their bases, form a breakwater of the British Mulberry at Arromanches. On platforms atop the caissons, antiaircraft guns face the English Channel. The gun crews had living quarters inside the caissons.

The British Mulberry could harbor 500 vessels at once. Ships entered from top right and lower left; the sheltered area lay within the breakwater of sunken ships and caissons at right. Supplies were unloaded at the floating piers at center and trucked to shore on the roadways at upper left.

On Utah Beach, a jumbled pile of discarded underwater obstacles, removed by Allied combat engineers during the landings, attests to the success of the invasion.

BIBLIOGRAPHY

Allied Forces, Supreme Headquarters, *Report by the Supreme Commander to the Combined Chiefs of Staff on the Operations in Europe of the Allied Expeditionary Force (6 June 1944 to 8 May 1945)*. Government Printing Office, no date.

American Forces in Action Series:
  Omaha Beachhead (6 June–13 June 1944). Historical Division, War Department, 1945.
  Utah Beach to Cherbourg (6 June–27 June 1944). U.S. Department of the Army, Historical Division, no date.

Barker, Theo, ed., *The Long March of Everyman, 1750-1960*. Penguin Books, 1978.

Belfield, Eversley, and H. Essame, *The Battle for Normandy*. B. T. Batsford Ltd., 1965.

Blumenson, Martin, *Eisenhower*. Ballantine Books, 1972.

Blumentritt, Guenther, *Von Rundstedt, the Soldier and the Man*. Odhams Press Limited, 1952.

Bostick, William A., *England under G.I.'s Reign*. Conjure House, 1946.

Bradley, Omar N., *A Soldier's Story*. Henry Holt and Company, 1951.

British Broadcasting Corporation, *War Report*. Oxford University Press, 1946.

Brown, Anthony Cave, *Bodyguard of Lies*. Bantam Books, Inc., 1976.

Buckley, Christopher, *The Second World War, 1939-1945: Norway, The Commandos, Dieppe*. His Majesty's Stationery Office, 1951.

Butcher, Captain Harry C., USNR, *My Three Years with Eisenhower*. Simon and Schuster, 1946.

Capa, Robert, *Images of War*. Grossman Publishers, 1964.

Carell, Paul, *Invasion—They're Coming!* E. P. Dutton & Company, Inc., 1963.

Churchill, Winston S.:
  The Second World War. Houghton Mifflin Company.
  Closing the Ring, 1951.
  The Hinge of Fate, 1950.
  Their Finest Hour, 1949.

Craven, Wesley Frank, and James Lea Cate, eds., *The Army Air Forces in World War II*, Vol. III, *Europe: Argument to V-E Day (January 1944 to May 1945)*. The University of Chicago Press, 1951.

Crookenden, Napier, *Dropzone Normandy*. Ian Allan Ltd., 1976.

Cruickshank, Charles, *The German Occupation of the Channel Islands*. Oxford University Press, 1975.

Desquesnes, Rémy, *Le Mur de l'Atlantique en Normandie*. Editions Heimdal, 1976.

Eisenhower, Dwight D., *Crusade in Europe*. Doubleday & Company, Inc., 1948.

Eisenhower Foundation, *D-Day, The Normandy Invasion in Retrospect*. The University Press of Kansas, 1971.

Ellis, Major L. F., *Victory in the West*, Vol. I, *The Battle of Normandy*. Her Majesty's Stationery Office, 1962.

Esposito, Brig. General Vincent J., USA (Ret.), chief ed., *The West Point Atlas of American Wars*, Vol. II, *1900-1953*. The Department of Military Art and Engineering, The United States Military Academy, Frederick A. Praeger, 1959.

Ewing, Joseph H., *29 Let's Go! (A History of the 29th Infantry Division in World War II)*. Infantry Journal Press, 1948.

Funcken, Fred and Liliane, *The Second World War, Part 4: Arms and Uniforms*. Ward Lock Limited, 1976.

Gamelin, Paul, *Le Mur de l'Atlantique, Les Blockhaus de l'Illusoire*. Archives de Guerre Collection Dirigée Par Gérard Guicheteau, Editions Daniel & Cie, 1974.

Goerlitz, Walter, *History of the German General Staff: 1657-1945*. Frederick A. Praeger, 1953.

Greenfield, Kent Roberts, ed., *Command Decisions*. Department of the Army, Office of the Chief of Military History, 1960.

Halle, Armin, *Tanks: An Illustrated History of Fighting Vehicles*. New York Graphic Society, 1971.

Howarth, David, *D-Day—The Sixth of June, 1944*. McGraw-Hill Book Company, Inc., 1959.

Icks, Lieut. Colonel Robert J., *Tanks and Armored Vehicles, 1900-1945*. WE Inc., no date.

Ingersoll, Ralph, *Top Secret*. Harcourt, Brace and Company, 1946.

Leasor, James, *Green Beach*. Corgi Books, 1975.

Leventhal, Albert R., *War*. A & W Visual Library, A Ridge Press Book, 1973.

Liddell Hart, B. H., ed., *The Rommel Papers*. Harcourt, Brace and Company, 1953.

Longmate, Norman:
  The G.I.'s: The Americans in Britain, 1942-1945. Hutchinson of London, 1975.
  How We Lived Then. Arrow Books, 1977.

Lund, Paul, and Harry Ludlam, *The War of the Landing Craft*. W. Foulsham & Co. Ltd., 1976.

McKee, Alexander, *Last Round against Rommel: Battle of the Normandy Bridgehead*. The New American Library, 1964.

Macksey, Kenneth:
  Armoured Crusader—A Biography of Major-General Sir Percy Hobart. Hutchinson of London, 1967.
  Tank Warfare, A History of Tanks in Battle. Stein and Day, 1971.

Macksey, Kenneth, and John H. Batchelor, *Tank: A History of the Armoured Fighting Vehicle*. Charles Scribner's Sons, 1970.

Maguire, Eric, *Dieppe: August 19th 1942*. Corgi Books, 1963.

Majdalany, Fred, *The Fall of Fortress Europe*. Hodder and Stoughton Limited, 1968.

Mallory, Keith, and Arvid Ottar, *The Architecture of War*. Pantheon Books, 1973.

Marshall, S. L. A., *Night Drop: The American Airborne Invasion of Normandy*. Little, Brown and Company, 1962.

Masterman, J. C., *The Double-Cross System in the War of 1939 to 1945*. Yale University Press, 1972.

Maule, Henry, *The Great Battles of World War II*. Galahad Books, 1972.

Mills-Roberts, Brigadier Derek, *Clash by Night: A Commando Chronicle*. William Kimber, 1956.

Montgomery of Alamein, Field Marshal the Viscount:
  The Memoirs of Field Marshal the Viscount Montgomery of Alamein, K.G. The New American Library, 1959.
  Normandy to the Baltic. Houghton Mifflin Company, 1948.

Moorehead, Alan, *Eclipse*. Harper & Row, 1968.

Mordal, Jacques, *Dieppe: the Dawn of Decision*. Souvenir Press, 1962.

Morgan, Lieut. General Sir Frederick, *Overture to Overlord*. Doubleday & Company, Inc., 1950.

Morison, Samuel Eliot, *History of United States Naval Operations in World War II*, Vol. XI, *The Invasion of France and Germany, 1944-1945*. Little, Brown and Company, 1975.

Moulton, J. L., *Haste to the Battle: A Marine Commando at War*. Cassell & Company Ltd., 1963.

Partridge, Colin, *Hitler's Atlantic Wall*. D. I. Publications, 1976.

Piekalkiewicz, Janusz, *Secret Agents, Spies and Saboteurs*. William Morrow & Company, Inc., 1973.

Pyle, Ernie, *Brave Men*. Henry Holt and Company, 1944.

Ramsey, Winston G., ed., *After the Battle: Number 5 (Dieppe, Eben-Emael)*. Battle of Britain Prints International Ltd., 1974.

Rapport, Leonard, and Arthur Northwood Jr., *Rendezvous With Destiny—A History of the 101st Airborne Division*. 101st Airborne Division Association, 1948.

Ridgway, General Matthew B., USA (Ret.), *Soldier: The Memoirs of Matthew B. Ridgway*. Harper & Brothers, 1956.

Robertson, Terence, *Dieppe, The Shame and the Glory*. Hutchinson of London, 1962.

Roosevelt, Eleanor B., *Day Before Yesterday: The Reminiscences of Mrs. Theodore Roosevelt, Jr.* Doubleday & Company, Inc., 1959.

Roskill, Captain S. W., *The War at Sea 1939-1945*, Vol. II, *The Period of Balance*. Her Majesty's Stationery Office, 1956.

Ryan, Cornelius, *The Longest Day*. Popular Library, 1959.

Ryder, Commander R. E. D., *The Attack on St. Nazaire, 28th March, 1942*. John Murray, 1947.

Saunders, Hilary St. George:
  The Green Beret: The Story of the Commandos 1940-1945. Michael Joseph Ltd., 1949.
  The Red Beret: The Story of the Parachute Regiment at War 1940-1945. Michael Joseph Ltd., 1950.

Shirer, William L., *The Rise and Fall of the Third Reich*. Simon and Schuster, 1960.

Speidel, Hans:
  Invasion 1944. Henry Regnery Company, 1950.
  We Defended Normandy. Herbert Jenkins Ltd., 1951.

Stacey, Colonel C. P., *The Canadians in the Second World War*, Vol. I, *Six Years of War: The Army in Canada, Britain and the Pacific*. Edmond Cloutier, 1955.

Stagg, J. M., *Forecast for Overlord, June 6, 1944*. W. W. Norton & Company, Inc., 1971.

Sulzberger, C. L., and the Editors of American Heritage, *The American Heritage Picture History of World War II*. American Heritage Publishing Co., Inc., 1966.

Summersby, Captain Kay, WAC, Army of the U.S., *Eisenhower Was My Boss*. Prentice-Hall, Inc., 1948.

Thompson, R. W.:
  Dieppe at Dawn: The Story of the Dieppe Raid. Hutchinson & Co. Ltd., 1956.
  The Price of Victory. Constable and Company Ltd., 1960.
  Spearhead of Invasion D-Day. Ballantine Books Inc., 1968.

Tourtellot, Arthur B., ed., *LIFE's Picture History of World War II*. Time Incorporated, 1950.

Turner, John Frayn, *Invasion '44 (The First Full Story of D-Day in Normandy)*. G. P. Putnam's Sons, 1959.

Tute, Warren, *D-Day*. Macmillan Publishing Co., Inc., 1974.

United States Army in World War II, The European Theater of Operations. Office of the Chief of Military History, United States Army:
  Harrison, Gordon A., *Cross-Channel Attack*, 1951.
  Pogue, Forrest C., *The Supreme Command*, 1954.
  Ruppenthal, Roland G., *Logistical Support of the Armies*, Vol. I, *May 1941—September 1944*, 1953.

Warlimont, Walter, *Inside Hitler's Headquarters 1939-45*. Frederick A. Praeger, 1964.

White, William, ed., *By-line: Ernest Hemingway*. Charles Scribner's Sons, 1967.

Wilmot, Chester, *The Struggle for Europe*. Collins, 1952.

Wilt, Alan F., *The Atlantic Wall: Hitler's Defenses in the West, 1941-1944*. The Iowa State University Press, 1975.

Young, Desmond, *Rommel, The Desert Fox*. The Berkley Publishing Corporation, 1965.

Young, Brigadier Peter, *Commando*. Ballantine Books, Inc., 1969.

PICTURE CREDITS

Credits from left to right are separated by semicolons, from top to bottom by dashes.

COVER and page 1—The Public Archives of Canada, Ottawa.

HITLER'S ATLANTIC WALL—6, 7: Bundesarchiv, Koblenz. 8: Ullstein Bilderdienst, Berlin—Courtesy Manfred Rommel, Stuttgart. 9: Ullstein Bilderdienst, Berlin. 10, 11: Bundesarchiv, Koblenz—Zentralbild, Berlin—Bildarchiv Preussischer Kulturbesitz, Berlin; Bundesarchiv, Koblenz; Bundesarchiv, Koblenz. 12, 13: Bundesarchiv, Koblenz, except left, Ullstein Bilderdienst, Berlin (2). 14, 15, 16: Bundesarchiv, Koblenz. 17: Bundesarchiv, Koblenz—Courtesy Hellmuth Lang, Captain (Ret.), Schwäbisch-Gmünd. 18, 19: Courtesy Hellmuth Lang, Captain (Ret.), Schwäbisch-Gmünd.

REHEARSALS FOR INVASION—22: *Daily Mail*, London. 24, 25: Imperial War Museum, London. 26: Map by Elie Sabban. 28: British Official. 30: Imperial War Museum, London.

AFTERMATH OF A TRAGIC RAID—34, 35, 36: Bundesarchiv, Koblenz. 37: Ullstein Bilderdienst, Berlin. 38: Bundesarchiv, Koblenz—Ullstein Bilderdienst, Berlin. 39: E.C.P. Armées, Paris. 40 through 43: Bundesarchiv, Koblenz.

OVERTURES TO OVERLORD—46: Map by Elie Sabban. 49: U.S. Army. 50: Imperial War Museum, London. 53: Bundesarchiv, Koblenz. 55: By kind permission of The Daily Telegraph, London. 57: U.S. Air Force—Public Records Office/Nautic Visual Services, London (2). 60: U.S. Air Force. 62: Imperial War Museum, London.

THE BIG BUILD-UP—64, 65: U.S. Army. 66: Radio Times Hulton Picture Library, London. 67: Bob Landry for LIFE. 68: U.S. Navy, National Archives. 69: Radio Times Hulton Picture Library, London. 70, 71: U.S. Army (2); Imperial War Museum, London. 72 through 75: U.S. Army. 76, 77: Bob Landry for LIFE.

SUPREME COMMANDER—78, 79: Popperfoto, London. 80: U.S. Army—Dwight D. Eisenhower Library. 81: Imperial War Museum, London. 82, 83: UPI—Derek Bayes, London; UPI. 84, 85: Bob Landry for LIFE—U.S. Office of War Information; Imperial War Museum, London—National Archives. 86, 87: Imperial War Museum, London; UPI (2). 88, 89: Dwight D. Eisenhower Library; Wide World.

THE AIRBORNE ASSAULT—92: Imperial War Museum, London. 94: U.S. Army. 96, 97: Map by Elie Sabban. 99: Imperial War Museum, London. 100: Bundesarchiv, Koblenz. 101: The Netherlands State Institute for War Documentation, Amsterdam. 103: Musée de Sainte-Mère-Eglise.

YANKS IN BRITAIN—106, 107: Imperial War Museum, London. 108: U.S. Army. 109: Radio Times Hulton Picture Library, London. 110: Keystone Press, London. 111: Imperial War Museum, London—Keystone Press, London. 112, 113: UPI—Topix, London—U.S. Army; U.S. Army. 114: *Punch*, London, except bottom right, Express Newspapers Ltd., London. 115: *Punch*, London (2)—Mrs. B. H. Stillings, Dorset; Strube for *The Daily Express*, courtesy John Frost Historical Newspaper Service, New Barnet, Hertfordshire. 116, 117: Radio Times Hulton Picture Library, London. 118, 119: Ralph Morse for LIFE; Imperial War Museum, London.

THE INVASION ARMADA—120, 121: U.S. Army. 122: Imperial War Museum, London. 123: Royal Canadian Navy. 124, 125: David E. Scherman for LIFE; Imperial War Museum, London—Imperial War Museum, London; David E. Scherman for LIFE—Frank Scherschel for LIFE; Imperial War Museum, London; David E. Scherman for LIFE. 126, 127: Imperial War Museum, London; National Archives.

AMERICAN LANDINGS—130: U.S. Air Force. 132, 133: Schutz Photo Panorama from Historical Print Division of Ankers Capital, Washington, D.C., courtesy Jack Mitchell. 135: Robert Capa for LIFE. 136: National Archives. 139: UPI.

ORDEAL AT OMAHA—142 through 151: Robert Capa from Magnum for LIFE.

BRITISH BEACHHEADS—154: Janusz Piekalkiewicz, Rösrath-Hoffnungsthal. 156: Public Records Office/Nautic Visual Services, London. 158: Ralph Crane for LIFE. 159: Helmut Laux.

BRITAIN'S SHOCK TROOPS—162, 163: Popperfoto, London. 164 through 171: Imperial War Museum, London.

THOSE WONDROUS TANKS—172, 173: Art by John Batchelor. 174: Imperial War Museum, London. 175: Art by John Batchelor—Imperial War Museum, London. 176, 177: Imperial War Museum, London; Art by John Batchelor—Art by John Batchelor; The Royal Armoured Tank Corps Museum, Dorset. 178: Art by John Batchelor—The Royal Armoured Tank Corps Museum, Dorset. 179: Art by John Batchelor—Imperial War Museum, London. 180, 181: Art by John Batchelor—Imperial War Museum, London; John Batchelor; Imperial War Museum, London—Art by John Batchelor.

THE FIGHTING INLAND—184, 185: U.S. Air Force. 186, 188: Imperial War Museum, London. 191: Popperfoto, London.

NEW WORK ON THE BEACHES—194, 195: Robert Capa from Magnum for LIFE. 196: UPI. 197: Imperial War Museum, London. 198, 199: U.S. Coast Guard, National Archives; UPI. 200, 201: U.S. Navy, National Archives; Popperfoto, London—The Netherlands State Institute for War Documentation, Amsterdam. 202, 203: U.S. Army.

ACKNOWLEDGMENTS

The index was prepared by Mel Ingber. For help given in the preparation of this book the editors wish to thank Dana Bell, U.S. Air Force Still Photo Depository, Arlington, Virginia; Antoinette de Bérender, Curator, Musée du Débarquement, Arromanches, France; Eva Bong, Ullstein Bilderdienst, Berlin; Carole Boutté, Senior Researcher, U.S. Army Audio-Visual Activity, The Pentagon, Washington, D.C., Cornell (Director) and Edith Capa, International Center of Photography, New York; Charles Chevrot, Montivilliers, France; Cécile Coutin, Curator, Musée des Deux Guerres Mondiales, Paris; Claude-Paul Couture, Barentin, France; V. M. Destefano, Chief, Reference Library, U.S. Army Audio-Visual Activity, The Pentagon, Washington, D.C.; Directorate of History, National Defense Headquarters, Ottawa, Ontario, Canada; Hans Dollinger, Wörthsee, Germany; Geneviève Duboscq-Troszczynski, Paris; Paul Gamelin, Nantes, France; Government Institute for War Documentation, Amsterdam; Jeanne Grall, Archives du Calvados, Caen, France; Charles R. Haberlein Jr., Photographic Section, Curator Branch, Naval History Division, Department of the Navy, Washington, D.C.; David Haight, Archivist, Dwight D. Eisenhower Library, Abilene, Kansas; Dr. Matthias Haupt, Bundesarchiv, Koblenz, Germany; Werner Haupt, Bibliothek für Zeitgeschichte, Stuttgart, Germany; T. C. Hine, Imperial War Museum, London; Heinrich Hoffmann, Hamburg; Colonel P. H. Hordern, D.S.O., O.B.E., The Royal Armoured Corps Tank Museum, Wareham, Dorset, England; Richard Huyda, Division Chief, National Photography Collection, The Public Archives of Canada, Ottawa, Ontario; Philip Jutras, Curator, Museum of Sainte-Mère-Eglise, France; Heidi Klein, Bildarchiv Preussischer Kulturbesitz, Berlin; Dr. Roland Klemig, Bildarchiv Preussischer Kulturbesitz, Berlin; Hellmuth Lang, Captain (Ret.), Schwäbisch-Gmünd, Germany; Roger Le Blanc, Mayor of Arromanches, France; William H. Leary, National Archives and Records Service, Audio-Visual Division, Washington, D.C.; James Leyerzapf, Supervisory Archivist, Dwight D. Eisenhower Library, Abilene, Kansas; J. S. Lucas, Imperial War Museum, London; Colonel Marcel Dugué MacCarthy, Curator, Musée de l'Armée, Paris; Peter Masters, Bethesda, Maryland; Brün Meyer, Bundesarchiv, Freiburg, Germany; Henri Michel, Président du Comité d'Histoire de la Deuxième Guerre Mondiale, Paris; Brigadier D. Mills-Roberts, C.B.E., D.S.O., M.C., North Wales; Jack Mitchell, Bedford, Virginia; Jonathan Moore, London; Meinrad Nilges, Bundesarchiv, Koblenz, Germany; J. W. Pavey, Imperial War Museum, London; Janusz Piekalkiewicz, Rösrath-Hoffnungsthal, Germany; Marianne Ranson, Comité d'Histoire de la Deuxième Guerre Mondiale, Paris; Manfred Rommel, Lord Mayor of Stuttgart, Germany; Professor Admiral Friedrich Ruge, Tübingen, Germany; Axel Schulz, Ullstein Bilderdienst, Berlin; Albert Speer, Heidelberg; Jim Trimble, National Archives and Records Service, Audio-Visual Division, Washington, D.C.; Michel de Vallavieille, Curator, Utah Beach Museum, Sainte-Marie-du-Mont, France; A. Williams, Imperial War Museum, London; Joy Williams, Reference Consultant, National Photography Collection, The Public Archives of Canada, Ottawa, Ontario; M. J. Willis, Imperial War Museum, London; Marjorie Willis, Radio Times Hulton Picture Library, London; Marie Yates, U.S. Army Audio-Visual Activity, The Pentagon, Washington, D.C.

INDEX

Numerals in italics indicate an illustration
of the subject mentioned.

92, 93, *170-171;* used in Normandy, 91, *92, 93, 95, 99,* 160-161, *184-185*
Gold Beach, 59, *map 96-97;* landings at, 141, 152-154, 156-157
Great Britain: build-up for Normandy invasion, *46, 47,* 50-51, *64-77;* security imposed in, before invasion, 58, 59; as supplier to U.S. forces, 51; U.S. troops in, 51, *106-119;* villages used for training, *68-69;* war brides, 116
Great Britain, Air Force of: at Dieppe, 30, 32, 33; and false invasion, 103; raids before invasion, 94
Great Britain, Army of: airborne forces depart, 91; airborne landings near Ranville, 95-97; airborne reinforcements to the Orne, 160-161; armored vehicles for invasion, 48, 54, 134, 153, *172-181;* at Bayeux, 184; near Caen, 183, 188, 189-192; at Dieppe, 23, 25-33; on D-plus-1, *182-183;* fictitious army, 55-56; first airborne landings, 92, 95, *99;* landing of supplies and reinforcements, 187-188, 196, 200-201; landings at Gold Beach, 141, 152-154, 156-157; landings at Juno Beach, 141, 152-154, 156, 157; landings at Sword Beach, 141, 152-154, *156,* 158-161; at Lebisey, 183; training of forces, 70. *See also* Commandos
Great Britain, Combined Operations Command, 20, 21, 22-23, 24, 25-29
Great Britain, Navy of: barrage on D-Day, 105, *126,* 128, 152; and construction of artificial harbors, 47, 196; midget submarines, *154;* and raid on Dieppe, 23, 25, 30, 31, 33; and raid on Saint-Nazaire, 24

H

Harbors, artificial, 47-48, 187, 196, 200; Mulberry A, 47, *200;* Mulberry B, 47, 157, *200-201*
Hartdegen, Alexander, 187
Hayn, Friedrich, 183
Hemingway, Ernest, 135, 138
Hennecke, Walther, 92, *93, 94*
Hermanville, *156,* 159
H-Hour, *126,* 128
Hitler, Adolf: and Atlantic Wall, 8; bunker hit by V-1, 193; concentrates European defenses at ports, 33; control over forces, 52; on D-Day, *155, 159;* divides control over armored divisions in France, 53; and intent of Allied invasion, 189; at meeting on Normandy front, 193; and new weapons, 193; orders forces to hold at Normandy, 193; orders V-1 used on London, 155; reinforces Normandy, 56; sends Strategic Reserves to Normandy, 105, 155
Hobart, Percy C. S., *174;* and development of tanks, 48, *174*
Howard, John, 92, 99
Huebner, Clarence R., 140
Hughes-Hallett, John: and artificial harbors, 47; and raid on Dieppe, 30, 32; and raid on Saint-Nazaire, 21

I

Ingersoll, Ralph, 191
Intelligence: Allied, on Atlantic Wall, 52, 53; Allied, on defenses at Omaha Beach, 132-134; Allied, on German deployment, 56; Allied, on German radar, 50; leaked about invasion, 55-56; German, on D-Day, 93; German, on *Neptune,* 56
Inter-Services Topographical Unit, 56, 57

J

Jahnke, Arthur, 105, 128-129, 131
Jodl, Alfred, *159;* orders Strategic Reserves withheld for Normandy, 105, 154; orders

V-1 used, 155
Jubilee, Operation, 23
Juno Beach, 59, *map 96-97;* Commandos at, 164; landings at, 141, 152-154, 156, 157

K

Keitel, Wilhelm, 155, 193
King, Ernest J., 48
Kirk, Alan G., 134
Krause, Edward C., 102

L

La Rivière, 156, 157
Landing craft: and choppy seas, 134; and landing of supplies and reinforcements, 187-188; shortage of, for Normandy invasion, 48, 52
Langrune-sur-Mer, 157
Laval, Pierre, 33
Le Hamel, 156
Lebisey, 160, 183
Leicester, B. W., on D-Day, 164
Leigh-Mallory, Trafford, *78-79;* on attack at Caen Canal, 99; as commander of Allied Expeditionary Air Force, 52, 59; opposes airborne operations on Cotentin Peninsula, 52
London Controlling Section, coordinates deceptive operations, 54-56
Loustalot, Edwin, 27
Lovat, Lord, *30;* on D-Day, 164, 169, 170; at Dieppe, *27,* 30

M

Marcks, Erich, and invasion, 104, 141, 160, 161
Marshall, George: and appointment of Supreme Commander for Normandy invasion, 51, 80; orders landing craft assigned to *Overlord,* 48; and plan for emergency invasion of France, 22
Maurice, F. J., 159-160
Merderet River, 100, 102, 183
Merville, 98-99
Meyer, Kurt, 183
Montgomery, Bernard L., *78-79, 188;* and attack on Caen, 189; determines time of day for invasion, 54; at final briefing, 59; as ground commander at Normandy invasion, 52, 152, 182; opinions of, 52; and specialized tanks, 174; and tank support at Normandy, 48
Moorehead, Alan, 153, 184
Morgan, Frederick E., 44, *49;* and COSSAC, 44; as deputy chief of staff for *Overlord,* 52; and landing craft, 45, 48; and opposition to *Overlord,* 49; and planning of *Neptune,* 45; and planning of *Overlord,* 44-45; on security precautions, 58
Moulton, James L., 182
Mountbatten, Louis: and Combined Operations Command, 21, 22, 33; and Morgan, 44

N

Neptune, Operation: planning of, 45, 47, 48, 52, 54, 59; postponed to June, 48, 52. *See also* Normandy, invasion of
Nickolls, L. A., 188
Normandy, invasion of: airborne forces depart for, 91; airborne landings on Cotentin Peninsula, 100-102; airborne landings at Merville, 98-99; airborne landings near Ranville, 75-97; and Allied advances after D-Day, 183-184, 186-193; Allied air superiority in, 187; assault area, *map 96-97;* boarding of ships for, 61, *121;* Channel crossing, *120-127;* Commandos at, 153, *162-171;* deceptions to hide, *50,* 54-56, 94, 103-104, 189; on D-plus-1, *182-183;* final plan

for, 59; first airborne landings, 92, 95; fleet assembles for, 90-91, 122; German early reactions to, 104-105; Germans unprepared for, 92; horrors of, 192; landing of supplies and reinforcements for, *196-201;* landings at Gold Beach, 141, 152-154, 156-157; landings at Juno Beach, 141, 152-154, 156, 157; landings at Omaha Beach, *126-127,* 128, 132-138, 140-141, *142-151;* landings prematurely announced, 63; landings at Sword Beach, 141, 152-154, 156, 158-161; landings at Utah Beach, 128-129, 131-132; naval barrage,105, *126,* 128, 140, 152; plan for, 45, 47, 48, 52, 59; postponed to June, 48, 52; and Resistance activity, 186; security provisions for, *54,* 58-59; status at end of D-Day, 161; tank warfare near Caen, 189-191; time and tide limitations of, 59, 61; training and briefing of forces for, 58; and weather, 59, 61, 62
Norway, fictitious invasion of, 55

O

Omaha Beach, 59, *map 96-97;* 132-133, *194-195;* on D-plus-1, 183; landing of supplies and reinforcements at, *198-199,* 200; landings at, *126-127,* 128, 132-134, *135,* 136-138, 140-141, *142-151*
Oppeln-Bronikowski, Hermann von, 160
Organization Todt, 8
Orne River, bridge attacked, 91, 92, 95
Otway, Terence, 98-99
Ouistreham, 169
Overlord, Operation: and appointment of Supreme Commander, 51; and build-up of forces in Britain, 50-51, *64-67, 72-77;* commanders, 51-52; disagreements among Allies over, 48-49; general briefing on, 59; goal of, 49-50; invasion launched, 63; planning of, 44-48; and security provisions, 54, 58-59; status at end of D-Day, 161, 182. *See also* Neptune; Normandy, invasion of

P

Paget, Bernard, 48; heads Combined Commanders, 22
Patton, George S., false army of, 55, 189
Pemsel, Max: reacts to invasion, 104; and unpreparedness for invasion, 92
Periers Rise, 159, 160
Pétain, Henri Philippe, and German victory at Dieppe, 33
Pointe du Hoc, *139,* 141
Port-en-Bessin, 140, 156, 183, 188, 192
Puttkamer, Karl Jesko von, 105
Pyle, Ernie, 108

R

Radar, tactics used against, *50,* 94, 103
Ramsay, Bertram H., *78-79;* as commander of Allied Naval Expeditionary Force, 52, 59, 134
Ranville, 95-97, 105
Ribbentrop, Joachim von, *159*
Ridgway, Matthew, 102, 183
River Aure, 183, 192
Roberts, John Hamilton "Ham", 22, 30, 31, 32
Römer, Helmut, 95
Rommel, Erwin, *8;* and "asparagus" obstacles, *100-101;* and Atlantic Wall, 8, 17, *18-19,* 53; as commander of armies defending invasion coast, 52; and defense of Cotentin Peninsula, 192, 193; on importance of repelling invasion on the beach, 53, 161; limited control of armor in Europe, 53; meeting with Hitler on Normandy, 193; orders armored attack near Caen, 183; proposes end of war, 193; rewards troops for maintaining shore defenses, 53; at start of invasion, 93, 105, 155
Roosevelt, Franklin D.: appoints Supreme